James H. Stark is a graduate of the New York University School of Law, where he was an Arthur Garfield Hays Civil Liberties Fellow and a member of the law review. He is presently practicing law in New York City.

Howard W. Goldstein, who is a partner in the New York City law firm of Mudge, Rose, Guthrie, Alexander and Ferdon, is a former chief appellate attorney in the office of the United States attorney for the Southern District of New York, Criminal Division. He is a graduate of New York University Law School, where he was also an Arthur Garfield Hays Civil Liberties Fellow and an editor of the law review.

AN AMERICAN CIVIL LIBERTIES UNION HANDBOOK

THE RIGHTS
OF
CRIME VICTIMS

James H. Stark and Howard W. Goldstein

General Editor of this series:
Norman Dorsen, President ACLU

BANTAM BOOKS
TORONTO • NEW YORK • LONDON • SYDNEY • AUCKLAND

THE RIGHTS OF CRIME VICTIMS
A *Bantam Book / published by arrangement with*
The American Civil Liberties Union

Bantam edition / April 1985

ISBN 0-553-24817-0

Published simultaneously in the United States and Canada

PRINTED IN THE UNITED STATES OF AMERICA

O   0 9 8 7 6 5 4 3 2 1

Contents

Preface

This guide sets forth your rights under the present law, and offers suggestions on how they can be protected. It is one of a continuing series of handbooks published in cooperation with the American Civil Liberties Union (ACLU).

Surrounding these publications is the hope that Americans, informed of their rights, will be encouraged to exercise them. Through their exercise, rights are given life. If they are rarely used, they may be forgotten and violations may become routine.

This guide offers no assurances that your rights will be respected. The laws may change and, in some of the subjects covered in these pages, they change quite rapidly. An effort has been made to note those parts of the law where movement is taking place, but it is not always possible to predict accurately when the law *will* change.

Even if the laws remain the same, their interpretations by courts and administrative officials often vary. In a federal system such as ours, there is a built-in problem of state and federal law, not to speak of the confusion between states. In addition, there are wide variations in the ways in which particular courts and administrative officials will interpret the same law at any given moment.

If you encounter what you consider to be a specific abuse of your rights, you should seek legal assistance. There are a number of agencies that may help you, among them, ACLU affiliate offices, but bear in mind that the ACLU is a limited-purpose organization. In many communities, there are federally funded legal service offices which provide assistance to persons who cannot afford the costs of legal representation. In general, the rights that the ACLU defends are freedom of inquiry and expression; due process of law; equal protection of the laws; and privacy. The authors in this series have discussed other rights (even though they sometimes fall outside the ACLU's usual concern) in order to provide as much guidance as possible.

These books have been planned as guides for the people directly affected; therefore, the question and answer format. (In some areas there are more detailed works available for "experts.") These guides seek to raise the major issues and inform the nonspecialist of the basic law on the subject. The authors of these books are themselves specialists who understand the need for information at "street level."

If you encounter a specific legal problem in an area discussed in one of these handbooks, show the book to your attorney. Of course, he or she will not be able to rely exclusively on the handbook to provide you with adequate representation. But if your attorney hasn't had a great deal of experience in the specific area, the handbook can provide helpful suggestions on how to proceed.

Norman Dorsen, President
American Civil Liberties Union

The principal purpose of this handbook, as well as others in this series, is to inform individuals of their legal rights. The authors from time to time suggest what the law should be, but their personal views are not necessarily those of the ACLU. For the ACLU's position on the issues discussed in this handbook, the reader should write to Librarian, ACLU, 132 West 43rd Street, New York, NY 10036.

Introduction

A book about the rights of crime victims could not have been written a decade ago. Some of the avenues open to crime victims that are discussed in this book (such as restitution, civil actions initiated by victims, and payments of witness fees to victims) have long existed. But public awareness of the opportunities available to victims and, indeed, the perception that they constitute "victims' rights," is a recent development; it is the outgrowth of a grass roots national movement whose goal is to provide assistance to victims, to help them maintain their dignity, to expand their opportunities for compensation for injuries or losses caused by crime and to increase the effectiveness of their participation in the criminal justice process.

The impetus for this movement has come from a growing awareness of the general social cost of crime and victimization, as well as from specific well-publicized instances of victimization.

Even the bare statistics describe a social problem so severe that it simply cannot be ignored:

1. In 1981, there were 41.5 million victimizations in the United States, 3 percent more than in 1980, and over 6.5 million Americans over the age of 12 were the victims of violent crime.

2. More than 18,500,000 households were victimized by burglary, larcency, or automobile theft;

3. There were over 5 million victims of assault,[1] and 178,000 persons were the victims of attempted or completed rapes.

4. In 1979, the total cost to Americans of residential burglary (including property destruction, the loss of money and valuables, and rehabilitation costs) was estimated at $3 billion. Larceny was estimated to cost Americans $2 billion per year and arson destroyed over $1 billion worth of property per year.[2]

5. A Harris poll conducted at the beginning of 1981 found that the average loss to victims in New York State, even after recovery from insurance or restoration of lost property, was in excess of $1,400 per victim; and that 43 percent suffered serious mental or emotional suffering as a result of their victimization; 53 percent agreed with the statement that "being the victim of a crime changed my whole life and made me more fearful about becoming a victim [again]."[3]

But even these statistics only give a rough idea of the real cost and impact of crime on its victims. Is it really meaningful to talk about the loss sustained in a robbery when the property stolen (which may have a market value of less than $1,000) consisted of a handicapped person's wheelchair or a deaf person's hearing aid or a television that is an elderly victim's only source of entertainment and, indeed, contact with the outside world? Statistics concerning automobile thefts may signify to the reader a certain number of adolescent joy rides; to the victim it may mean the loss of an automobile that was vital to the victim's livelihood.

If the magnitude of victimization has been one impetus for expanding victim rights, the other impetus may well be individual, well-publicized crimes; for example, when David Berkowitz—the Son of Sam killer who terrorized New York City by randomly shooting innocent victims—was offered a number of contracts for the rights to his "story," outraged New York legislators enacted a law that would escrow payments to criminals for the rights to their stories, preserving those funds for later distribution to the criminal's victims. Similarly, when the singer Connie Francis was raped in a motel, her well-publicized civil suit against the motel owner for negligence in failing to provide safe lodging inspired numerous other "third-party" civil suits seeking to compensate victims for crimes caused by the negligence of others. Indeed, the whole notion of state-funded compensation programs for crime victims originated with a British magistrate, Marjorie

Frye, who was said to have been inspired by her outrage at a single victimization.

Over the past several years, the plight of crime victims has become a recognized media "issue," the subject of multipart stories on television and in print. Politicians from both major parties have gone out of their way to identify themselves as advocates of victims' rights. In fact, the recent emergence of the crime victims' "issue" is simply the culmination of more than fifteen years of studies, legislation, organization, and litigation concerning the following matters vital to crime victims:

Compensation: Following the examples of victim compensation programs in Great Britain and New Zealand, California (1966) and New York (1967) instituted the first state-run publicly funded programs awarding compensation for out-of-pocket losses to victims of violent crime; now 39 states and the District of Columbia and the Virgin Islands operate such programs. In 1984, Congress passed the Victims of Crime Act which for the first time provided federal funding for up to 35% of the awards made by state compensation programs.

Assistance: In 1972, the first volunteer victims' assistance program was established in St. Louis; now there are over 500 programs throughout the United States, providing educational, counseling, and advocacy services to victims and their families, at both the state and local levels. Victim assistance has taken on national dimensions. The National Organization for Victim Assistance (NOVA)—a private non-profit association of victim and witness assistance practitioners, criminal justice professionals, researchers, and former victims—acts as a national clearinghouse for information on victims' assistance and victims' rights. And in 1981, 43 states and hundreds of local jurisdictions (following a proclamation by President Reagan) observed National Victim Rights Week, and in 1984, Congress provided up to $50 million in funding for victims assistance programs.

Restitution: In the late 1970s, and early 1980s, numerous states expanded existing statutes to include restitution for additional crimes, to permit restitution where the criminal was also sentenced to imprisonment (usually by use of split sentences or confinement to centers that allowed the criminal to be gainfully employed), to allow victims to participate in the ordering and scheduling of restitution payments and to make restitution mandatory or to require courts to state on the record why restitution was not granted in particular cases.

Civil Suits: Civil suits initiated by victims against criminals and third parties whose negligence allowed the crime to take place, have mushroomed in the past five years, resulting in publicized awards to victims, particularly multimillion dollar awards against corporate and governmental third parties. In addition, such suits became much easier to win as a result of statutes and court cases that expanded the obligation of third parties to prevent crimes, that expanded the potential liability of states and municipalities (which had long been immune to liability for such suits), that increasingly allowed the introduction of verdicts in criminal cases as evidence (or even irrefutable proof) of the criminal's civil liability and that eased what had been relatively short statutes of limitations for suits against criminals.

Intimidation: Since 1980, 5 states have greatly expanded victim protection against intimidation and retaliation by adopting the Model Code of the American Bar Association (ABA). In 1982, the federal government, for the first time, made it a crime to intimidate or retaliate against victims of federal crimes by enacting the Federal Victim Witness Protection Act. In 1984, the federal Bail Reform Act made the safety of victims and witnesses a factor in refusing or revoking pre- and post-trial bail.

Son of Sam Statutes: In 1977, New York enacted the first so-called Son of Sam statute escrowing compensation to criminals for movies or books based on their version of the crimes and making it easier for victims to recover judgments against such criminals; by 1982, 22 other states had also enacted such statutes and Congress enacted its own form of "Son of Sam" statute in 1984.

In the past 10 years there has also been a substantial expansion of victims' opportunities for alternative dispute resolution (including the establishment of a statewide program in New York in 1980, and the current operation of more than 180 centers across the country). Concern for the victims' interests has led to changes in the prosecution of sex crimes (including increased assistance for rape victims and new laws easing prosecution while protecting victims from unwarranted cross-examination at trial): and to greater protection against domestic violence (with the enactment of statutes in 43 states and the District of Columbia allowing for broad civil protection orders against abuse of victims and the enactment of legislation making spouse abuse a separate criminal offense in 11 states). The rights of elderly victims are also being upheld (including active crime prevention programs and assistance aimed at this group, increased penalties for crimes against the elderly, and statutes requiring the reporting of abuse of the elderly).

Unlike, for example, the rights of reporters, criminals, or prisoners, there is no provision in the federal Constitution guaranteeing the rights of victims. Thus (unlike many of the handbooks in this series) this handbook does not primarily discuss federal constitutional issues, or even federal statutes. The few cases that do in fact refer to constitutional issues when deciding questions relevant to victims are mentioned. There is also some discussion of (1) the threshold questions of a victim's standing to raise constitutional challenges when he is not even a party to the prosecution of his crime; (2) a proposed constitutional amendment (giving victims a guaranteed role in the criminal process); and (3) such potential theoretical bases for victims' constitutional rights as the First Amendment (with its guaranteed right to petition for the redress of grievances), and the Fourteenth Amendment (which guarantees victims, as well as other Americans the right to due process and equal protection).

Instead, what are commonly referred to as victims' rights are really a broad range of rights, privileges, policies, and practices that are to be found in a variety of state codes or, where not yet codified, have become accepted practices in the criminal justice system as it functions in particular jurisdictions. In general, these "rights" relate to the following general areas affecting victims of crime: (1) compensation for victims of violent crimes; (2) restitution for injury or loss of property; (3) the right to commence civil litigation to recover damages caused by criminals, accessories, or the negligence of third parties; (4) procedural rights of victims to participate with dignity and appropriate representation in the criminal justice process; and (5) the rights to be free of intimidation and retaliation, to pursue alternative forms of dispute resolution, and to share in profits received by criminals who sell their story of the crime.

Because the source of these "victims' rights" is primarily to be found in *state* and *municipal* court decisions, ordinances, and practices (as distinct from the *federal* Constitution, cases, or statutes), these rights have not been uniformly enacted or applied; for example, whereas forty-one jurisdictions have now enacted compensation programs for victims of violent crimes, each of these programs has its own complicated rules governing eligibility for awards, the size and nature of benefits to be awarded, and application and review procedures. Although these programs tend to address similar concerns about, for example, eligibility and benefits, each of them addresses these concerns in a slightly different way.

The state of the law with respect to restitution and the procedural rights of victims to participate in the criminal justice process is, if anything, even more varied. While the compensation programs are purely statutory, both restitution and the victim's role in the criminal process are, most often, a function of the particular practices of one prosecutor's office or a particular court. As a result, not only do these practices, and therefore the victims' rights, change from jurisdiction to jurisdiction (and indeed, from courthouse to courthouse) but since they are not always codified, they are extremely difficult to determine with any precision.

Because of this diversity (and the magnitude of recent developments—including new legislation, proposed reforms, and new case law—in this area) there are substantial obstacles to writing a handbook that can provide specific practical advice in a question and answer format for a national audience of victims. The authors have attempted to deal with this problem in a number of ways. Where a clear majority of the jurisdictions have enacted legislation or adopted procedures or precedents that recognize or deny the particular right at issue, the answer will indicate that such a position has "probably" been adopted in "most jurisdictions." Where there is no majority rule, the answer will state that "it depends on the jurisdiction" or that it will "vary" from jurisdiction to jurisdiction. Where there is a practice or procedure in a particular jurisdiction of particular interest to a national audience of victims (often practices that are more expansive in recognizing victims' rights, or the federal practice), the authors have attempted to identify it because of its potential interest to a large number of victims.

This handbook also contains appendixes: a chart analyzing provisions of state compensation programs (Appendix A); a list of administrators of state compensation programs (Appendix B); suggestions concerning legal representation of crime victims (Appendix C); a list of alternative dispute resolution centers around the country (Appendix D); and a state-by-state list of citations to domestic violence statutes (Appendix E).

As a practical matter, then, this handbook cannot provide you with a detailed description of all of your rights and privileges or all of the problems that are likely to confront you as a victim both of crime and of the criminal justice system. Moreover, as an editorial judgment, certain types of crimes and victimizations are only touched on here. Although this book deals with some of the problems of "white-collar" crime victims, for example, no attempt is made to provide a comprehensive outline of all of their potential rights, problems, and remedies for two reasons. First, civil recovery in connection with such crimes has spawned its own elaborate and very complex literature. Second, such suits are usually brought by businesses or by individuals who are represented by attorneys experienced in civil litigation; the presentation of legal issues in this handbook (which, after all, is intended for a layman) would not add a great deal to the knowledge of the attorneys retained by victims to pursue such litigation.

The last three chapters of this book deal all too briefly with the specialized problems of elderly crime victims, victims of rape and sexual abuse, and the victims of domestic violence. The information provided in these chapters is far from an exhaustive survey of the very difficult problems faced by these victims or the variety of statutes, procedures, and services relevant to their situation. In order to produce a manageable handbook that addresses in some reasonable fashion the general problems faced by victims of crime throughout the United States, their problems could only be sketched in the broadest outlines. However, there are a number of excellent articles and texts (which were relied on to a great extent in preparing the material found in these chapters); these publications, which are identified in the footnotes at the end of the chapters, can be consulted in your general library or local law library (if it is open to the public).

As the disclaimer at the beginning of this book explains, the discussion of victims' rights contained here is not meant to reflect the policy of the American Civil Liberties Union. The goal of the authors has been to provide an overview of the emerging issues for crime victims, accurately and comprehensively. While their descriptions and explanations do not represent an attempt to formulate an ACLU policy in this important new area, wherever possible the authors have tried to be mindful of the traditional ACLU concerns for protecting the rights of both the accused and prisoners, as well as protecting the right of freedom of speech. The authors feel strongly that crime victims deserve the rights described in this book and that in most instances these rights do not conflict with the concerns of accused persons, prisoners, and free speech. In those relatively few areas where the authors have perceived a conflict, they have noted the existence of these significant competing concerns and, wherever possible, have cautioned the reader of the existence of legitimate interests that may conflict with that of the victim or have suggested how the rights of victims and these competing concerns might be balanced. Ultimately, it will be for the courts to make the difficult decisions that will establish the frontiers of victims' rights and determine where their legitimate rights end, and where the rights of others (accused persons, prisoners, and the press) begin.

Naturally, the "rights" discussed in this handbook do not, by any stretch of the imagination, include the sum total of all the "rights" that the most aggressive advocates of victims' rights have proposed or that may become the focus of victims' rights debates. The future advocacy of victims' rights may include calls for any or all of the following:

1. A constitutional amendment creating the right of citizens to be protected from crime or unnecessary violence;

2. A federal scheme to provide compensation for victims who are injured as a result of crime;

3. A comprehensive national correctional industries program capable of funding mandatory restitution for all crime victims;

4. The creation of tripartite criminal proceedings in which victims are active parties represented by lawyers and where trials result both in a disposition of criminal charges and in a civil judgment;

5. The recognition of the right of crime victims to be represented by lawyers in all criminal and civil proceedings and the establishment of programs for victims comparable to the public defender and legal aid programs that currently provide legal assistance to indigent criminals.

The history of the victims' rights movement clearly indicates that activism and innovation beget activism and innovation. The broader the information about victims' rights is disseminated and the more victims who exercise their rights, the more deeply those rights become entrenched in the legal and criminal justice system and the more demand and need there is to expand those rights. If this book can disseminate information to victims who were previously unaware of the extent of their rights and provide them with a simple explanation of how these rights can be asserted, it will have accomplished its objectives. It is the hope of the authors that in doing so, in some small way, they will help to expand the frontiers of crime victims' rights.

This handbook, compiled by the authors in a relatively short time, relied on the conscientious work and experience of a variety of experts in the victims' rights field. If it succeeds in providing a realistic overview of this field, it does so only because the authors were fortunate enough to be the recipients of aid from the following dedicated individuals who generously shared with us their time, their research, their experience, and their expertise: Daniel McGillis; Alan Harland, John Stein, Paul Hudson, Susan Hillenbrandt, Norman Bloch, George Nicholson, Paul Austern, Victoria Jaycox, Lee Pearson, James Bergstein, Frank Carrington, Chris Whipple, Karen Morello, Lucy Friedman, Franci Livingston, Peggy Davis, Lisa Lerman, Leigh Bienen, Alan Shortell, Bruce Keller, Richard Emery, Steve Shapiro, and Marcia Paul, and the following organizations: New York Crime Victims' Board, Center for Women Policy Studies, ABA Committee on Criminal Justice, ABA Special Committee on Alternative Dispute Resolution, President's Task Force on Crime Victims, American Association of Retired Persons, National District Attorney's Association, National Counsel of Senior Citizens, New York Legislative Task Force on Victims (R. Gottfried, Chairman), Abt Associates, San Francisco Community Boards Program, National Organization for Victim Assistance, Victim Assistance Legal Organization (VALOR), the New York Civil Liberties Union, Insurance Information Institute, and all of the state crime victim compensation boards and local prosecutors' offices that responded to the authors' inquiries. For the difficult and far from glamorous job of assisting the authors in researching and editing this book, James Stark wishes to thank Demetra McBride, Howard Cohn, and Lori Andrews and Howard Goldstein wishes to thank Gail D'Italia and Michelena Hallie. Both of the authors wish to express their appreciation for the concern, guidance, and patience of Norman Dorsen, President of the ACLU and General Editor of the series of ACLU handbooks, and for the patience and support of their law firms: Greenbaum, Wolff & Ernst, Morril & Paul, and Mudge Rose Guthrie Alexander & Ferdon.

Last, but not least, the authors wish to thank those who physically prepared this text (in the face of constant revision); James Stark expresses his appreciation to Brenda Foster, Cindy Treibitz, Yung Jin Kim, and especially Diane York who had the almost impossible job of putting together in final form text and footnotes; Howard Goldstein expresses his thanks to Cathy Ienuso, who was appropriately skeptical when she was told months ago that she was working on the "last" draft.

Notes

1. A. Paez, "Criminal Victimization in the U.S." (Washington, D.C.; Bureau of Justice Statistics, Mar. 1983) (N.C.J.–87577).
2. *Campaign for Victim Rights* (Washington, D.C.: NOVA, 1981), p. 3.
3. L. Harris et al., "A Pilot Survey of the Crime Victims in New York State," (Albany: N.Y. Crime Victims Compensation Board) (Mar. 1981), study no. 802516, pp. 1, 2.

I

Victims and Their Rights

What is a victim?
Generally speaking, anyone who suffers a loss or injury as the result of an act that constitutes a crime under a federal, state, or local law has been victimized. This includes individuals as well as corporations, relatives, and dependents of persons who themselves are injured or killed during the course of a crime and even Good Samaritans who may be harmed during the act of preventing a crime or while preventing the perpetrator from leaving the scene.

Which "victims' rights" are discussed in this handbook?
This book deals with the victims' right to—

1. participate in the criminal justice system;

2. obtain benefits from a fund established by the state to compensate crime victims;

3. receive restitution ordered by the criminal court;

4. recover a judgment for damages in a civil action against the criminal, accessories, or negligent third-party defendants;

5. be free of intimidation;

6. share in profits from exploitation of the criminal's version of the crime;

7. seek alternative dispute resolution.

In addition, there are brief chapters on the special rights and problems of elderly victims and victims of rape and domestic violence.

Is there a crime victims' "bill of rights"?

A number of states, including Washington, Wisconsin, Nebraska, Rhode Island, Florida, and Oklahoma, have enacted Victims' Bills of Rights. These states have provided victims of crimes the right to be informed of state victim compensation programs, to be treated with dignity and compassion, to be provided with counseling and other forms of assistance by agencies established specifically to serve crime victims and to have certain procedural rights in the prosecution of the crime in which they were victimized, including the right to be notified of important developments in the case and to be heard on such questions as sentencing and parole.

As used in this book, however, the "rights of victims" encompasses much more than these state statutory "bills of rights." The rights described in this handbook are not codified in any single statute; some are explicit in, or implied by, a variety of state and federal statutes, some are part of the common law and can be found only by examining opinions written by courts in a variety of cases, and others exist only by virtue of practices and procedures adopted by particular courts and jurisdictions and may not be written down at all. As a result, these rights vary greatly from state to state, city to city and even from courthouse to courthouse.

Will this handbook give the victim a detailed description of the rights available in his particular jurisdiction?

No. In a book this size, a detailed description of all of the rights available to all victims of crime in a particular jurisdiction is clearly impossible. Instead, this handbook is intended as a general introduction to the type of problems faced by victims and the kinds of rights that are commonly recognized by different jurisdictions. If you have specific questions about the practice or policy in your jurisdiction that are not answered in the text or footnotes, consult the appendixes, which include a state-by-state chart identifying many of the important features of the state victim compensation programs, and a listing of state domestic violence statutes. If you still have questions about practices in your jurisdiction, contact the victim assistance program in your area (often such programs are affiliated with the office of your local United States attorney, district attorney, or prosecutor) which may well operate a "victims' hotline" listed in your telephone directory. If you have trouble locating the victims' assistance group in your area, you can obtain information about local victims' assistance by contacting the National Organization for Victim Assistance, 1757 Park Rd., N.W., Washington, DC 20010. Victims with special problems may also find it valuable to contact specialized victims' assistance agencies in their area that operate domestic violence shelters, rape clinics, hotlines for rape victims or family abuse victims, or senior citizens' organizations providing services to elderly crime victims. To find out additional information about your state's victim compensation program (many of which provide victim hotlines), you can contact your state's victim compensation program administrator; a list of their names and addresses is contained in Appendix B.

If after consulting this handbook and your local victims' assistance agency or specialized victims' program you wish additional information, you may wish to consult an attorney knowledgeable in the rights and problems of crime victims. Some suggestions for locating knowledgeable attorneys in your area are contained in Appendix C.

Although the specific information about victims' rights that you are seeking may not be included in this handbook, it is hoped that the categories of rights discussed and the answers to the questions posed here can provide a framework for your own further investigation.

Are victims guaranteed any rights to participate in the criminal justice system?

Yes. Victims have always had a role in criminal prosecutions, but this role has changed radically over time. In England (before the eighteenth century) and in colonial America, the victim typically initiated and pursued criminal prosecution. With the rise of a permanent public police force and public prosecutors, the victim's role in the arrest, trial, and prosecution of criminals virtually disappeared. Although the victim in many cases still signed the complaint that technically commenced a criminal proceeding and in most cases appeared as a witness at the trial of the accused, victims were eventually viewed as "pieces of walking evidence." Critics called the victim the forgotten man of the criminal justice system and spoke of victims as being "twice victimized"—once by the criminal and once by the criminal justice system itself.

In recent years, there has been a trend back toward recognizing the fact that victims have the right to be actively involved in the prosecution, sentencing, and probation of the person responsible for their victimization. Increasingly, practices and procedures are being implemented that seek to reduce the cost to the victim of participating in criminal prosecutions in time, money, and lost dignity. In addition, more and more jurisdictions are providing victims with a right to participate in important decisions regarding the prosecution and sentencing of criminals. A step-by-step description of the victim's role in the criminal justice system and a discussion of these emerging rights is contained in chapter II.

Does the government compensate victims for injuries or lost property?

Yes. Thirty-nine states, the District of Columbia, and the Virgin Islands presently have compensation programs for crime victims. In general, these programs provide limited compensation (with states paying average awards of three thousand dollars) to victims of violent crimes to reimburse medical expenses, lost wages, and, in some jurisdictions, certain types of essential property. There are numerous restrictions (which vary from state to state) on eligibility and benefits. A variety of agencies administer the programs (including state court systems and workmen's and independent crime victims' compensation boards) and the procedure for application, determination, and review of claims differs from state to state. In 1984, Congress began providing partial federal funding for state compensation programs and also set up a small federal program to compensate victims of crimes committed by certain persons under the protection of federal law enforcement officers.

The most common limitations on eligibility and benefits as well as a general description of the purpose and procedures used by most of the state crime victims' compensation programs is described in chapter III. A recent state-by-state analysis of the most important features of the thirty-eight crime victim compensation programs is contained in a table in Appendix A and a list of the addresses and telephone numbers of these programs is in Appendix B.

What is restitution and how can crime victims obtain it?

Although judges have long had the power to order criminals to pay restitution to their victims, for a variety of reasons, it was only rarely mandated. In the last decade there has been a renewed interest in restitution as judges are increasingly using their power to enforce restitution by convicted criminals, states are establishing programs that will allow persons convicted of crimes to earn sufficient money to provide at least some restitution to victims, and statutes are being enacted that make restitution mandatory or that require judges to state on the record their reason for failing to order it. The powers of judges to order restitution (which may be grounded in specific statutes or simply in the judge's broad powers to impose sentencing) vary from state to state and cases have established different standards for (1) the type of loss or injury to the victim that can be compensated; (2) the proof that the victim must provide; (3) the criminal acts that may give rise to restitution; and (4) the procedural requirements for a valid award. Naturally the criminal's ability to pay restitution will also vary, depending in large part on whether programs exist in a particular jurisdiction that allow persons convicted of crimes to earn wages to satisfy awards to victims. An explanation of how restitution works can be found in chapter IV.

Do victims have the right to be free from threats of intimidation and retaliation by persons who want to prevent them from reporting a crime or testifying in a criminal trial?

Yes. Although studies indicate that intimidation of victims and witnesses is widespread, and many states have statutes on the books that make intimidating conduct a crime, prosecutions for intimidation have been rare. While criminal statutes have long made it a felony to intimidate a subpoenaed witness, intimidation of a victim who had not yet reported the crime, or who had not been called to testify, could only be prosecuted (where there was no physical violence) as harassment, coercion, or a similar misdemeanor.

In 1980, the Criminal Justice Section of the American Bar Association issued a report on the problem of victim and witness intimidation and drafted a model statute making it a crime to intimidate a victim or witness under certain circumstances. This statute has now been enacted in a number of states. A statute making it a federal crime to intimidate or retaliate against victims or witnesses in connection with violations of federal law and trials in federal courts was enacted in 1982, and in 1984 Congress enacted legislation which permitted judges to refuse or revoke bail where the accused or convicted person represented a threat to the safety of a victim or witness.

These statutes (along with their effects on defendants' rights) and the use of such measures to reduce intimidation as victim hotlines, police patrols, and relocation are discussed in chapter VII.

Can a crime victim initiate his own civil action for damages to recover the cost of his injury or property loss?

Yes. Acts that constitute crimes also give rise to civil claims. Victims who suffer property loss or personal injury can initiate their own civil actions against the person guilty of the criminal act to recover damages. A criminal conviction can be used as evidence of liability in a civil action, but civil actions do not require a criminal conviction. In fact, the burden of proof in a civil case is not so high as the standard of proof required for conviction of a crime. However, as a practical matter, the value of such a civil suit depends in large part on the victim's ability to identify the person who committed the crime and the ability of the defendant to satisfy any resulting judgment.

Since many criminal defendants are without financial resources and are "judgment proof," in recent years there has been an increasing interest in civil suits brought against persons whose negligence made it possible for someone else to commit a crime. Parties other than the criminal defendant—"third parties," such as parole boards or mental institutions who negligently release dangerous criminals; innkeepers (restaurant, bar, and hotel owners) and landlords who negligently fail to provide safe or secure premises; cities that negligently fail to provide promised police protection; and employers who negligently hire dangerous employees—have increasingly been objects of civil suits for damages.

Chapter V describes the procedural problems that are involved when a civil action is brought against the person who committed the crime, accessories or persons whose negligence have allowed the crime to take place. Using a number of actual cases as examples, this chapter demonstrates, among other things, how a prior criminal conviction, investigative police reports, and grand jury materials can be used as evidence in a civil case, where and when third parties have a duty to keep victims safe from crime and the circumstances in which a governmental body, such as a school board, prosecutor's office, police, or parole board will be immune from civil suits.

Do victims have any right to share in the profits that criminals make from movies, books, or articles depicting the crime?

Yes. Since 1977, when New York enacted its "Son of Sam" Statute (specifically intended to allow victims of the Son of Sam killer to share in lucrative offers that he was receiving for his "story") twenty-one additional states and the federal government have enacted similar statutes stipulating that all such compensation be paid directly into escrow funds administered by state agencies. Such funds make it easier for victims to satisfy civil judgments against the criminal and give them other procedural advantages, including a longer period of time in which to commence damage actions against the criminal. Victims' rights under these statutes and the cases applying them are described in chapter VI. This chapter also discusses criticisms of these statutes, including the argument that they violate the First Amendment by chilling the publication of the criminal's story.

Where the crime is part of an ongoing relationship between the offender and the victim, do victims have any alternatives to going to court to bring a criminal prosecution or a civil action?

Yes. Victims involved in ongoing relationships with offenders have long reached private settlements with the offenders or, in some communities, have referred their ongoing dispute to a community dispute resolution organization. Increasingly, local alternative dispute resolution centers and neighborhood justice centers (many established by the local prosecutor's office or the court) are being used by victims to obtain redress (including restitution, payments of damage, and agreements on future conduct) for minor crimes and civil disputes related to them. A description of these alternative dispute resolution mechanisms and how they affect victims is in chapter VIII, and a list of the addresses of 180 such programs across the United States can be found in Appendix D.

Do all crime victims face the same problems?

No. Obviously, the impact of a minor property theft and of rape on the respective victims is enormously different. This difference manifests itself not only in the victim's perception of the impact of the crime on his or her life, but also on how they subsequently deal with the criminal justice system and their chances for obtaining what they consider to be adequate compensation or restitution.

In general, the rights described in this handbook will be available to all victims, where relevant and in effect in the victims' jurisdiction. However, certain victims—victims of domestic violence, rape, and the elderly—face special problems not faced by other crime victims. The literature describing the problems of these three groups, the special services that are being made available to them, and the increasing rights and protections being afforded to them by the criminal justice system are extensive. Chapters IX, X, and XI attempt to briefly describe some of the particular problems of these victims and several areas in which their specific rights have been expanded.

II

The Right to Participate in the Criminal Justice System

A. The Victim's Role in the Criminal Justice System— Mistreatment and the Move Towards Reform

Are victims parties to a criminal proceeding?

No, the victim is not a formal party to a criminal proceeding. As in civil proceedings, there are two parties to a criminal proceeding. The plaintiff is the party who brings or prosecutes the action, and the defendant is the party against whom the action is brought. In criminal cases, the state or government is the plaintiff, and the accused offender is the defendant.

Does the fact that the victim is not a party to a criminal proceeding have any legal consequences?

Yes. Because the victim is not a formal party to the criminal proceeding, his input into the process is limited. The victim cannot force the prosecutor to take actions advocated by the victim or prevent him from taking steps opposed by the victim. In legal terms, the victim lacks *standing*, or the legal right to be heard by a court, with respect to prosecutorial decisions. Crime victims fall within the classic definition of persons with standing, because they suffer "injury in fact" and the laws that they seek to enforce, that is, criminal statutes intended to deter certain injuries to individuals, make their claims "arguably within the zone of interest" for which the statute was enacted.[1] Nonetheless, the Supreme Court has held that victims lack standing in criminal proceedings. "A citizen lacks standing to contest the policies of the prosecuting authority when he himself is neither prosecuted nor threatened with prosecution . . . a private citizen lacks a judicially cognizable interest in the prosecution or nonprosecution of another."[2]

But isn't the whole purpose of bringing the criminal to justice to avenge or punish the wrong inflicted on the victim?

No. Our criminal justice system proceeds on the premise that a criminal act is a wrong perpetrated against society. While an injury to an individual victim begins the criminal justice process, the wrong committed by the accused is viewed as a social wrong, and public officials—police, prosecutors, judges, and correction agencies—investigate the crime, arrest the accused, institute formal proceedings for determining the accused's criminal responsibility, fix the appropriate punishment and carry it out.[3]

Was the victim always excluded from the criminal justice system?

No. In colonial America, individuals victimized by crime initiated arrests and prosecutions, aided by officials who charged for their services. In eighteenth-century Boston, for example, the victim arrested a criminal with the help of a watchman or constable, paid for a warrant where necessary, investigated the case himself (with the help of information obtained by posting rewards) and then retained an attorney to have an indictment written and to prosecute the offender. A successful prosecution led to an award of restitution or even multiple damages. If the offender was indigent, the victim could sell the defendant into servitude until the damages were paid off; jail was not an alternative unless the victim himself compensated the government for the cost of incarceration.[4]

Indeed, until the 1780s, jails were not used as places of punishment except in extraordinary cases in New York, Connecticut, Massachusetts, and Pennsylvania.[5]

When did this system change?

After the American Revolution, the formerly private functions of investigating and prosecuting crime gradually were assumed by the government, and public prosecution replaced private prosecution as the dominant means for pursuing criminal trials. With hard labor the usual punishment for crime rather than restitution or multiple damages, the victim no longer had the same interest in pressing criminal prosecutions.[6] By the early 1800s incarceration in penitentiaries became the primary object of the criminal process, rather than providing restitution to the victim.[7] Similarly, by the early nineteenth century, citizens rarely helped peace officers make arrests. Because paying private fees to policemen resulted in corruption, reformers called for a salaried police force responsible to the community as a whole. By the beginning of the 1830s, the professional police force on the public payroll had replaced the law enforcement officers for hire of the eighteenth century.[8]

Does this mean that there is no role in the contemporary criminal justice system for the victim?

No. The victim still plays several essential roles in the criminal justice system: (1) The individual's victimization, although viewed as a social wrong, still provides the basis for most criminal charges. (2) Police investigators rely upon victims to report crimes and depend upon victim cooperation and information. (3) Victim identification of the accused can be crucial to a decision to prosecute, and their testimony and evidence are frequently the principal bases of the prosecution's case.[9]

But doesn't the victim have a constitutional right to participate in the criminal justice system?

No. Victims' rights are not guaranteed by the Constitution. Indeed, the absence of a constitutional basis for the victim to participate in the criminal justice system led the President's Task Force on Victims of Crime to propose an addendum to the Sixth Amendment (which provides the accused with the right to a jury trial, counsel, cross-examination of the witnesses against him, and "to be informed of the nature and cause of the accusation") that would add the following language: "Likewise, the victim in every criminal prosecution shall have the right to be present and to be heard at all critical stages of judicial proceedings."[10]

In a few cases, arguments have been made that the Constitution confers a particular right on victims of crime; for example, in several cases, women victims of domestic violence have argued that police and prosecutorial policies of refusing to arrest and prosecute their abusers amounted to selective enforcement of the laws against domestic violence, an arbitrary and discriminatory classification scheme in violation of the equal protection clause of the Fourteenth Amendment.

At least one court has held that such a claim states a cause of action cognizable under the Constitution.[11]

As another example, a victim could commence an action pursuant to the federal Civil Rights Act[11a] where property seized during a search or recovered by the police was never returned. A refusal by police to return property seized in a criminal investigation, when there has been a timely demand by the owner for its return and where there are no pending or impending criminal proceedings, constitutes a deprivation of property that violates the due process clause of the Fourteenth Amendment.[12]

Do victims have any legislatively recognized rights?

Yes. A variety of state and federal statutes have been enacted to increase the victim's information about, influence over, and participation in, the criminal process. These reforms have resulted in part from the grass roots victims' movement described in the Introduction, and in part from prosecutors' reactions to sociological evidence that victims' perceived mistreatment by the system results in their failure to participate in investigations and cooperate in prosecutions.[13]

What are these statutory rights?

A number of states, including Nebraska, Rhode Island, Washington, Wisconsin, Oklahoma, and Florida, have enacted victims' bills of rights.[14] As this book went to press, Illinois and South Carolina also enacted victims' rights legislation.[14a]

These statutes (which have all been enacted since 1979) were motivated by a legislative recognition of the "civic and moral duty of victims and witnesses of crimes to fully and voluntarily cooperate with law enforcement and prosecutorial agencies" and the importance of such cooperation to the criminal justice system.[15]

What rights are protected or created by these victims' rights statutes?

The victims' "bills of rights" dictate that victims and witnesses be "treated with dignity, respect, courtesy, and sensitivity." They grant victims and witnesses certain specific rights that "are to be honored and protected . . . in a manner no less vigorous than the protections afforded criminal defendants."[16]

Most of the state statutes confer the following rights on victims and witnesses:

1. To be informed of the final disposition of the case;

2. To be notified if any court proceeding for which they have received a subpoena will not occur as scheduled;

3. To receive protection from victim intimidation and to be provided with information as to the level of protection available;

4. To be informed of the procedure for receiving witness fees;

5. To be provided, whenever practical, with a secure waiting area not close to where the defendants wait;

6. To have personal property in the possession of law enforcement agencies returned as expeditiously as possible, where feasible, photographing the property and returning it to the owner within ten days of being taken;

7. To be provided with appropriate employer intercession so that loss of pay and other benefits resulting from court appearances will be minimized.

These rights are extended not only to victims and witnesses but also to families of victims, whether or not they are witnesses.[17]

In addition, Wisconsin and Nebraska provide victims and witnesses with the right to "a speedy disposition of the case in which they are involved." Washington's bill of rights contains the right "of access" to immediate medical assistance and the right not to be detained for an unreasonable length of time by a law enforcement agency before having such assistance administered. Rhode Island requires that notice be given to the victim of the status of an investigation, and Rhode Island and Florida require that notice be given of the accused's arraignment and release from custody, and give the victim a right of input in sentencing and parole decisions.[18]

Are these rights enforceable by the victim in a lawsuit?
It is not yet clear whether these statutes create legally enforceable rights. The statutes in Washington and Wisconsin mandate that these rights be honored, protected, and, presumably, enforced by all law enforcement agencies, prosecutors, and judges. The Nebraska statute requires the

state Commission on Law Enforcement and Criminal Justice to select public and private nonprofit agencies as victim and witness assistance centers and to do everything necessary to carry out the statutory provisions. Rhode Island places responsibility with the department of the attorney general to make certain that victims receive the notice required by the statute. The Oklahoma statute, by contrast, only places a burden on the district attorney's office to inform "as far as practical" victims and witnesses of the "services" indicated by the bill "to the discretion of the district attorney."[19] The Florida statute specifically provides that nothing in it shall be construed as creating a cause of action against the state or its agencies.[19a]

Are these five statutes the only sources of victims' rights?

No. California has also enacted something of a victims' bill of rights by means of a 1982 voter-approved criminal justice initiative. However, although this initiative amended the California constitution and penal law to make restitution mandatory (except in extraordinary cases), to make public safety (presumably including threats to the victim) relevant in the decision to release the accused on bail, to eliminate plea bargaining, and to give victims the right to be heard in sentencing and parole proceedings, the bulk of the bill dealt with issues that do not relate to the victims' right to participate in the criminal justice system, such as the right to be assured safe schools, the use of evidence that had previously been excluded for constitutional reasons, and changes in the substantive rules of sentencing.[20]

New York enacted victims' rights legislation in February 1984, authorizing state officials to "promulgate standards for the treatment of the innocent victims of crime," including the provision of emergency social and medical services and the provision of information regarding the availability of compensation and counseling and treatment programs; the stages of the criminal justice process in which the victim will be involved; protection from intimidation; and the progress of the criminal case against the accused. The New York fair treatment standards law also grants crime victims the right (1) to be consulted by the district attorney in serious felony cases for their views regarding disposition of the criminal case by dismissal, guilty plea, or trial; release of the defendant pending trial; and the availability of sentencing alternatives such as community supervision and restitution; (2) to be provided, where possible, with a separate, secure waiting area when awaiting court appearances; (3) to have property that has been held for evidentiary purposes promptly returned; and (4) to be provided with assistance in informing their employers that the need for victims' cooperation may necessitate absences from work, and informing their creditors of circumstances that may affect their ability to meet obligations.[20a]

The New York legislation specifically addresses the issue of enforceability, providing that "[n]othing in this article shall be construed as creating a cause of action for damages or injunctive relief against the state or any of its political subdivisions or officers or any agency thereof."[20b]

Also, at least one local county has promulgated a victims' bill of rights. In 1982, law enforcement officials in Jefferson County, Kentucky, which includes the city of Louisville, voluntarily executed a policy statement containing a fourteen-point bill of rights that declares the victim's rights, among others, to be—

1. free from intimidation;

2. informed of the status of the criminal proceeding;

3. advised of the availability of compensation under the Kentucky Crime Victims' Compensation Board;

4. informed of the availability of social services and reimbursement for travel expenses;

5. informed of continuances, possible plea bargains, and the potential release of the defendant (including the right to be "notified and consulted before a defendant is released on parole");

6. have property returned "as expeditiously as possible."[21]

Do victims outside of states with bills of rights have any rights?

With these exceptions, the states generally have not enacted comprehensive victims' bills of rights. Instead, the emerging rights of victims with respect to the criminal justice system are the result of statutes enacted piecemeal to deal with specific aspects of the system, practices that have been adopted by law enforcement agencies, prosecutors, or judges, and programs and services provided by hundreds of local and state victim/witness assistance agencies throughout the country.

Is there a statutory source of victims' rights in federal cases?

Yes. In passing the Victim and Witness Protection Act of 1982, Congress recognized the importance of victim and witness cooperation with the criminal justice system and attempted to address some of the inequities that result from "contact with the criminal justice system unresponsive to the real needs of the victim."[22]

The act deals with the subjects of bail, restitution, and sentencing. Under the act, a court may impose as a condition of a defendant's release, the requirement that he not commit a witness intimidation offense.[23] The court is explicitly authorized to order restitution as part of a sentence under the act, and, in fact, is required to state its reasons for not doing so if restitution is not ordered.[24] In addition, the act amended Rule 32 of the Federal Rules of Criminal Procedure to require the use of "victim impact statements"—statements describing the impact of the crime on its victim—in the preparation of presentence reports.

The act also strengthened the government's ability to deal with witness intimidation by making it a crime to intimidate or harass a person to influence or prevent testimony in any official proceeding or to hinder, prevent, or delay the communication of information relating to the commission of a federal offense.[25] Congress further made it a crime to retaliate against anyone participating or presenting information in an official proceeding.[26] Under the act, the government can commence a civil action and apply for a temporary restraining order prohibiting witness harassment.[27]

In addition to these substantive provisions, Congress called on the Justice Department to prepare guidelines for the treatment of victims and witnesses in federal cases. These guidelines were issued by the attorney general on July 9, 1983,[28] and mandate that "components of the Department of Justice engaged in the detection, investigation, or prosecution of crimes" establish mechanisms to provide victims and witnesses with the following services:

1. Information on, and assistance in, contacting agencies that

provide emergency medical and/or social services, compensation, and counseling;

2. Information on case status and the availability of protection from intimidation;

3. Prompt notification of scheduling changes in court proceedings;

4. Prompt notification of the release of the accused on bail and the eventual outcome of the case;

5. Notification of the sentencing date, the victim's opportunity to address the court at sentencing, the sentence imposed, and the defendant's parole eligibility date;

6. Advance notification of the defendant's release from custody;

7. Consultation with the victim during various stages of prosecution, including the negotiation of a plea or the placement of the accused in a pretrial diversion program;

8. Separate waiting areas for defense and prosecution witnesses;

9. Prompt return of property;

10. Employer intercession;

11. Training of law enforcement personnel and victim assistance;

12. Such general victim assistance as providing transportation, parking, and translators, where necessary.

On October 12, 1984, the President signed legislation which makes sweeping changes in the federal criminal laws. In addition to changes in the areas of bail, sentencing, parole, the insanity defense, and witness protection, which are discussed elsewhere in this chapter, the legislation included a chapter entitled the Victims of Crime Act of 1984. Among other features, the Victims of Crime Act of 1984 creates a federal Crime Victims Fund, from which the Attorney General is to make annual grants to eligible state crime victim compensation programs. The fund is to be funded by fines collected from persons convicted of federal crimes, a special penalty assessment to be levied on all persons or organizations convicted of federal crimes (without regard to the sentence), the proceeds of forfeited bail bonds and collateral, and money ordered to be paid into the fund pursuant to a newly enacted federal "Son of Sam" law. The Act also requires the Attorney General to appoint a Justice Department official to the position of Federal Crime Victim Assistance Administrator. Among other duties, the Federal Crime Victim Assistance Administrator is to be responsible for coordinating federal victim services with other victim services and for monitoring compliance with the fair treatment guidelines issued under the Victim and Witness Protection Act of 1982. [28a]

What are victim/witness assistance agencies?

In the last decade, victim/witness assistance programs have spread across every state and province in the United States and Canada.[29]

Although these programs share the goal of ameliorating the victim's trauma, they vary widely in how they are organized, how they are funded, and the kinds of services that they provide. Typically, these victim/witness programs are sponsored by the local police or prosecutor's office, by community-based organizations specifically dedicated to serving victims or witnesses, and by such other host organizations as hospitals, mental health centers, or universities. Typically, they operate on a county- or citywide basis, although some organizations serve more than one county. Most of these organizations were started in 1975, or thereafter. In 1984, Congress enacted the Victims of Crime Act which created a Crime Victims Fund (funded by fines in federal criminal cases, specially created penalty assessments and forfeited appeal and bail bonds) which provided up to $50 million over four years to states for victim services. In addition to federal funding, many of these programs also receive funding from the city or county in which they are located.[30]

What type of services do these agencies provide?

About one-third of these programs operate twenty-four-hour telephone hotlines that allow victims and witnesses immediate access to someone knowlegeable about their problems. Most of the programs provide some counseling by trained professionals, and all provide victims with referrals to other sources of assistance. Most will also assist victims in making victim compensation claims, escorting victims to police or court appearances, and ascertaining the status of police investigations.[31]

These agencies also routinely provide public education on

victims' rights and problems; they also train police departments on how to deal with victims and witnesses.[32]

A number of these programs are operated by prosecutors' offices to assist victims and witnesses in negotiating the byways of the criminal justice system. In particular, victim/witness units in prosecutors' offices provide victims and witnesses with notification of court schedules and case dispositions (followed by reminder telephone calls if necessary), operate programs that allow victims and witnesses the option of being alerted by telephone rather than waiting in the courthouse to see if they are called for scheduled court appearances, maintain witness reception areas in the courthouse, and provide orientation to court procedure. In addition, they frequently provide escort or transportation to the courthouse, assistance in obtaining witness fees and restitution, intervention with employers to ease the strain of missing work, and act as liaisons with the police in situations of victim or witness intimidation.[33]

Are any emergency services available if victims (particularly victims of violent crimes) need emergency assistance?

Yes. The victim/witness assistance agencies in most jurisdictions provide some emergency services to victims, including short-term emergency food and shelter (particularly in situations of domestic violence), immediate repair to locks and other security devices, and very limited emergency financial assistance.[34] A 1979 National Institute of Justice survey indicated that many of the victim assistance projects in 70 jurisdictions provided emergency medical care (54 percent), emergency food or shelter (69 percent), security repairs (36 percent), financial assistance (56 percent), and crisis intervention (23 percent) to at least one client per month.[35]

In addition, victim programs that do not provide these services often distribute information, typically made available to victims at the scene of the crime or in hospital emergency rooms (in the form of brochures or wallet-size cards), which provides victims with the names, addresses, and telephone numbers of agencies that provide these services. All victim/witness projects surveyed indicated that they made such referrals.

Victim service agencies generally rely on information obtained through the police to identify potential clients; 83 percent of the programs routinely screened police crime reports to find crime victims in order to contact them.[36] A number of victim service agencies, usually at the request of the police officer called to the scene, or by monitoring the police radio, actually intervene to assist victims at the crime scene.[37]

A number of police departments have training programs so that officers will be able to deal with the immediate needs of traumatized victims. Indeed, victims often speak highly of the understanding treatment received from the police officer who investigated their case. The President's Task Force on Victims of Crime specifically recommended in its 1982 report that training police officers to deal with the victim's initial reaction to his victimization, including providing "psychological first aid," become a departmental priority.[38]

Do victims have a statutory right to obtain information about available services?

In most states, no. However, the victims' rights bills in Nebraska, Rhode Island, Oklahoma, Wisconsin, Washington, Florida and Jefferson County, Kentucky, explicitly grant victims the right to be notified of available financial assistance and other social services.[39] At least three other states, New York, Pennsylvania, and Ohio, have enacted statutes requiring either the police or the court to notify victims of the existence of a victim's compensation program.[40] The 1983 Justice Department Guidelines require officials to insure that victims receive information about community-based compensation and treatment programs.

A specific example of such mandatory notification is the statutory requirement in Oklahoma whereby investigating officers are obligated to inform victims of rape, forceable sodomy, or domestic abuse of the existence of a twenty-four-hour hotline and to read to them a statement of their rights, including the right to press charges, to protection from harm and to be informed of financial assistance, including in the case of rape victims the right to a free medical examination. The notice is to be handed to the victim at the initial interview.[41]

B. The Victim and the System

The manner in which crimes are investigated and prosecuted varies from state to state, and sometimes even from jurisdiction to jurisdiction within a single state. However, processing by the criminal justice system generally involves the following stages:

1. initial victimization;

2. report of the victimization;

3. investigation of the crime;

4. arrest;

5. charging a person with the crime;

6. determination of bail;

7. pretrial conferences and appearances;

8. plea bargaining or trial;

9. sentencing;

10. release of the convicted defendant, including probation and parole.

Since the nature of these stages can vary substantially from jurisdiction to jurisdiction, the remainder of this chapter will attempt to give only an overview of the victim's involvement and rights in connection with each of these stages of the criminal process. To learn how a case is processed in the victim's own jurisdiction, the victim should contact the local victim/witness assistance program or the local law enforcement or prosecutor's office. The questions posed in this chapter can serve as an outline of the kinds of information that the victim should seek and the kinds of rights that the victim should assert.

C. Initial Victimization

Do Americans have the right to be protected from crime? In other words, is there a right not to be a victim?

No. No court has ever concluded from any federal or state constitution or statute that citizens are guaranteed the right to be free from crime. Under certain circumstances, however, the government may assume a "special duty" to protect an individual or to prevent the commission of a crime by some particular person: for example, some cases have held that where the police promise protection against certain threats or release a person from custody whom they knew or should have known would commit a crime, the government has assumed a special duty to prevent the commission of a crime and is liable to victims in civil suits for damages.[42]

Recently, the New York Court of Appeals upheld an $800,000 award to the family of a woman who was killed by a burglar after her 911 emergency telephone call was mishandled by the police. The city and county had contended that they could not be held liable for negligence in the performance of a governmental function, including police protection, unless a special relationship existed between them and the injured party. The court concluded, however, that

> [c]onsidering the fact that she was merely a block and a half from the local police station, . . . and was not yet at the mercy of the intruder, it cannot be said as a matter of law that this assurance [that the police would respond "right away"] played no part in her decision to remain in her home and not seek other assistance. Unfortunately, it only increased the risk to her life.[43]

Does a victim have the right to defend himself against crime?

To some extent, yes. A victim who reasonably believes he is threatened with injury or death is justified in using sufficient force to prevent the attack or to protect himself from the threatened harm. If his life is in serious danger, he may use force calculated to seriously harm or even kill his assailant.[44] In a number of states, however, a person may not kill his assailant even in self-defense if he can safely retreat, unless he is attacked in his own house.[45] The privilege of self-defense extends to the defense of others in most jurisdictions, and to the defense of one's property, although the use of deadly force generally is not justified in order to protect property.[46] If the victim is prosecuted on criminal charges or is sued in a civil damage action by his assailant for the injury he inflicted, he is relieved from liability if he reasonably acted in self-defense.

The privilege of self-defense extends only to the amount of force reasonably necessary to fend off an imminent danger. If the force used is considered excessive, a jury may hold the victim liable for the harm he inflicts that goes beyond the real or apparent necessities of his own defense. Nor is the victim justified in using violence after his assailant is disarmed or the danger is clearly past; "revenge is not defense."[47]

D. Report of the Victimization

Does a victim have an obligation to report the crime to the police?

Generally, no. Informing police of the commission of most crimes in most jurisdictions is strictly voluntary. A statistical survey indicated that in 1981, only 35.5 percent of the crimes actually committed were reported to the police.[48]

There are some circumstances in which failure to report the commission of a crime is itself a separate crime, which could result in charges being brought against the victim; for example, "misprision" of a felony is a crime under federal law. A victim or witness can be guilty of misprision if he has actual knowledge of the commission of a felony (possibly as a witness) and conceals the crime and fails to report it to the authorities "as soon as possible."[49]

Prosecution for misprision, which is rare, requires that the crime involved be a serious one (a felony), and further requires more than mere silence or failure to report to the police: there must, in addition, be an affirmative act of concealment of the crime's commission.[50]

A few states have laws whereby certain kinds of offenses must be reported to the police. Under these statutes, the failure to report the particular offense when it is discovered is a misdemeanor.[51] A Colorado statute provides that it is the duty of every corporation or person who has reasonable grounds to believe that *any* crime has been committed to promptly report the suspected crime to law enforcement authorities; the statute does not prescribe any punishment, however, for failure to make such a report.[52] In at least 35 states, it is a crime for certain persons to fail to report instances of abuse or neglect of the elderly.[53]

Why do such a large number of victims not report crimes?

According to a survey conducted in 1972, by the Law Enforcement Assistance Administration, the most common reasons cited by victims for not reporting crimes were their beliefs—

1. their belief that nothing could be done or that there was a lack of proof; (34 percent);

2. that the victimization was "not important enough" (28 percent);

3. that the police would not want to be bothered (8 percent);

4. that it was not convenient for the victim to get involved with the criminal justice system (5 percent);

5. that the matter was "private or personal" (4 percent);

6. that they were afraid of reprisal from the offender if they reported the crime to the police (2 percent).[54]

Should victims report the commission of crimes to the police?

Absolutely. If crimes can be committed with the knowledge that a substantial percentage of victims will not report them to the police, there is little or nothing to deter criminals from committing future crimes. Without police involvement, there is little chance that the victim will ever learn the identity of the criminal or have his property returned. In addition, uniform reporting of crimes (even if they are not solved) can lead to greater attention being given to specific kinds of victims and to the problem of crime in dangerous neighborhoods. Accurate reporting can lead to more resources being devoted to law enforcement in those areas.

Are there any practical reasons for victims to report crimes?

Yes. Victims may lose valuable rights by failing to report crimes promptly. All of the existing programs providing compensation for crime victims stipulate that victims promptly report the commission of crimes to the police in order to be eligible. The victim is required to report the crime within periods ranging from twenty-four hours (the Virgin Islands), to three months (New Jersey), unless there is cause for his failure to do so (such as an injury from the crime that places the victim in the hospital).[55] Under the Wisconsin victims' bill of rights, for example, a victim is eligible for the enumerated rights only if the crime is reported to law enforcement authorities within five days of its occurrence or discovery, unless he had a reasonable excuse not to do so.[56]

Similarly, police reports are necessary if the victim intends to claim an income tax deduction for lost property or medical expenses. Where the victimization results in the loss of property or valuable documents, insurance companies and agencies often require "proof of loss"—usually including a police report—before offering reimbursement or replacing lost documents.[57]

Where does the victim go to report a crime?

Most crimes involving physical injury or property loss fall within the jurisdiction of local law enforcement officials and should be reported to the police or to the district attorney in the county in which the crime occurs. Certain crimes—for example, fraud involving the use of the mails, extortion, and kidnapping—may also fall within the jurisdiction of federal law enforcement officials and can be reported either to a federal investigative agency (for instance, the FBI or the United States Postal Inspectors) or to the federal prosecutor (the United States attorney). The victim need not be concerned whether he has chosen the wrong agency or prosecutor, since he will be directed to the appropriate agency if necessary.

This discussion assumes that the victim is seeking to report a crime *after* its occurrence. If a victim is seeking assistance during the commission of a crime, the local police should be notified. All citizens should be familiar with the procedure in their county for contacting the police in an emergency.

Is it illegal to make false statements or reports to the police about the commission of a crime?

Yes. In most states and in cases involving federal jurisdiction, it is illegal to volunteer false information to the police concerning the commission of a crime.[58] The purpose of such statutes is to protect private citizens from false accusation and the resulting embarrassment, annoyance, and aggravation.[59]

Generally, the report must be given *gratuitously* in order to convict a victim or witness of the crime of making a false report that is, the information must be volunteered and unsolicited. The victim or witness cannot be prosecuted if the allegedly false information was given in answer to questions by the police during the course of an investigation.[60]

Can the victim be sued if he mistakenly identifies the wrong person as the perpetrator of the crime or testifies against him?

Generally, no. Although civil actions for damages are sometimes instituted by a criminal defendant against a person who initiated the criminal proceedings or testified against him, such actions are rarely successful.

As discussed in this chapter, witnesses may be subject to criminal sanctions for knowingly making false reports to the police, or for falsely testifying at any stage of the legal proceedings. However, perjury is considered an offense against the public only, and is punishable only by the criminal law.[61]

Historically, witnesses have been immune at common law from civil liability for their testimony in judicial proceedings.[62] Therefore, actions in state courts in which criminal defendants later attempt to sue a witness who testified against them are rare, and are uniformly dismissed on the basis of witness immunity.[63]

Criminal defendants have also sued witnesses for damages in federal courts, alleging that their constitutional right to a fair trial was violated by a witness's false testimony either before a grand jury or at trial. Witness immunity from subsequent civil suits extends to such claims under the federal Constitution and civil rights laws, however, and these suits have also been unsuccessful.[64]

The policy behind the doctrine of witness immunity is that witnesses should be encouraged to cooperate with law enforcement authorities and to make full disclosures of all pertinent information within their knowledge.[65] Even where the immunity doctrine does not strictly apply, courts have held that the same policy protects a witness who, in good faith and without malice, mistakenly identifies the wrong person as the perpetrator of the crime.[66]

While the immunity rule protects a witness from liability for simply furnishing information in good faith to the proper authorities, or appearing in court and testifying during criminal proceedings, the witness who actively instigates a wrongful criminal prosecution for his own improper motives can be held liable to the accused for malicious prosecution. In order to prevail, the accused must demonstrate that the criminal proceedings were instituted against him by, or at the instance of, the witness, maliciously and without probable cause, and that the prosecution terminated in the accused's favor. Proof that the witness knowingly made a false identification or false statements in a criminal complaint, or unduly influenced the authorities to commence the criminal proceeding can support the accused's claim that the witness caused the prosecution to be initiated. Where the criminal proceedings are instituted by the prosecutor on his own decision or after an independent investigation, or pursuant to a valid grand jury indictment, however, the witness is not liable simply because he supplied information in good faith and approves of the prosecution, and he is immune from civil suit for his testimony thereafter.[67]

Can the victim settle his dispute privately without reporting the commission of a crime to the authorities?

Under certain circumstances, yes. Agreements between victims and offenders to settle their disputes privately are permissible for certain kinds of crimes, most typically shoplifting, passing bad checks, and the fraudulent use of credit cards. State "civil compromise" statutes recognize this practice and authorize victims to negotiate a settlement, under court supervision, with the perpetrators of offenses such as the above property crimes and simple assault and battery. The crimes for which compromise is permissible are generally offenses that are also civil torts giving rise to a private cause of action for damages against the offender. Under the civil compromise statutes, the victim must appear before the court and submit a written acknowledgment that he has obtained satisfaction of the injury from the defendant and obtain consent from the court or prosecutor to a dismissal of criminal charges. The court then stays further proceedings and discharges the defendant after he pays court costs.[68]

Absent formal sanction by the court of such a settlement, however, the victim who accepts private reparation from an offender in exchange for a promise not to initiate prosecution may himself be the object of criminal charges for the offense of "compounding." It is a crime in many states if a person receives anything of value in return for his promise either to conceal the fact that a crime has been committed, or to refrain from initiating or aiding in the prosecution of the offender.[69] Such statutes enforce the concept that the original crime was an offense "against society" for which public prosecution is the only remedy; it is not for the victim to redress a personal grievance. It is an affirmative defense to a charge of compounding in some states, however, that the agreement merely involved restitution to the victim in an amount reasonably related to the offense committed.[70]

Civil compromise statutes generally do not permit settlement of serious crimes; a victim or witness may be charged with misprision of felony under federal law if he conceals the commission of a felony of which he has actual knowledge.[71]

In particular cases, for instance, family or neighborhood situations, where the relationship between the victim and offender may make the victim reluctant to prosecute relatively minor offenses, a number of community programs have been instituted to provide mediation and arbitration services in an effort to address the underlying problems and resolve them privately, outside the criminal court.[72]

E. Investigation of the Crime

What happens when a victim reports a crime to the police?

Usually, a patrol officer travels to the scene of the crime, questions the victim and any witnesses and prepares an initial report. If the victim reports the crime by going to the police station, the questioning of the victim takes place at the police station.[73]

If the person who committed the crime is not arrested at the scene or cannot be identified by the victim, the case will be assigned to a detective. In larger police departments, the detective will probably be a specialist in the investigation of certain kinds of cases; for instance, homicide, burglary, theft, or sexual assault. In addition to obtaining written statements from witnesses and analyzing physical evidence, the detectives investigating the case often request the assistance of victims in providing additional details, thoroughly examining the scene of the crime, reviewing photographs in order to identify the offender and arranging a lineup. When the detectives assigned to the case have finished their investigation, they write a final report and present the case to the local prosecutor.

Can the victim obtain a copy of the initial police report?

Yes. Victims can and should obtain a copy of the initial police report, which may be required by an insurance company or the state's victim compensation law in making insurance or compensation claims. Depending upon the jurisdiction, there may be a small fee for obtaining the report.

In addition, the victim should take careful note of the investigating officer's badge number and of the case number assigned to the particular crime (which will appear on the police report). Subsequent inquiries about the status of the case should refer specifically to the case number and, if possible, to the badge number of the investigating officer.

Do the police have the right to keep a victim's property to help them in their investigation or prosecution of the crime?
Yes. Police have broad powers to keep a victim's recovered property if that property will assist them in the investigation of crime or in the prosecution of a criminal action.[74]

Are there any limits on this right to keep property?
There must be a reasonable basis to believe that the property will be useful in an investigation or prosecution. The victim has a right to receive an itemized list, signed by the officer taking possession of the property, indicating each and every item belonging to the victim or witness that was taken into police custody.[75]

When will this property be returned to the victim?
It depends upon the jurisdiction and the circumstances of the case. In general, the prosecutor or the police will retain the victim's property until they determine that it will no longer be needed in an investigation or prosecution. In Rhode Island, Nebraska, Wisconsin, Oklahoma, Florida, and Washington, a victim has the right to have property "expeditiously returned" when it is no longer needed by law enforcement agencies.[76] The Wisconsin, Oklahoma, and Washington statutes, while still leaving the determination of when property is no longer needed to the discretion of law enforcement officers, provide that where "feasible," all victim property "shall be photographed" so that the photographs can be used to assist prosecution and investigations and the actual property can be returned.[77] The Washington statute provides for the return of photographed property "within ten days" of receiving the property.[78] The Nebraska statute also provides for return of property within ten days, although it does not specify that the property be photographed.[79] Each of these statutes, except the Florida and Rhode Island laws, exempts weapons, currency, contraband, property subject to evidentiary analysis, and property to which ownership is disputed.[80]

A similar statute in Kansas explicitly provides that law enforcement officers may photograph property involved in a robbery or burglary and prepare a statement indicating the description of the property, the name of the owner, the location of the robbery, and the name of the investigating officer and photographer. The statement and photograph are deemed "competent evidence" and are "admissible in the prosecution to the same extent as if the property had been introduced as evidence." After the photograph is taken, the property can be returned to its owner. [81]

What happens to the victim's property in states without such statutes?

It depends upon the jursidiction. In some states, the victim must actually pay the state the cost of maintaining property held as evidence. [82] In some states, the release of property being held as potential evidence in a criminal prosecution requires the explicit approval of a judge. [83] In other jurisdictions, the return of property can be accomplished by instruction from the prosecutor or investigating officer to the clerk (usually a police department employee) who maintains the property.

Prosecutors in many jurisdictions will routinely maintain custody of all property taken as evidence until after the trial and after the exhaustion of all appeals. If a victim or witness has need of his property, a specific application for release of that property should be made to the prosecutor involved. [84]

Although not required to do so by statute, many prosecutors' offices, as a matter of policy, photograph evidence so that property can be returned to the victim. [85] Where the photographing and return of evidence is an office policy rather than a legal requirement, the cooperation or consent of counsel for the accused is usually required. [86] The President's Task Force on Victims of Crime has made it a priority for prosecutors, police, and judges to facilitate the prompt return of property to victims through the widespread use of photography and the admission of photographs as evidence at trial. [87] The Justice Department Guidelines promulgated pursuant to the Victim and Witness Protection Act of 1982, also provide that "property of any victim or witness which is held for evidentiary purposes should be maintained in good condition and promptly returned."

In those jurisdictions with no established policy for photographing and promptly returning property, the victim can— and should—appeal to the prosecutor or law enforcement officer in charge of his case. If the request is refused, the victim should ask for a document explaining the reasons for maintaining custody of the property pending trial. If the victim is dissatisfied with the response, he should appeal to a superior of the law enforcement official or to appropriate employees of the local victim/witness assistance agency.

What can a victim do if the prosecutor or police who recovered or took custody of his property, damage, destroy, lose, or otherwise fail or refuse to return that property?

A survey conducted in 1975, in Alameda County, California, indicated that in thirty percent of the cases where the police had recovered victims' property and used it in court, it was never returned to the victims.[88] In a survey conducted in 1979, one-third of the victim/witness units in prosecutors' offices had assisted victims or witnesses in obtaining property return on at least one occasion each month.[89]

The state may retain validly seized property for use as evidence in the criminal proceedings. Such retention has been called unquestionably lawful.[90] Once the criminal proceedings have terminated, however, or where the property has been seized without a search warrant or under an invalid search warrant, the owner is entitled to its return.[91] If the authorities believe that the property is contraband, or if ownership of the property is disputed, a hearing must be provided; the property is presumed to be rightfully owned by the claimant from whom it was seized unless the authorities present evidence that he does not in fact own it.[92]

The victim has several potential civil claims against the officials responsible for custody and return of his property if they fail or refuse to restore it to him. He can bring an action in conversion or replevin to secure the return of his property.[93] He can also seek a writ of mandamus to compel restoration of his property.[94] The state can also be compelled to compensate the owner for the delay in returning his property.[95]

The victim may also be able to maintain an action against the responsible individuals for negligent breach of duty, if they have failed to exercise reasonable diligence to keep the property safe while in their custody. Suits on this basis appear to be rare. However, as a general matter, public officers can be held liable to a person who is injured by their negligent failure to perform their official ministerial duties.[96]

Finally, where officials responsible for custody of his property refuse to restore it to the victim, he may also have a basis for initiating action under the federal Civil Rights Act[96a] for deprivation of property without due process of law.[97] However, since "public officials acting in good faith and without malice in their sphere of official responsibility are entitled to a 'qualified good faith immunity . . . from liability for damages' under section 1983,"[98] the victim must show that the officer responsible deprived him of his rights, and knew or reasonably should have known that the action he took within his official sphere would violate the victim's constitutional rights; for instance, by disregarding or being ignorant of, settled, indisputable law.[99] If the victim can meet the difficult burden of showing that the property clerk or other responsible officer acted according to some policy or widespread practice of failing to properly protect and restore property to the rightful owners, which was approved or acquiesced in by his superiors, those superiors may also be held liable under section 1983.[100]

Are victims obligated to cooperate with the police in investigations of crimes?

No. The victim's cooperation with the police is strictly voluntary. However, as a realistic matter, there is little likelihood that the offender will be arrested unless the victim cooperates with the police investigation. In over ninety percent of those crimes that are "solved" (that is, in which the offender is identified and an arrest made), the victim has cooperated in the investigation.[101]

How is the victim expected to cooperate during an investigation?

If the victim was present during the commission of the crime, he will play a critical role in developing an adequate factual foundation for the police to proceed in their effort to locate and arrest the offender. The police will first ask the victim for a detailed statement of what occurred. Frequently, the victim is interviewed more than once, and the victim's statement is expanded and refined.

After the initial interview with the police, the victim may be asked to participate in any of several procedures to identify the offender. The victim may be asked to view hundreds of photographs, attend a lineup, or do both. The victim may be asked to tape-record telephone calls or, with respect to crimes such as blackmail and extortion, to meet with the offender and record the conversation by means of a device taped to the victim's body. These latter types of cooperation present a degree of risk to the victim, are less typically requested of the victim, and are subject to close supervision by police and prosecutors.

What happens during a lineup?

During a lineup, the victim views a number of persons, usually five or six, and is asked whether any of those persons is the offender. Frequently, the persons in the lineup are asked to repeat the words that were uttered by the offender at the time of the crime.

At the lineup, the victim usually views the suspects from a projection room, through a one-way mirror, or by means of some other device that prevents the suspect from seeing the victim. The suspect is entitled to counsel at a lineup to insure that the procedures used by the police are not unduly suggestive.[102] However, some jurisdictions allow the police or prosecutor to withhold the victim's name from defense counsel and to have the victim make any selection outside defense counsel's presence, so long as the latter has had an opportunity to participate in selecting the "array" and in choosing the manner of display.[103]

Are victims compensated for expenses incurred during investigations?

To some extent, yes. Few jurisdictions reimburse victims for expenses incurred in connection with police investigations. Massachusetts provides transportation costs and mileage fees for victims who assist the district attorney in criminal investigations.[104] Additional aid, such as transportation to and from the police department, remains a policy decision of the local police department or district attorney's office. Most district attorneys' offices that responded to a questionnaire reported informal transportation services for victims.[105] Some limit such service to emergency situations.[106]

The situation changes when an investigation reaches the grand jury stage.[107] Just over half of the states have enacted legislation providing for some compensation for victims who appear as witnesses during grand jury investigations. Such compensation is usually limited to travel expenses and minimal witness fees. Witness fees range from $.50 a day[108] to $30.00 a day.[109] The average witness fee is $10.75 a day. Mileage reimbursements average $.12 per mile. Only a few jurisdictions reimburse witnesses for lodging, meals, and other expenses incurred while attending criminal proceedings.[110]

Do victims have the right to be notified of the progress of the investigation of their case or whether an arrest has been made?

In most states, no. A survey in 1975 (Alameda County, California), showed that twelve percent of the victims surveyed were never notified that an arrest had been made in their cases.[111]

The victims' bills of rights in Nebraska, Rhode Island, Washington, and Wisconsin specifically provide that victims have the right to know whether a case has been "closed" by the police.[112] The New York Fair Treatment Standards Law provides that the agencies which compromise the criminal justice system of the state shall promulgate standards to insure that victims, witnesses, and the relatives of homicide victims receive information regarding the progress of their case, including whether the accused has been arrested, released and the status of any formal criminal proceeding.[112a] The victims' bill of rights in Jefferson County, Kentucky, provides that victims have the right "to be informed whenever possible by local law enforcement agencies, or the county or commonwealth's attorney of the current status of their case and to be informed of the final disposition of that case."

In those states where there is no statutory right to be notified of the progress of an investigation, the victim should feel free to contact the patrol officer or detective involved in the victim's case and to request information concerning the status of the investigation. As a matter of policy, many law enforcement agencies and prosecutors attempt to keep victims so informed. A growing number of victim/witness assistance groups provide notice to victims of the progress of the investigation, the defendant's arrest, and the status of the case as it proceeds through the system. Units in Boulder, Colorado; Clark County, Nevada; St. Louis, Missouri; Sacramento County, California; and Minneapolis/St. Paul, Minnesota, are among those providing this service.[113] A recent survey of victim and witness assistance programs indicated that approximately one-fifth of these programs will check the status of police investigations for victims.[114]

What happens after the police have finished their investigations?

After the police have concluded their reports, the detective or officer in the case presents the written reports, along with his own oral explanation and recommendations, to the local prosecutor. If the prosecutor is satisfied that the police report provides sufficient evidence of the commission of a crime by the alleged offender identified in the report, and further decides that the case has a reasonable probability of success at trial, the prosecutor will take the necessary steps to formally charge the defendant. In many cases, the prosecutor will wish to discuss the charges with the victim or witness before proceeding, in order to satisfy himself that the person identified as committing the crime actually committed it and that the victim or witness will cooperate with the prosecution.

What if the police are unable to identify the person who committed the crime or are unable to obtain sufficient evidence against an identified offender?

After a certain period of time, the police will close their investigation. The length of time that an investigation remains open depends upon the jurisdiction and the offense; in general, the more serious the offense, the longer the police will continue their investigation.

Can the victim force the police to continue an investigation?

No. There are no formal means by which a victim can compel the police to continue conducting an investigation they otherwise wish to drop. The judicial remedy most frequently used in attempts to force official action—the writ of mandamus—is generally unavailable to victims dissatisfied with the way their case has been handled.

What is a writ of mandamus?

Mandamus is "a command in the name of the government directed to an official that orders the official to perform a particular duty."[115] Such writs are available only "to enforce a clear legal right."[116]

Why is the writ of mandamus generally unavailable to victims?

Courts will not issue writs of mandamus unless the party seeking the writ can show that he is "beneficially interested" in the action being ordered. Courts will also not issue writs of mandamus where the official's duty involves the use or exercise of discretion; mandamus is only available to force an official to carry out what are referred to as ministerial tasks.[117]

Where the victim can demonstrate that he suffered injury by the commission of a particular crime, different from that suffered by society at large, courts have held that he is a "party beneficially interested" in the prosecution or investigation of the crime sufficient to justify his standing to bring a mandamus action.[118]

However, because courts will not issue the writ in matters committed to the discretion of the official involved, and because the power to investigate and prosecute crime is committed to the discretion of the executive arm of the government, courts are wary of interfering.[119]

What should the victim do if he is not satisfied with the conduct of the police investigation?

If the victim is not satisfied with the way in which an investigation is being conducted, or is dissatisfied because the police have closed an investigation, he should discuss the matter with a senior official of the police department or with a prosecutor, both of whom have the authority to override a lower-level decision to close a case. In cases where more than one law enforcement agency has jurisdiction, the victim can seek to interest another jurisdiction, typically the federal prosecutor, in pursuing the case.

Do victims have a right of access to police investigative reports?

No. Nearly every state exempts law enforcement investigative files—as opposed to the initial police report—from the general requirements of their laws requiring that public records be open to inspection ("freedom-of-information" or "sunshine" laws). In many states where such an exemption has not been expressly provided by statute, courts have held, or the state attorney general has stated in a written opinion, that investigative files are not public records and thus are not open to public inspection.

One exception to this general rule is that the victim can obtain police investigative reports relating to closed investigations as part of discovery in a civil suit.[120]

F. Arrest

If an arrest is not made at the scene of the crime, by what process is the accused usually arrested?

After the prosecutor has filed a formal charging instrument—usually a complaint or indictment—with the court, the prosecutor requests that a judge sign a warrant authorizing the police to arrest the accused.

If the accused is not arrested at the scene of the crime, what are the chances that the police's investigation will identify him and produce an arrest?

Very slight. In general, only twenty percent of all victimizations involving serious offenses result in an arrest.[121]

Can a police officer called to the scene of a crime make an arrest without a warrant?

It depends upon the crime and the circumstances. Most states allow a policeman to make a warrantless arrest where the officer has probable cause to believe that the defendant committed a felony, even though the crime is not committed in the officer's presence.[122] In general, crimes that carry maximum prison sentences of more than a certain length of time (usually one year) are considered felonies[123]

If the alleged crime is a misdemeanor and is not actually committed in the officer's presence, many states prohibit a police officer from making a warrantless arrest.[124]

Does the officer appearing at the scene of the crime have any discretion in deciding whether or not to make an arrest?

Yes. Officers have a wide degree of discretion in determining when to make an arrest.[125]

What kinds of considerations affect the officer's decision to make an arrest?

In those situations where the officer does not witness the crime's commission, the officer must make his own assessment whether a crime was committed, whether the person or persons identified by the victim or witnesses actually committed the crime, and whether there is sufficient evidence, based upon the officer's experience and training, to demonstrate to a prosecutor and to a judge that the accused committed the crime. In large part, the officer's assessment will depend upon—

1. the severity of the crime;
2. the age of the complainant;

3. the identity (if known) of the offender;

4. the officer's evaluation of the victim's credibility;

5. the officer's evaluation of the extent to which the victim will "follow-through" with a prosecution;

6. the victim's description of how the crime was committed.[126]

Does the victim's desire to press aggressively for a suspect's arrest affect the officer's decision?

Yes. Surveys indicate that where the offense is minor and where the victim does not want an arrest to be made, the officer will usually comply with the victim's wishes. Where the crime is severe and the accused is someone whom the police suspect of prior criminal conduct, the victim's wishes to prosecute will be honored.[127]

Is a police officer free to use his discretion not to make an arrest even if a crime is committed in his presence?

In a few states it is a criminal offense for an officer to neglect to make an arrest where the crime is actually committed in his presence.[128] Victims can also argue that there is a common law rule that officers are bound to make arrests for felonies committed in their presence.[129]

Is there any legal means by which a victim can force the police to make an arrest?

No. Courts have not been sympathetic to attempts by victims or others to force police officers to make arrests.[130]

Have any arguments been made that police are required to make certain arrests?

Yes. A variety of arguments can and have been made why arrests should be required; for example, the New York City Police Department previously had a standing policy and practice of not making arrests in cases involving domestic violence. This policy was rooted in the belief that battered wives brought violence upon themselves and/or were unlikely to pursue prosecution. In *Bruno v. Codd*, a class action was brought on behalf of battered women who had been deprived of police cooperation in making arrests. Plaintiffs argued that the police had a duty under New York City's charter "to preserve the public peace, prevent crime, detect and arrest offenders

. . . and to arrest *all* persons guilty of violating any [criminal] law or ordinance";[130a] and the police practice violated the battered wives' constitutional right to equal protection under the laws, because it constituted discrimination based on sex and was irrational.[131]

Although this argument was not adopted by the court, the litigation did produce a consent settlement with the police department. As part of the settlement, the police department adopted a policy of advising domestic violence victims of their rights and not automatically refusing to make arrests solely because the assaulter and victim are married.[132]

Police departments in a number of other cities have also adopted such policies as a result of litigation brought by battered wives.[133]

If the officer fails or refuses to make an arrest does the victim have any civil redress against the officer?

Generally, no. Most courts have rejected claims that an officer has any civil liability to a victim for failure to make an arrest.[134]

An exception to the general rule has been made in situations where the police have undertaken a "special duty" to an individual; for instance, offered to protect him against the threats of a particular criminal.[135]

Once a victim or witness swears out a complaint and a judge issues a warrant, are the police obligated to make an arrest?

Yes. In some states it is a criminal offense for an officer to refuse or neglect to make an arrest once a warrant has been issued.[136]

Are there circumstances under which the victim can make a warrantless arrest of the person who committed the crime?

Yes. Although the requirements vary with the kind of offense and with the jurisdiction, in most states a victim acting in good faith can make an arrest without a warrant.[137]

Where a jurisdiction requires that the offense be committed in the victim's presence and that arrest follow immediately, these requirements will be strictly enforced; for example, in *Protective Life Insurance Co. v. Spears*,[138] a victim who had nearly been run down by a reckless driver attempted to arrest his attacker hours after the incident. The court held that because the offense involved a breach of the public peace, and an arrest did not take place when the crime was being committed, nor was pursuit for the purpose of arrest begun immediately, the attempted arrest long after the offense was completed was invalid.[139]

Are such citizen arrests common?

No. They are extremely rare.[140] In addition to the personal risk involved in any attempt to make a citizen's arrest, the victim might be liable to the person arrested for damages for false arrest, false imprisonment, or both if it turns out that the person arrested did not in fact commit the crime, that the victim was negligent in believing that the accused had committed the crime, or even that some of the technical requirements of the statute were breached.[141]

Are the police obligated to assist a victim making a citizen's arrest?

In most states, yes. Typically, if the victim requests a police officer's aid, the officer must take the arrested person into custody and bring him before the appropriate local court.[142] However, there may be an exception to this requirement where the police officer has reasonable cause to believe that the arrested person did not commit the alleged offense or that the arrest was otherwise unauthorized.[143]

G. Charging a Person with a Crime

How are people charged with a crime?

The precise details, as well as the names of the stages of the charging process differ from jurisdiction to jurisdiction. In broad outline, however, most jurisdictions adhere to the following procedures:

If the accused is arrested at the scene of the crime, or is otherwise arrested without a warrant, the initial charging document is a criminal complaint. A complaint is a sworn statement that identifies the criminal statute violated and sets forth the facts upon which the police or prosecutor bases the accusation of the defendant. Depending upon the jurisdiction and the nature of the crime, the complaint may be signed by the prosecutor or police officer, but often the victim or witness who reported the crime is asked to sign a complaint. The complaint must set forth "probable cause" to believe both that a crime has been committed and that the defendant committed the crime. "Probable cause" consists of "facts and circumstances . . . sufficient to warrant a prudent man in believing that the [accused] had committed or was committing an offense."[144] A neutral judicial officer makes the determination whether probable cause is established by the complaint.[145]

Within a short time after the filing of a complaint, the accused is entitled to a hearing, frequently denominated the "preliminary examination." In federal courts, the preliminary examination must be held within a "reasonable time" after arrest, but no later than 10 days after arrest if the defendant is in custody or 20 days after arrest if the defendant is not in custody.[146] The time periods in state and local courts may differ; for example, in New York, the preliminary examination must take place within 120 hours of the arrest if the defendant is incarcerated.[147]

What happens at a preliminary examination?

At the preliminary examination, the prosecution must establish through evidence that there is "probable cause" to hold the defendant. The defendant is entitled to have counsel, to cross-examine the witnesses against him and to introduce evidence on his own behalf.[148] In many jurisdictions, the prosecution may present hearsay testimony at the preliminary examination.[149] In such jurisdictions, the victim does not have to testify at the preliminary examination; the prosecution usually establishes probable cause through the testimony of the investigating police officer. Other jurisdictions restrict the prosecution to nonhearsay evidence.[150] In these jurisdictions, the victim's testimony is usually required at the preliminary examination.

The President's Task Force on Victims of Crime has recommended that federal and state legislation be enacted "to ensure that hearsay is admissible and sufficient in preliminary hearings, so that victims need not testify in person."[151] The task force characterized victim testimony at preliminary examinations as "an enormous imposition that can be eliminated."[152]

What happens after the preliminary examination?

If the prosecution does not establish "probable cause," the defendant is released. In felony cases, if the prosecution establishes "probable cause" at the preliminary examination, the defendant is generally held for action by the grand jury. The grand jury is a body of citizens who determine, upon the prosecutor's recommendation, whether to charge the defendant with a crime. The charging instrument issued by the grand jury and on which the defendant stands trial is called an indictment. The indictment is a "probable cause" finding by the grand jury. Barring extraordinary circumstances, the grand jury's finding of probable cause is binding upon the court.[153] Therefore, where a grand jury returns an indictment prior to the scheduled date of a preliminary examination, the preliminary examination is not required.[154]

The Fifth Amendment's guarantee that "[n]o person shall be held to answer for a capital, or otherwise infamous crime (*i.e.*, a felony), unless on a presentment or indictment of a Grand Jury . . ." does not apply to the states.[155] The states, therefore, are free to adopt their own procedures for charging persons with serious crimes. In states with grand jury systems, there are differences both with respect to the quality and the quantum of proof required for an indictment.

How are people charged with crimes if they are not arrested at the scene of the crime?

A defendant who is not arrested at the time of the crime may be subject to some or all of the aforementioned procedures. Thus, after an investigation the police may file a complaint, obtain a warrant, arrest the defendant, and proceed with a preliminary examination and presentation before a grand jury. On the other hand, a prosecutor may decide to present the results of the police investigation directly to a grand jury or otherwise file the state's formal charge.

Is the victim or witness responsible for any false statements in the complaint or to the grand jury?

Yes. Federal law[156] makes it a crime punishable by a fine of up to $10,000 or imprisonment of up to 5 years, or both, to make any false material declaration under oath in any proceeding before a federal court or grand jury. Since the statements in the complaint or to a grand jury are sworn statements, the complainant or witness is subject to punishment under this statute if his statements are knowingly false.

In addition, a person who makes false statements under

oath with respect to material matters in a criminal proceeding is guilty of perjury under various state statutes.[157]

Do victims have the right to counsel before a grand jury?

In most jurisdictions, a grand jury witness's counsel may not be present while the witness is testifying. If a witness wishes to be accompanied by counsel, counsel must remain outside the grand jury room.[158] In those jurisdictions that allow the witness's counsel in the grand jury room, fewer than half expressly provide the right to appointed counsel if the victim cannot afford to retain his own. [159] In Virginia, a witness is entitled to counsel "of his own procurement."[160]

A few of the jurisdictions that allow the witness's counsel to be present in grand jury hearings have imposed restrictions on this rule. Several allow counsel only for those who are "targets" of investigations.[161] Other states provide automatic immunity from prosecution to grand jury witnesses and provide representation only for those witnesses who waive such immunity.[162]

Almost all jurisdictions limit the role of counsel in grand jury proceedings. Although he may consult with his client and advise him of his rights, counsel may not cross-examine a witness or make any arguments to the grand jury.

Can a victim refuse to testify before a grand jury?

No. Unless he has a basis for asserting his Fifth Amendment right not to incriminate himself, a victim who has been subpoenaed to testify before a grand jury—like all citizens—has a legal duty to testify.[163] A willful refusal to testify subjects the victim to penalties for both civil and criminal contempt of court.[164]

Can the victim call witnesses before the grand jury?

No. Only the prosecutor has authority to call witnesses to appear before the grand jury. However, the victim can suggest to the prosecutor that certain witnesses be called to testify before the grand jury.

Who decides what crimes the defendant is to be charged with?

Ultimately, the prosecutor determines what charges will formally be brought against the defendant. If the accused has not already been formally charged in a complaint or indictment at the time of arrest, the police officer will tentatively charge the accused with commission of one or more specific crimes. After reviewing the police officer's report, and perhaps consulting witnesses or the victim, the prosecutor decides with which specific crimes the accused will be charged. Where grand jury action is required, the prosecutor makes a recommendation to the grand jury and drafts the indictment. The prosecutor's recommendations to the grand jury are rarely rejected.[165]

Can the victim compel the prosecutor to seek an indictment or charge the defendant with a particular crime?

Generally, no. Except as already noted, courts have consistently refused to issue writs of mandamus or otherwise act to compel a prosecution.[166] As the Supreme Court has noted, the decision whether to prosecute is solely within the discretion of the prosecutor.[167]

Can the victim initiate prosecution?

In some states, yes. One method by which a criminal prosecution may be initiated is through the filing of a written complaint with a judge or magistrate, alleging that a crime has been committed. The complainant may be examined under oath, together with any witnesses he produces, to determine whether he has a reasonable basis for making the complaint.[168] The judge or magistrate will then issue a summons or arrest warrant for the person charged in the complaint.

In a few states, if a court finds that the prosecutor's refusal to prosecute is unjustified and unreasonable, the judge is authorized by statute to order the prosecutor to institute criminal proceedings after a private citizen has submitted an affidavit that a crime has been committed.[169] As a general rule, however, the prosecutor has absolute discretion in deciding whether to institute criminal proceedings and the nature of the offenses with which the accused will be charged, and in the absence of clearly improper conduct the courts will not interfere with those determinations.

The private citizen who initiates prosecution against the accused must, of course, have a reasonable basis for believing that a crime has been committed and that the person named in the complaint committed it. In Alaska, the name of a person who voluntarily appears before a judge to prosecute a person in any criminal action must be endorsed on the complaint as a private prosecutor. If the court trying the action later determines that the prosecution is malicious or without probable cause, the court will render judgment against the private prosecutor for the costs of the action.[170] Furthermore, if the accused is acquitted after trial, he may institute a civil action for malicious prosecution against the complainant.

Have any challenges to prosecutorial discretion with respect to charging the defendant been successful?

Yes. In Ohio and New York, battered women sought to change police and prosecutorial policies of inaction in cases of domestic abuse. Both cases resulted in consent decrees obligating defendants to provide greater legal assistance to abused women.[171]

What role can counsel hired by the victim play after a prosecution has been commenced?

After prosecution is initiated, whether by citizen complaint or indictment or information, the victim can employ a private attorney who may, at the request or with the consent of the public prosecutor, assist in the prosecution. Although this practice is authorized by statute in only a few states,[172] the courts in most states have permitted the practice so long as the public prosecutor retains control of, and supervision over, the case.[173] Only a few courts have expressly held that privately employed attorneys may not assist the public prosecutor.[174]

Where the prosecutor does not consent to formal participation by a victim's attorney, the court has discretion to permit the attorney to appear as *amicus curiae* (a "friend of the court") and file briefs, or even make motions, argue, introduce evidence or object to examination questions on behalf of the victim. Prosecutors have also worked informally with victims' groups and lawyers and sought their input on trial issues.[175]

What are "victim advocates"?

In some parts of the country, experiments have been conducted with "victim advocates." These advocates are attorneys or private citizens associated with victim/witness services groups who represent the victim's interests on an informal basis during criminal proceedings to insure that the victim's views are considered in bail decisions, plea bargaining, sentencing, and so forth.[176] In some jurisdictions, victim advocates have informally assumed certain legal functions; for instance, conducting witness interviews.[177] However, victim advocates have not yet become widely recognized participants in the criminal justice system. The American Bar Association has recently discussed legislation passed or proposed in some states and the benefits of advocacy programs in providing information to the victim and enhancing his participation in the justice system.[178]

Does the victim need his own lawyer in a criminal proceeding?

No. Absent unusual circumstances, the victim does not need separate representation by counsel in the criminal prosecution of the accused.[179] The victim's concerns with respect to the prosecution can be addressed by the victim/witness agency, a victim's advocate, or the prosecutor. However, contrary to statements made by many prosecutors to the effect that they are "the victim's lawyer," prosecutors represent the state, not the victim. Where the victim's personal concerns conflict with the needs of the prosecution (for example, where a victim's fear leads to an unwillingness to testify), the prosecution's duty is to represent the state's interests rather than the victim's interests.

Where can the victim get a lawyer?

The victim is not entitled to a lawyer provided by the state; he must hire his own lawyer; he should contact his local victim's assistance agency or bar association.

H. The Process After the Charge

What happens after the accused has been charged with a crime?

The arrest of the accused triggers a series of hearings before judges in one or more courts. The order and timing of these hearings, as well as the level of court at which they are held, varies from jurisdiction to jurisdiction. Recognizing that most victims are unfamiliar with criminal procedures, many prosecutors' offices have in recent years prepared pamphlets to explain the criminal process to the victim-witness. In general, after the accused is charged, the following procedures take place:

1. an "arraignment;"

2. pretrial conferences and hearings;

3. pretrial diversion (where permitted and appropriate);

4. "plea bargaining" or trial;

5. sentencing if the defendant is convicted;

6. the release of the defendant.

What is an arraignment?

If the accused has not already been indicted at the time of his arrest, a criminal complaint will be filed. Upon the filing of a complaint, or shortly thereafter, the accused is "arraigned" before a magistrate or judge. At the arraignment, the charges are explained to the defendant, and the court makes sure that the defendant understands his constitutional rights, including the right to an attorney. If the defendant cannot afford to retain an attorney, arrangements are made at this proceeding to obtain an attorney for him (typically a public defender or an attorney associated with a Legal Aid Society). The accused is not asked to plead guilty or not guilty at an arraignment on a complaint.

The arraignment is also the first stage of the criminal process at which bail is set. The conditions for bail are subject to review at every subsequent stage of the criminal process.[180]

At the conclusion of the arraignment, the court fixes a date for the preliminary examination or hearing. The process then continues with the preliminary hearing, grand jury presentation, and arraignment of the accused on the indictment.

An accused who has already been indicted at the time of his arrest is also brought before a judge for an arraignment. The arraignment of a person on an indictment differs from the arraignment on a complaint only in that the accused is required to plead "guilty" or "not guilty" to the indictment. If the defendant pleads guilty, the judge schedules a future time when sentence will be imposed. If the defendant pleads not guilty, the judge will consider the defendant's request to be released on bail pending trial of the action and will typically set a schedule for the filing of pretrial motions by the defendant.

What are "pretrial conferences"?

The accused's arraignment on an indictment is typically followed by one or more pretrial conferences and hearings. These are more and more becoming the true battleground of the criminal justice system, for it is during these proceedings that the court takes evidence and rules on an assortment of frequently outcome-determinative motions made by defendants. Defendants frequently seek by such motions to (1) dismiss the indictment because of improper conduct by the prosecutor; (2) "suppress" physical evidence on the ground that it was unconstitutionally seized; (3) "suppress" a confession or other statement of the defendant on the ground that it was unconstitutionally obtained; and (4) "suppress" the identification testimony of a victim or witness on the ground that it is the product of unduly suggestive identification procedures. At the pretrial conference, the court will also rule on motions by codefendants for separate trials, motions for continuances, and defense requests for "discovery," or information about the prosecution's case. The question of bail is also a proper subject for review at pretrial conferences.

What is the victim's role in pretrial proceedings?

If the defendant does not make any pretrial motions, the victim's role during the pretrial stage will be limited to preparing for his ultimate testimony as a trial witness. This frequently requires a series of meetings with the prosecutor and the police at which the facts of the crime are reviewed at length. Often, defense counsel will want to interview the victim (as well as other witnesses) at this stage in the process. The victim is free to talk to defense counsel if he chooses, but is not required to do so. For that matter, the victim is not required to talk to the prosecutor prior to trial, although a lack of cooperation by the victim may lead a prosecutor to dismiss the charges against the defendant for fear of being unable to prove the government's case. By issuing a subpoena, both the prosecutor and defense counsel can require the victim to attend the trial.

If the defendant makes pretrial motions, the victim may be required to testify at a hearing on the defendant's motions; for example, if the victim will identify the defendant at trial, the defense may try to suppress such an identification by arguing that it is the product of an unduly suggestive pretrial identification procedure. If such a motion is made, the victim may be cross-examined about the circumstances that give rise to the identification.

What is the victim's role in the determination of bail?

No state has granted an express right to crime victims to present their views at a defendant's bail hearing. In recent years, however, a growing consciousness of the victim's concerns has been reflected in state laws and in the procedures followed by prosecutors with respect to bail decisions. In response, for example, Florida recently enacted legislation that permits the victim to be heard if the defendant seeks modification of a bail condition prohibiting him from contact with the victim.[180a]

The Eighth Amendment provides that excessive bail shall not be required, and thus, by implication, an accused has a constitutional right to release on bail at some level. Most state constitutions specifically grant persons charged with a crime the right to be released on bail, except in capital cases. Traditionally, the only factors relevant to a judge's decision in setting the amount of bail, or in releasing the defendant on his promise to appear at trial (recognizance), are those factors bearing on the likelihood that the defendant will appear before the court as required. Those factors include the defendant's assets and liabilities, his family ties, his character and mental condition, his prior record of convictions and appearances in court, and the weight of the evidence against him on the present charge.

Do courts consider the defendant's potential danger to society in setting bail?

Traditionally, no. However, many study groups and victims' advocates, among them the Attorney General's Task Force on Violent Crime, have urged the amendment of state laws to enable judges to consider the danger posed by the defendant to the community in setting bail.[181] Recent constitutional amendments and legislation in a number of states have effected such a change and now require the judge to consider, in addition to the traditional factors, the potential danger to the victim and the community if the defendant is released pending trial or pending an appeal of his conviction. If the judge believes there is a threat of such danger, he can refuse to release the defendant on his own recognizance and can set bail at a higher amount.[182]

A growing number of states authorize the judge to order that the defendant be detained in jail after his initial arrest for a specified limited time, generally either sixty or ninety days (most of those states also require that the trial begin within that time), if he is charged with a dangerous crime, or if the prosecutor demonstrates that the defendant has threatened or has attempted to injure a prospective witness.[183] Other states authorize the judge to order the defendant held without bail only in cases where the defendant was initially released on bail and during that time committed a crime or threatened or intimidated a prospective witness.[184]

Statutes which permit the pretrial imprisonment, without bail, of accused individuals, on the ground that they present a danger to society—"preventive detention" statutes—raise serious due process concerns, because they incarcerate the accused without an adjudication of guilt. The Supreme Court has not determined whether such statutes are constitutional when applied to adults.[184a] However, noting that the liberty interests of juveniles may be subordinated to the *parens patriae* interests of the state, the Supreme Court recently upheld the constitutionality of a New York preventive detention statute applicable to juvenile cases in Family Court.[184b]

On October 12, 1984, the President signed the Bail Reform Act of 1984, which includes the first federal preventive detention law. The Act—which the ACLU opposed as unconstitutional—makes danger to the public a factor to be considered in determining bail. Under the Act, a defendant's release can be conditioned upon his avoiding all contact with the victim and potential witnesses, and the court can hold a defendant without bail if the court concludes that no set of conditions will assure the defendant's presence for trial or the safety of any person and the community. A detention order can only be entered after a hearing. However, in certain cases involving narcotics, crimes of violence and repeat offenders, there is a rebuttable presumption that no condition or combination of conditions will reasonably assure the safety of any other person and the community. [184c]

Is a defendant entitled to be released on bail after being convicted?

Yes. A number of states follow the standard of the federal Bail Reform Act of 1966[185] with respect to release after conviction.[186] Under that standard, a convicted person is to be released under the least restrictive conditions necessary to assure his appearance for sentencing or appeal, unless the court finds that the defendant is likely to flee or will pose a danger to the community. The judge may also order the detention of a convicted defendant pending appeal if the appeal is found to be frivolous or taken for the purpose of delay.

Is danger to the community a relevant consideration in determining bail after conviction?

Yes. The risk of danger posed by the defendant is considered a relevant factor in the case of release after conviction. Despite that fact, the federal standard has been criticized for presumptively favoring release unless a clear showing of such a threat is made. The Attorney General's Task Force on Violent Crime recommended that release on bail not be presumed for convicted persons sentenced to a term of imprisonment and that release be available, at the court's discretion, only to those defendants who are able to provide convincing evidence that they will not flee, or pose a danger to the community, and who can demonstrate that their appeals are likely to result in a reversal of their conviction or an order for a new trial.[187] Adopting that standard, the Bail Reform Act of 1984 provides that a sentenced defendant shall be detained pending an appeal unless the court finds (1) by clear and convincing evidence that the person is not likely to flee or pose a danger to the community and (2) that the appeal is not taken for the purpose of delay and raises a substantial question of law or fact likely to result in reversal or an order for a new trial.[188]

Do victims have a right to speak at bail hearings?

No. Laws requiring consideration of the safety of victims and witnesses imply an expectation that victims and witnesses will have an opportunity to demonstrate that they will be threatened with harm if a defendant is released on bail. Generally, however, victims do not have the right to address the court formally at bail hearings.[188a] One informal procedure practiced by a few prosecutors, which is encouraged by victim/witness services groups, involves a discussion between the victim and prosecutor prior to the bail hearing and presentation of the victim's concerns and supporting evidence by the prosecutor at the hearing.[189] Sometimes the police officer who initially interviewed the victim will transmit the victim's opinion to the court at the hearing. Moreover, because criminal proceedings are public the victim is entitled to *appear* at the bail hearing.[190]

What is "pretrial diversion"?

Many jurisdictions have programs designed to give a "second chance" to first offenders and to others who have committed less serious crimes. Generally under these programs, the accused agrees to submit to the probation department's supervision for a fixed period of time without entering a guilty plea or otherwise being convicted. At the expiration of the fixed time period, the probation department renders a report on the accused's compliance with the terms and conditions of his supervision, which can include restitution. If the report is favorable, the initial charges are dismissed. If the report is unfavorable, the accused is prosecuted.[191]

How are criminal cases resolved?

Criminal cases that are not resolved by pretrial motion, pretrial diversion, or by voluntary dismissal by the prosecutor are disposed of in one of two ways; either the accused pleads guilty to the charges in the indictment or to some lesser charges agreed to by the prosecutor, or the accused stands trial before a judge or jury.

If the accused stands trial, the prosecution must prove its case against the defendant "beyond a reasonable doubt."[192] This is done by the presentation of documentary exhibits and live testimony—including the testimony of the victim—to the trier of fact. At the trial, the accused has the right to be represented by counsel, to confront and cross-examine witnesses against him and not to be compelled to incriminate himself.

Not all criminal trials resolve the charges against the accused. If the jury is unable to agree upon a verdict, a "mistrial" is declared. The prosecutor must then reevaluate his case and decide whether to retry the defendant. If there is a retrial, the victim and other witnesses must testify a second time.

What is "plea bargaining"?

Plea bargaining is the term commonly used to describe the attempt by the defendant and the prosecutor to reach a negotiated settlement disposing of a criminal case. Once such an agreement is reached, the court is generally free to accept or reject the terms.[193]

From seventy to ninety-five percent of the criminal charges filed are disposed of by guilty pleas.[194] Therefore, if the victim is to have any meaningful role in the criminal prosecution, the parties must involve the victim in plea bargaining.

What type of "bargaining" takes place?

A plea agreement can be reached at any time before sentencing, even before the accused is indicted. The accused may agree to plead guilty to certain charges if other charges are dropped; to plead guilty to a less serious offense than that charged; or to plead guilty to all or some of the charges if the prosecutor promises to recommend an agreed-upon sentence.

If the prosecutor agrees to dismiss certain charges, he must ask the court for approval. Such approval is usually granted as a matter of course.[195] Court approval is also required before the defendant is permitted to plead guilty to a less serious offense.[196] Finally, state statutes make it quite clear that any agreement concerning sentencing does not bind the court: the judge is free to accept or reject the agreement.[197]

Why do parties engage in plea bargaining?

Plea bargaining reduces the congestion of the courts. Its proponents argue that without plea bargaining, the courts would be unable to process all of the charges filed.[198] Court congestion is not, however, the only reason why many observers support plea bargaining. The Supreme Court has described plea bargaining as "an essential component of the administration of justice. Properly administered, it is to be encouraged," because it permits prompt and final disposition of a case and minimizes the time which the accused spends in jail before trial.[199] The New York Court of Appeals has pointed out that plea bargaining relieves parties of the risks involved in a trial, allows law enforcement officers to exchange a promise of leniency for important information, and satisfies the ends of justice by permitting sentencing that is individualized to the particular offense and offender.[200] Plea bargaining also allows the prosecutor to make arrangements with the defendant, where applicable, for the voluntary return of the victim's property and for the defendant to get a commitment from the prosecutor for a lower bail.[200a]

Do all states allow plea bargaining?

No. Some observers are critical of plea bargaining. They argue that it denies the defendant his constitutional right to be presumed innocent until proven guilty at trial and that it gives too much power to the prosecutor.[201] In 1975, Alaska eliminated plea bargaining. California has disallowed plea bargaining for twenty-five types of felonies, including murder, rape, arson, and burglary.[202]

A study of the effect of the elimination of plea bargaining in Alaska shows that while the rate of trials increased, the expected onslaught never occurred. One reason why the number of trials remained manageable is that many defendants pleaded guilty even though they had no agreement with the prosecutor.[203] The report also found that on the average, harsher sentences were imposed for relatively minor offenses, drug charges, and embezzlement after plea bargaining was eliminated. Violent offenders did not receive a similar increase in sentencing.[204]

What effect does a plea agreement have on a victim's attempt to receive restitution?

In most situations, a plea agreement can include provisions for restitution. Therefore, the victim seeking restitution should ask the prosecutor to include a restitution provision in any plea agreement with the defendant. If charges are dismissed as part of a plea agreement, some courts may refuse to order restitution for the dismissed offenses.[205]

Do victims have the right to be consulted during plea-bargaining discussions?

Generally, no. While almost half of the state legislatures have enacted statutes regulating plea bargaining, practically all of these provisions remain silent as to the role of the victim. Instead, they focus on the defendant's rights and on the judge's duty to remain separate from any plea discussions.[206]

However, several jurisdictions have expressly provided for victim participation in plea bargaining. The Justice Department Guidelines promulgated in July 1983, provide that department officials should consult with victims of serious crimes concerning plea agreements. In Florida, the state's attorney is required to consult with the victim or his family concerning any plea agreement.[206a] In Nevada, a court may interview witnesses, including the victim, to determine if the offense is

more serious than the plea submitted.[207] A judge in Indiana
may not consider a prosecutor's recommendation of a felony
plea bargain unless the prosecutor has notified the victim of
the plea discussions, the prosecutor's recommendation, and
the victim's right to be present in court when the judge
considers the plea.[208] Similar New York legislation was recently vetoed by the governor, who explained that it would
"significantly delay the disposition of cases."[209]

Of those jurisdictions that do not expressly provide for
victim participation in plea bargaining, several allow indirect
participation by permitting judges to order and review presentence reports that include victim impact statements prior to
accepting the plea.[210] Thus, even though the victim is not
present in court, his statements to the probation officer concerning the effect the offense has had on him are given
consideration.

Victims in the remaining jurisdictions must rely on informal practices of the local prosecutors' offices. Many such
offices regularly consult with the victim before finalizing a
plea agreement.[211]

What is the victim's role at trial?

At trial, the victim is typically called to testify as a witness
for the prosecution. As a witness, it is the victim's duty to tell
the court and jury exactly what happened. Because the evidence heard by the court and jury must conform to certain
legal rules, witnesses do not tell their stories in narrative
form. Rather, the witness is asked to answer specific questions posed by the prosecutor. This process is called direct
examination.

After the prosecutor has finished questioning the victim,
the defendant's lawyer has the right to ask further questions,
known as cross-examination. The prosecutor then has the
right to ask further questions, or to "redirect" examination.
This process continues until both the prosecutor and defense
attorney excuse the witness.

What can defense counsel ask the victim on cross-examina-
tion?

Evidentiary rules vary from jurisdiction to jurisdiction, and
a detailed study of the many rules relating to cross-examination
is beyond the scope of this book. Generally, however, defense counsel has wide latitude to question the victim about

all matters covered during the victim's direct testimony, as well as matters relating to the victim's bias, motive, interest, and credibility in general.[211a]

How does the victim know what to expect as a witness?

Prior to testifying, the prosecutor will meet with the victim to review the facts and to acquaint the victim with courtroom procedure. At that time, various "rules" of courtroom procedure are discussed with the witness. As part of their victim-witness programs, many prosecutors have published these "rules" in pamphlet form.

The defendant's lawyer, or a defense investigator, may also wish to speak to the victim prior to the trial. The victim is free to speak to a defense representative or to decline to do so as the victim chooses.

Is the victim always called as a witness?

No. In some cases, the victim may not be called to testify by the prosecutor. This occurs when there are other witnesses to the crime and when the prosecutor concludes that for some reason—for example, fear, nervousness, or lack of recollection—the victim will not be a good witness. A decision by the prosecutor not to subpoena the victim does not necessarily relieve the victim of the obligation to testify. Like all other witnesses, the victim can be subpoenaed as a witness by the defendant.

Can the victim insist on testifying?

No. The victim cannot insist on testifying if he is not called as a witness by the prosecution or the defense.

Are trial witnesses compensated for their attendance at trial?

Yes. Witnesses appearing at trial are entitled to witness fees in most jurisdictions.[212] Such fees are usually limited to traveling expenses and to a nominal daily allowance.[213] However, some courts provide fees only for those witnesses who were subpoenaed to appear.[214] Victim/witness services agencies will assist the victim or witness in filling out forms and complying with any other procedural requirements relating to obtaining witness fees.

Can a victim be forced to attend trial?

Yes. A party may subpoena a victim or witness to testify. A

subpoena is a court order commanding the recipient to appear; if the recipient fails to appear, he is in contempt of court and may be subject to a fine or imprisonment.

In addition, almost all jurisdictions have enacted material witness statutes. Under these statutes, a police officer or a party to a criminal proceeding may submit an affidavit to the court stating that a certain witness's testimony is material and that the witness will probably not appear at trial. The court may then order the prospective witness to appear in court where a hearing is held to determine his materiality. If the court determines that the witness is material, he may have to provide a surety or undertaking to guarantee his appearance. If he refuses, he may be detained until trial or, if appropriate, until his deposition is taken.[215]

Material witness statutes generally do not set out the rights of material witnesses. Fewer than a quarter of the states expressly provide the right to counsel. Under federal law, counsel is appointed "whenever the United States magistrate or the court determines that the interests of justice so require and such person is financially unable to obtain representation."[216] Most of the other jurisdictions imply a right to counsel by providing that right, either at arraignment[217] or at the initial appearance.[218]

Can a victim get a subpoena set aside?

Yes. A victim, like any other witness, can make a motion to set aside, or "quash," a subpoena. Because the victim's testimony will rarely be irrelevant or privileged,[219] such motions are not frequently made or granted. Generally, a victim cannot quash a subpoena to testify on the grounds that compliance would be embarrassing, emotionally traumatic, or dangerous.[220] Where the witness has already testified on behalf of the prosecution and has been cross-examined by the defendant, further defense subpoenas have been quashed as "oppressive."[221]

Can family members remain in the courtroom during trial to provide emotional support for the victim?

Testifying is a traumatic event for the victim. Often he or she will want family members in the courtroom to provide support and to minimize this trauma.[222] Since most courts are open to the public, family members can usually attend. Defense counsel can, however, deny the victim this means of support by serving family members with subpoenas. Even if the defense has no intention of calling them, the family members are thus designated as witnesses. The defense attorney may then ask the judge to clear the court of all witnesses not presently testifying, including the family of the victim.[223] This technique, although it is used, is an abuse of the subpoena process, and such subpoenas can be challenged and quashed.

Does the rule excluding witnesses from the courtroom permit defense counsel to exclude the victim?

Yes. In fact, the President's Task Force on Victims of Crimes "time and again" heard the complaint that victims were excluded from the trial by this tactic. Recognizing the unfairness of this strategy, the task force has recommended that victims and families of victims be excepted from the rule excluding witnesses from the courtroom. In particular, the task force recommends that one designated person be allowed to be present as support for the victim, even if that person has been served with a subpoena.[224]

Are trial schedules usually adhered to?

No. If either party desires additional time before the commencement of trial, he may move for a continuance. Although records are not routinely kept on the number of continuances granted, one study reported that almost fifty percent of the major misdemeanor cases in the District of Columbia had been delayed at least once.[225] There are an average of two and a half continuances granted in each criminal case in the Bronx.[226] According to a 1972 study, twenty-six percent of the cases alerted for trial each week in the District of Columbia were formally continued, while numerous others were repeatedly postponed until the next day.[227]

How do postponements of trial dates affect victims?

Institutional participants in the criminal process frequently find continuances advantageous. The defense attorney requests them to help prepare for trial, or in some cases in the hope that the prosecution witness's memory will fade or the witness will become unavailable. In addition, a defendant who is released on bail can avoid imprisonment for a longer period of time if his attorney delays conviction by requesting continuances. The district attorney will often ask for a continuance because his schedule is too full to allow him to prepare for trial.[228] Finally, the court will often grant a continuance because of its congested calendar.

The victim, however, does not benefit from continuances. Victims are often required to take time off from work or to arrange for child care in preparation for their court appearances. When a trial is postponed after the victim has arrived at court, his inconvenience and expense must be duplicated. Such postponements also prolong the trauma to which the victim is exposed.[229]

Have these hardships on the victim been recognized?

Yes. Many district attorneys' offices have tried to minimize the hardships that result from continuances by having their witnesses "on call": if a witness can be reached by telephone and can arrive in court fairly quickly, he need not appear until notified by telephone.[230]

The President's Task Force on Victims of Crime has made several recommendations that would further aid the victim. As for prosecutors, the task force recommends that (1) the prosecutor should vigorously oppose continuances unless legitimate investigation is incomplete, or the victim's schedule so requires; and (2) the prosecutor should determine in advance if a continuance is necessary, and inform the victim of such a continuance before he arrives at court.[231]

As for the judiciary, the task force recommends that (1) the court should grant continuances sparingly and only for good cause; and that when a court does grant a continuance, it should state clearly on the record why the continuance was granted, and who had requested it.[232]

Can an employer fire a victim or witness for work time lost due to his participation in criminal proceedings?

Unfortunately, although most states have laws prohibiting an employer from discharging or imposing any other penalty on an employee who is summoned for jury duty, only a few provide similar statutory protection to victims and witnesses subpoenaed to testify in a criminal case.[233]

Even those states that forbid the dismissal of employees do not require that employers pay employees for time lost as a result of court appearances. However, victim/witness programs try to encourage employers to continue paying the employee's wages.[234] A victim/witness assistance unit associated with the St. Louis, Missouri, city circuit attorney's office stated in response to a recent survey that in the relatively rare case in which they are unable to persuade an employer to pay its employee for the time spent in court, the unit itself pays lost wages on an hourly basis after receiving verification that the hours were docked. That system appears to be unique.

Do any of the victims' bills of rights recognize the employment-related problems of being a victim?

Yes. The states that have passed victims' bills of rights, Nebraska, Rhode Island, Oklahoma, Washington, Florida, and Wisconsin—as well as the federal guidelines, all stipulate that victims and witnesses be provided with "employer intercession services" to ensure that the employers of victims and witnesses will cooperate with the criminal justice process in order to minimize an employee's loss of pay and other benefits resulting from court appearances.[235] Even in those states that have not yet enacted specific legislation, many victim/witness services groups provide aid to employees by notifying their employers about the criminal proceedings and discussing with them the need for their cooperation. By improving witness notification procedures, these service groups also attempt to minimize the amount of work time lost.

What kinds of protection against intimidation or retaliation are available to witnesses?

Victims and witnesses are sometimes intimidated and harassed by the accused and, depending upon the circumstances, can only be protected by one or all of the following: (1) protection against disclosure of their addresses and, in some cases, their names; (2) the right to give testimony by deposition or in closed courtrooms during hearings and trial; (3) orders prohibiting the defendant from having any contact with them; and (4) police protection. Under current laws, however, these rights are limited.

Is the accused entitled to know the victim's name and address?

Generally, yes. In many states, the complaint, indictment, or information, a copy of which must be given to the defendant, is required to state the names, and sometimes the addresses, of all witnesses whom the state expects to testify at trial.[236] Other states require that witnesses' names and addresses be disclosed by the prosecutor during pretrial discovery.[237] Information is thus usually available to the defendant in the very early stages of prosecution when he is often free on bail or recognizance, which enables him to locate a witness in order to harass him. Moreover, the initial police reports are available for inspection as public records in most jurisdictions. Finally, the defendant often learns the names and home addresses of victims and witnesses through newspaper and television reports, even if his own attorney withholds from him the information disclosed by the prosecutor. While the courts have the power to prevent disclosure of a witness's name or address, they generally require convincing evidence of an actual threat to the witness's safety before finding nondisclosure permissible.[238]

Have any steps been taken to permit victim anonymity?

Yes. The general policy favoring disclosure of the victim's identity is being reexamined. A number of states, (among them, California, Florida, and Georgia) have statutes that protect police officers and other experts from disclosure of their addresses when they are called as witnesses. A few states have recently passed laws that also authorize that names and addresses of other witnesses be withheld; for example, Illinois[239] allows the court to deny disclosure if it finds that there is a substantial risk of physical harm, intimidation, or unnecessary annoyance. Connecticut[240] specifically protects any victim of a sexual assault from divulging his or her address, and a number of states limit public disclosure of any information that may identify a minor victim of a sexual offense.[241] A bill was introduced in Rhode Island in 1981, which would have prohibited the publication or broadcasting of the name and address of a victim of a criminal offense, unless the victim gave written consent.[242] The bill failed to pass the assembly, however.[242a] A bill is presently pending before the New York State Senate that contains broad protections against disclosure of the identities and addresses of victims of, or witnesses to, violent crimes. The bill would also prohibit disclosure of the identities of crime witnesses who specifically request nondisclosure.

Some of these laws apparently are intended to protect victims more from the embarrassment of public disclosure than from intimidation by the defendant. A Connecticut statute, for example, provides that unless the court specifically orders disclosure, a victim's name and address shall be kept confidential but shall be made available to the defense (presumably to permit defendant's counsel to interview him).[243]

The defendant and his counsel often have a legitimate need to learn the identity and address of the victim or a witness. Proper preparation of a defense can require investigation relating to the victim or a witness, and balancing the defendant's rights and the victim's rights cannot be done in the abstract. Both the President's Task Force on Victims of Crime and the Justice Department Guidelines have recommended that, to the extent possible, the addresses of victims and witnesses not be made public *or* available to the defense, absent a clear need as determined by the court. At the present time, no state law provides such broad protection.[243a]

Can the victim give testimony behind closed doors?

Generally, no. In most cases, a witness must give his testimony publicly at the trial of the accused. Criminal trials are presumptively open to the public and the press, both historically and as a constitutional right.[244] The U.S. Supreme Court recently invalidated a Massachusetts statute that required trial judges to exclude the press and public from the courtroom during the victim's testimony in trials for specified sexual offenses involving victims under the age of eighteen.[245] The court made it clear that state laws containing mandatory closure rules are unconstitutional. Therefore, it is up to the trial judge to decide, on a case-by-case basis, that concern for a crime victim's well-being necessitates closure of the courtroom during his testimony.

Are trials ever broadcast on television?

Yes. Although the U.S. Judicial Conference has consistently opposed televising federal judicial proceedings,[245a] twenty-six states now permit television coverage of trials. The advent of television into the courtroom can increase the trauma of testifying at trial. Surveys have shown that the presence of television cameras in the courtroom causes witnesses to be distracted, nervous, and self-conscious.[246] It has also been suggested that subjecting a witness to being televised over his objection constitutes an invasion of his right to privacy.[247] Nevertheless, the Supreme Court has ruled that it is not unconstitutional to televise trials, absent a showing on appeal that such media coverage interfered with the jury's ability to adjudicate fairly.[248] Although in most states the trial judge has the power to prohibit the televising of witnesses in appropriate situations, he is not required to respect the witness's wishes; for example, the Florida Supreme Court in *In re Post-Newsweek Stations, Florida, Inc.*,[249] specifically mentioned three cases in which the trial judge refused requests by witnesses and victims not to have their testimony televised. In each case the trial judge's decision was upheld on appeal. One case involved the widow of a murder victim; another, a prison inmate who feared retaliation; and the third, a sixteen-year-old rape victim.[250]

Do the victim's privacy interests ever permit closure of a trial?

Yes. Judges occasionally exclude the press and public from the courtroom, or refuse a request to televise a particular trial, or permit specific witnesses to testify in the judge's chambers, particularly in cases of rape or sexual offenses against children. No general rule can be formulated, however, and the procedure in a given case depends a great deal on the judge's sensitivity regarding the potential psychological harm to the victim if he or she is required to testify publicly.

Can a victim's testimony be taken prior to trial and then read to the jury?

Sometimes. In rare cases, a witness may be permitted to testify by deposition prior to the actual trial, and not appear in court at all. The circumstances in which testimony by deposition is permitted, however, are usually limited to those where the witness will not live until the trial or will be too ill to testify.[251]

Are there laws against victim/witness intimidation?

Yes. Both the states and the federal government have laws making it a criminal offense to injure, threaten, intimidate, or harass a witness in order to influence or prevent his testimony.[252] The judge may routinely require as a condition of a defendant's pretrial release that he not have any contact with the victim or witnesses, or even go near their neighborhoods.[253] If the defendant violates this type of condition, stricter additional conditions can be imposed, or his bail can be revoked. Many victim/witness services groups intercede on behalf of a fearful victim or witness and warn the suspect of the consequences of any threatening act or notify his attorney to do so, recommend conditions of release or pretrial detention, notify the police to investigate any threats that occur, and even file charges against the suspect.[254]

Under the federal Victim and Witness Protection Act of 1982, the court may issue a restraining order prohibiting harassment of a victim or witness when there are reasonable grounds to believe such harassment exists or is threatened.[255]

Do police offer physical protection to witnesses?

In extreme cases police protection may be provided for the victim or witness, or they may be relocated so that the accused will not find them.[256] Relocation programs are controversial and are often criticized as offering inadequate protection to, and imposing undue hardship upon, the witness or relatives of the witness.[257] It is ironic indeed that in cases involving relocation, it is the victim or witness—involuntarily made a critical part of the prosecution—who has to give up his home, job, identity, and often family ties, while the defendant frequently remains at home.

As a practical matter, police departments simply do not have adequate resources to provide protection for victims and witnesses in all cases. It is often difficult for the victim of intimidation to prove that the accused has threatened him, since many threats are made by anonymous telephone calls. The intervention of victim/witness assistance units has proved successful in many areas, however, in responding to the fears of victims and providing counseling and liaison procedures with regular law enforcement; for example, in St. Louis, Missouri, "an informal but real" arrangement between the victim assistance unit and the detective bureau of the police department, as well as officers assigned to the city attorney's office, includes police contact with the victim and members of his family, help to the victim or witness in moving within the area, and provision of funds for transportation to enable the victim or witness to leave town temporarily to avoid harassment. Such services can be invaluable because they are undertaken informally, without the problems of proof involved in formal legal action or unnecessary strain on the resources of regular law enforcement.

Does the victim have any recourse if the defendant is acquitted after trial?

Generally, no. The constitutional guarantee against double jeopardy protects a defendant from any further prosecution after acquittal. The policy behind the guarantee against double jeopardy is that the prosecution should not be allowed to make repeated attempts to convict a person for an alleged offense, thereby subjecting him to expense and embarrassment and forcing him to live in a continuing state of insecurity about his personal freedom.[258] Indeed, the double jeopardy clause precludes the prosecution from appealing from an acquittal. "A judgment of acquittal, whether based on a jury verdict of not guilty or on a ruling by the court that the evidence is insufficient to convict, may not be appealed and terminates the prosecution when a second trial would be necessitated by a reversal."[259]

Are successive prosecutions in different jurisdictions barred by an acquittal?

No. Successive prosecutions in different jurisdictions are not barred by the double jeopardy clause. Under the principle of dual sovereignty, the same transaction may give rise to different criminal offenses for double jeopardy purposes when each is defined as a crime by a separate sovereign government. Thus, federal prosecution after a state trial (or vice versa), or prosecutions by separate states that each have appropriate jurisdiction, would not be barred.[260]

Federal prosecutors generally request a dismissal of federal charges after a state trial following an established policy that there should be no federal prosecution after a state trial, unless there is a compelling federal interest supporting dual prosecution.[261] New York prohibits subsequent prosecution of an offense tried in another jurisdiction, unless the previous trial was dismissed by a court order expressly founded on the insufficiency of the evidence to establish some element of the offense that is not required to be established in New York.[262] The Supreme Court of Michigan has held that the Michigan constitution bars successive federal-state prosecutions unless the state's interest in the prosecution is distinctly different from the federal government's interest.[263] Many states follow the dual sovereignty rule, however, and permit prosecution of a defendant, with specific exceptions, after he has previously been tried in a different jurisdiction.

How does the court determine what sentence to impose?

If the accused is convicted—either by a guilty plea or after trial—the court sets a date for sentencing. Prior to the sentencing date, the probation department will conduct an investigation into the defendant's background and the circumstances of the crime. The results of that investigation, as well as any recommendation by the probation department as to an appropriate sentence, are set forth in a report and transmitted to the judge.

At the sentencing hearing, the defendant and his counsel have the right to present to the judge any facts in mitigation of punishment. They may also comment on the probation department's presentence investigation report, a copy of which is usually made available to them.

In some states, particularly in capital cases, a separate hearing devoted solely to the question of sentencing is held before the jury, which then fixes a sentence; under many such statutes, the jury's sentencing decision is advisory only, and the judge retains final responsibility for imposing the sentence.[264]

What are the common sentencing alternatives?

After a defendant is convicted of a misdemeanor, the sentencing court will usually order him to pay a fine, place him on probation, suspend his sentence, or sentence him to a period of imprisonment.[265] If the misdemeanor conviction is the result of the defendant's agreement to plead guilty to a misdemeanor in exchange for a dismissal of a felony charge, the defendant is more likely to receive a prison term. Indeed, in California more than fifty percent of such convictions result in imprisonment.[266] If the charge was originally a misdemeanor, it is unlikely that the defendant will spend time in prison.[267]

A defendant convicted of a felony will usually receive a prison sentence or be placed on probation. A third to half of those convicted of felonies receive prison sentences. An individual defendant's chance of imprisonment depends upon whether he previously has been convicted and the seriousness of his offense.[268]

The period of imprisonment for a particular offense, or the range of possible penalties, is set by statute. Some jurisdictions require that the court set a fixed period of imprisonment within statutory limits; most allow the court to set a maximum and a minimum sentence that fall within statutory boundaries.[269] In such an instance, the defendant's actual release date is determined by the parole board.

Under the federal Sentencing Reform Act of 1984, enacted on October 12, 1984, a Sentencing Commission is established. The Commission will promulgate guidelines containing sentencing ranges for offenses to be used by federal courts in sentencing defendants. Once the guidelines and other aspects of the new system go into effect, a defendant will serve the sentence imposed by the court, with credit off for good behavior; the parole system will be abolished.[269a]

What are the nonincarceration alternatives?

The sentencing court generally has the discretion to place a convicted offender on probation. Probation is usually imposed when the court finds that a prison sentence is not necessary for the defense of society, but that the defendant does need supervision.[270] The court has the discretion to decide the length and terms of probation. Terms often include paying a fine, refraining from criminal activity, and reporting regularly to the probation officer.[271] The terms of probation may also include restitution to the victim.[272] Such a term is more likely if the victim has initiated civil suit.[273]

Restitution may be a factor in the disposition of a case without regard to whether the defendant is placed on probation.[274] Thus, the offender may be required, as part of his sentence, to make restitution to the victim. Such a disposition is usually limited to nonviolent property crimes. If the offender fails to make restitution after it has been ordered as part of his sentence, he may be held in contempt.[275]

Under the Sentencing Reform Act of 1984, the court may order the defendant to make restitution, under specified conditions, in addition to any sentence of imprisonment, fine or probation. In felony cases, if the court places a defendant on probation, one of the conditions of probation must be either a fine, community service or restitution. An order of restitution entered by the court can be enforced by the victim as a civil judgment. Moreover, without regard to a restitution order, the court can order a defendant convicted of an offense involving fraud to give notice of his conviction to the victims of his offense. Presumably, such notice will enable the victims to institute civil actions.[275a]

What happens to a defendant acquitted by reason of insanity?

A defendant found not guilty by reason of insanity has formally been acquitted and is not subject to the regular sentencing procedures. Nonetheless, such a defendant cannot be discharged in most states without a court order.[276] Indeed, many defendants who are adjudicated insane face longer confinement than they would have faced if found guilty.[277]

The court usually has the authority to order the temporary detention of a defendant found to be insane for purposes of observation.[278] After the initial observation period, most states provide an adversarial hearing to determine whether the defendant should be committed to a mental hospital.[279] There is, however, no consensus on certain aspects of the hearing. Some states require a finding of potential danger to society by clear and convincing evidence, while others require only a preponderance of evidence.[280] Some courts impose a presumption of danger to society, while others require a *de novo* determination.[281] Finally, certain jurisdictions do not allow the defendant to be committed for a period longer than the authorized prison sentence for the offense charged, while others impose no such limitation.[282]

Under the Federal Insanity Defense Reform Act of 1984, a hearing must be held within forty days of the verdict where a defendant is found not guilty only by reason of insanity. At the hearing, the defendant has the burden of proving that his release would not create a substantial risk of bodily injury to another person or serious damage to the property of another due to a present mental disease or defect. The defendant must make such a showing by clear and convincing evidence if the crime involved bodily injury to another, serious damage to the property of another, or a substantial risk of such injury or damage. In all other cases, the showing must be made by a preponderance of the evidence. If the defendant fails to make such a showing, he is committed to a "suitable facility" until such time as the director of the facility certifies to the court that the standard described above has been met.[282a]

Although the victim is not generally permitted to participate in the commitment hearing, he may have the right to notice before the victim is released or placed in a less secure facility.[283]

Do courts consider victims' statements in determining sentences?

In may states, yes. Several jurisdictions have enacted statutes allowing victims to speak at sentencing hearings.[284] Of these jurisdictions, a few allow counsel or a family representative to appear on behalf of the victim.[285]

Several other jurisdictions provide indirectly for victim participation in sentencing hearings by permitting the court to hear witnesses if the court so chooses or if a party so requests.[286] Of course, victims are always free to address a letter to the sentencing judge, stating their views on an appropriate sentence.

What is a victim impact statement?

Statutes in roughly one-quarter of the jurisdictions, including the federal courts, require that the presentence report prepared by the probation department to aid the court in determining an appropriate sentence include a victim impact statement.[287] Local prosecutors' offices in other jurisdictions informally provide victim impact statements or reports.[288] Such a statement usually details any physical, emotional, or financial impact the crime has had on the victim, or on the family of a homicide victim, as well as any attempts by the victim to receive restitution.[289] Depending upon the jurisdiction, either the victim supplies a statement or the probation officer compiles the information and submits a report.

Most states providing for victim impact statements require that they be automatically included in the presentence report. Several jurisdictions, however, require a victim impact statement only after the offender is convicted of a felony or a crime of violence.[290] In some jurisdictions, they are not required at all. In Virginia, for example, the court must demand the statement.[291]

Of those jurisdictions that do not expressly provide for victim impact statements, one-third have enacted general provisions that allow the court to request such a report.[292] The majority of jurisdictions therefore make available a victim impact statement, either automatically or upon demand.

What is "parole"?

Parole is the supervised release of a prisoner before he has served his entire sentence. Eligibility for parole is fixed by statute or by the sentencing judge.[293] A prisoner is generally eligible for parole after serving his minimum term of imprisonment.[294] In most states, those eligible for parole may request a hearing so that they can explain why they should be released.[295] However, neither a hearing nor the parole system is constitutionally required.[296] Indeed, under the federal Sentencing Reform Act of 1984, the federal parole system will be replaced by a system of sentences in accordance with guidelines promulgated by a federal sentencing commission.[296a]

Typically, an administrative body—the "parole board"—makes the decision as to whether or not to release an eligible prisoner. If the board chooses to grant parole, it may qualify release on the prisoner's promise to meet certain conditions. These conditions are decided by the board, and commonly include—

1. refraining from any criminal activity or association with criminals;

2. abstaining from liquor;

3. carrying no firearms;

4. performing some community service;

5. reporting regularly to a designated parole officer.[297]

The parolee may also have to agree to pay restitution to the victims of the crimes he committed.[298] In addition, some parole boards may stipulate that the prisoner admit that he committed the crimes for which he was convicted.[299]

Although a parolee is no longer in prison, the state continues to impose restrictions on the parolee's freedom. Indeed, states view parole as a type of confinement. In New York, for example, those on parole are "in the legal custody of the division of parole until expiration of the maximum term or period of sentence."[300]

What impact does public opinion have on the parole decision?

The public may disagree with the parole board's decision, but it probably cannot force the board to change its mind. The parole board's decision is required to be made on the basis of the defendant's rehabilitation while incarcerated and not on the community's memories of the initial crime. In direct response to public outcry over its original determination, a parole board (Marin County, California) rescinded its decision to grant parole to a convicted rapist and murderer.[301] The superior court found that this reaction violated the prisoner's due process rights: the parole decision must rest on relevant, articulated grounds. The board had not stated why public opinion was relevant to its decision.[302]

What if a parolee violates the conditions set by the parole board?

If a parole officer has reason to believe a parolee has violated any conditions of his parole, the officer may report the violation to the board. The board may then issue a warrant for the arrest of the parolee.[302] Officers and boards are usually given a great deal of discretion in deciding when such a violation has occurred.[304]

After a parolee is arrested and threatened with revocation of parole and imprisonment for the remainder of his sentence, the Constitution provides him with certain rights.[305] Initially he is entitled to a preliminary hearing to determine whether there was probable cause to arrest him for violation of parole.[306] He must be given notice of when the hearing will occur, as well as the opportunity to present evidence and cross-examine witnesses.[307] If probable cause is found, the parolee may demand a revocation hearing at which it will be decided whether parole should be revoked.[308] The parolee is entitled to notice of this hearing, disclosure of the evidence against him, the right to cross-examine witnesses and present his own evidence, and an impartial hearing body.[309]

Do parole boards consult the victim before granting his assailant parole?

Generally, no. Fewer than one-fifth of the states expressly provide for victim attendance at parole hearings.[310] Of those states that provide for such attendance, most allow attendance only if the offense was serious.[311]

The remaining states do not expressly disallow public parole hearings.[312] Several provide that victims or families of victims are to receive notice of parole hearings.[313] Such notice is either given personally to the victim or published in a local newspaper. Presumably, if victims receive a notice of hearings, they are permitted to attend them.

In June 1984, the United States Parole Commission promulgated rules which provide that victims who request it will be given advance notice of a parole hearing, so that they may present their views, either orally or in writing.[313a] Then, in October 1984, legislation was enacted which specifically provides for Parole Commission consideration of oral or written statements by victims.[313b] Several states also allow victims or their families to submit written statements to parole boards.[314] A few other jurisdictions include such statements in presentence reports, which are then made available to the parole board.[315]

In California, a victim or the relatives of a dead victim have the right to appear before the parole board.[316] In one recent case, a convicted murderer agreed to pay the victim's parents $100,000 to settle a civil wrongful death suit against the murderer. As part of the settlement, the victim's parents agreed not to oppose the defendant's parole.[317]

Notes

1. *Data Processing Service Org. Inc. v. Camp*, 397 U.S. 150 (1970); *See also Worth v. Seldin*, 422 U.S. 490 (1975); Goldstein, "Defining the Role of the Victim in Criminal Prosecution," 52 *Miss. L. J.* 515, 552 (1982) [hereafter "Goldstein"].

2. *Linda R. S. v. Richard D. et al*, (410 U.S. 614, 619 (1973). *See also Leeke v. Timmerman*, 454 U.S. 83 (1981); *Commonwealth v. Malloy*, 450 A.2d 689 (Sup. Ct., Pa. 1982).

3. Hall, "The Role of the Victim in the Prosecution and Disposition of a Criminal Case," 28 *Vand. L. Rev.* 931, 932 (1975) [hereafter "Hall"]; W. LaFave and A. Scott, *Handbook on Criminal Law* (1972), pp. 11, 14.

4. McDonald, "Towards a Bicentennial Revolution in Criminal Justice: The Return of the Victim," 13 *Amer. Crim. L. Rev.* 649, 651–53 (1976) [hereafter "McDonald"]; R. Lane, *Policing the City—Boston 1822–1885* (New York: Atheneum, 1971), pp. 6–10; Nelson, *Emerging Notions of Modern Criminal Law in the Revolutionary Era: An Historical Perspective, Criminal Justice in America* (1975), p. 108.

5. McDonald, *supra* note 4, at 656 n.41; E. H. Sutherland and D. R. Cressey, *Principles of Criminology* (Philadelphia: Lippincott, 1966), p. 503.

6. McDonald, *supra* note 4, at 659–61.

7. *Id* at 657–58.

8. *Id* at 666–68.

9. Despite the criminal justice system's practical dependence upon the victim, until recently victims have been routinely denied input into the crucial decisions relating to arrest and prosecution. Indeed,

victims routinely find that they are not even given information concerning the status of their case. R. Lynch, "Improving the Treatment of Victims: Some Guides for Action," in *Criminal Justice and the Victim*, W. McDonald, ed., pp. 172–73 (Sage, 1976) [hereafter "Lynch"].

10. President's Task Force on Victims of Crime, "Final Report" (Dec. 1982), p. 114 [hereafter "Task Force Final Report"].

11. *Doe v. City of Belleville*, No. 81–5256 (S.D. Ill. Mar. 22, 1982). *See also Bruno v. Codd*, 90 Misc. 2d 1047, 396 N.Y.S.2d 974 (Sup. Ct. 1977), *rev'd in part, appeal dismissed in part*, 64 A.D.2d 582, 407 N.Y.S.2d 165 (App. Div. 1978), *aff'd*, 47 N.Y.2d 582, 419 N.Y.S.2d 901, 393 N.E.2d 976 (1979), and *Raguz v. Chandler*, No. C74–1064 (N.D. Ohio, filed 1974) (both domestic abuse complaints that terminated in consent decrees); *Commonwealth v. Franklin*, 385 N.E.2d 227 (Mass. 1978) (claim of selective enforcement of laws based on race).

11a. 42 U.S.C. §1983.

12. *Davis v. Fowler*, 504 F. Supp. 502 (D. Md. 1980); *Covington v. Winger*, 562 F. Supp. 115 (W.D. Mich. 1983).

13. Cronin and Bourque, "Assessment of Victim/Witness Assistance Projects" (1981), National Evaluation Program Phase 1 Report, series A, no. 24, National Institute of Justice, U.S. Dept. of Justice [hereafter "NIJ Assessment"]; Williams, "The Role of the Victim in the Prosecution of Violent Crimes" (1978) 30, PROMIS Research Project publn. 12, Institute for Law and Social Research [hereafter "INSLAW Project"].

14. Neb. Rev. Stat. §81–1423; R.I. Pub. L. 1983 ch. 265 (to be codified at R.I. Gen. Laws §12–28); Wash. Rev. Code §7.69.020; Wis. Stat. §950.04; Okla. Stat. §215.33; 1984 Fla. Stat., ch. 84–363.

14a. 1984 Ill. Laws 83–1432; 1984 S.C. Acts 487. Unfortunately, these bills were not reported by statutory reporting services in time for more detailed inclusion in this book.

15. Wash. Rev. Code §7.69.010; Wis. Stat. §950.01.

16. *Id*.

17. Okla. Stat. §215.33; Wash. Rev. Code §7.69.030; Wis. Stat. §950.04; R.I. Gen. Laws §12–28–3 (except does not specifically provide for photographing property); Neb. Rev. Stat. §81–1423(6) (same).

18. Wis. Stat. §950.04(9); Neb. Rev. Stat. §81–1423; Wash. Rev. Code §7.69.030(8); R.I. Gen. Laws §12–28–3(1), (10) and (11); 1984 Fla. Stat., ch 84–363, adding §§921.143 and 960.30 (1)(d)(1)–(3).

19. Okla. Stat. §215.33.

19a. 1984 Fla. Stat., ch. 84–363, adding §960.30(3).

20. *See* Cal. Const. art. I, §28(e); Cal. Penal Code §§1191.1; 1192.7; 3043.

20a. N.Y. Exec. Law §§640–42.

20b. N.Y. Exec. Law §645.

21. The Bill of Rights was signed on Apr. 21, 1983, by the Jefferson County judge executive, the commonwealth's attorney, the county sheriff, the chief judge of the district court, the mayor of Louisville, the county attorney, the district supervisor of probation and parole, and the chief judge of the circuit court, after proposed statewide legislation was defeated in the legislature.

22. Pub. L. 97–291, 96 Stat. 1248 §2(1), (2).

23. 18 U.S.C. §3146.

24. *Id.* at §3579.

25. *Id.* at §1512.

26. *Id.* at §1513.

27. *Id.* at §1514.

28. 33 *Crim. L. Rptr.* 3329.

28a. Victims of Crime Act of 1984, H.J. Res. 648, Chap. XIV (Oct. 12, 1984).

29. National Organization for Victim Assistance, "The Victim Service System: A Guide to Action 1983," Introductory letter from Marlene A. Young, executive director.

30. NIJ Assessment, *supra* note 13, at 9.

31. *Id.* at 12–13.

32. *Id.* at 15.

33. *Id.* at 16–20.

34. *Id.* at 14.

35. *Id.*

36. *Id.* at 12.

37. *Id.*

38. Task Force Final Report, *supra* note 10, at 58–59.

39. 1984 Fla. Stat., ch. 84–363, adding §960-30 (1)(a); Neb. Rev. Stat. §81–1423(6)(4); R.I. Gen. Laws §12–28–3(9); Wis. Stat. §950.04(4); Okla. Stat. §215.33(3); Wash. Rev. Code §7.69.020. *See also,* Minn. Stat. Ann. §611A-02.

40. 71 Pa. Cons. Stat. §180–7.17; Ohio Rev. Code Ann. §2929.14 (D) and 2929.22(G). The New York legislation was signed into law in Feb. 1984.

41. Okla. Stat. §40–44.

42. *See, e.g., Chambers-Castanes v. King County,* 100 Wis.2d 275 (1983) (a special duty arose from the police dispatcher's statements that police were on the way); *Nearing v. Weaver,* No. TC26761 (Sup. Ct. Oreg. Oct. 4, 1983) (a special duty created by a statute requiring the arrest of protection order violators); *Rieser v. Dist. of Columbia,* 563 F.2d 462, 478–79, *vacated en banc,* 563 F.2d 482, (1977), *reinstated in relevant part en banc,* 580 F.2d 647 (D.C. Cir. 1978) (the District of Columbia and the parole board were held liable to the victim's survivor for aiding the assailant in obtaining employment in the victim's apartment building); *Robillitto v. State,* 104 Misc.2d 713, 721–22, 429 N.Y.S.2d 362, 368–69 (Ct. Cl. 1980) (the state was found liable for releasing a juvenile with a long history of trouble with the plaintiff); *Gardner v. Chicago Ridge,* 71

Ill. App. 2d 373, 219 N.E.2d 147 (1966), (the police were liable for failing to protect a summoned witness); *Schuster v. New York*, 5 N.Y.2d 75, 180 N.Y.S.2d 265, 154 N.E.2d 534 (1958) (the state was liable when a witness was murdered after supplying information); 46 A. L .R. 3d 1064 (a national survey concerning the government's liability for failing to provide police protection) Note, "Holding Governments Strictly Liable for the Release of Dangerous Parolees," 55 *NYU L. Rev.* 907 (1980).

43. *Delong v. Erie County*, 60 N.Y.2d 296 (1983), *affirming* 89 A.D.2d 376, 455 N.Y.S.2d 887 (App. Div. 1982), discussed in *N.Y. Times*, Nov. 2, 1983, at B11, col. 1. For a fuller discussion of such civil suits for failure to protect and for negligent release see chap. V.

44. *See, e.g.*, N.Y. Penal Law §35.30(4) (a private person may use deadly physical force not only to defend himself or a third person from deadly physical force, but also to effect the arrest of a person who has committed murder, first-degree manslaughter, robbery, forcible rape, or forcible sodomy and is in immediate flight).

45. *See, e.g., State v. Johnson*, 261 N.C. 727, 136 S.E.2d 84 (1964); *Crawford v. State*, 231 Md. 354, 190 A.2d 538 (1963).

46. W. L. Prosser, *The Law of Torts* §§19–21, at 108–17 (1971) [hereafter "Prosser, *Torts*"].

47. *Id.* note 46, at 110. *See also* Seligman, "Keeping Up," *Fortune*, Oct. 3, 1983, at 29, col. I (reporting on a jury verdict of $75,000 awarded to a burglar who stole $150 in goods from a car and who was apprehended and shot in the foot by the victim while awaiting the police).

48. Bureau of Justice Statistics Technical Report, "Criminal Victimization in the U.S.," at 2 (Mar. 1983).

49. 18 U.S.C. §4.

50. *U.S. v. Johnson*, 546 F.2d 1225 (5th Cir. 1977) (mere failure to report insufficient); *U.S. v. Daddano*, 432 F.2d 1119 (7th Cir. 1970), *cert. denied*, 402 U.S. 905 (1971); *Lancey v. U.S.* 356 F.2d 407 (9th Cir.), *cert. denied*, 385 U.S. 922 (1966).

51. Fla. Stat. §827.07 (any person who has reason to believe a child has been abused is required to report it to the Health Department); Tenn. Code Ann. §38–1–205 (anyone who discovers unattended human body or parts thereof must report the discovery immediately).

52. Colo. Rev. Stat. §18–8–115.

53. See Chapter IX *infra*.

54. LEAA, Crime in the Nation's Five Largest Cities: National Crime Panel Surveys of Chicago, Detroit, Los Angeles, New York, and Philadelphia: (Washington, D.C.: Government Printing Office, Apr. 1974), p. 5.

55. McGillis and Smith, *Compensating Victims of Crime: An Analysis of American Programs*, 73 (National Institute of Justice, May 1983) [hereafter "McGillis and Smith"].

56. Wis. Stat. §950.03.

57. *Cf. State v. Moose*, 36 N.C.App. 202, 203, 243 S.E.2d 425, 427 (1978).

58. *See, e.g.*, N.Y. Penal Law §§240.50, 240.55, making it a misdemeanor to circulate false reports about the alleged occurrence of a crime, falsely report a crime that did not occur to the police or to provide the police with false information about an actual offense or incident; 18 U.S.C. §1001, making it a felony to make a false or fraudulent statement in any matter within the jurisdiction of a department or agency of the United States; *People v. Meyers*, 72 Misc.2d 1003, 340 N.Y.S.2d 505 (Crim. Ct. 1973) (there is a common-law duty of reasonable conduct in truthfully reporting to the police; *Daas v. Pearson*, 66 Misc.2d 95, 319 N.Y.S.2d 537 (Sup. Ct. 1971), *aff'd*, 37 A.D.2d 921, 325 N.Y.S.2d 1011 (App. Div. 1971) (same); *U.S. v. Rodgers*, 35 Cr. L. Reporter 3047 (Sup. Ct. Apr. 30, 1984) (false statement to the FBI and the Secret Service to institute criminal investigation violates 18 U.S.C. §1001).

59. *People v. Komosa*, 47 Misc. 2d 634, 263 N.Y.S.2d 153 (Civ. Ct. 1965).

60. *People ex rel. Morris v. Skinner*, 67 Misc.2d 221, 323 N.Y.S.2d 905 (Sup. Ct. 1971).

61. *Stolte v. Blackstone*, 213 Neb. 113, 328 N.W.2d 462 (1982).

62. 1 F. Harper and F. James, *The Law of Torts*, §5.22, at 424 (1956) [hereafter "Harper and James"]; *Imbler v. Pachtman*, 424 U.S. 409, 421 (1976).

63. *See, e.g.*, *W. G. Platts, Inc. v. Platts*, 73 Wash.2d 434, 438 P.2d 867 (1968); *Kantor v. Kessler*, 132 N.J.L. 336, 40 A.2d 607 (1945).

64. *Warren v. Applebaum*, 526 F. Supp. 586, 587 (E.D.N.Y. 1981); *Brawer v. Horowitz*, 535 F.2d 830, 836 (3d Cir. 1976); *Kincaid v. Eberle*, 712 F.2d 1023 (7th Cir. 1983).

65. *Harper and James, supra* note 62.

66. *Shires v. Cobb*, 271 Or. 769, 534, P.2d 188, 189–90 (1975); *Manis v. Miller*, 327 So.2d 117, 118 (Fla. Dist. Ct. App. 1976).

67. Prosser, *Torts, supra* note 46, at 836–37.

68. *See, e.g.*, MAINE REV. STATE ANN. tit. 15, §891; VA. CODE §19–2–151. *See also* OHIO REV. CODE ANN. §2921.21(B) (2).

69. *See, e.g.*, IOWA CODE ANN. §720.1; KAS. STAT. ANN. §21–3807.

70. *See, e.g.*, Harland, "Monetary Remedies for the Victims of Crime: Assessing the Role of the Criminal Courts," 30 *UCLA L. Rev.* 52, 64–65 (1982) [hereafter "Harland"].

71. See p.——, *supra*.

72. Goldstein, *supra* note 1, at 526; INSLAW Project, *supra* note 13, at 24–25, see Chapter VIII, *infra*.

73. National District Attorneys' Association, *The Victim Advocate*, 1 (1977).

74. *See, e.g.*, MICH. STAT. ANN. §28.1259(5) (property and things seized shall be safely kept by the officer as long as necessary for the purpose of being produced or used as evidence in any trial); N.J.

Stat. Ann. §2C:64–4 (nothing in this chapter shall impair the right of the state to retain evidence pending a criminal prosecution); N.C. Gen. Stat. §15A–242, 253 (property subject to seizure as evidence of criminal offense).

75. *See, e.g.,* Fla. Stat. Ann. §§933.12, 933.13; N.C. Gen. Stat. §15A–254.

76. R.I. Gen. Laws §12–28–3(8); Neb. Rev. Stat. §81–1423(6) (7); Okla. Stat. §215.33(7); Wis. Stat. §950.04 (7); 1984 Fla. Stat., ch. 84–363, adding §960.30(1)(f); Wash. Rev. Code §7.69.030(6).

77. *Id. See also,* 1984 Fla. Stat., ch. 84–363, adding §914.16.

78. Wash. Rev. Code §7.69.030(6).

79. Neb. Rev. Stat. §81–1423(6) (7).

80. *Id.*

81. Kan. Stat. Ann. §60–472(1).

82. *See* Harland, *supra* note 70, at 61.

83. *See* N.Y. Penal Law §450.10; *People v. Davis,* 105 Misc.2d 409, 432 N.Y.S.2d 350 (Civ. Ct.), *aff'd,* 109 Misc.2d 230, 439 N.Y.S.2d 798 (County Ct. 1981) (retention of property for 14 months found justifiable, and unilateral release by prosecutor not permissible).

84. *See* Witness Assistance Brochure, Victim/Witness Division, Montgomery County, Ohio, prosecutor's office (property kept until 30 days after sentencing); California Victim/Witness Assistance Program Guidelines, 15 (Office of Criminal Justice Planning); *N.Y. Times,* Nov. 25, 1980, at B6.

85. *See, e.g.,* responses to a survey made in connection with this book from New Orleans, Louisiana, district attorney; Louisville, Ky., commonwealth attorney [hereafter "Responses to questionnaire"].

86. *See, e.g., People v. Angelo, NYLJ,* May 5, 1983, at 1, col. 3 (discussing the policy of the police and the D.A. with respect to photographing and returning property involved in shoplifting cases, and cautioning that the New York law requires that defense be notified and be given the opportunity to examine and photograph property, and court approval is to be obtained before its return).

87. Task Force Final Report, *supra* note 10, at 57, 63, 73.

88. Lynch, *supra* note 9.

89. NIJ Assessment, *supra* note 13, at 19.

90. *Davis v. Fowler,* 504 F. Supp. 502, 504 (D. Md. 1980).

91. *U.S. v. LaFatch,* 565 F.2d 81, 83 (6th Cir. 1977), *cert. denied,* 435 U.S. 971 (1978); *Search Warrants C-419847 & C-419848 v. State,* 665 P.2d 57, 58 (Ariz. 1983).

92. *U.S. v. Wilson,* 540 F.2d 1100, 1104 (D.C. Cir. 1976); *People v. Superior Court, Alameda County,* 100 Cal.App.3d 154, 160 Cal. Rptr. 663 (Ct. App. 1979). *See also Matter of Search Warrant (Encore House),* M–9–150 (S.D.N.Y. Oct. 20, 1983), reported in *NYLJ,* Oct. 25, 1983, p. 1, col. 2 (the court ordered the government to return to companies subject to a criminal investigation checks valued at $1 million that were seized through search warrants, where

checks had been retained for more than 3 months and companies offered to submit copies of checks or summaries of data contained therein at trial; the government was given 15 days to submit evidence that checks are "fruits of a crime").

93. *In re Caggiano*, 78 Misc.2d 187, 342 N.Y.S.2d 203 (Sup. Ct. 1973), *aff'd*, 44 A.D.2d 828, 355 N.Y.S.2d 170 (App. Div. 1974).

94. *W. Mason, Inc. v. Jackson County Prosecutor*, 95 Mich. App. 447, 451, 291 N.W.2d 76 (1980); *Caggiano*, 342 N.Y.S.2d at 206; *Gay Cottons, Inc. v. Hogan*, 55 Misc. 2d 126, 284 N.Y.S.2d 684 (Sup. Ct. 1967); *Ballard v. Superior Court*, 64 Cal.2d 159, 49 Cal. Rptr. 302, 410 P.2d 838 (1966).

95. *See W. Mason, Inc. v. Jackson County Prosecutor*, 95 Mich. App. 447, 452, 291 N.W.2d 76 (1980) (a plaintiff was entitled to compensation for reasonable rental value of a bulldozer seized as evidence during a period when he was unjustifiably deprived of its use); *Kubli v. Rosetti*, 40 A.D.2d 4, 6, 337 N.Y.S.2d 147, 149 (App. Div. 1972), *rev'd on other grounds*, 34 N.Y.2d 68, 356. N.Y.S.2d 29, 312 N.E.2d 167 (1974) (judgment awarded, with interest, from the date the plaintiff became entitled to the return of his property).

96. *See generally Tcherepnin v. Franz*, 570 F.2d 187, 191 (7th Cir.), *cert. denied*, 439 U.S. 876 (1978); *Hayward Lumber and Investment Co. v. Biscailuz*, 47 Cal.2d 716, 306 P.2d 6 (Sup. Ct. 1957).

96a. 42. U.S.C. §1983.

97. *See Davis v. Fowler*, 504 F.Supp. 502 (D.Md. 1980) (the police were ordered to return to the plaintiff-owner his motorcycle and equipment that were seized as suspected stolen property and not returned, where no criminal proceedings were instituted and where no hearing was held to determine that the property was contraband). *See also Covington v. Winger*, 562 F.Supp. 115 (W.D. Mich. 1983) (claim that the defendant police officer's failure to return property because it had been misplaced or lost was willful and in reckless disregard of the plaintiff's rights; a rehearing was ordered to determine whether the plaintiff had property interest in the firearms seized).

98. *Hazo v. Geltz*, 537 F.2d 747, 750 (3d Cir. 1976) [quoting *Wood v. Strickland*, 420 U.S. 308, 318 (1975)].

99. *Wood*, 420 U.S. at 308–9; *Harris v. City of Roseburg*, 664 F.2d 1121, 1128 (9th Cir. 1981).

100. *See generally Wolf-Lillie v. Kenosha City Sheriff*, 504 F.Supp. 1, 6–7 (E.D.Wis. 1979) *vacated on other grounds*, 699 F.2d 864 (7th Cir. 1983).

101. McGillis and Smith, *supra* note 55, at 73. Victims may also be required to cooperate with the police in order to be eligible for an award under victim's compensation statutes. *See, e.g.*, N.Y.C.R.R. §525.4.

102. *U.S. v. Wade*, 388 U.S. 218 (1967).

103. *See, e.g.*, *U.S. v. Tolliver*, 569 F.2d 724 (2d Cir. 1978), and cases cited therein.

104. Mass. Gen. Laws, ch. 262, §29.
105. *See, e.g.*, Office of the prosecuting attorney, Detroit.
106. *See, e.g.*, Alabama district attorneys' office.
107. See pp. 79–86, 98–99, *infra*.
108. CONN. GEN. STAT. §52.260.
109. 28 U.S.C. §1821; N.H. REV. STAT. ANN. §516.16.
110. *See, e.g.*, 42 PA. CONS. STAT. §5903; 28 U.S.C. §1821; NEB. REV. STAT. §81–1897.
111. Lynch, *supra* note 9, at 172.
112. NEB. REV. STAT. §81–1423(6)(1); R.I. Gen. Laws §12–28–3(12); WASH. REV. CODE §7.69.030(1); WIS. STAT. §950.04(1).
112a. N.Y. Exec. Law §641.
113. *See* Task Force Final Report, *supra* note 10, at app. 2.
114. NIJ Assessment, *supra* note 13, at 14, 19.
115. Hall, *supra* note 3, at 965.
116. *Id.*
117. *Poulos v. New Hampshire*, 345 U.S. 395, 411 (1953) (quoting *Royall v. Virginia*, 116 U.S. 572, 582–83 (1886). *See also* Hall, *supra* note 3, at 965).
118. *See, e.g.*, *Miles-Lee Auto Supply Co. v. Bellows*, 26 Ohio Ops.2d 452, 197 N.E.2d 247 (1964) (finding-standing by a competitor for bringing action seeking a writ of mandamus to prosecute Sunday closing laws). *But see State ex rel. Skilton v. Miller*, 164 Ohio St. 163, 128 N.E.2d 47 (1955) (no standing by a private citizen to bring a writ of mandamus to compel prosecution of a store owner for remaining open in violation of Sunday closing law); *State ex rel. Naramore v. Hensley*, 53 N.M. 308, 310, 207 P.2d 529, 530 (1949) (holding that the state, not the parents of a murder victim, was the party "beneficially interested" in the prosecution of the alleged killer and could not be compelled by mandamus to bring the prosecution). The conclusion of these courts that victims have such standing has been cast into serious doubt by the *Linda R. S.* case discussed *supra*, note 2. *See Inmates of Attica Correctional Facility v. Rockefeller*, 477 F.2d 375 (2d Cir. 1973).
119. *See Moses v. Kennedy*, 219 F. Supp. 762, 764–65 (D. D.C. 1963) (refusing to grant a writ to compel FBI agents to arrest Mississippi law enforcement officials who allegedly violated the petitioners' constitutional rights); *Restivo v. Degnan*, 191 Misc. 642, 77 N.Y.S.2d 563 (Sup. Ct. 1948) (no writ to compel the magistrate to issue a warrant to arrest persons identified by the victim as his assailants); *Hassan v. Magistrate's Court*, 20 Misc.2d 509, 511, 191 N.Y.S.2d 238, 240 (Sup. Ct. 1959) (no writ to compel the arrest of a police officer accused by the petitioner of perjury in a traffic violation case). *See also O'Connor v. State of Nevada*, 507 F.Supp 546 (D. Nev. 1981) *aff'd*, 686 F.2d 749 (9th Cir.), *cert. denied*, 103 S.Ct. 491 (1982).
120. See Chapter V, *infra*.

121. Y. Kamisar, W. LaFave, and J. Israel, *Modern Criminal Procedure*, 15 (1980) [hereafter "Kamisar, LaFave, and Israel"].

122. *See* 5 Am.Jur.2d Arrest §§25 *et seq*. (1962).

123. *See*. *e.g.*, 18 U.S.C. §1; N.Y. Penal Law §10.00.

124. 5 Am.Jur.2d Arrest §30 (1962).

125. *See*, Goldstein, "Police Discretion Not to Invoke the Criminal Process: Low-Visibility Decisions in the Administration of Justice," 69 *Yale L. J.* 543, 575 (1960); Comment, "Police Discretion and the Judgment That a Crime Has Been Committed—Rape in Philadelphia," 117 *U. Pa. L. Rev.* 277, 291 (1968).

126. Hall, *supra* note 3, at 937–44; W. LaFave, *Arrest: The Decision to Take the Suspect into Custody*, 21, 51, 106, 107, 112, 117–19, 286 (Amer. Bar Foundation 1965) [hereinafter "LaFave"].

127. Hall, *supra* note 3, at 937–44.

128. La Fave, *supra* note 126, at 78–79.

129. 5 Am.Jr.2d Arrest §24 (1962).

130. *See*, *e.g.*, *Moses v. Kennedy*, 219 F. Supp. 762 (D.D.C. 1963) (refusing to compel FBI agents to arrest law enforcement officials who allegedly violated the petitioner's constitutional rights); *Matter of Restivo v. Degnan*, 191 Misc. 642 77 N.Y.S.2d 563 (Sup. Ct. 1948) (mandamus will not lie to compel police justice to issue arrest warrant).

130a. NYC Charter and Code §435(a) (1976).

131. *Bruno v. Codd*, 90 Misc.2d 1047, 396 N.Y.S.2d 974 (Sup. Ct. 1977), *rev'd in part, appeal dismissed in part*, 64 A.D.2d 582, 407 N.Y.S.2d 165 (App. Div. 1978) *aff'd*, 47 N.Y.2d 582, 419 N.Y.S.2d 901, 393 N.E.2d 976 (1979). The background of this litigation and its eventual settlement (challenging not only police procedures but also the procedures of the New York City Department of Probation and the clerks of the family court) is described in Woods, "Litigation on Behalf of Battered Women," 5 *Women's Rights L. Rep.* 7 (1979) [hereafter "Woods"].

132. Woods, *supra* note 131, at 32–33.

133. *See also Nearing v. Weaver*, No. TC26761 (Sup. Ct. Oreg., Oct. 4, 1983) (*en banc*) (discussing Oreg. legislative response to domestic violence by enacting a statute *requiring* the police to arrest violators of protective orders). For a more complete discussion, see Chapter X.

134. *See* 41 A.L.R.3d 700; Comment, "Crime Victim: Recovery for Police Inaction and Underprotection," 1970 *Law and Soc. Order*, 279, 286–87.

135. *See Nearing v. Weaver*, No. TC26761 (Sup. Ct. Oreg. Oct. 4, 1983) (*en banc*) (statutory duty to arrest where there is probable cause to believe a protective order has been violated); *Baker v. City of New York*, 25 A.D.2d 770, 269 N.Y.S.2d 515 (App. Div. 1966) (special duty created by a family court protective order); *Sorichetti v. City of New York*, 95 Misc.2d 451, 408 N.Y.S.2d 219 (Sup. Ct. 1978) (same).

136. Hall, *supra* note 3, at 938. *See also* 5 Am.Jur.2d Arrest §4 (1962).
137. *See, e.g.,* N.Y. Crim. Proc. Law §140.30 (felony and misdemeanor); Cal. Penal Code §837 (felony and misdemeanor constituting "breach of peace"); Tenn. Code Ann. §40–816 (same); 5 Am.Jr.2d Arrest §36 (1962).
138. 231 So.2d 510 (Miss. 1970).
139. *See also People v. Martin,* 225 Cal.App.2d 91, 36 Cal. Rptr. 924 (Ct. App. 1964) (a citizen's arrest for a misdemeanor offense neither committed nor attempted in the citizen's presence held invalid despite reasonable cause to believe the offense had in fact been committed); 5 Am.Jur.2d Arrest §35, 36 (1962).
140. Hall, *supra* note 3, at 938.
141. Prosser on Torts, *supra* note 46, at §§11, 26.
142. N.Y. Crim. Proc. Law §140.40(1).
143. *Id.* at (4). *See also People v. Foster,* 10 N.Y.2d 99, 217 N.Y.S.2d 596, 176 N.E.2d 397 (1961) (affirming a citizen's right to make an arrest and receive police assistance notwithstanding that the offense was not committed within the presence of the officer).
144. *Beck v. Ohio,* 379 U.S. 89, 91 (1964).
145. *Id.*
146. Fed. R. Crim. P. 5(c).
147. N.Y. Crim. Proc. Law §180.80. *See also* responses to the questionnaire from the San Diego County, California, district attorney (a preliminary hearing must be held within 10 days after arraignment); Milwaukee County, Wisc., district attorney (a preliminary hearing must be held within 10 days after initial appearance if defendant is in custody, and within 20 days if he is released on bail or on recognizance).
148. *See, e.g., Coleman v. Alabama,* 399 U.S. 1 (1970), Fed. R. Crim. P.5.1(a).
149. *See, e.g.,* Fed. R. Crim. P. 5.1(a); Iowa R. Crim. P. 2(4) (b); Ariz. R. Crim. P. 5.4(c).
150. *See, e.g.,* N.Y. Crim. Proc. Law §180.60.
151. Task Force Final Report, *supra* note 10, at 17, 21–22.
152. *Id.* at 21.
153. *U.S. v. Calandra,* 414 U.S. 338 (1974).
154. *See, e.g.,* Fed. R. Crim. P. 5(c); Ohio R. Crim. P. 5(B); Tex. Code Crim. P. art. 16.01.
155. *Hurtado v. California,* 110 U.S. 516 (1884); *Watson v. Jago,* 558 F. 2d 330, 337 (6th Cir. 1977); *U.S. ex rel. Wojtycha v. Hopkins,* 517 F.2d 420, 425 (3d Cir. 1975).
156. 18 U.S.C. §1623.
157. *See, e.g.,* N.Y. Penal Law §210.15 (false testimony is first-degree perjury, a felony punishable by a term of up to 7 years).
158. *U.S. v. Mandujano,* 425 U.S. 564 (1976).
159. *See, e.g.,* S.D. Codified Laws Ann. §23A–5–11; Wash. Rev. Code §10.27.120.
160. Va. Code §19.2–209.

161. Ariz. Rev. Stat. Ann. §21–412; N.M. Stat. Ann. §31–6–4. A "target witness" is a "person as to whom the prosecutor or the grand jury has substantial evidence linking him to the commission of a crime and who, in the judgment of the prosecutor, is a putative defendant." *United States Attorney's Manual* §9–11.250 (Oct. 31, 1979).

162. N.Y. Crim. Proc. Law §190.52; Minn. Crim. Proc. R. §18.04.

163. See *U.S. v. Nixon*, 418 U.S. 683, 709–10 (1974).

164. See, e.g., *In re Irving*, 600 F.2d 1027, 1031 (2d Cir.), *cert. denied*, 444 U.S. 866 (1979).

165. *Hawkins v. Superior Court*, 22 Cal.3d 584, 589–90, 150 Cal. Rptr. 435, 438, 586 P.2d 916, 919 (1978); Note, 7 *Harv. C.R.-C.L.L. Rev.* 432, 498–99 (1972).

166. Hall *supra* note 3, at 967–68, and cases cited therein.

167. *Leeke v. Timmerman*, 454 U.S. 83 (1981) (per curiam). See also *Smith v. U.S.*, 375 F.2d 243 (5th Cir.), *cert. denied*, 389 U.S. 841 (1967) (discretion of the attorney general in choosing whether to prosecute is absolute); *People ex rel. Daley v. Moran*, 94 Ill.2d 41, 445 N.E.2d 270 (1983) (state's attorney has discretion whether to charge the defendant with crime and what charge to press); *Manning v. Municipal Court of the Roxbury District*, 372 Mass. 315, 361 N.E.2d 1274 (Mass. 1977) (victim cannot compel the district attorney to act); *Inmates of Attica Correctional Facility v. Rockefeller*, 477 F.2d 375 (2d Cir. 1973) (courts will not intervene in the discretionary determination of the prosecutor whether to prosecute).

168. See, e.g., Mass. Gen. Laws Ann. ch. 276, §22.

169. See, e.g., Colo. Rev. Stat. §16–5–209 ("arbitrary and capricious" refusal); Kans. Stat. Ann. §22–2301 ("in extreme cases"); Mich. Comp. Laws §767.41 (if the court is "not satisfied" with the prosecutor's statement of reasons for not filing an information). A few jurisdictions permit the court to appoint a substitute prosecutor if the district attorney fails or refuses to prosecute. See, e.g., Pa. Stat. Ann. tit. 16, §4408; Tenn. Const. art. 6, §5; Utah Const. art. VIII, §10; *People ex rel. Hoyne v. Newcomer*, 284 Ill. 315, 120 N.E. 244 (1918) (the court may commit prosecution of an offense punishable only by imposing a fine to a person other than the prosecutor if the latter declines to act).

170. Alaska Stat. §12.45.150.

171. *Raguz v. Chandler*, No. C74–1064 (N.D. Ohio, filed 1974); *Bruno v. Codd*, 90 Misc.2d 1047, 396 N.Y.S.2d 974 (Sup. Ct. 1977), *rev'd in part, appeal dismissed in part*, 64 A.D.2d 582, 407 N.Y.S.2d 165 (App. Div. 1978), *aff'd*, 47 N.Y.2d 582, 419 N.Y.S.2d 901, 393 N.E.2d 976 (1979).

172. For example, Kas. Gen. Stat. §19–717 provides that counsel hired by the prosecuting witness in any type of criminal action will be recognized as an associate prosecutor. See also Oreg. Rev. Stat. §135.165, permitting an attorney hired by the complainant to appear against the defendant at every stage of the preliminary proceedings, subject to the control of the district attorney.

173. *See, e.g.,* Dession, "Private Prosecution: A Remedy for District Attorneys' Unwarranted Inaction," 65 *Yale L. J.* 209, 220 n.60 (1955); *Hopkins v. State,* 429 So.2d 114 (Ala. Crim. App. 1983) (special prosecutor entered an appearance at the request of the victims' families and with the consent of the district attorney); *Woods v. State,* 240 Ga. 265, 239 S.E.2d 786 (1977) (the special prosecutor hired by the family and friends of the victim to assist the district attorney participated in the trial under the district attorney and delivered part of the closing argument); *State v. Misenheimer,* 304 N.C. 108, 282 S.E.2d 791 (1981) (several witnesses hired a private prosecutor who aided in the preparation and who sat with the district attorney at trial); *Commonwealth v. Malloy,* 304 Pa. Super. 297, 450 A.2d 689 (Sup. Ct. 1982) (the victim's attorney represented the state at the preliminary hearing, with the consent of the district attorney). If the victim is involved in a civil action against the defendant where the same facts are at issue as in the criminal case, however, the attorney representing him in the civil action may not aid in the criminal prosecution. *See, e.g.,* Mich. Comp. Laws Ann. §§49, 158, 776.18; *Commonwealth v. Tabor,* 376 Mass. 811, 384 N.E.2d 190 (1978); *State v. Jensen,* 178 Iowa 1098, 160 N.W. 832 (1917).

174. *See, e.g., Biemel v. State,* 71 Wis. 444, 37 N.W. 244 (1888) (the attorney paid by private parties and appearing for the prosecution, but without any appointment from the court, was not the proper attorney to aid in the prosecution); *State v. Harrington,* 534 S.W.2d 44 (Mo. 1976) (private prosecutor employed by private individual not permitted); *McKay v. State,* 90 Neb. 63, 132 N.W. 741 (1911) *modified,* 91 Neb. 281, 135 N.W. 1024 (1912) (the private attorney employed by the victim's family may not prosecute the case, even with the court's permission; the district attorney must select an assistant if one is required, and the court must formally appoint him as the special prosecutor).

175. *See* Woods, *supra* note 131, at 13–14, discussing *People v. Mandel,* 61 A.D.2d 563, 403 N.Y.S.2d 63 (App. Div. 1978) (feminist antirape groups worked with the district attorney and submitted trial memorandum on the issue of the exclusion of the victim's prior sexual history).

176. *See, e.g.,* Fresno County, Calif., Probation Dept., Victim Service Project, discussed in McDonald, *supra* note 4, at 671; and a similar program in Chicago, discussed in Goldstein, *supra* note 1.

177. National Organization for Victim Assistance, *The Victim Service System: A Guide to Action 1983,* 123 (1983).

178. ABA Section of Criminal Justice, Victim Witness Assistance Project, *Victim/Witness Legislation: Considerations for Policymakers,* 39–42 (1981).

179. Although the victim may not need formal representation by an attorney in the criminal proceedings, an attorney can provide useful counseling on a victim's legal rights and prospects with respect to

civil recovery, restitution, compensation, benefit programs, witness fees, protection from intimidation, a speedy trial, property return, and procedures and rights to obtain timely information and notification of developments in the criminal case.

180. Wice, *Bail and Its Reform: A National Survey* (1973).

180a. 1984 Fla. Stat., ch. 84–363, adding §930.047(2).

181. Attorney General's Task Force on Violent Crime (Final Report) Recommendation 38, at 51 (U.S. Dept. of Justice, Aug. 17, 1981) [hereafter "Attorney General's Report"].

182. *See, e.g.*, Mass. Gen. Laws Ann. ch. 276, §42A. *See also* Cal. Const. art. 1, §28(e) (public safety shall be the primary consideration in setting, reducing or denying bail; no person charged with commission of any serious felony shall be released on his or her own recognizance).

183. *See, e.g.*, D.C. Code Ann. §23–1322; Wis. Stat. §969.035.

184. *See, e.g.*, Ind. Code §35–33–8–5; Mass. Gen. Laws Ann. ch. 276, §58. A survey of state pretrial release laws is contained in Gaynes, *Typology of State Laws Which Permit the Consideration of Danger in the Pretrial Release Decision* (1982) (available from the Pretrial Services Resource Center, 918 F Street, NW. Washington, DC 20004).

184a. *Bell v. Wolfish*, 441 U.S. 520, 534n.15 (1979). *See Sellers v. U.S.*, 89 S.Ct. 36, 38 (1968) (bail pending appeal) (chambers opinion of Justice Black).

184b. *Schall v. Martin*, 35 Cr.L. 3103 (U.S. June 4, 1984).

184c. Bail Reform Act of 1984, H.J. Res. 648, Title II, Chap. 1 (Oct. 12, 1984), adding new 18 U.S.C. §3142. It should be noted that the ACLU was in the forefront of those opposing this new Bail Act on the grounds, among others, that pre-trial detention violates the accused's right to a presumption of innocence and to reasonable bail.

185. 18 U.S.C. 3148.

186. *See, e.g.*, Fla. R. Crim. P. 3, 130(b) (4) (i).

187. Attorney General's Report, *supra* note 181, at 52. *See also* Ariz. R. Crim. P. 7.2(b) (the defendant bears the burden of proving that his conviction will probably be reversed on appeal in order to be granted release after conviction).

188. Bail Reform Act of 1984, H.J. Res. 648, Title II, Chap. 1 (Oct. 12, 1984), adding new 18 U.S.C. §3143.

188a. *But see* n.180a, *supra*.

189. Hall, *supra* note 3, at 945 (discussing interviews with prosecutors).

190. *Id.* (citing interviews with several judges).

191. *See, e.g.*, N.Y. Crim. Proc. Law §170.55 (charges are automatically dismissed if the people do not move for reinstatement within 6 months of adjournment); *Singleton v. City of New York*, 632 F.2d 185. (2d Cir. 1980) *cert. denied*, 450 U.S. 920 (1981) (discussing §170.55); N.J. Rev. Stat. §2C:43–12 (providing for supervisory treat-

ment for first offenders as an alternative to trial and imprisonment). *See also* 18 U.S.C. §3161(h) (2).

192. *In re Winship,* 397 U.S. 358 (1970).

193. *See generally* Kamisar, LaFave, and Israel, *supra* note 121, at 1220–22.

194. Hyman, "Bargaining and Criminal Justice," 33 *Rutgers L. Rev.* 3 (1980); Kamisar, LaFave and Israel, *supra* note 121, at 1222.

195. Kamisar, LaFave, and Israel, *supra* note 121, at 1222.

196. *Id.*

197. *See, e.g.,* N.J. Rev. Stat. §3:9–3; Iowa Code §813.2; Calif. Penal Code §1192.5.

198. *People v. Selikoff,* 35 N.Y.2d 227, 360 N.Y.S.2d 623, 318 N.E.2d 784 (1974), *cert. denied,* 419 U.S. 1122 (1975). *See also* Hughes, "Pleas Without Bargains," 33 *Rutgers L. Rev.* 753 (1981) (discussing this argument).

199. *Santobello v. New York,* 404 U.S. 257, 260 (1971).

200. *Selikoff,* 35 N.Y.2d at 233–34, 360 N.Y.S.2d at 629, 318 N.E.2d at 788.

200a. Klein, *Let's Make a Deal* (Lexington Books 1976).

201. *See* Alschuler, "Book Review," 12 *Crim. L. Bull.* 629, 632 (1976); Alschuler, "The Prosecutor's Role in Plea Bargaining," 36 *U. Chic. L. Rev.* 50 (1968).

202. Cal. Penal Code §1192.7.

203. *Id. See also* White, "Plea Bargaining: Can Alaska Live Without It?" *Judicature* 266 (1978) [hereafter "Can Alaska"].

204. *Id.*

205. *See* Dawson, *Sentencing: The Decision as to Type, Length, and Conditions of Sentence,* 108 (Boston: Little, Brown, 1969) [hereafter "Sentencing"].

206. Many jurisdictions have enacted provisions requiring that the defendant's lawyer be present during all discussions, and that the judge has the right to refuse any recommendation of the prosecutor. *See, e.g.,* Cal. Penal Code §1192.5; Fed. R. Crim. P. 11.

206a. 1984 Fla. Stat., ch. 84–363, adding §960.30(1)(c).

207. Nev. Rev. Stat. §174.055.

208. Ind. Code §35–35–3–2. *See also* Me. Rev. Stat. Ann. tit. 15, §812 (similar provisions); Jefferson County, Ky., *Victim's Bill of Rights* (1982) (requiring that the victim be notified of a plea agreement); Minn. Stat. Ann. §611A.03 (same).

209. State of New York, Executive Chamber, "Message to the Senate" (Aug. 8, 1983) (vetoing S. 3735, 1983–84) (Regular Sessions 1983).

210. *See, e.g.,* N.J. Rev. Stat. §3:9–3. *See infra* text accompanying notes 287–292.

211. In response to the questionnaire, prosecutors' offices in Dayton, Birmingham, Jacksonville, and Cincinnati referred to routine consultations with victims during plea discussions.

211a. A defendant's first-degree rape conviction was recently reversed in New York because the prosecutor did not inform defense counsel of the victim's intention to sue the defendant upon the conclusion of the criminal case. The court held that this information related to the victim's motive to lie and should have been disclosed so that defense counsel could cross-examine the victim about it. *"People v. Wallert"* N.Y. *Law Journal*, Jan. 25, 1984, p. 1.

212. *See, e.g.,* N.Y. Civ. Proc. Law §8001; Del. Code Ann. tit. 10, §8903; Mass. Gen. Laws Ann. ch. 262, §29.

213. *See, e.g.,* Miss. Code Ann. §25–7–47; Mont. Code Ann. §26–2–50. *But see* N.D. Cent. Code §31–01–18 (an indigent witness paid a reasonable sum for necessary expenses).

214. *See, e.g.,* 42 Pa. Cons. Stat. 5903.

215. *See, e.g.,* Cal. Penal Code §1332; Mont. Code Ann. §46–12–102; N.Y. Crim. Proc. Law §620.30.50.

216. 18 U.S.C. §3006A(g).

217. *See, e.g.,* N.Y. Crim. Proc. Law §620.40; Minn. Stat. Ann. §692.54.55.

218. *See, e.g.,* Tenn. Code Ann. §40–11–110; S.D. Codified Laws Ann. §23A–43–2; Va. Code §19.2–127. The right to counsel is sometimes more specifically acknowledged by including the material witness provisions in the sections addressing arraignments and the right to bail. *See, e.g.,* Tenn. Code Ann. §40–11–110; S.D. Codified Laws Ann. §23A–43–2; Va. Code §19.2–127. In so placing the statutes, the legislatures seem to imply that the material witness has the same rights as the accused at arraignment.

219. *See, e.g., U.S. v. Orsini,* 424 F. Supp. 229 (E.D.N.Y. 1976), *aff'd,* 559 F.2d 1206 (2d Cir.), *cert. denied,* 434 U.S. 997 (1977); *Bias v. State,* 561 P.2d 523 (Ct. Crim. App., Okla.), *cert. denied,* 434 U.S. 940 (1977).

220. *See State v. Gilbert,* 109 Wis.2d 501, 326 N.W. 2d 744 (1982).

221. *See, e.g., U.S. v. Raineri,* 670 F.2d 702 (7th Cir.), *cert. denied,* 103 S.Ct. 446 (1982); *Amsler v. U.S.,* 381 F.2d 37 (9th Cir. 1967); *State v. Blunt,* 197 Neb. 82, 246 N.W.2d 727 (1976).

222. *See* Cal. Penal Code §865.5 (the victim of sexual abuse is entitled to have one person of his choosing to provide support during a preliminary hearing or trial).

223. Task Force Final Report, *supra* note 10, at 80. The judge, at his discretion, can exclude witnesses, presumably to guard against a fabrication of testimony. This rule is generally provided in case law rather than by statutes. *See* 23 C.J.S. *Criminal Law* §1009 (a national survey of the rule). *See, e.g., People v. Legget,* 55 A.D.2d 990, 391 N.Y.S.2d 195 (App. Div. 1977); *People v. Felder,* 32 N.Y.2d 747, 344 N.Y.S.2d 643, 297 N.E.2d 522, *app. dismissed,* 414 U.S. 948 (1973). *But see* Fed. R. Evid. 615.

224. Task Force Final Report, *supra* note 10, at 80.

225. Gorman, "Excessive Delay In the Courts: Toward a Continuance Policy Relating to Counsel And Parties," 21 *Cleve. St. L. Rev.* 118 (1972) [hereafter "Excessive Delay"], [quoting *Report of The Comm. on the Admin. of Justice to the Comm. on the District of Columbia,* 91st. Cong., 2d Sess., Court Management Study (1970)].

226. Vera Institute Study, 1978, Reported by Colleen Cosgrove of Vera Institute Research.

227. "Excessive Delay," *supra* note 225.

228. Task Force Final Report, *supra* note 10, at 67. *See also* Goldstein, *supra* note 1, at 524 (1982) (a general description of continuances).

229. Task Force Final Report, *supra* note 10, at 67.

230. Responses to questionnaire from, *e.g.*, district attorney's office, Birmingham, and city prosecutor's office, Phoenix.

231. Task Force Final Report, *supra* note 10, at 68.

232. *Id.* at 75.

233. *See, e.g.*, CONN. GEN. STAT. §54–85(b); ILL. REV. STAT. ch. 38, §155–3; N.Y. Jud. Law §750 and Penal Law §215.11; and WIS. STAT. §103.87.

234. *See* National Organization for Victim Assistance, *The Victim Service System: A Guide to Action 1983*, 117 (1983).

235. NEB. REV. STAT. §81–1423; R.I. Gen. L. §12–28; OKLA. STAT. §215.33(7); WASH. REV. CODE §7.69.030(7); 1984 FLA. STAT., ch. 84–363, adding §960.30(1)(g); WIS. STAT. §950.04(8). *See also* N.Y. Exec. Law §642(4).

236. *See, e.g.*, COLO. REV. STAT. §16–5–203; Ark. R. Crim. Pro. 43–1004; KANS. STAT. ANN. §22–3201; Iowa R. Crim. P. 5.

237. *See, e.g.*, Ariz. R. Crim. P. 15.1(a)(1); ILL. REV. STAT. ch. 110A, §412.

238. *McGrath v. Vinzant*, 528 F.2d 681 (1st Cir.), *cert. dismissed*, 426 U.S. 902 (1976); *People v. Benjamin*, 52 Cal. App.3d 63, 124 Cal. Rptr. 799 (Ct. App. 1975).

239. ILL. REV. STAT. ch. 110A, §412(i).

240. CONN. GEN. STAT. §54–86d.

241. *See, e.g.*, ME. REV. STAT. ANN. tit. 30, §508; N.Y. Civ. Rights Law §50.b.

242. R.I. Assembly Bill 81–50472.

243. CONN. GEN. STAT. §54–86e.

244. *Press-Enterprise Co. v. Superior Court*, 78 L. Ed.2d 629 (1984); *Richmond Newspapers, Inc. v. Virginia*, 448 U.S. 555 (1980).

245. *Globe Newspaper Co. v. Superior Court for the County of Norfolk*, 457 U.S. 596 (1982).

245a. *N.Y. Times*, Sept. 21, 1984.

246. Comment, "The Prejudicial Effects of Cameras in the Courtroom," 16 *U. Richmond L. Rev.* 867, 878 n.81 (1982).

247. Douglas, "The Public Trial and the Free Press," 33 *Rocky Mtn. L. Rev.* 1, 7 (1960).

248. *Chandler v. Florida*, 449 U.S. 560 (1981).

249. 370 So.2d 764, 778 (Fla. 1979).

250. 16 *U. Richmond L. Rev.* at 880 n.95.

251. *See, e.g.*, La. Code Crim. P. 295; Fed. R. Crim. P. 15(e).

252. *See, e.g.*, Calif. Penal Code §136.1; ILL. REV. STAT. ch. 38, §32–4(b); 1984 FLA. STAT., ch. 84–363, adding §§914.22, 914.23. 42 U.S.C. §1985.

253. *See, e.g.*, Ariz. R. Crim. P. 7.3(b); 18 U.S.C. §3146.

254. *See, e.g.*, the victim/witness units in Honolulu, Detroit, Minneapolis, Baltimore, and numerous others.

255. 18 U.S.C.§1503, 1514. *See also*, FLA. STAT., ch. 84–363, adding §914.24.

256. *See* Public Law 91–452, Title V, §§501–504, Oct. 15, 1970, 84 Stat. 933, 18 U.S.C. preceding §3481 (federal "Witness Protection Program"). *See also* the responses to the questionnaire from city cir. atty., St. Louis; and dist. attys., Milwaukee, San Diego, and Louisville.

257. *See* Note, "The Dilemma of the Intimidated Witness in Federal Organized Crime Prosecutions: Choosing Among the Fear of Reprisals, the Contempt Powers of the Court, and the Witness Protection Program," 50 *Fordham L. Rev.* 582, 585–90, 604–6 (1982). *See generally, Franz v. United States*, 707 F.2d 582 (D.C. Cir. 1983), *addendum* 712 F.2d 1428 (D.C. Cir. 1983); *Doe v. Civiletti*, 635 F.2d 88 (2d Cir. 1980). On October 12, 1984, the Witness Security Reform Act of 1984 was enacted. H.J. Res. 648, adding new 18 U.S.C. §§3521–3528. Among other features, the Act provides means by which the visitation rights of a non-custodial parent can be honored in cases where a child is relocated with a parent having custody of the child.

258. *Green v. U.S.*, 355 U.S. 184, 187–88 (1957).

259. *U.S. v. Scott*, 437 U.S. 82, 91 (1978). There is an exception to this rule when a trial judge, after a guilty verdict, sets aside the jury's verdict and enters a judgment of acquittal. In such a case, because an appellate reversal would not require a new trial, the prosecution may appeal. *U.S. v. Wilson*, 420 U.S. 332 (1975).

260. *See U.S. v. Lanza*, 260 U.S. 377 (1922); *U.S. v. Wheeler*, 435 U.S. 313 (1978). *See generally* Note, "Double Jeopardy and Federal Prosecution after State Jury Acquittal," 80 *Mich. L. Rev.* 1073 (1982).

261. *See* United States Attorneys' Manual, Title 9, §§2.142; *Petite v. U.S.*, 361 U.S. 529 (1960).

262. N.Y. Crim. Proc. Law §40.20.

263. *People v. Gay*, 407 Mich. 681, 289 N.W.2d 651 (1980).

264. *See, e.g.*, FLA. STAT. §921.141 (capital offense); TEX. CRIM. PROC. CODE ANN. §37.071(b) (capital offense). *See also* MO. REV. STAT. §565.006 (capital offense); Ga. Code §27–2534 (recidivists).

265. Kamisar, LaFave, and Israel, *supra* note 121, at 24.

266. *Id.*

267. *Id.*

268. *Id.*

269. *Id.*

269a. Sentencing Reform Act of 1984, H.J. Res. 648 (Oct. 12, 1984).

270. Sentencing, *supra* note 205, at 67. *See also* N.Y. Penal Law §65.00(1).

271. Sentencing *supra* note 205, at 101.

272. *Id.* at 105. *See, e.g.*, N.Y. Penal Law §65.10.2(g). *See also* ch IV; Harland, *supra* note 70, at 72.

273. Sentencing, *supra* note 205, at 107.

274. *See generally* Harland, *supra* note 70, at 64 *et seq*.

275. *See* J . L. Barkas, *Victims of Crime* (New York: Scribner, 1977); p. 182; Harland, *supra* note 70, at 71–72.

275a. Sentencing Reform Act of 1984, H.J. Res. 648 (Oct. 12, 1984), adding new 18 U.S.C. §§3555, 3556, 3563, 3625.

276. Note, "Commitment and Release of Persons Found Not Guilty by Reason of Insanity: A Georgia Perspective," 15 *Ga. L. Rev.* 1065, 1071 (1981) [hereafter "Commitment"].

277. *Id.* at 1066.

278. Note, "Rules for an Exceptional Class: The Commitment and Release of Persons Acquitted of Violent Offenses by Reason of Insanity," 57 *NYU L. Rev.* 281, 282.

279. *Id.* at 282.

280. *Id.* at 304.

281. *Id.*

282. Commitment, *supra* note 276, at 1072. *See, e.g.*, ILL. ANN. STAT. ch. 38, §1005–2–4(b), OREG. REV. STAT. §161.327. *See generally*, Ennis and Emery, *Rights of Mental Patients*, (Avon/Discus, 1978).

282a. Insanity Defense Reform Act of 1984, H.J. Res. 648, Chap. IV (Oct. 12, 1984), adding new 18 U.S.C. §§20, 4241–4247.

283. *See, e.g.*, N.Y. Crim. Proc. Law §730.60 (4-day notification to those reasonably expected to be the victim of an assault by an offender to be released or transferred from a mental health facility). *See also* ILL. REV. STAT. ch. 38 §104–30 (police authorities in a county where the offense occurred must be notified before the defendant's release).

284. *See, e.g.*, ARIZ. REV. STAT. ANN. §13–702(F); Cal. Penal Code §1191.1; CONN. GEN. STAT. §54–91c; FLA. STAT. §921.143; Wash. Rev. Code §9.94A.110.

285. *See* ARIZ. REV. STAT. ANN. §13–702(F). Cal. Penal Code §1191.1; Wash. Rev. Code §9.94A. 110 (eff. 1984). *See also* Task Force Final Report, *supra* note 10, at 66 (recommending that victims have the right to speak at sentencing hearings and send written statements to the court).

286. *See, e.g.*, MINN. STAT. §631.20; N.D. Cent. Code §29–26–17.

287. *See, e.g.*, N.Y. Crim. Proc. Law §390.30; ILL. REV. STAT. ch. 38, §1005–3–2; Fed. R. Crim. P. 32(c)(2)(C).

288. Responses to questionnaire, *supra* note 85. (Such cities include Minneapolis, Washington, D.C., and Honolulu).

289. *See, e.g.*, ARIZ. REV. STAT. ANN. §12–253.4; Wash. Rev. Code §9.94A (will be effective in 1984); ILL. REV. STAT. ch. 38, §1005–4–1.

290. *See, e.g.*, Iowa Code §901.3; Va. Code §19.2–297.

291. Va. Code §19.2–299.

292. *See, e.g.*, Ala. R.Crim. p. 3 (requiring the investigator to include, in addition to information concerning the defendant, "any other information required by the court").

293. C. L. Newman, *Parole: Legal Issues, Decision-Making, Research* 26 (1974).

294. Kamisar, LaFave, and Israel, *supra* note 121, at 24.

295. Newman, *Parole* 26.

296. *Greenholtz v. Inmates of the Nebraska Penal and Correctional Complex*, 442 U.S. 1, 7 (1979).

296a. *See* n.269a, *supra*.

297. Newman, *Parole* 35; *Morrissey*, 408 U.S. at 478.

298. *See, e.g.*, N.J. STAT. ANN. §30:4–123.45 *See also* Note, "Criminal Procedure," 12 *Seton Hall L. Rev.* 164 (1981).

299. Press release by Jonathan S. Landay, proprietary to the United Press International (Apr. 25, 1983) (available on NEXIS, Regional News Section, N.Y. Metro Distribution, 464 words, keyword "Trantino") (mentioning the Trenton, parole board's use of this condition). *But see Hines v. State Bd. of Parole*, 293 N.Y. 254, 257, 56 N.E.2d 572, 573 (1944) (seeming to disallow such a condition in N.Y.).

300. N.Y. Exec. Law §259–i(b).

301. *In re Fain*, 139 Cal.App.3d 295, 188 Cal. Rptr. 653, *later app'd*, 145 Cal.App.3d 540, 193 Cal. Rptr. 483 (App. Dep't. Sup. Ct. 1983).

302. *Id*. When the governor tried to prevent the defendant's subsequent parole release, the appellate court ruled that such action was beyond the governor's power. *In re Fain*, 145 Cal. App. 3d 540, 193 Cal. Rptr. 483 (App. Dep't. Sup. Ct. 1983). The state supreme court refused to review the lower court's decision. *N.Y. Times*, Oct. 2, 1983, at §A.

303. *See, e.g.*, N.Y. Exec. Law §259–i(3); Ind. Code §11–13–3–8.

304. *Morrissey*, 408 U.S. at 479.

305. *Id*.

306. *Id*. at 485.

307. *Id*.

308. *Id*. at 487.

309. *Id*. at 489.

310. *See, e.g.*, Ark. Stat. Ann. §§43–2819, 43–2819–1, 43–2819–2; Cal. Penal Code §3043; Del. Code Ann. tit. 11, §4350; Mass. Gen. Laws Ann. ch. 127, §133A; N.J. Rev. Stat. §30:4–123.55; Tenn. Code Ann. §40–28–107. Vermont permits oral statements to the parole board by "attorneys or other persons with an interest in the case before the board." T.28 Vt. Stat. Ann. §502 (b).

311. *See, e.g.*, Del. Code Ann. tit. 11, §4350 (victim's family may testify at hearing only where offender was sentenced for first-degree murder); Mass. Gen. Laws Ann. ch. 127, §133A (victim or family may testify only where offender was sentenced to life imprisonment for offense other than first-degree murder); Tenn. Code Ann. §40–28–107 (victim may testify where offender was sentenced to term of 10 years or more).

312. *But see* Ky. Rev. Stat. §61.810(1) (parole board meetings are closed to the public).

313. *See, e.g.,* Ariz. Rev. Stat. Ann. §31–411(F). *See also*, Minn. Stat. Ann. §611A.06 (notice of release).
313a. *N.Y. Times*, June 1, 1984, at A22.
313b. H.J. Res. 648 (Oct. 12, 1984), amending 18 U.S.C. §4207.
314. *See, e.g.,* Ariz. Rev. Stat. Ann. §31–411; Iowa Code §906.7.
315. *See, e.g.,* Md. Ann. Code art. 41, §124.
316. Cal. Penal Code §3043.
317. *The National Law Journal*, Apr. 2, 1984, at p. 4.

III

The Right to Compensation

Can crime victims receive compensation by the government for their injuries?

Yes, in most states. In thirty-nine states and the District of Columbia and the Virgin Islands, victims of violent crimes who have suffered personal injuries (and certain dependents of deceased crime victims) can be compensated for loss of earnings or support and certain out-of-pocket loss (including reasonable medical expenses) which directly result from the crime.[1]

Which states have no crime victim compensation programs?

As of 1984, there is no compensation program in Arizona, Arkansas, Georgia, Idaho, Maine, Mississippi, New Hampshire, South Dakota, Utah, Vermont, and Wyoming, or in the Commonwealth of Puerto Rico.

Is government compensation for loss resulting from crime a new idea?

No. The Babylonian Code of Hammurabi (in use in 2380 B.C.) provided that "if a robber has not been caught . . . the city and governor in whose territory and district the robbery was made, shall replace for [the victim] his lost property" and

The authors would like to express their gratitude to Daniel McGillis and Paul Hudson for their assistance in the preparation of this chapter and would also like to acknowledge that any generalizations about state compensation programs would have been impossible without the pioneering survey of such programs contained in McGillis and Smith, *Compensating Victims of Crime: An Analysis of American Programs* (Washington, D.C.: National Institute of Justice and Abt Associates Inc., May 1983) (No. J-LEAA-013-78).

that "if it was a life that was lost, the city and governor will pay one mina of silver to [the victim's] heirs."[2]

What is the origin of modern crime victim compensation?

The recognized originator of the present-day government compensation programs for victims of violent crimes is Margery Fry, an English magistrate and reformer, who, inspired by the injury to a man blinded in an assault in 1951, began writing and speaking in favor of such a program.

As a result of the debate that followed Ms. Fry's proposals, New Zealand enacted a law in 1963, creating a three-person panel to investigate claims and to award compensation (including medical expenses and lost wages within certain limits) to victims of violent crimes. There was no requirement that the criminal be arrested prior to an application for compensation. In 1964, Britain created its own Criminal Injuries Compensation Board which, with certain restrictions, compensated victims of violent crimes or their dependents, if the victims themselves were deceased.[3]

When did state compensation of crime victims begin in the United States?

The first crime victim compensation program in the United States was enacted in California in 1965, after Superior Court Judge Francis McCarty (San Francisco) urged that victims (such as a middle-aged woman he knew who had been robbed and beaten and was forced to incur over a thousand dollars in unreimbursed medical expenses) should be compensated by the state of California. While this first California program (which has since been substantially modified) was followed by more detailed and sophisticated compensation programs enacted in New York (1966), Hawaii (1967), Maryland and Massachusetts (1968), and New Jersey (1971).[4]

Is there a separate federal compensation program?

Not really. After two decades of bills to create a separate federal program for victims of federal crimes, Congress passed the Crime Victims Act of 1984. The Act created a Crime Victims Fund which provides federal funding for victims assistance programs as well as qualifying state compensation programs. The Fund can make grants to states operating qualifying programs of up to 35% of last year's awards. To qualify, among other things, state programs must compensate victims of federal crimes.

In 1984, Congress also created a very limited federal program to directly compensate victims of crimes committed by persons who had been accepted into the Federal Witness Protection Program. This program is to operate under guidelines issued by the Attorney-General, provides for awards (if the victim is killed) of up to $50,000 and requires the victim to first seek restitution, state compensation or recovery through a civil action; the federal government will only provide compensation equal to the damages which have not been recovered from these other sources.

What are the usual justifications for enacting these programs?

It depends on the state. Most often, supporters of these programs argue that they are a humanitarian response to help victims who cannot afford the medical expenses and other losses that result from crime. Another frequent rationale is that the risk of suffering a loss due to crime should be spread over the entire society and particular individuals should not be forced to bear the entire cost. A number of practical reasons have also been suggested including improving citizen cooperation with law enforcement (a prerequisite for most compensation awards), increasing publicity concerning the cost of crime and increasing incentives for society as a whole to prevent crime. One rationale that is rarely, if ever, embraced by those who enact state compensation programs is the idea that such programs are required in light of the state's failure in its obligation to protect all of its citizens from crimes.[5]

Are the state compensation programs all the same?

No. The forty-two existing programs vary widely in their stated purpose, restrictions on eligibility and benefits, funding, organizational structure, and procedures for processing claims.

What type of agency administers a state compensation program?

It depends on the state. With the exception of New Mexico (which has a fully independent agency), all of the other compensation programs are affiliated with, or sponsored by, other state agencies. Most of the operational programs are affiliated with state workers' compensation or industrial safety boards, with the courts, with departments of public safety or protection, or with the state attorney general's office.

In fact, there is a bewildering variety of combinations of these affiliations; for example, in Texas, the attorney general's office investigates claims that are made to the Industrial Accident Board. In West Virginia, the attorney general investigates claims made to the Court of Claims but awards can only be approved by the legislature. Of those states where claims are handled by workers' compensation agencies, some (such as Florida) have a staff that handles only victim compensation claims; others (such as Montana) handle victims' claims as part of their general responsibilities to review all claims for compensation. In the states where compensation is administered by the state courts, the Delaware program is affiliated with the courts only for budgetary reasons and is otherwise an independent program. In Illinois, Ohio, and West Virginia, the programs are affiliated with the state's Court of Claims, or another specialized court while in Massachusetts, Rhode Island, and Tennessee, the programs are affiliated with the general trial court system. Moreover, although technically affiliated with other state agencies, seven programs (in addition to the New Mexico program) are functionally independent.[6]

Sometimes the affiliation of a compensation program with another state agency can create unforeseen problems; for example, in one Massachusetts case, the prosecutor for the state's criminal case also represented the victim in a compensation proceeding; an appellate court rejected the defendant's claim of a conflict of interest but ordered a new trial on the ground that the prosecutor violated an unrelated provision of Massachusetts law that bars prosecutors from being concerned as counsel for either party in a civil action depending upon the same facts as the prosecution.[7]

How can a victim find out about the availability of victim compensation in his or her state?

A victim can request relevant information and application forms from any of the administrators of a state victims' compensation program (see Appendix B). In addition, these programs' services are described in public service advertising and brochures, posters and cards that are commonly distributed by police and sheriffs' departments; victims' service organizations, prosecutors' offices, crisis centers, senior citizens' groups, and other social service organizations.

Approximately a third of the programs require police officers to notify victims of their rights to compensation.[8] This notice usually takes the form of a wallet-size card distributed by police officers to victims. A number of programs have arranged for relevant literature to be distributed to victims at the emergency rooms of hospitals where they are treated. In those states (such as New Jersey and New York) which maintain a "victim hotline"—a telephone number that can be called toll-free twenty-four hours a day for information on compensation and victim assistance—perhaps the easiest way to obtain victim compensation information and materials is to request this information over the telephone.

How can a victim apply for compensation?

It depends on the state. Each of the compensation programs has its own application form, which can be obtained from the administrator of the program and from some or all of the sources just discussed.

Several states (including Minnesota, Illinois, and Virginia) have a two-step application process. After the victim completes a preliminary claim form requesting such information as the claimant's identity, relationship to the offender, a brief description of any physical injury, and the crime and the name of the officer to whom the crime was reported, the claim is screened and if it meets the statutory criteria, a more detailed application form is sent to the claimant.

In the other states, the claimant will receive an application form after his initial inquiry. These forms vary a great deal in the amount of information being sought. Typically, an applicant is asked for some or all of the following information: identity of victim and claimant, nature of crime, itemized medical expenses and economic loss, itemized funeral expenses and lost wages and support, list of dependents of the victim, and collateral sources of reimbursement (identity and amount). After the claimant returns the completed application, typically the program will acknowledge receipt of the application by letter or by telephone and inform the victim at that time if any additional information is required.[9]

Is there an application fee?

Many states have application fees of five to ten dollars that are waived if the claimant is indigent.[10]

Is the victim required to submit any documentation verifying the claim?

Yes. Typically, compensation programs will require that claims be supported by some or all of the following documentation:

1. Police reports (to prove that crime occurred and was reported);

2. Medical or funeral bills (to prove expenses);

3. Employer's report (to document lost wages) or tax forms (to demonstrate lost revenue and/or financial hardship);

4. Prosecutor's report (to indicate cooperation);

5. Witnesses' reports (to determine any victim misconduct);

6. Insurance information (to identify collateral sources of payments or benefits).[11]

Depending on the state, the responsibility for obtaining this documentation may be placed on the victim or on the compensation program's own staff. Programs report that delays in processing claims often result from the victim's failure to properly provide this documentation or by the failure of medical personnel and law enforcement agencies to properly respond to requests for such information. In fact, in some states, a very high percentage of claims are abandoned during processing due to the victim's inaction, or due to a failure to respond to requests for further information.[12]

Where can the victim receive assistance in preparing applications or providing verification?

Virtually all victims' assistance groups provide assistance in preparing compensation applications. In several states (including California) there is even formal coordination between compensation programs and victim/witness assistance programs in the processing of applications. Typically, the victim's assistance program will confer with claimants providing advice about how to complete the application forms (or even complete them for the victim) and sometimes will take responsibility for providing necessary documentation or verification of the claim.

Does a victim need an attorney in order to apply for victims' compensation?

It depends on the state and the nature of the victim's claim. Most state programs discourage victims from retaining attorneys on the grounds that the claim procedures are simple and that the compensation board will make an honest effort to treat claimants fairly. However, the Maryland compensation program reports that attorneys are involved in ninety percent of its claims. Whether the victim needs an attorney depends in large part on the nature of the particular procedures used by the program in the victim's state, and on the complexity of the victim's claim. In states with informal application procedures (particularly where program staff personnel or victim service agencies are available to help the victim complete applications) no attorney may be necessary. In those states where trial courts adjudicate claims after a formal hearing, the services of an attorney may be desirable, or even indispensable. In addition, if it is questionable whether the victim is eligible for compensation or whether the victim is seeking benefits that are not clearly allowable under the program's provisions, an attorney may be helpful or even necessary.[13]

What is the maximum amount of time after the crime that a victim can file a claim for compensation?

It depends on the state. The statute of limitations for filing claims varies from state to state from as little as three months to up to two years. In some states, these periods can be extended once only for an additional period of time for good cause.[14]

In general, these deadlines for filing claims are strictly enforced and claims are denied that are filed after the time period indicated in the statute (as extended where the claimant can show good cause). New York courts have repeatedly declined to ignore New York's deadline, even where there were extenuating circumstances; for instance, if the claimant moved out of state or if the claimant was a minor.[15] However, in other states courts have allowed victims to file claims after the deadline where there were compelling equitable considerations; for example, where a city police department failed to provide a victim with the proper claim forms, a California court held that the police department's error prevented the compensation board from refusing a claim even though it was filed more than one year after the crime.[16] The New Jersey Supreme Court allowed an incapacitated victim of a brutal assault and rape to file her claim six and a half weeks after the end of the statutory period for filing a claim had expired, since the victim was hospitalized for ten days after the attack and the physical and psychological effects of her rape trauma syndrome continued for at least seven weeks after the assault.[17]

Must an offender be arrested or convicted of the crime in order for a victim to be eligible for an award?

No. If the conduct producing the injury constitutes a crime, neither prosecution nor conviction is necessary for the victim to claim compensation.[18] Even if the state technically has no jurisdiction to prosecute, if the conduct producing the injury could have been prosecuted as a crime, the victim is eligible for compensation.[19] While it is not determinative of the compensation board's decision, the results of a criminal prosecution can be considered by the board in deciding whether there was a crime and who committed it. A Maryland appellate court has specifically held that acquittal in a criminal trial could be considered and used as a basis for the compensation board's conclusion that a particular defendant had not committed the crime for which a victim was claiming compensation.[20]

If there is a criminal prosecution pending when a victim files his claim, the compensation board may defer consideration of an award until after the criminal trial (although the victim may be eligible for an emergency award during the trial).[21]

If there is a prosecution and the accused was acquitted, does that prevent the victim from receiving compensation?

No. An acquittal or failure to prosecute does not bar the victim from recovering compensation. While the board may consider an acquittal or a failure to prosecute as evidence that there was no crime or that a particular defendant is innocent,[22] it is not conclusive evidence and the claimant can dispute it.[23]

If the crime was committed by someone who was technically incapable of committing a crime because of drunkenness, insanity, senility, or other condition, can the victim receive compensation?

Yes. The victim is eligible for compensation under the

provisions of virtually all of the statutes under such circumstances.[24]

Is every crime victim eligible for compensation?

No. In general, programs compensate victims and certain other persons who are killed or injured as a direct result of certain acts, omissions, or conduct that are punishable under that state's criminal laws. However, all programs have a variety of restrictions on eligibility that depend on (1) the residency of the victim; (2) the location of the crime; (3) the type of crime; (4) the victim's relationship to the offender; and (5) the victim's own background.

In order to recover, the burden is on the victim to demonstrate that he is entitled to an award.[25]

In general, courts in most states broadly interpret provisions making victims eligible and narrowly interpret restrictions on compensation.[26] However, some courts (treating the victims' compensation statute as a limited departure from the common law) have held that its provisions should be strictly construed.[27]

Is the location of the victim's residence relevant to his eligibility?

It depends on the state. All of the existing programs will accept claims if the claimant resides in the state being asked to make the award, but some states will not consider claims made by nonresidents. Twenty-three programs provide compensation regardless of the residency of the claimant.[28] In addition, some states that do not otherwise compensate nonresident claimants have entered reciprocal agreements that allow residents of other states to make claims for compensation where the programs in the states in which they reside allow their residents to make claims. As of 1984, there are still a number of states—including New Mexico, Nevada, Florida, and California—which do not compensate nonresident claimants, and place the burden of proving he is a resident on the claimant in order to be eligible for the award.[29]

Beginning in 1985, increasing numbers of states can be expected to provide compensation for non-residents as a result of Congress's enactment of the Crime Victims Act of 1984. That act provides substantial federal funding to qualifying state compensation programs; in order to qualify a state must compensate non-residents victims on the same basis it compensates its own residents.

Even where residence is required, however, there is no requirement that the claimant's residency in the state making the award be "lawful" and a California appellate court has reversed a denial of compensation to an illegal alien residing in California on the ground that no such exclusion is explicit in the state's compensation statute.[30]

Does the denial of compensation to a victim solely on the ground that he is not a resident in the state making the award violate the victim's constitutional rights?

It is not clear. One California appellate court upheld the denial of an award on residency grounds to a New York tourist shot in the leg on a trip to California.[31] The court found that distinguishing between residents and nonresidents for purposes of compensation did not create a "suspect classification" and that, because the statute required no particular duration of residency in order to qualify for an award, there was no interference with the victim's fundamental right to travel; since the statute did not create a suspect classification or abridge a fundamental right, the court rejected the claimant's argument that it violated equal protection because exclusion of nonresidents is rationally related to the state's legitimate goal of reducing the cost of a compensation program. The California court also held that the statute did not violate the privileges and immunities clause of Article 4 of the United States Constitution.

However, a federal court came to a different conclusion in a case involving the denial of an award to an Austrian national as a result of the residency requirement of the Virgin Islands' Criminal Victim's Compensation Act.[32] In that case, the court held that distinguishing between Virgin Islands residents and aliens created a suspect classification (similar to a classification based on race) and that the statute could be upheld only if the state could demonstrate a compelling and overriding state interest for the statute. Observing that the purpose of the statute was to provide incentives for public cooperation with law enforcement and the criminal justice system, the court held that a classification based on residency (rather than, for instance, cooperation with police) was irrational and violated the equal protection guarantees of the Fourteenth Amendment.

Can a victim recover from the compensation program in his state if the crime took place in another state?

No. Most programs are limited to crimes that take place in the state administering the program. A small number of states (such as Wisconsin) provide their residents who suffer injury or death due to crimes in other states with the same rights as if they were injured at home if the state or territory in which the crime occurred will not compensate the victim.[33]

If the victim has a family or household relationship with the person who committed the crime, is the victim still eligible for compensation?

It depends on the state. Twenty-six of the existing programs prohibit at least some persons who are "family members" of the criminal from receiving compensation.[34] In most of these states, the victim is considered to be in the same "family" with the offender if (1) he is related by blood or marriage to the offender (often within "the third degree of consanguinity or affinity"); (2) he is maintaining a sexual relationship with the offender; or (3) he is residing in the same household with the offender.[35]

This has excluded victims killed by their spouses from recovering compensation in a number of cases on the ground that the victim had an "affinity" to the person committing the crime (despite the creative argument in one New York case that this exclusion was only intended to keep the family of a perpetrator who injured himself during commission of the crime from claiming compensation).[36] The Maryland Supreme Court has also rejected an attempt to limit the effect of the statute to legitimate children of the perpetrator, upholding the denial of an award where the claimant was the child of a woman allegedly stabbed to death by a man who was conceded to be the child's biological father.[37]

However, a Florida appellate court, relying on an 1899 Florida Supreme Court case, allowed a claimant allegedly slashed by her estranged husband to recover compensation on the ingenious grounds that a husband and wife are not related within any degree of affinity (since they are not related by marriage but married to each other); the court observed that the legislature, if it wanted to bar spouses from recovering compensation, could and should have simply used the word *spouse* in listing ineligible claimants.[38]

A Maryland court reversed denial of an award to the family

of a victim allegedly killed by his sister's husband, observing, with respect to affinity, that an affine of one spouse is not related to his affine of the other spouse (that is, a person is not related to his in-laws' spouses).[39]

The complications and irrationality that can result from applying exclusions "within three degrees of consanguinity or affinity" is clearest in a 1978 decision of the Maryland Supreme Court involving a claim by a homicide victim's wife and children.[40] The victim was reportedly killed by his brother-in-law and nephew. After defining consanguinity as a relationship by blood and affinity as a relationship by marriage, the court attempted to determine what was meant by "degrees." There are two separate and very different possibilities: under common or canon law, the number of generations is counted from the common ancestor down to the descendant whose degree of relationship is to be ascertained; civil law ascends by generations from either of the two relatives to the common ancestor and then down the collateral line to the other. As a result, the number of degrees under civil law is exactly double that under common law. Observing that the statute had a remedial purpose, the court adopted the civil law method of determining degrees. Then, after an analysis that required five pages, the court determined that (1) the wife was related to the nephew within three degrees of affinity; (2) the children were only related to the nephew within four degrees of consanguinity (and therefore were not excluded from recovering against him), but (3) the children were related to the brother-in-law within three degrees of affinity. Since each of the claimants was related to one of the alleged coperpetrators of the crime within the degree of relationship indicated by the statute, neither the children nor the wife could recover. However, if the murder had been committed by either the nephew or the brother-in-law alone, the wife or children could have recovered but not both.

Reacting to the criticism, irrationality, and complicated administration of such provisions, a number of states have proposed or enacted legislation to limit or repeal this exclusion.

Are there states that allow "family members" to receive compensation under certain circumstances?

Yes. While at least fifteen states have made "family members" absolutely ineligible for compensation, in certain states they can receive compensation under particular circumstances. In

Wisconsin, Illinois, Virginia, and Minnesota, for example, a victim who separates from the offender and cooperates in the prosecution is eligible to make a claim.[41] Indiana allows nonspousal dependents of the offender to receive compensation "where justice requires"; while spouses are ineligible for awards, there is a separate fund in Indiana for spouse abuse victims.[42] In New York an injured victim can recover if the related offender does not benefit from any award and if the victim has been living separate from the perpetrator for one year, there is a divorce or separation decree in effect, the offender is a fugitive or has been convicted, or the victim is an emancipated minor.[43] Some states, such as Hawaii and Michigan, allow relatives of the offender to recover out-of-pocket expenses or expenses paid to third-party medical providers.[44]

Why are victims related to the offender, or living in the same household, ineligible for compensation?

There are three reasons typically given to justify this exclusion.[45] First, there is the assumption that victims related to, or living with, the offender contribute to their own victimization. Second, the close relationship creates a potential for fraud and trumped up claims. Finally there is the fear that providing compensation to the victim under such circumstances may directly or indirectly benefit the offender.

This exclusion has been severely criticized.[46] Virtually all studies of domestic violence are highly critical of the assumption that the victim contributes to his or her own victimization. On the contrary, without publicly funded counseling and financial assistance, it may be impossible for an abused and dependent family member to leave the household that he or she shares with the offender. Similarly, compensation programs could reduce the potential for fraud or for unjustly enriching the offender simply by giving the compensation program the discretion to make an award to a "family member" where it would serve "the interests of justice" (as in Minnesota, Ohio, and North Dakota) or where it does not unjustly enrich the offender (as in a number of states including Kansas).[47]

Are other victims ineligible for compensation?

Yes. In general, there are two other categories of victims who are ineligible to make claims. First, in most states, persons who are victimized in the course of their normal work with criminals—police officers and firemen—are not eligible for compensation; typically their losses are compensated by workers' compensation. Some states however do compensate firemen and policemen with victims' compensation awards to the extent that they have not already been reimbursed by workmen's compensation, and in Indiana there is blanket compensation (without need for proof that the injury was directly caused by the crime) for law enforcement officers or firemen injured or killed while performing official duties.[48]

Second, there are a series of restrictions intended to prevent the offender or persons with a criminal background from benefiting from crime victim compensation. In New Mexico, North Dakota, Washington, and Pennsylvania, prisoners in state institutions who have been injured or killed by crimes committed by other inmates are ineligible for crime victim compensation.[49] Ohio enacted a provision (following a claim for victims' compensation by the wife of an alleged organized crime figure for losses caused by the death of her husband when a bomb in his car exploded), which excludes persons with a history of past felonies from receiving compensation.[50] Similarly, a number of states exclude all claims that would unjustly benefit the offender or an accomplice.[51]

In addition, Nebraska has a unique limitation on eligibility.[52] It mandates that a victim's prior social history be assessed before granting an award; if the victim comes from an undesirable background he can be denied an award.

Does a victim have to be "financially needy" in order to receive compensation?

It depends on the state. Two thirds of the existing programs have no financial need requirement.[53] The remaining programs have some form of financial hardship requirement in order to qualify for compensation.

The tests for financial need vary greatly from state to state. Some states have been liberal in allowing victims with assets to receive compensation; in California, victims are denied compensation only if they have more than $30,000 in liquid assets, and the staff of the compensation program in Connecticut (which has a financial needs test) reports that no one has ever been denied an award for lack of financial need.[54]

By contrast, until 1983, New York placed the burden on victims to show that they suffered "serious financial hardship" before they could qualify for an award. This restriction on eligibility was so strictly enforced that New York appellate courts invalidated an award of $600 to a retired person because of stocks and savings amounting to less than $29,000 and an award of $450 for unreimbursed medical expenses to a claimant who had been unemployed for 8 months (and whose sole income was unemployment insurance and interest on his savings) because of his $25,000 savings account and ownership of $60,000 in stocks. As a result of these rulings, less than 1 percent of all victims in New York would be eligible for victims' compensation.[55] Responding to heavy criticism of this limitation on eligibility, in 1983, the New York legislature amended the compensation statute to allow compensation where the victim could show "financial difficulty," which was to be determined by the crime victims board by considering—

1. the victim's net financial resources and whether they were likely to be exhausted during his lifetime;

2. how many dependents the victim had;

3. his reasonable living expenses;

4. his employment situation;

5. any indebtedness;

6. the existence of any special needs.[56]

In determining the extent of the financial hardship suffered by the victim, typically states can take into account a wide variety of financial loss; for example, a Maryland appellate court has ruled the cost of the crime to the victim (for purposes of determining financial hardship) is not limited to out-of-pocket expenses and includes (in a case where seven children claimed compensation for the death of their mother) the loss of maternal services, and their cost of replacement.[57]

States differ on whether to consider all or only part of the victim's total financial resources in determining whether the injury caused by the crime constitutes a "hardship." The Texas attorney general issued an opinion in 1981, which required the Texas compensation program to consider all the victim's resources in determining "financial stress," including benefits received for vacation or sick leave. After an appellate court ruling the New York's Crime Victim Board could not exempt any assets in determining financial hardship, the legislature amended the statute to include a specific formula for determining the victim's "net financial resources" that excludes—

1. the value of the victim's home up to $100,000 or 5 years' rent;

2. clothing;

3. personal property;

4. furniture;

5. appliances;

6. business tools;

7. retirement and health benefits;

8. the family car and life insurance (except for death benefits).

The board also was given discretion to exempt up to $100,000 in annual income or business inventory.[58]

What is the justification for this financial means test?

In line with the humanitarian justification for crime victims' compensation, this requirement is an attempt to restrict compensation to the truly "needy." Obviously, such provisions are also intended to reduce the costs of a state's compensation program. However, these restrictions have been strongly criticized for (1) increasing the cost of administration of compensation programs by requiring a screening of claimants' finances; (2) punishing frugal individuals who have built up savings or assets and (3) causing victims additional unnecessary trauma and violations of privacy.[59] It is for just these reasons that a number of programs that presently have financial needs tests are considering limitations on them (as New York did in 1983, by requiring a showing of "financial difficulty" rather than "financial hardship") or outright abolition.[60]

Is the victim's own conduct relevant to his claim for compensation?

Yes. In all of the programs, the board is entitled to weigh the victim's responsibility for his own injury or death against that of the offender and reduce or deny the award accordingly.[61]

What constitutes conduct that would reduce or prohibit an award?

In general this is left to the discretion of the board. Some statutes specify that conduct constituting "provocation" is one basis for reducing or denying an award.[62]

Where the claimant's innocence has been raised as an

issue, the burden is on the victim to show that he did not incite, provoke, or consent to the crime.[63] In two Washington appellate cases, courts have upheld the denial of benefits where there was evidence that a victim had prepared an ambush for the person who caused the injury (and had even fired first) and where a victim, while drunk, shouted abuse at an acquaintance, backed the acquaintance up against the wall and thus provoked a knifing. After an award to the widow of an alleged organized crime figure killed by a car bomb, Ohio made any victim whose conduct even remotely contributed to his own victimization ineligible for compensation.[64]

The method by which boards weigh the extent of a victim's responsibility for the injury varies.[65] In Florida, four staff members make independent estimates and the final figure is arrived at by compromising all of these estimates. Some program administrators use a personal "rule of thumb" (such as the program administrator who stated that assault victims who ventured into bad neighborhoods were at least ten percent responsible for their own injury). In some states (such as Wisconsin) up to thirty-three percent of all claims are denied because the victim's conduct contributed to his injury.

Is there any requirement that the victim cooperate with law enforcement officers in order to obtain compensation?

Yes. Virtually all of the programs require that the victim report the crime to the appropriate law enforcement agency within a specified period of time after its occurrence. The time period varies widely from twenty-four hours (the Virgin Islands) to three months (New Jersey).[66] In most states the time limit can be extended upon a showing of good cause (for example, if the victim was ill or hospitalized); in some states (such as Nebraska and Pennsylvania), hospital emergency rooms treating victims of violent crimes are required to file reports that satisfy this requirement. In addition, most states require continuing cooperation with law enforcement officers, including assistance in investigating the crime, identifying the suspect and appearing as a witness in any prosecution.[67]

The reason for this requirement is to encourage citizen participation in law enforcement (one of the purposes of providing victim compensation) and to reduce the possibility of fraud. In one case, where an award was allegedly denied because the victim had failed to cooperate with a workmen's compensation proceeding, the court reversed the board's denial, strictly construed the requirement of cooperation with a "law enforcement agency" to include only agencies involved in the investigation of a crime or the apprehension or prosecution of a criminal, and generally held that such provisions were not meant as a barrier to recovery but simply intended to require some general showing of cooperation by the victim with police and prosecutors.[68]

Is the type of crime relevant to whether a victim is eligible to receive compensation?

Yes. All of the compensation programs only reimburse victims for injury or loss due to certain kinds of violent crimes.

Which are the compensable violent crimes?

It depends on the state. Most states require that the conduct producing injury (1) occur or is attempted within the state to which the claim is made; (2) pose a substantial threat of personal injury or death; and (3) is punishable by fine, imprisonment, or death or would be so if the person engaged in the conduct possessed the requisite legal capacity to commit the crime.[69] Approximately a quarter of the programs list specific violent crimes for which injury is compensable. Although the lists vary from state to state, typically they include murder, manslaughter, assault, kidnapping, rape, sodomy, and sexual abuse.[70]

The burden is on the claimant to prove that a compensable crime was committed. In one New York case, where a claimant was injured when she fell down a flight of stairs leading to the subway, the court upheld the denial of the claim on the ground that she had not met her burden of showing that she was pushed, or that any crime was committed.[71] On the other hand, a New Jersey appellate court has ruled that the compensation board is not bound by a determination by the police that a death was not the result of homicide.[72]

Are injuries from motor vehicle accidents covered by victims' compensation statutes?

No. Ninety percent of the victims' compensation programs explicitly exclude any injury resulting from ownership or operation of a motor vehicle except where the injuries were intentionally inflicted;[73] in many states, such as Hawaii and Kentucky, this restriction is extended to include operation of a boat or aircraft.[74]

Where the statute does not explicitly exclude victims of an automobile accident, and the driver's acts amount to manslaughter, assault, or some other violent crime, the victim is eligible for compensation.[75]

In those states that exclude injuries caused by motor vehicles, the fact that the driver's conduct could be prosecuted as a separate compensable crime has not been sufficient to justify an award. For example, courts in Florida and Kentucky have barred compensation even where the driver was a hit-and-run motorist who intentionally fled the scene of the accident or was intoxicated and fleeing from another crime.[76] Even where the driver was found guilty of the intentional crime of third-degree murder, a Pennsylvania court upheld the widow's ineligibility for compensation on the ground that the exception for intentional crimes did not apply to an automobile accident unless the driver's actions were committed with the specific purpose of causing the injury or that he knew that injury or death was the inevitable consequence of his act; proof of "intent" for purposes of murder did not mean the injury was intentionally inflicted under the compensation statute.[77]

Do any of the compensation programs allow claims for injuries due to hit-and-run driving or driving while intoxicated?

Yes. Recognizing the severe loss that a victim can suffer as a result of such injury, California, Oregon, and West Virginia permit claims arising from reckless driving violations (including hit-and-run driving and driving under the influence of alcohol) and Ohio compensates victims injured by persons fleeing from the scene of a felony.[78] Similar proposals are now pending in other states.

Is anyone besides a victim eligible for compensation?

Yes. Where a victim has died due to a crime, almost every state will allow dependents or family members to recover compensation. In some states, under certain other circumstances, third parties can also make claims.

Are a homicide victim's dependents eligible for compensation?

Yes. In all the programs, dependents are eligible for benefits if the victim died as a direct result of the crime and if they relied upon the victim for their principal support.[79]

Can family members receive compensation if they are not dependent for their principal support on a deceased victim?

Yes. Most states also provide for compensation to any surviving spouse, parent, or child of a victim who died as a direct result of a crime, regardless of dependency.[80] However, a minority of states require that family members be dependents of the victim or restrict the benefits available to nondependent relatives. As a result of such a provision, in one New Jersey case, the parents of a murdered child were held not to qualify for compensation because they were not financially dependent on the crime victim.[81] Hawaii restricts parents and adult children of a deceased victim to compensation for hospital, medical, and burial expenses.[82]

Are persons who are not family members or dependents of a deceased victim permitted to file for compensation?

Generally, no. Typically such compensation is limited to members of the victim's family or dependents, but in some states, any private individual assuming medical expenses for a victim who dies can obtain compensation. Burial expenses can be recovered by nonrelatives in New York and also in Indiana (if the victim is unmarried).[83]

If the victim is injured by a crime but dies before he receives an award, is his estate eligible to receive compensation?

It depends on the state. In the Virgin Islands, estates are specifically permitted to bring claims. By contrast, one court held that New York's compensation program is intended for living claimants; a claim does not vest in a victim until there has been an actual award, and therefore if a victim dies before an award is granted, his estate has no right to compensation.[84]

Are good samaritans eligible for compensation?

Yes. In eighty-five percent of the victim compensation programs, there are also provisions that allow for compensation to persons who are injured or killed in the act of aiding a crime victim, preventing a crime or apprehending a person reasonably suspected of engaging in a crime. In some states with compensation programs, awards are more liberally granted for "good samaritans" than for other victims. For example, in New York "good samaritans" are exempt from the financial means test, are allowed to recover regardless of whether they contributed to their own injury and are permitted to recover up to $5,000 in damage to property.[85] The Georgia State Claims Advisory Board, while not authorized to compensate

crime victims in general, is authorized to compensate good
samaritans who sustain injury, property damage, or death in
attempting to prevent the commission of a crime or to aid a
police officer at the officer's request; however, the Georgia
board has reviewed and paid only one such claim in the last
fifteen years.[86]

What kinds of loss or damage can be compensated?

It varies from state to state. Typically victim compensation
programs compensate for (1) medical expenses; (2) lost wages;
(3) funeral expenses; and (4) loss of support to the dependents
of a deceased victim. In order to qualify for grants from the
federal Crime Victims Fund, state programs must provide
compensation for medical expenses (including mental health
counseling), loss of wages due to physical injury and a victim's
funeral expenses. However, states vary widely in the particular kinds of expenses that they will compensate, how the
victim's loss is calculated, ceilings on the maximum award for
a particular loss or for the total award, and what deductions
will be made from the actual loss to determine the award.
Programs are not, however, required to award victims all of
the damages to which they would be entitled in a civil suit.[87]

Does the victim's loss have to directly result from the crime?

Yes. However, compensation statutes do not generally define which injuries "directly result" from a crime. Many
states do, however, limit compensable injury to the victim to
"bodily injury," presumably in order to place the burden on
the victim to prove a discreet, identifiable injury, which did
not exist prior to the crime, but is closely connected to it; for
example, in one Florida case, the son of a victim killed in a bar-
room fight was denied compensation for psychiatric treatment
related to his obsession with his father's murder on the ground
that the son's injury was not "a direct result of a crime."[88]

In general, what "lost earnings" are compensable?

It depends on the state. "Loss of earnings" may be defined
in the statute, but typically compensation programs make
their own determinations about what constitutes recognizable
losses; their decisions (whether in a particular case or in
connection with the adoption of a general rule or regulation)
can only be overturned if they are arbitrary, capricious, or an
abuse of discretion.[89]

Courts in some states have ruled that wages lost because a victim missed work by testifying at criminal proceedings and loss of overtime, sick leave, and vacation benefits were not to be considered "lost earnings."[90] A New York court has even ruled that a victim who was unemployed for eight months prior to the crime cannot collect lost wages (despite an injury that prevented him from seeking work) because the statute required the board to consider "an amount equal to the *actual* loss sustained" and in his case, any loss was purely speculative.[91] In addition, a New York court denied claims by uniformed police officers injured in the line of duty on the ground that there was no actual loss because job benefits reimbursed such losses; they were not entitled to recover night shift or overtime work lost as a result of injury because this did not represent a "serious financial hardship."[92]

However, other courts have been far more liberal in allowing compensation for lost earnings.[93]

What constitutes compensable "loss of support"?

In making awards based on "loss of support," boards compensate claimants who are financially dependent on the victim for lost future payments for support and maintenance.[94] Courts in Michigan and Pennsylvania have held that separated wives of homicide victims are eligible to recover lost support (even if the husband was not currently making support payments) as long as the victim, at the time of his death, had a legal obligation to support the claimant.[95] However, courts have upheld decisions by compensation boards not to compensate as loss of support payments for babysitting and housekeeping services incurred due to the death of the claimants' mother.[96] In determining how much compensation to provide for loss of support, compensation boards need not pay for all damages that the dependent is entitled to recover in a civil action.[97]

How do boards calculate how much earnings or support is lost?

In general, compensation boards have discretion in determining how to calculate the exact amount of the lost support or earnings.[98] The burden is on the claimant to provide sufficient evidence to support any alleged economic loss.[99]

In calculating future support and future earnings lost due to the death of a victim, courts have relied on actuarial tables and evidence about the particular victim's life expectancy, multiplied his expected life span by a percentage of his actual annual earnings (often adjusted to the victim's net after tax income), and then subtracted from this total any income that the dependent may receive from other sources, including social security payments, expenses avoided by reason of the victim's death, and even earnings by the dependents themselves.[100] Some states (such as New York) calculate the amount of loss by projecting the victim's actual earnings into the future without making any adjustment for inflation or potential increases in earnings. Where a self-employed victim's earnings varied from year to year, some states provide for a mathematical average to be used in determining lost future earnings according to tables developed by the state's workmen's compensation program.[101]

Are the costs of rehabilitation compensable?

Yes, in most of the programs. Rehabilitation expenses can be reimbursed as medical expenses or under special provisions, such as a provision of the Wisconsin law that permits compensation of costs that "may be reasonably required to cure and relieve the effects of the injury, and to attain efficient use of artificial members and appliances."[102]

Can a victim disabled by a crime receive victim compensation for expenses related to his disability?

Probably not. Most of the programs do not provide for disability payments above and beyond payments for a limited amount of lost wages and out-of-pocket medical expenses. However, nine programs do provide disability payments when the victim's continuing disability results from the crime.[103] In many states, such provisions adopt the disability benefit schedules contained in the state's workmens' compensation laws; the Washington Supreme Court has upheld the use of such schedules to compensate disabled crime victims as reasonable and not a violation of equal protection.[104]

Does victims' compensation cover psychiatric treatment or counseling expenses?

Yes. In most cases, this is reimbursable as a medical expense. In addition, victims' assistance organizations can provide victims with information about obtaining free counseling in connection with the victimization. In some states, however, there are special provisions that authorize reimbursement for counseling expenses. Some of these, like the one in California, do not stipulate that the victim suffer any actual physical injury in order to obtain reimbursement for psychological counseling.[105]

While Florida's statute does not specifically refer to compensation for psychiatric treatment and defines a victim as "any person who suffers personal physical injury as a direct result of a crime," a Florida appellate court held that a victim could recover as out-of-pocket loss unreimbursed psychiatric treatment for nervous tension and memory disorder.[106] In Massachusetts and Virginia counseling expenses are only recoverable in cases of sexual assault.[107]

Can the victim of sexual assault be compensated for the costs of pregnancy?

It depends on the state. In a number of states (including Wisconsin and Delaware), the victim of a sexual assault can recover the costs related to treatment of resulting pregnancies.[108]

Will the compensation programs compensate victims for pain and suffering resulting from the crime?

In general, no. The fear of fraud, the difficulty in assessing claims of mental anguish and determining their causes, and the potential cost of such compensation have led most states to bar recovery for pain and suffering. However, some programs (including Delaware, Hawaii, Rhode Island, and the Virgin Islands) do allow for compensation for pain and suffering.[109] In fact, in Hawaii, in 1981, fifty-one percent of total awards were attributed to payments for pain and suffering.[110] In a few other states (including West Virgina, North Dakota, Tennessee, Oregon, and Wisconsin), victims of sexual assault can receive compensation for pain and suffering or for "nervous shock."[111]

In situations where a victim is incapacitated or deceased and the victim or a dependent must hire someone to provide services the victim would normally perform, is compensation available?

Yes, in about a third of the programs. Typically, payments are made for loss reasonably incurred in obtaining ordinary and necessary replacement services, such as services in the home where the homemaker is incapacitated or killed by crime and where the housekeeping must be done by someone else. Wisconsin, for example, specifically provides that homemaker replacement services are to be compensated.[112]

Where the statute is not explicit, some states (such as Maryland) have allowed payment for "homemaker's services" or "maternal services," while others have denied such awards on the grounds that they are not the result of an out-of-pocket loss or loss of support.[113] In calculating the cost of replacing lost homemaker's services, the Ohio Court of Claims has ruled that the compensation board is to consider the actual cost of the replacement services used and not a projection of potential costs; in so doing the court rejected the argument that such a requirement discriminates in favor of victims who can afford to advance such payments and against those who cannot.[114]

Will state compensation programs compensate victims for lost or damaged property?

No. There is no compensation program that generally compensates victims for lost property. Moreover, federal grants are not available to reimburse compensation awards due to property loss. The rationale for this exclusion is that property losses are less devastating than physical injury and that states cannot afford the cost of compensating victims for all property losses. However, there are limited exceptions to this rule. New York, Hawaii, and California, for example, do allow recovery of property loss for good samaritans.[115] Recognizing that for the handicapped and elderly, the loss of eyeglasses, hearing aids, prosthetic devices, wheelchairs, and even television sets can be devastating, New York has enacted a provision that compensates victims who also suffer physical injury and elderly victims (even if they are not physically injured) for the loss or damage of "essential property" up to $250. Colorado provides reimbursement up to $100 for the deductible amount of a residential insurance policy and for damage to doors, locks, windows, and security-related residential property up to $250. Colorado specifically excludes such awards from the victim's income for state income tax and welfare eligibility purposes.[116]

Some states now award compensation for such losses (and for other expenses that might not otherwise be reimbursable such as childcare, relocation costs, or transportation) by relying on statutory language that gives compensation boards discretion to provide "reasonable" compensation for victims' expenses or pecuniary loss.[117]

What is the maximum total award that a victim can receive?

It varies widely from state to state.[118] Almost half the programs pay maximum awards of less than $15,000. Only Alaska, Maryland, New York, and Texas allow maximum awards of more than $40,000, and then, only under certain circumstances.

Are there limits on compensation for specific expenses or losses?

Yes. Most states have ceilings for at least some kinds of expenses, for example, most states impose a ceiling on allowable funeral expenses of between $500 (Ohio) and $2,500 (Virgin Islands).

With respect to lost wages, some states pay up to a certain maximum amount per month or per week until the claimant reaches the overall maximum permitted by that program; for example, in different programs, claimants will be compensated for wage losses up to a maximum of $750 per month (Illinois), up to a maximum of $100 per week (Michigan), and up to $150 per week (Kentucky).

Some programs will compensate the claimant up to a certain proportion of his usual wages or of the average wages in that state. Florida, the Virgin Islands, and Montana will compensate a victim for up to two-thirds of the victim's lost earnings or gross income (but in Montana, the ceiling on such compensation is $125 per week).

Although administrators of some programs have reported that only a very small percentage of awards reach or exceed the statutory maximum, the low limits on maximum awards (which have not typically been adjusted for inflation) and, in particular, the low ceilings on compensable monthly and weekly earnings have been strongly criticized.[119]

Is compensation for medical expenses included in these overall limits on the total award?

Yes, in most states. In some states, there are separate ceilings for medical expenses. In California and Oregon there is a separate $10,000 maximum award for medical expenses and another $3,000 ceiling specifically for rehabilitation expenses. In two states, New York and Texas, awards for medical expenses have no maximum limits (although New York does have medical fee guidelines which limit reimbursement for particular items of medical care). In addition, the compensation programs in Florida, New Jersey, and New Mexico have used their economic leverage as the payer of last resort to negotiate reduced fees with hospitals (within the program's maximum allowable payments) which will allow the boards to pay in full the medical expenses incurred by the claimant. One program administrator reports that he successfully negotiated with hospitals to accept as little as 30 percent of their usual charges in full compensation for medical services provided by the hospital to a crime victim.[120]

Is any minimum loss required?

Yes. In most of the programs, there are minimum loss requirements from as low as $25 (Delaware) to $300 (South Carolina).[121] Typically, such programs prohibit claims for compensation unless the victim has lost at least $100 in out-of-pocket earnings or two continuous weeks of earnings.

What is the purpose of these minimum loss requirements?

To cut administrative costs, to save time, and to reduce the program's workload. However, these minimum loss restrictions have also been criticized. Commentators have argued that they do not result in significant savings. In addition, they discriminate against rape victims (who may not incur such out-of-pocket loss or loss of earnings) and the poor, elderly, and disabled (for whom any loss of earnings or out-of-pocket expenditures may be devastating).[122] As a result of such criticism, New York eliminated minimum loss requirements in 1982. Sexual assault victims are eligible for reimbursement of out-of-pocket medical expenses in Washington regardless of whether they meet minimum loss requirements, and states such as Pennsylvania and Virginia have exempted victims who are elderly and on fixed incomes.[123] Such exemptions are being considered in other states.

Are awards subject to any standard deductibles?

Yes. In Connecticut ($100), Illinois ($200), Massachusetts ($100), Minnesota ($100), Oregon ($250), and Virginia ($100), there are deductibles (similar to the deductibles used by insurance companies) which are subtracted from any award to a crime victim. These deductible provisions have been criticized for the same reason as the minimum loss requirement and at least one state (Virginia) exempts elderly victims from the $100 deductible.[124]

Are awards reduced by any compensation that the victim receives from other sources?

Yes. All of the programs have so-called collateral source deductions that have the effect of reducing the award by benefits received or to be received by the victim from other sources. Some of these restrictions are phrased in very general terms allowing deductions for amounts or benefits from any source.[125] Other statutes list specific sources. Typically, they require that the award will be reduced by the amount of any payments to the victim from—

1. the person who committed the crime;

2. public insurance programs (including workers' and unemployment compensation);

3. public funds;

4. private insurance contracts;

5. any emergency awards that the claimant has already received from the compensation program.[126]

Are proceeds from public insurance programs, such as social security and welfare, deductible from compensation?

Yes.[127] One Washington Supreme Court case held that public insurance did not include benefits received from Federal Old Age Survivors and Disability Insurance Act (OASI) and social security payments.[128] However, the Washington legislature amended the statute explicitly to make such payments deductible.[129]

Courts have differed on the effect of allowing deduction for such insurance where OASI or social security payments during a given year would exceed what a homicide victim would have earned. A New Jersey appellate court has ruled that the compensation board rightly denied compensation to the widow of a murder victim because social security benefits exceeded the amount of support provided by the decedent at the time of his death.[130] However, a Pennsylvania court has held that the fact that social security payments during certain years were higher than what the victim would have provided to his widow was irrelevant since the statute only dictated deduction of the total social security payments from any lost earnings.[131]

Are private insurance proceeds deductible as collateral resources?

In most states, yes. Many statutes explicitly include proceeds from private insurance as deductible, but even where the statute is silent, such proceeds (and in some states this includes life insurance policies payable to the family of a homicide victim) are deductible from economic losses for purposes of determining the award.[132] Included among the types of private insurance proceeds deductible from compensation are any amounts received by a victim under wage continuation programs maintained by his employer.[133]

There are exceptions. Hawaii explicitly exempts death benefits from the provisions mandating collateral source deductions.[134] Pennsylvania does not deduct the proceeds from medical insurance that pays expenses incurred in connection with the loss of an eye from the amount of an award.[135]

The deduction of proceeds from private insurance has been challenged on constitutional grounds by a victim who argued that such exclusions discriminate against persons who prepare for potential injury by investing in insurance and in favor of persons who invest in other assets or make no provision for potential future loss. The Washington Supreme Court (after observing that the statute applies equally to all victims and reasonably prevents double recovery by any individual victim) held that the legislature had a rational basis for reducing awards by amounts obtained from private insurance and that the statute did not violate equal protection or the privileges and immunities clause of the United States Constitution.[136]

How do these deductions work? Are the amounts that the claimant receives from outside sources deducted from his total loss? Or is the maximum permissible award determined first and then the collateral source income deducted from that amount?

None of the statutes is explicit about when the collateral source deduction should be made. However, decisions by the Massachusetts Supreme Judicial Court and the Hawaii Supreme Court dictate that the compensation board should (1) first determine the total recognized loss; (2) deduct collateral source payments; and (3) pay an award up to the program's maximum for all unreimbursed injuries or expenses.[137]

If a victim uses an attorney to represent him in making a claim, will the compensation board pay the attorney's fees?

It depends on the state. Most of the programs will pay attorney's fees, but a number of states (including Florida, New Mexico, Oklahoma, Oregon, Virginia, and Washington) have no provision for paying attorney's fees. In the absence of a specific provision allowing for the payment of attorney's fees, a Florida appellate court has ruled that Florida's compensation board cannot award fees to the claimant's attorney. Where the program awards the attorney's fee, the attorney is not permitted to charge the victim an additional fee and in some states, any attorney who does so is guilty of a crime.[138]

Is there a limit on the amount of attorney's fees that these programs will pay?

Yes. About half of the programs awarding fees will pay "reasonable" fees as determined by the program.[139] The remaining states will pay fees up to a certain percentage of the award, typically between ten and fifteen percent of the total award.[140]

In determining what fee is reasonable, the North Dakota Supreme Court has ruled that a number of factors should be considered, including the—

1. legal and clerical time spent;

2. novelty of the claim;

3. attorney's skill;

4. customary fee for such claims;

5. time constraints;

6. amount of the ultimate award;

7. experience and reputation of the attorney;

8. awards in similar cases;

9. attorney's relationship with his client.[141]

Unless the statute specifically provides for payment of the fee in installments, the fee should be paid in full when the award is made to the victim.[142]

Are attorney's fees paid in addition to the other compensation for which the victim is eligible?

It depends on the state. Slightly more than half the states paying attorney's fees pay them in addition to the compensation for which the victim is eligible. The remaining states deduct the amount paid in attorney's fees from the victim's award.[143]

Who determines whether the victim's claim for compensation will be approved?

Typically, an investigator employed by the compensation board will review the application and supporting documentation, make any necessary inquiries and then recommend denial of the claim or an award in a specified amount. The administrator or board of the program then will review this recommendation.

Are victims allowed to see the investigator's recommendation?

Yes. In some states, such as New Jersey, victims receive copies of the recommendations before a final decision and are allowed to present additional evidence in support of their claim. Typically, however, the claimant must specifically request access to such reports.

Does the victim have a right to a hearing on his claim?

Yes. In general, there is no right to a hearing in the first instance. However, where there are questions remaining after an investigation, the program itself may initiate a hearing and notify the victim where and when to appear. If it is not clear from the notification, the victim should specifically request detailed information about the reason for the hearing and any additional information or documentation that the program demands.

Even where the statute does not explicitly provide a hearing, courts have held that the victim is entitled to a hearing if his claim is denied.[144] However, compensation board hearings, like other administrative hearings, need not provide participants with the full procedural guarantees of, for example, a criminal trial.[145] To assist him in preparing for the hearing, upon a showing of necessity, the victim may request that the board provide him or his attorney with the opportunity to review reports prepared or consulted by the board, to take depositions of witnesses or to obtain a copy of the transcript of the criminal trial.[146]

When and how will the victim learn whether he will receive an award?

The victim is usually notified by letter; the amount of time required to process the claim varies from one or two months (Kansas, Michigan, Montana, Nebraska, North Dakota, Oklahoma, and Oregon) to over a year (Minnesota and the

Virgin Islands).[147] Delay is considerable in West Virginia where the legislature must approve all decisions even after the claim has been fully processed by the compensation program. However long the delay until the actual award, the claimant is not entitled to receive interest from the date of the crime to the date of the award.[148] Often, notification of a final decision will consist of a simple denial without further explanation. In such situations, the victim should specifically request copies of the investigative reports or other materials related to the program's determination to make a denial.

The Hawaii Supreme Court has ruled that Hawaii's compensation board's decisions must conform to the state's Administrative Procedure Act that stipulates that decisions denying claims be in writing, accompanied by separate findings of fact and conclusions of law and a ruling on each factual assertion by the victim.[149]

When a claim is approved, does the board have to make the award in one lump sum?

No. The compensation board has a great deal of discretion as to when and how an award is to be paid. A Pennsylvania case upheld the board's right to defer payment of the award to the wife of a homicide victim until after she had received a certain number of monthly social security payments, and a court in New Jersey upheld a decision to pay the 73-year-old mother of a murder victim her $10,000 award in monthly payments of $75 a month (on the ground that it was reasonable for the board to attempt to distribute its funds in small amounts among the largest number of victims).[150]

Is there any way that a victim can receive an emergency award prior to review of his claim?

Yes. Three quarters of the programs allow for the payment of emergency awards ranging from $500 to $1,500; several of these states, including New York, require that these awards be paid in partial payments of $500, as needed.[151] In all of these jurisdictions, the amount of any emergency award is subtracted from the final award and if the final award is denied or is less than what has been paid, the victim must reimburse the program for the difference.[152]

Under what circumstances are such emergency awards granted?

The standards vary from state to state. While some programs will simply accept a victim's statement that he needs immediate assistance, other programs require a determination that a final award will probably be made to that victim or that the victim will suffer some undue financial hardship if an immediate award is not made.[153]

How long does it take to obtain an emergency award?

It varies from state to state. A study of emergency awards indicated that the average processing time lasted from several days or less (Alaska, Connecticut, New York, Texas, and Wisconsin) to as much as six months (Tennessee).[154] Emergency award procedures have been strongly criticized where (as in the case of Tennessee) applications for emergency assistance are treated like all other pending claims, or where (as in some states), an emergency award is authorized and then there is a delay of weeks or months until the program actually generates and transmits the check to the claimant.[155]

If conditions change after a victim has received an award, can he apply for a supplemental award?

Yes. Most programs allow for such supplemental awards, provided that the initial and supplemental award do not in the aggregate exceed the maximum award allowed in that state. Such awards may be granted as a result of changed circumstances, typically unanticipated additional economic loss or the failure to obtain expected collateral source benefits.[156] There are usually limits on how long after an initial award a claimant can file for a supplemental award, although this varies from state to state.[157]

Can a victim appeal an unsatisfactory award or denial of a claim?

Yes. Only New Mexico, Rhode Island, and Tennessee make no provision for appeals; in the other programs, there are as many as three levels of appeal.[158] Typically, the first level of appeal involves reconsideration by the administrators who made the initial determination. After this initial reconsideration, there is often an additional opportunity for an appeal to the full board at a formal hearing. Two thirds of the programs then allow, as a last resort, judicial review of the board's decision. In some states, such as North Dakota (which provides for an appeal to the state's supreme court) a victim has an explicit right to judicial review of the board's decision on a claim.[159] In many states the compensation statute itself does not outline the procedure for appeal, but the state's Administrative Procedures Act (which covers appeals from all administrative decisions) applies. Even where the compensation statute itself makes no explicit provision for appeal by a victim, the courts may have inherent residual power to review the board's exercise of its administrative powers. The Maryland Supreme Court in such a case specifically held that victims could seek judicial review where the board's action was arbitrary, illegal, capricious, or unreasonable.[160]

Can the perpetrator of the crime appeal an award?

No. While victims have a right to appeal adverse rulings, the criminal has no standing to appeal from a board determination to award compensation.[161]

Under what circumstances can a court overturn a board's decision on a claim?

Typically, courts can reverse the board's decision only where it is arbitrary; capricious; clearly erroneous on the record and in light of the policy behind the compensation statute; or if it represents an error of law.[162]

How often is compensation awarded?

This varies a great deal from state to state. When considered in terms of the total number of "claims processed" (the sum of awards and denials in a given year), it varies from 24 percent (Texas) to 99 percent (the Virgin Islands), and the average award rate for all compensation programs is 60 percent.[163]

How much do victim compensation programs award to claimants?

In a recent survey, the amount awarded ranged from $57,686 (Nebraska), to $15,270,141 (California).[164] The average award for all of the existing victim compensation programs was approximately $3,000.

Where do the compensation programs get their funds?

Most state programs are funded partially by the state and partially by the federal government. Thirteen of the programs (approximately a third) receive state funds solely from the state's general revenues.[165] State crime victims' compensation boards are wholly at the mercy of state legislatures or revenue-collecting mechanisms for their year-to-year financing. Where the legislature has refused to allocate funds for a state crime victims' compensation board, most courts have ruled that they are powerless to force a transfer of necessary funds from other state agencies or to award a judgment against the state to the victim.[166] However, the Massachusetts Supreme Judicial Court in one case did uphold a victim's judgment against the state for a compensation award, even though the legislature had not funded the compensation program.[167]

The remaining programs receive funds from fines and penalties assessed on persons convicted of state or municipal crimes, but the amount of the fine varies from state to state.[168] Some states (such as Maryland, which orders all persons convicted of crimes to pay $10 in costs to the compensation fund) have fixed fines or penalties. In some states, the amount of the fine varies with the offense. Thus, in Connecticut, there is a $15 fine on all motor vehicle and driving under the influence offenses and misdemeanors and a $20 fine in all felony convictions. In other states, there may be judicial discretion to impose fines within certain limits; for example, in Oklahoma, for violent felony convictions, a judge has discretion to order payment of a fine between $25 and $10,000. A number of states (including Delaware, Florida, and Montana) impose surcharges on fines and penalties otherwise charged to persons convicted of all or certain crimes; for example, in Montana, there is an 18 percent surcharge on certain traffic offense convictions (processed by the Montana Highway Patrol) which goes to the victims' compensation program. To supplement state funding, Congress created the Crime Victims Fund in 1984. The Fund is authorized to provide qualified state programs with grants of up to 35% of their prior year's awards for non-property related losses. States qualify for grants by meeting certain eligibility and benefit requirements (e.g. compensating non-residents and victims of federal crimes and compensating for lost wages, funeral expenses and medical expenses, including mental health counseling). However, each state must certify that the federal funds are not supplanting state funds which could be used for compensation. The moneys for the Fund come from fines in federal criminal cases, special penalty assessments and forfeited bail and appeal bonds.

Is the use of fines and penalties to finance a victims' compensation program fair or efficient?

It is not clear. The use of fines to finance victim compensation has been criticized as a violation of equal justice on the ground that "offenders" such as those who receive traffic tickets are not any more responsible than anyone else in society for the harm caused to the class of persons who receive "victims'" compensation for injury due to violent crime.[169] A constitutional challenge to the Florida victim compensation program on the grounds that its five-percent surcharge on offenders (including traffic offenders) violated equal protection was upheld by a lower court. However, on appeal the court held that the surcharge could "quite properly be considered as a form of punishment for the offense" and that it was not so excessive or harsh as to be "plainly and undoubtedly in excess of any reasonable requirements for redressing the wrong."[170]

While the use of such fines offers an expedient way to fund compensation programs in an era when taxpayers are increasingly unwilling to pay higher taxes, the actual assessment and collection of fines and surcharges has met, as a practical matter, with mixed success. In Tennessee, for example, in the first year of the operation of a fine system, only a thousand dollars was collected statewide; it took the personal efforts of a legislator traveling throughout the state and threatening clerks with mandamus actions before the fines were widely assessed and collected.

Similarly, in New York there has been disappointing results from the institution of a fine system, apparently because the fines go to general revenues rather than specifically to victims' compensation; New York is now considering legislation that would make these fines directly payable to the compensation program in hopes of encouraging more widespread assessment in collection.

In New Jersey, there is a full-time court monitor who travels to the various courts of the state and audits the court's docket books in order to ascertain that appropriate fines have been assessed and that the revenues have been submitted to the victims' compensation program. In addition, in New Jersey such checks are payable directly to the program rather than being routed through the state's finance department.[171]

Are there other sources for revenue for victims' compensation programs?

Yes. A variety of additional techniques are used in different jurisdictions; for example, part of the salaries received by prisoners on work release programs in some states are payable to the victims' compensation fund under certain circumstances (Indiana, Tennessee, and New Jersey).[172]

In addition, in most of those states with "Son of Sam" statutes that create escrow funds for the royalties received by criminals for books describing their crimes, some portion of those funds may be used to finance victims' compensation programs.[173] Using rights granted to the state by virtually all of the state compensation statutes, programs can recover all or part of any award from funds recovered by the victim in any civil suit for damages under the state's subrogation rights.[174]

Under what circumstances is the victim obligated to reimburse the state out of money he receives as compensation awarded to him in a civil suit?

Typically, compensation statutes provide that acceptance of an award by the victim grants the state subrogation rights; that is, the right to recover the amount of the award from any claim that the victim may have for damages resulting from the crime.[175] Not only can the state initiate such damage actions but it also has the right to intervene in any action brought by the victim or claimant to recover damages in any civil action, and the right to share in any settlement or judgment the victim obtains.[176]

This affects victims in a number of ways. First, in many states any recovery by the victim from anyone (including a negligent third party or even a recovery by the victim from the state Workmen's Compensation Board) can be claimed by the state.[177] There is an exception to this in states where the statute limits the state's right to subrogation to sums received from the criminal offender or "from any person on behalf of the offender"; such a provision in the Virgin Islands barred the state from recovering any portion of twenty-five-thousand-dollar damage award to the victim in a third-party action against the government for its negligence in allowing a police officer to carry a revolver when he was unfit to carry a weapon.[178]

Second, even if the victim settles his civil action for only a small portion of his total damages, the state may be entitled to recover its entire award; since virtually all compensation statutes are specific in permitting full recovery by the state, at least one court has held that the trial judge in the victim's civil action is not entitled to reduce the amount of the state's recovery, even if the victim settles for a small part of his total loss.[179] However, after the New York attorney general ruled that even the state's Crime Victims Board lacked the power to compromise or reduce the amount that the state is entitled to receive through subrogation, the legislature amended the compensation statute to explicitly grant the board the power to settle subrogation claims for an amount less than the victim was awarded.[180]

Third, typically the state has absolutely no obligation to participate in, or pay for, the victim's suit.[181] In many situations where a person commences and actively pursues a civil suit that creates a fund benefiting the state, the state can be compelled to pay its share of the attorney's fees required to create this "common fund."[182] However, the California attorney general and an appellate court in Washington have both specifically rejected arguments that the state should pay its proportionate share of the victim's attorney's fees in obtaining a civil recovering under a "common fund" theory.[183] One exception to this rule is New York that provides that the victim's attorney's fees in obtaining a civil recovery are to be deducted before the amount to be recovered through subrogation is determined.[184]

Notes

1. The following state statutes authorize victim compensation: ALASKA STAT. §§18.67.010-.180 (1981); CAL. GOV'T CODE §§13959–13974 (West 1980 & 1981 Cal Legis. Serv. 3 & 4); CONN. GEN. STAT. ANN. §§54-201 to -217 (West Supp. 1981); DEL. CODE ANN. tit. 11, §§ 9001-9017 (1979); FLA. STAT. ANN. §§960.01-.25 (West Supp. 1982); HAWAII REV. STAT. §§351-1 to -70 (1976 & Supp. 1980); ILL. ANN. STAT. ch. 70, §§71–90 (Smith-Hurd Supp. 1981–1982); IND. CODE ANN. §§16-7-3.6-1 to .6-20 (Burns Supp. 1981); KAN. STAT. ANN. §§ 74–7301 to –7318 (1980); KY. REV. STAT. §§346.010-.190 (1977 & Supp. 1980); MD. CODE ANN art. 26A, §§1–17 (1981 & Supp. 1981); MASS. GEN. LAWS ANN. ch. 258A, §§1–8 (West Supp. 1981); MICH. COMP. LAWS ANN. §§18.351-.368 (West 1981); MINN. STAT. ANN. §§ 299B.01–17 (West Supp. 1981); MO. ANN STAT. §§595.010-.070 (Vernon Supp. 1982); MONT. REV. CODES ANN. §§53–9–101 to –133 (1979 & Supp. 1981); NEB. REV. STAT. §§81–1801 to –1842 (Supp. 1980 & 1981); NEV. REV. STAT. §§217.010-.350 (1979 & Supp. I, III 1981); N.J. STAT. ANN. §§52:4B–1 to –21 (West Supp. 1981–1982);

N.M. Stat. Ann. §31–17–1 (1977); N.Y. Exec. Law §§621–635 (McKinney 1972 & Supp. 1981–1982); N.D. Cent. Code §§65–13–0110–20 (Supp. 1981); Ohio Rev. Code Ann. §§2743.34–.72 (Baldwin 1977); Okla. Stat. Ann. tit. 21, §§142.1–.18 (West Supp. 1981–1982); Or. Rev. Stat. §§ 147.005–.365 (1979); Pa. Stat. Ann. tit. 71, §§180–7 to 7.17 (Purdon Supp. 1980–1981); R.I. Gen. Laws §§12–25–1 to –14 (1981); Tenn. Code Ann. §§29–13–101 to –208 (1980 & Supp. 1980); Tex. Rev. Civ. Stat. Ann. art. 8309–1, §§1–18 (Vernon Supp. 1982); Va. Code §§ 19.2–368.1 to .18 (Supp. 1981); Wash. Rev. Code Ann. §§ 7.68.010–.910 (Supp. 1981); W. Va. Code §§14–2A–1 to -27 (Supp. 1981); Wis. Stat. Ann. §§949.01–.18 (West Supp. 1981–1982); V.I. Code Ann. ch. 7, tit. 34 §§151–53, 156–58, 161–66, 169 (Supp. 1983); Iowa Code Ann. §912.1 *et seq*. (Supp. 1983); Colo. Rev. Stat. §§24–4.1–102 to –119 (Supp. 1983); D.C. Code §§3–401 to –415 (Supp. 1983); S.C. Code §§16–3–1110 to 1340 (Supp. 1983). The federal Crime Victims Fund was created by H.J. Res. 648, Chap. XIV, Sec. 1402, 98th Cong., 2d Sess. (October 4, 1984). A table comparing many of the most important provisions of these statutes is contained in Appendix A. This table was prepared by the National Organization for Victim Assistance from a comprehensive survey contained in D. McGillis and P. Smith, *Compensating Victims of Crime: An Analysis of American Programs* (Washington, D.C.: Natl. Instit. of Justice and Abt Associates, Inc.; May 1983) (No. J-LEAA-013-78) [hereafter "Abt Survey"]. Legislation in three other states was passed after this chapter was written:

    1. In 1984 Alabama and Louisiana also established compensation programs.

    2. North Carolina passed legislation, H.B. 177 (1983), to create a victims' compensation program but as of 1984 this program was not operating due to lack of appropriations; as this book went to press, the legislature was considering amendments to fund a scaled down program.

2. Cyrus H. Gordon, *Hammurabi's Code: Quaint or Forward Looking?* (New York, 1960), p. 6.

3. Abt Survey, *supra* note 1, at 2–4; G. Mueller, "Compensation for Victims of Crime: Thought and Afteraction," 50 *Minn. L. Rev*., 213, 217 (1965); M. Fry, *Arms of the Law* (London: Victor Gollancz, 1951), p. 124; Fry, "Justice for Victims" *The Observer*, London (July 7, 1957) [reprinted in 8 *J. Public L.*.192 (1959)]

4. Abt Survey, *supra* note 1, at 28; R. Childres, "Compensation for Criminally Inflicted Personal Injury," 50 *Minn. L. Rev*. 271, 279 (1965).

5. Abt Survey, *supra* note 1, at 12, 49. *See* V.I. Code Ann. tit. 34 §152.

6. *Id*. at 49–60.

7. *Commonwealth v. Tabor*, 376 Mass. 811 (1978); Mass. Gen. Laws Ann. c.12, §30.

8. *See, e.g*., N.Y. Exec. Law §625–a.

9. For a description of the application process of various states *see* Abt Survey, *supra* note 1, at 95–97.

10. *Id.* at App. A, Table IV, B.

11. *Id.* at p. 97.

12. *Id.* at p. 98.

13. *Id.* at p. 84.

14. *See, e.g.,* N.Y. Exec. Law §625(2).

15. *In re Renta v. Van Rensselaer,* 54 A.D.2d 796, 387 N.Y.S.2d 736 (3d Dept. 1976) (rejecting the claim filed 1 year and 1 month after the crime despite the claimant's move to Puerto Rico); *Hayes v. Van Rensselaer,* 69 Misc.2d 315, 329 N.Y.S.2d 900 (Sup. Ct., N.Y. Co. 1972) (no extension for the claimant's infancy or disability); *Johnsen v. Nissman,* 39 A.D.2d 578, 331 N.Y.S.2d 796 (2d Dept. 1972).

16. *Hartway v. State Bd. of Control,* 69 Cal. App.3d 502, 137 Cal. Rptr. 199 (1st Dist. 1977).

17. *White v. Violent Crimes Compensation Bd.,* 76 N.J. 368, 388 A.2d 206 (1978). At least one commentator has severely criticized the use of equitable tolling under these circumstances, however humanitarian. Note, "Tolling of Substantive Statutes of Limitation—White v. Violent Crimes Compensation Board," 33 *Rutgers L. Rev.* 95 (1979).

18. *Dept. of Labor v. Sargeant,* 27 Wn. App. 1, 615 P.2d 519 (Ct. App., Div. 2 1980).

19. *Id.*

20. *Criminal Injury Compensation Bd. v. Remson,* 282 Md. 168, 384 A.2d 58 (Ct. App. 1978).

21. *Id.*

22. *Id.*

23. *In re Saferstein,* 160 N.J. Super. 393, 390 A.2d 137 (1978).

24. *See, e.g.,* N.Y. Exec. Law §621(3).

25. *Stafford v. Dept. of Labor,* 33 Wash. App. 231, 653 P.2d 1350 (Ct. App., Div. 2 1983).

26. *Application of Edmundson,* 63 Haw. 254, 625 P.2d 372, 377 (1981); *In re Application of Mary Horner,* 55 Haw. 514, 518, 523 P.2d 311, 314 (1974); *Haddenham v. State,* 87 Wash.2d 145, 550 P.2d 9 (1976); *Criminal Injuries Compensation Bd. v. Gould,* 273 Md. 486, 331 A.2d 55 (1974).

27. *Regan v. Crime Victims Compensation Bd.,* 57 N.Y.2d 190, 455 N.Y.S.2d 552, 441 N.E.2d 1070.

28. Abt Survey, *supra* note 1, at 63, App. A, Table II.

29. *Compare* OHIO REV. CODE ANN. §2743.51 (A)(1)(B) *with* Cal. Govt. CODE §13960 (a).

30. *Cabral v. State Bd. of Control,* 112 Cal. App.3d 1012, 169 Cal. Rptr. 604 (2d Dist. 1980).

31. *Ostrager v. State Bd. of Control,* 99 Cal. App.3d 1, 160 Cal. Rptr. 317 (1st Dist. 1979), *appeal dismissed,* 449 U.S. 807 (1980).

32. *Sailor v. Tonkin,* 356 F. Supp. 72 (D.V.I. 1973).

33. *See, e.g.,* WIS. STAT. ANN. §949.035(1).

34. Abt Survey, *supra* note 1, at 64, App. A, Table II.

35. *See, e.g.,* Ky. Rev. Stat. §346.020(4); Wis. Stat. Ann. §949.08(2).
36. *Weisinger v. Van Rensselaer,* 79 Misc.2d 1023, 362 N.Y.S.2d 126 (Sup. Ct., Sullivan Co. 1974).
37. *Gossard v. Criminal Injuries Compensation Bd.,* 279 Md. 309, 368 A.2d 443 (1977).
38. *Ocasio v. Bureau of Crimes Compensation,* 408 So.2d 751 (Fla. D.C.A., 3 Dist. 1982).
39. *Alimo v. Criminal Injuries Compensation Bd. of Maryland,* Superior Court of Baltimore City, 1973/824/138213 (Liss, J.).
40. *Remson, supra* note 20.
41. Abt; Survey, *supra* note 1, at 64–65; *See, e.g.,* Wis. Stat. Ann. § 949.08 (2)(a); Ill. Ann. Stat. ch. 70 §76.1(d).
42. Ind. Code Ann. §§4–23–17.5, at 16–7–3.6–5(b).
43. N.Y. Exec. Law. §624(2).
44. *See, e.g.,* Hawaii Rev. Stat. §351–33(1); Mich. Stat. Ann. §18.354(c).
45. Abt Survey, *supra* note 1, at 64.
46. *Id.*
47. *See, e.g.,* Minn. Stat. Ann. §299B.03(1)(c).
48. Ind. Code Ann. §36–8–4–5.
49. *See, e.g.,* Wash. Rev. Code Ann. §7.68.070(e).
50. Ohio Rev. Code Ann. §2743.60(E)–(G).
51. *See, e.g.,* Wis. Stat. Ann. §949.08(3).
52. Neb. Rev. Stat. §81–18, 16(1).
53. Abt Survey, *supra* note 1, at 69–71.
54. *Id.* at 70, 160.
55. *Regan, supra* note 27; *New York State Dept. of Audit and Control v. Crime Victims Compensation Bd.,* 76 A.D.2d 410, 431 N.Y.S.2d 598 (3d Dept. 1980).
56. N.Y. Exec. Law §631 (b) (Supp. 1984).
57. *Holmes v. Criminal Injury Compensation Bd.,* 278 Md. 60, 359 A.2d 84 (Ct. App. 1976).
58. *Compare* Op. Tex. Att. Gen. No. M.W.–369 (Sept. 23, 1981) *and New York State Dept. of Audit and Control, supra* note 55 *with* N.Y. Exec. Law §631(6)(b).
59. Abt Survey, *supra* note 1, at 70, 71.
60. *See, e.g.,* N.Y. Exec. Law §631(6).
61. *See, e.g.,* Hawaii Rev. Stat. §351–31(c); Wis. Stat. Ann. §949.06(5).
62. *See, e.g.,* Hawaii Rev. Stat. §351–31(c).
63. *Stafford v. Dept. of Labor,* 33 Wn. App. 231, 653 P.2d 1350 (Div. 2 1982).
64. *Id.* (shootout); *Hansen v. Dept. of Labor,* 27 Wn. App. 223, 615 P.2d 1302 (Div. 1 1980); Ohio Rev. Code Ann. §2743.60(E)–(G).
65. Abt Survey, *supra* note 1, at 71–72.
66. *Id. See, e.g.,* Wis. Stat. Ann. §950.03 (5 days); N.Y. Exec. Law § 631(1) (1 week).
67. *See, e.g.,* Wash. Rev. Code Ann. §7.68.070(11).
68. *Criminal Injuries Compensation Bd. v. Gould,* 273 Md. 486, 331 A.2d 55 (1975).

69. Abt Survey, *supra* note 1, at 65–66. *See, e.g.,* Ky. Rev. Stat. Ann. § 346.020(3).

70. Abt Survey, *supra* note 1, at 65–66. *See, e.g.,* Hawaii Rev. Stat. §351–32.

71. *Regan, supra* note 27.

72. *In re Saferstein, supra* note 23.

73. Abt Survey, *supra* note 1, at 66. *See, e.g.,* Fla. Stat. Ann. §960.03(3).

74. *See, e.g.,* Ky. Rev. Stat. Ann. §346.020(3).

75. *In re Application of Horner,* 55 Haw. 514, 523 P.2d 311 (1974).

76. *Davis v. Bureau of Crimes Compensation,* 406 So.2d 1189 (Fla. D.C.A., Div. 1 1981) (hit-and-run driver); *Crime Victims' Compensation Bd. v. Miller,* 607 S.W.2d 424 (Ky. 1980).

77. *In re Turner,* 44 Pa. Cmwlth. 326, 403 A.2d 1346 (Pa. Cmwlth. 1979).

78. *See, e.g.,* Or. Rev. Stat. §147.005(4); Ohio Rev. Code Ann. § 2743.51(C).

79. *See, e.g.,* Conn. Gen. Stat. Ann. §54–210.

80. *See, e.g.,* N.Y. Exec. Law §625(b); Ky. Rev. Stat. §§346.050(1)(b).

81. *In re Carr,* 136 N.J. Super. 344, 346 A.2d 406 (1975).

82. Hawaii Rev. Stat. §351–31(a) (4).

83. *See, e.g.,* N.Y. Exec. Law. §§624(1)(d); Wis. Stat. Ann. §§949.05(1)(b); Hawaii Rev. Stat. §351–31(a)(4).

84. *Gryziec v. Zweibel,* 74 A.D.2d 9, 426 N.Y.S.2d 616 (1980).

85. Abt Survey, *supra* note 1, at 63. *See, e.g.,* Ky. Rev. Stat. §346.020.

86. Ga. Code Ann. §47–518 to 526; Abt Survey, *supra* note 1, at 151.

87. *Gloeckl v. Commonwealth,* 57 Pa. Cmwlth. 28, 425 A.2d 877 (1981).

88. Abt Survey *supra* note 1, at 67; Ind. Code Ann. §16–7–3.6–8(a); *Bureau of Crimes Compensation v. Trass,* 421 So.2d 50 (Fla. D.C.A., 2 Dist. 1982). *See also Wolf v. State,* 325 So.2d 342 (La. App., 4th Cir. 1976).

89. *Jerome v. Crime Victims Compensation Bd.,* 119 Mich. App. 648 (1982).

90. *Id.;* *Hughes v. North Dakota Crime Victims' Reparations Bd.,* 246 N.W.2d 774 (N.D. 1976) (testimony); *New York State Dept. of Audit and Control, supra* note 55 (overtime); Op. Tex. Att. Gen., No. MW–369 (Sept. 23, 1981) (sick leave and vacation benefits).

91. *New York State Dept. of Audit and Control, supra* note 55.

92. *New York State Dept. of Audit and Control v. Crime Victims' Compensation Bd.,* 76 A.D.2d 405, 431, N.Y.S.2d 602 (3d Dept. 1980).

93. *Gurley v. Commonwealth,* 363 Mass. 595, 296 N.E.2d 477 (1973) (future earnings); *Peterson v. Commonwealth,* 45 Pa. Cmwlth. 72, 404 A.2d 1364 (1979) (future earnings); *Holmes, supra* note 58 (maternal services).

94. *Peterson, supra* note 93; *Gurley, supra* note 93; *Levato v. Commonwealth,* 458 A.2d 665 (Pa. Cmwlth. 1983).

95. *Archer v. Crime Victims Compensation Bd.*, 104 Mich. App. 537 (1981); *Levato, supra* note 94.

96. *Jerome, supra* note 90; *Gloeckl, supra* note 87.

97. *Worthington v. State Bd. of Control*, 266 Cal. App. 2d 697, 72 Cal. Rptr. 449 (1st Dist. 1968); *In re Carr, supra* note 81.

98. *In re Eader*, 70 Ohio Misc. 17 (Ct. Cl. 1982).

99. *In re Martin*, Ct. Cls. No. V77-1308, *aff'd*, Dec. No. 79–027 (Ohio).

100. *See* Fla. Stat. Ann. §960.13(3); *Division of Workers' Compensation v. Brevda*, 420 So.2d 887 (Fla. D.C.A., 1st Dist. 1982).

101. *Gurley, supra* note 93 (use of actuarial tables); *Peterson, supra* note 93 (percentage of earnings times life expectancy minus total social security payments); *In re Eader, supra* note 98 (net taxable income minus dependents' expenses avoided and dependents' earnings).

102. Wis. Stat. Ann. §949.06(1). In addition, Wisconsin allows for compensation of "Christian Science treatment in lieu of medical treatment." *Id.*

103. Abt Survey, *supra* note 1, at App. A, Table II.

104. *Haddenham v. State*, 87 Wn.2d 145, 550 P.2d 9 (1976); Wash. Rev. Code Ann. §7.68.070(5).

105. Cal. Govt. Code §13965(a)(1).

106. *Division of Workers' Compensation v. Brevda, supra.*

107. *See, e.g.*, Mass. Gen. Laws Ann. ch. 258A §5.

108. *See, e.g.*, Wis. Stat. Ann. §949.01(5); Del. Code Ann. §9002(7).

109. *See, e.g.*, V.I. Code Ann. tit. 3, §153(7).

110. Abt Survey, *supra* note 1; at 67–68. State of Hawaii, Criminal Injuries Compensation Commission, Annual Report, 1981 p. 3.

111. *See, e.g.*, Wis. Stat. Ann. §949.01(5).

112. Wis. Stat. Ann. §946.06(2)(c). *See also* Ohio Rev. Code Ann § 2743.51(J).

113. *Compare Holmes, supra* note 58 (allowing award) *with Jerome, supra* note 90 (denying award).

114. *In re Eader, supra* note 98.

115. *See, e.g.*, Hawaii Rev. Stat. §351–52(4).

116. N.Y. Exec. Law §631(2); Colo. Rev. Stat. §24–4–102, 109.

117. *See, e.g.*, Hawaii Rev. Stat. §351–33(5).

118. For comparisons of limits imposed on compensation awards by different states see Abt Survey, *supra* note 1, at 168–170, and Appendix A of this book.

119. Abt Survey, *supra* note 1, at 76.

120. *Id.*

121. *See* Abt Survey, *supra* note 1, at 20.

122. *Id.*

123. *See, e.g.*, Pa. Stat. Ann. tit. 71 §180–7.5; Wash. Rev. Code Ann. § 7.68.170.

124. Va. Code §19.2–368.11(B).

125. *See, e.g.*, Hawaii Rev. Stat. §351–63(a).

126. *See, e.g.*, Wis. Stat. Ann. §949.06.

127. *See, e.g., Peterson, supra* note 93 (social security); Op. Att. Gen.
Tenn., 80–158 (Mar. 12, 1980) (workmen's compensation); *Gurley,
supra* note 93 (welfare payments).

128. *Standing v. Dept. of Labor and Industries,* 92 Wash.2d 463, 598
P.2d 725 (1979).

129. Wash. Rev. Code. Ann. §7.68.020(7), 130 (Supp. 1984–5). *See
also Fairley v. Dept. of Labor and Industries,* 29 Wn. App. 477,
627 P.2d 961 (Ct. App. Div. 2 1981).

130. *David v. Violent Crimes Compensation Bd.,* 145 N.J. Super. 337,
367 A.2d 1174 (1976).

131. *Peterson, supra* note 93; 404 A.2d 1364 (1979).

132. *Hoffman v. Commonwealth,* 46 Pa. Cmwlth. 54, 405 A.2d 1110
(1979); *Peterson, supra* note 93; 404 A.2d 1364 (1979); *Gloeckl,
supra* note 87; Op. Att. Gen. Tenn., 80–158 (Mar. 12, 1980).

133. Op. Tex. Att. Gen., No. M.W. 369 (Sept. 23, 1981).

134. Hawaii Rev. Stat. §351–63(a).

135. *Sciulli v. Commonwealth,* No. 1690 C.D. 1981 (Pa. Cmwlth. Apr. 28
1983).

136. *Standing v. Dept. of Labor,* 92 Wn.2d 463, 598 P.2d 725 (1979) (*en
banc*).

137. *Application of Walter R. Edmundson,* 63 Haw. 254, 625 P.2d 372
(1981); *Gurley, supra* note 93.

138. Abt Survey, *supra* note 1, at 84–86, Ex. 4.3. *Bureau of Crimes
Compensation v. Williams,* 405 So.2d 747 (Fla. App. Div. 2 1981),
petition denied, 412 So.2d 471 (Fla. 1981). *See also* Ind. Code.
Ann. §16–7–3.6–14.

139. *See, e.g.,* Wis. Stat. Ann. §949.14.

140. *See, e.g.,* Pa. Stat. Ann. tit. 71, §180–7.2.

141. *Hughes v. North Dakota Crime Victims Reparations Bd.,* 246,
N.W.2d 774 (N.D. 1976).

142. *In re Hollywood,* 124 N.J. Super. 50, 304 A.2d 747 (1973).

143. Abt Survey, *supra* note 1, at 85.

144. *Fitch v. Crime Victims' Compensation Bd.,* 99 Mich. App. 363, 366,
297 N.W.2d 667 (1980); *Archer, supra* note 95.

145. *United Mutual Insurance Co. v. Zamenick,* 76 Misc.2d 1 (Sup. Ct.,
Orange Co. 1973).

146. *In re Thomas, N.Y.L.J.* p. 12, cl.1 (Sup. Ct., N.Y.C. Dec. 5, 1979);
Zimney v. North Dakota Crime Victims Reparation Bd., 252
N.W.2d 8 (N.D. 1977).

147. Abt Survey, *supra* note 1, at 99, 171–76.

148. *Gurley, supra* note 93.

149. *Horner v. Criminal Injuries Compensation Commission,* 54 Haw.
294, 506 P.2d 444 (1973).

150. *In re Hollywood, supra* note 142; *Peterson v. Commonwealth,
supra* note 93.

151. Abt Survey, *supra* note 1, at 81–83, Ex. 4.2. *See, e.g.,* N.Y.
Exec. Law §630.

152. *Id.* at §631.

153. Abt Survey, *supra* note 1, at 81. *See, e.g.*, N.Y. Exec. Law §630.
154. Abt Survey, *supra* note 1, at 81–83, Ex. 4.2.
155. *Id.*
156. *See, e.g.*, Fla. Stat. Ann. §960.14(2).
157. Abt Survey, *supra* note 1, at 83.
158. *Id.* at p. 99.
159. *See, e.g.*, Hughes, *supra* note 141; *Zimney v. North Dakota Crime Victims Reparations Bd.*, *supra* note 146.
160. *Gould, supra* note 68.
161. *United Mutual Insurance Co. v. Zamenick*, 76 Misc.2d 1 (Sup. Ct., Orange Co. 1973).
162. *Hansen, supra* note 64; *Gould, supra* note 68.
163. Abt Survey, *supra* note 1, at 103.
164. *Id.* at pp. 116, 117, Ex. 6.4.
165. *Id.* at p. 123.
166. *State Ex. rel. Indiana State Bd. of Finance v. Marion County Superior Court*, 396, N.E.2d 340 (Ind. 1979); *Wolf v. State*, 346 So.2d 320 (La. Ct. App. 1977) (reversing a judgment against the state growing out of an award granted to a victim where the state had failed to fund a crime victims' compensation program and later repealed it). *Cf. Gillespsie v. State*, 619 S.W.2d 128 (Tenn. Ct. App., West Sect. 1981) (no jurisdiction to pay an award to a victim if the injury occurred after the statute was enacted but before it was effective); *Taylor v. Florida Crimes Compensation Commission*, 367 So.2d (Fla. App., Div. 3 1979).
167. *Gurley, supra* note 93.
168. Abt Survey, *supra* note 1, at 121–25.
169. S. Thorvaldson and M. Krasknik, "On Recovering Compensation Funds from Offenders," 5 *Victimology* 18, 21 (1980).
170. *State v. Champe*, 373 So.2d 874, 880 (Fla. 1979).
171. Abt Survey, *supra* note 1, at 123–24.
172. *Id.* at 24–25.
173. *See, e.g.*, N.Y. Exec. Law §632–a(11)(b).
174. *See, e.g., id.* at §634.
175. *Id.*
176. *United Mutual Insurance Co. v. Zamenick Co.*, *supra* note 161 (the criminal cannot oppose the state's intervention in civil action on the grounds that the award was not justified).
177. *Hulsey v. Commonwealth* 620 S.W.2d 890 (Ky. Ct. App. 1982) (the state has subrogation rights over victim's workmen's compensation awards).
178. *Richards v. Government of Virgin Islands*, 579 F.2d 830 (3d Cir. 1978).
179. *Aylward v. Dragus*, 82 Ill. App.3d 283 (1980). *See also Dept. of Labor v. Dillon*, 28 Wn. App. 853, 626 P.2d 1004 (Wn. App. Div. 1, 1981) (the state is entitled to recover the full payment even where there was a partial settlement).

180. *Compare* Op. N.Y. Att. Gen. May 23, 1977, *with* N.Y. Exec. Law §634(2).

181. *Dillon, supra* note 179.

182. *See e.g., Quinn v. State*, 15 Cal.3d 162 (1975).

183. 64 Ops. Cal. Atty. Gen. 540 (July 3, 1981); *Dillon, supra* note 181. *But see* Cal. Gov. Code §13966 (allowing a victim litigant to receive 25 percent of the recovered amount).

184. N.Y. Exec. Law §634(2) (allowing for the recovery of reasonable attorneys' fees).

IV

The Right to Restitution

What is restitution?
In all states, under certain circumstances, defendants in criminal cases may be ordered by the court to pay restitution; that is, to compensate victims for expenses, losses, or injury to persons or property. In some instances, restitution (or reparation as it sometimes is called)[1] may involve the return or repair of stolen or damaged property, or even a requirement that the defendant personally perform certain services for the victim.[2]

Does restitution have any advantages over victim compensation or civil actions as a means for compensating victims?
Yes. In many cases, the expense of bringing a civil action against an offender for damages (particularly where the amount of damages suffered by the victim is negligible) makes such actions impractical. Many victims who would be ineligible for victim compensation (for example, because they are not victims of violent crimes or are related to the offender) are eligible for restitution. Moreover, restitution typically provides compensation for losses not usually covered by victim compensation statutes, such as losses due to stolen, lost, or damaged property. In those fourteen states without a functioning victim compensation program, restitution may be the only means (short of a civil action) for an uninsured victim to obtain compensation for his injury.

The authors express their gratitude to Professor Alan Harland, Temple University, for the assistance that he provided in preparing this chapter and gratefully acknowledge that much of the material contained in this chapter comes from Harland, "Monetary Remedies for the Victims of Crime: Assessing the Role of the Criminal Court," 30 *UCLA L. Rev.* 52 (1982).

Are there problems in obtaining restitution?

Yes. Some states limit the kinds of losses that can be recovered as restitution with the result that victims will not receive as much as they could be awarded in a civil action. Others strictly limit restitution to direct victims of the specific crime for which the defendant was charged; persons indirectly injured or victims of related crimes may not be eligible.

There are also important (sometimes insurmountable) practical obstacles. First, unlike victim compensation, restitution is impossible unless the perpetrator of the crime has been arrested and charged and has been convicted, pled guilty, or assigned to a pretrial diversion program. Even in such cases, an order of restitution is meaningless unless the convicted offender has the means to pay restitution and the court or some other state agency enforces the restitution order.

Given these limitations, is restitution a realistic way for victims to obtain compensation?

Yes. Despite the limitations, millions of dollars each year are paid to victims as restitution and there has been a trend in recent years toward enacting more comprehensive restitution statutes.

While the practical obstacles remain, they often are exaggerated; for example, some commentators have argued that restitution is illusory because most criminals lack the means to pay restitution. However, most victimizations do not involve substantial monetary losses; for example, in 1974, there were more than 2,000,000 cash thefts in the United States, but 78 percent of these amounted to less than $50; only 5 percent of these cash thefts involved more than $1,000. Of the 30.5 million cases of property loss or damage in that year, only 6 percent involved losses or damage of more than $499, and only 3 percent exceeded $999.[3]

In fact, individual victims across the country have received restitution from defendants. One Oklahoma victim, for example, received $1,424 from the college student who stole her collection of gold and silver coins; another Oklahoma woman received $100 restitution from the defendant who stole and wrecked her car. One restitution program operated by the district attorney in Portland, Oregon, collected almost $35,000 in restitution during 1981 alone. New York officials estimate that between 20 and 25 percent of criminals convicted in the

New York courts have sufficient assets to pay restitution to some of their victims; however, New York judges have only issued restitution orders in 4 percent of the eligible cases.[4]

Is restitution a new idea?

No. Restitution for crime victims was employed in biblical times. According to the bible, "[i]f a man steals . . . [h]e shall make restitution. . . ." The Code of Hammurabi also provides for restitution.[5] The amount of restitution varied with the circumstances; for example, Mosaic Law provided that the penalty for highway robbery could include restitution up to five times the value of the goods taken, while the ancient Greeks (according to the Ninth Book of Homer's *Iliad*) had "death fines" that required murderers to pay a certain amount to the families of their victims.[6]

Restitution was also an important part of early English common law. In the seventh century, the Anglo-Saxon king, Ethelbert, promulgated a detailed code that provided for payments to be made in connection with a variety of crimes; including theft, adultery, assault, and murder.[7] Intended to control violent retaliations for crimes by the victim's clan against the criminal's clan, the code specifically provided for "payments" (the *Wergild*); part of this payment was to be made by the criminal's clan to the victim's clan (the *Bot*) and part went to the king for a violation of the "king's peace" (the *Wit*). These payments were mandatory and varied according to the social rank of the victim, the particular part of the body that was injured, whether property was lost or whether the victim died.[8] Over time, the portion of the *Wergild* that went to the king increased while the payments to clans decreased. Eventually Anglo-Saxon law developed the concept of a *Botless* crime (a crime that was punishable solely because it was a breach of the king's peace). As the state progressively monopolized the criminal process and the punishment of crimes, restitution fell into disuse.[9] If a victim wanted compensation he was forced to initiate a separate civil suit against the criminal for damages.

What is the origin of the modern practice of restitution?

In the nineteenth century, a number of commentators (including the English philosopher Jeremy Bentham, the American jurist, Oliver Wendell Holmes, and the Italian philosopher, Enrico Ferri) criticized the popular distinction between criminal or penal sanctions (meant to redress an injury to society) and restitution to the victim, on the ground that both were meant to redress the same criminal act.[10]

The resurgence of restitution as part of the American criminal justice system is the result of the enactment of penal laws permitting suspended sentences and probation. By the late 1930s, at least eleven states specifically allowed courts the discretion to make restitution or reparation one of the conditions of probation.[11]

In the last two decades, several factors have significantly contributed to the increasing use of restitution. First, the Model Penal Code (which has been adopted virtually in its entirety by a number of states) explicitly provides for sentences of restitution or the use of restitution as a condition of probation.[12] Second, in the last decade, the federal government [through the Law Enforcement Assistance Administration (LEAA)] spent millions of dollars supporting the establishment, operation, and evaluation of restitution programs; its efforts have resulted in the passage of additional legislation providing for restitution in a number of states as well as the establishment of scores of functioning programs to administer restitution ordered by the courts.[13] Finally, and perhaps most important, the "victims' movement" has produced a greater awareness among judges of the needs of victims, the increased discretionary use of restitution and, in some states, the enactment of statutes that make restitution a mandatory condition of probation or require judges to state why restitution is not being ordered.[14]

At what stage in the criminal proceeding can the court order restitution?

At several different stages. The court can order restitution with the agreement of the defendant as part of a pretrial diversion,[15] or restitution can be part of the defendant's sentence after a trial or a guilty plea. When restitution is ordered at sentencing it may constitute the sentence itself,[16] it may be ordered as a condition of probation or a suspended sentence,[17] or it may be ordered in addition to a term of imprisonment.[18]

Is restitution available for all crimes?

Yes. Most state statutes and the federal statute authorize restitution without limiting the court's authority to specific crimes or offenses.[19] In addition, a number of states authorize restitution for specific types or degrees of crime or make restitution mandatory for particular offenses.[20] Some of these statutes also prohibit restitution for certain minor offenses such as traffic violations.[21]

Who is eligible for restitution?

Most of the statutes and cases authorizing restitution limit restitution to "aggrieved parties."[22] One New York case has defined an aggrieved party as "the party whose rights, personal or property, were invaded by the defendant as a result of which criminal proceedings were successfully concluded."[23] The federal statute authorizes restitution "to any victim of the offense."[23a] Thus, in virtually all cases, the direct victim of the crime will be eligible for restitution, although other persons who indirectly sustain losses may not be eligible.

Are persons who reimburse the direct victim for his loss (such as insurers) eligible for restitution?

It depends on the jurisdiction. Most states have case law or statutes that allow insurers to obtain restitution in connection with amounts paid to victims as a result of claims growing out of injury or losses incurred.[24] However, there are exceptions. Iowa and South Dakota, for example, permit the insurer to seek restitution in its own name only if it has no right of subrogation and if the victim has no duty to pay proceeds of restitution to the insurer.[25] North Carolina and a number of other states generally exclude insurers and other third parties who are obligated to indemnify the victim from obtaining restitution.[26]

As of 1983, the Victim Witness Protection Act specifically allowed federal courts, where they determine it is "in the interest of justice," to order restitution to any person who has compensated a victim for a loss due to crime to the extent of the compensation.[27] However, if the order also provides restitution to the victim, the statute specifically states that all restitution to victims will be paid prior to reimbursement of the insurance company.

Are family members of victims entitled to restitution?

Yes. Although not direct victims themselves, the family of homicide victims in virtually all states and in the federal courts can recover certain kinds of losses resulting from the homicide.[28] However, in many states recovery is limited to the victim's medical or funeral expenses. In addition, under the 1982 federal law, restitution can be awarded to the estate of a person who died after being victimized.[29]

Are governmental entities that incur the expense of prosecuting the defendant or incarcerating him entitled to restitution?

The word *restitution* is sometimes used to describe orders requiring a criminal defendant to make payments to the state as part of a sentence. As used here, *restitution* is limited to payments to victims to compensate them for their losses due to crime. In this sense, the payments that may be ordered to governmental entities are not *restitution* (unless specifically intended to compensate the government for a specific loss directly resulting from the crime), although they could be properly called fines, fees, or costs.

In a number of states courts have issued orders (sometimes in reliance on the state's general restitution statute) which required defendants to pay the costs of investigation, prosecution, and extradition of his case, or to pay an amount to the state compensation fund; other courts have disallowed such awards.[30] A number of cases have even upheld orders requiring indigent criminal defendants to repay the cost of court-appointed attorneys, rejecting defendants' arguments that such awards may chill the exercise of the defendants' Fifth- and Sixth-Amendment rights to counsel and a fair trial.[31]

Is anyone excluded by statute from receiving restitution?

Yes. Many states specifically prohibit restitution to accomplices or coparticipants in the defendant's crime.[32]

Must the victim obtain a civil judgment in order to qualify for restitution?

No. Unlike damages awarded after a civil trial (which are intended to fully compensate the victim for his loss), an order requiring the payment of restitution is primarily intended to aid in the criminal defendant's rehabilitation by increasing his sense of responsibility for the victim's loss and by instilling a feeling of obligation to repair the injury he caused. In fact, one appellate federal court (in a fraud case) upheld an order requiring the defendant to pay restitution even where he was absolved of personal liability in a subsequent civil suit against him.[33]

What type of loss or injury can be considered in ordering restitution?

It varies from jurisdiction to jurisdiction. The courts in most states limit restitution to recovery by the victim of "actual" or pecuniary losses (including out-of-pocket and other economic losses) which are liquidated or "easily ascertainable."[34] In ordering restitution in such jurisdictions, courts will refuse to consider such noneconomic injury to the victim as inconvenience, pain and suffering, or even physical impairment and will refuse to include in a restitution order punitive damages.[35]

The 1982 federal statute takes a similar approach to victims' losses.[36] That statute directs the courts to consider the following types of losses in ordering defendants to pay restitution: (1) in property cases, if return of the property is impossible or impractical, an amount equal to the greater of either the value of the property on the date of damage or the value of the property on the date of sentencing less any property returned; (2) in cases of bodily injury to the victim, an amount equal to the cost of necessary medical and related professional services (including psychiatric care) plus the cost of necessary physical or occupational therapy or rehabilitation and any lost income; and (3) in cases of death of a victim due to bodily injury, an amount equal to the cost of necessary funeral and related services. However, a separate provision of the statute explicitly directs that the amount of restitution ordered shall be "as fair as possible to the victim" without unduly complicating or prolonging sentencing.

A number of states are more liberal in calculating the amount of restitution. Some (such as North Carolina) authorize restitution for all damages or losses that could ordinarily be recovered by the victim in a civil action.[37] One state—Washington—allows the sentencing court to order restitution equal to twice the amount of the victim's loss or the offender's gain as well as awarding the victim damages for pain and suffering.[38] Some courts have also allowed restitution awards greater than the precise economic value of the victim's loss by adding an amount to pay for inconvenience or other injury to the victim.[39]

What types of loss are considered in awarding restitution to families of homicide victims?

In addition to out-of-pocket expenses for medical care for the victim or funeral expenses, some states (such as Washington), have permitted the court to award amounts as general damages to the victim's family.[40] Several states also authorize orders of restitution, without limitation on amount, for damages incurred by the victim's wrongful death.[41]

If the victim is eligible for restitution, is the judge required to order it?

It depends on the jurisdiction and the circumstances. In general, judges have a great deal of discretion in the sentencing of defendants and are not compelled to order them to pay restitution or to impose any other sentence.[42] However, in some states, restitution is mandatory for particular crimes (usually property crimes) and is a mandatory condition for admission of the convicted person into certain pretrial diversion programs.[43] In addition, statutes in an increasing number of jurisdictions now require judges to order restitution or to state on the record their reasons for failing to do so.[44] Such provisions create a presumption of restitution that then places the burden on the defendant to show that he is incapable of paying it.

Is the victim entitled to participate in the decision to order restitution?

Yes, but the extent of the victim's participation varies greatly from jurisdiction to jurisdiction. In part, this depends on the stage in the criminal process restitution is ordered, victims generally have rights to participate in decisions relating to pretrial diversion, probation, sentencing, or parole (see chapter II).

Since restitution orders must be supported by evidence in the record concerning damages, the court ordinarily must ascertain information on the victim's loss or injury prior to ordering restitution. Increasingly, facts about the victim's loss or separate victim impact statements are required by statute to be part of the presentencing report considered by the judge.[45] Such reports include various kinds of facts about the victim's loss or injury due to the crime; for example, in the federal courts, the victim impact statement must contain information assessing the financial, social, psychological, and medical impact upon, and cost to, the victim.[46]

This obligation to present a report to the court on the

crime's effect on the victim has not always been thoroughly complied with; for example, in one federal case in Alabama where a kidnap victim was hit in the head with a shotgun, saw her boyfriend dead on the floor of their home, was stripped naked, threatened with death and then forced to engage in oral sex with the defendants, the Federal Probation Service suggested restitution of $599 to cover medical expenses. The court strongly criticized this lack of compliance with the spirit and letter of the federal law concerning victim impact statements, pointing out that no measure of damages was requested for the serious psychological injury suffered by the victim, or her lost income, and no application for restitution was made at all on behalf of the estate of the murdered boyfriend or the owner of an automobile used by the defendants during the kidnapping.[47]

In many jurisdictions that have no statutory requirement of a victim impact statement, prosecutors have instituted formal procedures for obtaining information about the victim's loss; for example, in Pima County (Tucson), Arizona, victims are asked by the prosecutor's office to complete a statement of "Victim's Itemized Financial Losses" that provides detailed information on unrecovered property or cash, damaged property, medical expenses, job-related losses, and other financial losses.

In Multnomah County (Portland), Oregon, the district attorney's office has initiated a program called Project Repay whose staff investigates and documents the victim's loss, calculates an equitable amount of restitution and then monitors the offender's payments to insure that the victim actually receives the restitution award. In two years of operation, the program documented approximately $1.5 million in victims' losses that produced over 1,500 restitution plans.

In many jurisdictions, victims also have a voice in whether restitution is to be ordered. In some restitution programs, the victim's consent is required before a criminal defendant will be assigned to a pretrial diversion program for purposes of satisfying a restitution order.[48] In some states (such as Alabama), the victim, by statute, is entitled to present his views on restitution to the court at any hearing in which restitution is considered.[49] Even in states without any formal provisions for allowing victims to document their losses or participate in restitution decisions, the victim may pass on his views on restitution to the prosecutor or judge through the victim/witness assistance program in his jurisdiction or may transmit his views by letter or through phone calls to the prosecutor or the judge himself.

If the victim's loss increases substantially after the defendant's sentencing, can the trial judge reconsider restitution and order a greater amount?

Yes, in most jurisdictions.[50]

Is the offender's ability to pay relevant to the court's determination whether to order restitution?

Yes. In virtually all jurisdictions, the court is only permitted to order "reasonable" or "appropriate" restitution.[51] Where satisfying the restitution order would be beyond the offender's financial means, courts have limited the amount of restitution ordered or prohibited restitution altogether on the grounds that restitution under such circumstances would be impossible to achieve and would not have any meaningful rehabilitative effect on the offender. A Pennsylvania court, for example, strongly criticized an order that required a foundry worker convicted of arson to pay restitution of $1.5 million. In another arson case, an Illinois court modified an order requiring payments of $1,000 per month when the defendant's annual earnings were $6,500 per year; the modified order required only that the defendant pay 10 percent of his net income monthly for 5 years or until he had paid $53,000.[52]

While the defendant must have the financial ability to pay the award, the court may require him to make financial sacrifices or even to temporarily change his life-style or standard of living if that is necessary to allow him to make restitution. In a number of cases, for example, courts have required defendants to sell or mortgage their homes in order to make restitution.[53]

Which of the offender's circumstances are considered relevant in determining how much restitution to order?

It varies from jurisdiction to jurisdiction. Decisions and specific provisions of restitution statutes in a number of states require that courts consider some or all of the following factors:

1. the physical and mental health of the offender;
2. his age and education;

3. his job or potential for employment or vocational training;

4. the needs and circumstances of the defendant's family;

5. his financial conditions;

6. what plan of restitution would be most effective in aiding his rehabilitation.[54]

Is the burden on the offender to show that he is unable to pay the amount of restitution proposed by the court?
Yes.[55]

Where the offender has other lawful financial obligations such as support of his family or payment of fines or court costs, does restitution to the victim take priority?
It depends on the state. In some states, the offender must pay restitution before fines, court costs, room and board, or even support of his dependents. In other states, priority is given to room and board, job-related expenses, or support of the offender's dependents.[56] In still other states, only a certain percentage of the money earned by the offender while incarcerated or on parole is to be used for restitution (typically twenty or thirty percent) and the remainder is to be retained by the offender or to be used for other purposes (such as supporting his family).[57]

Is a finding of guilt required before a defendant can be ordered to pay restitution?
Ordinarily, yes. For example, if the defendant is tried and acquitted, the court (barring extraordinary circumstances, has no power to impose any sentence, including an order to pay restitution.

Is there an exception where the defendant has agreed to pre-trial diversion before a finding of guilt?
Yes. If there is no finding of guilt because the prosecutor specifically agreed with the defendant not to prosecute in return for restitution to the victim, the defendant may be subject to an order requiring him to pay restitution. At least ten states have enacted preadjudicative procedures that include some arrangement for the defendant to provide restitution to the victim. Such states as Kansas, Oregon, New Jersey, Pennsylvania, and South Carolina have authorized prosecutors to divert defendants who request diversion into

special programs that provide restitution to the victim in lieu of prosecution; these programs may also provide that the defendant participate in community service, treatment, or therapy as a condition of diversion.[58] The general requirements for admission to such programs and a description of pretrial diversion can be found in chapter II. Courts have explicitly held that restitution may be imposed as a condition of pretrial diversion without a verdict of guilt because it is in the nature of reparation to the victim and not a form of punishment imposed by the state.[59] However, the defendant's agreement to participate in such programs must, on balance, be voluntary; if his decision to participate was the result of coercion, such procedures would violate the defendant's right to due process.

Where a defendant is charged with a number of offenses, is restitution limited to those offenses on which he is convicted or to which he pleads guilty?

It depends on the jurisdiction. The statutes in a number of states authorize restitution only for "the offense for which the conviction was had."[60] Courts have strictly construed this limitation and have permitted restitution only for the specific counts on which the defendant was convicted or pleaded guilty. Courts in a number of states have limited restitution to the specific counts for which the defendant was found or pleaded guilty, even where the statute was not explicit.[62]

In the jurisdictions that have adopted this limitation on restitution, when will it prevent victims from obtaining restitution?

First, where the defendant is charged with a specific crime involving a stated amount of damage or loss, this limitation has been used to bar victims from recovering any greater amount, despite testimony at trial that proved the eventual loss was greater than the amount stated in the indictment.[63] A federal appellate court, for example, reversed a restitution order for $1,989.35 on the ground that the defendant had pleaded guilty to embezzling $262.12 even though trial testimony indicated that the victim's real loss (which was only discovered after indictment) was the greater amount.[64] Second, where the defendant is involved in an ongoing scheme or has committed the same crime against a number of different victims, failure to obtain a plea or conviction for all of the counts will bar some of the victims from obtaining restitution.[65] In one case, the defendant was charged with 17 counts of fraud in connection with a veterans' home loan scheme.[66] The defendant was convicted of only 6 counts involving 6 different veteran-victims; a federal appellate court overturned a restitution order that would have provided restitution to all of the 17 victims plus an additional veteran who was not named as a victim in the indictment. This specific prohibition against restitution has been strongly criticized, particularly as it has been applied to instances of embezzlement or check forgery.[67] It is common practice for prosecutors (particularly in check forgery cases) to charge only 1 or 2 counts of check passing in exchange for a negotiated guilty plea;[68] but in states that have adopted this particular limitation, restitution is barred for all of the bad checks written by the defendant except for those one or two involved in the count that resulted in conviction.[69]

The third group of victims excluded from restitution as a result of this limitation are those who are injured by an aspect of the defendant's activity that violates the criminal laws but for which the defendant was not charged or convicted. In one Florida case, for example, the victim was barred from recovering for injuries due to an automobile accident when the defendant was convicted not for violation of the traffic laws in creating the accident, but for leaving the scene of the accident; since the injuries were not directly related to this so-called confliction offense, the victim was denied restitution. In one Illinois case, where the defendant set fire to a college dormitory, the court ruled that a conviction for arson (destruction by fire of the college's property) did not support an order requiring the defendant to pay students for property that was destroyed or damaged as a result of the fire.[70]

In these states, do courts ever order restitution greater than the amount contained in counts on which the defendant pleads guilty or is convicted?

Yes. As part of a plea bargain or sentencing proceeding, the defendant may agree with a judge or prosecutor to admit responsibility for crimes in addition to the specific crimes to which the defendant is pleading guilty or has been convicted. Most courts have upheld restitution to victims of losses due to these admitted acts as well as losses due to acts for which the defendant actually pleaded guilty.

It should be emphasized, however, that such restitution orders are the result of a voluntary agreement by the defendant to admit responsibility and to pay restitution for these additional offenses in return for the prosecutor's agreement to accept a guilty plea for some but not all the offenses charged. Only rarely will such plea negotiations include a specific amount that the defendant agrees to pay in restitution; typically, the plea agreement only states that the defendant will agree to admit to certain additional crimes or to undertake to pay restitution for those crimes or to certain victims. In general, the amount of the restitution and the manner of payment is formulated later, in the presentence report that is prepared by the prosecutor's office; typically it also reflects proposals made by the defendant or his lawyer. In passing sentence, the court cannot substantially increase the amount or change the nature of restitution beyond what is contained in the plea agreement without offering the defendant the opportunity to withdraw his plea.[71] A federal appellate court also has upheld a restitution order in an amount exceeding that involved in the convicted offense where the defendant had voluntarily entered into a previous civil consent judgment in which he agreed to pay the victim for losses caused by criminal activity that went beyond the offenses for which he was convicted.[72]

In some states that have adopted this general limitation on restitution to convicted offenses, there are even cases where broader restitution orders have been upheld without the defendant's agreement on the ground that restitution in a larger amount was supported by evidence in the trial record.[73]

Are there any states that do not limit restitution to the specific offenses for which there has been a finding of guilt?

Yes. Courts in a number of states (including California, Michigan, and Illinois) permit restitution in amounts greater than that specified in the charging instrument, and for losses caused by other criminal acts, even if they involved other victims.[74] In one California case, a building contractor was convicted of one count of grand theft in a fraudulent home-remodeling scheme; he was ordered to pay the victims identified in that specific count $821. Eight months later, the court increased the restitution to $2,000 for the original victims and added $6,600 in restitution to other customers not named in the count for which the defendant was convicted. In uphold-

ing the restitution order, the appellate court stated that restitution was designed to rehabilitate the defendant and therefore
should be based "on the realities of the situation" and not on
technical limitations of the definition of the offense for which
the defendant was actually convicted.[75] An Illinois case upheld a probation condition calling for restitution to victims of
a confidence game in addition to the original complainants
and a Michigan appellate court upheld an order requiring the
defendant to pay restitution for the whole value of the property stolen from a victim even though he was only convicted
of receiving part of it.[76]

In fact, the California courts have gone so far in one widely
criticized case as to order restitution where the defendant
was acquitted of the charge. In that case, the defendant was
convicted of one count of defrauding a victim and acquitted of
another, but ordered by the court to pay the total amount
involved in both counts; the appellate court upheld the restitution (even though its effect was to overrule the jury verdict
of acquittal) because the trial judge had elicited testimony
after the trial that indicated the defendant had perjured himself in denying his guilt in connection with the count on
which he was acquitted.[77]

Is it necessary for the court to specifically spell out the terms of the restitution?

Yes. In general, courts are required to specify the amount
and schedule of restitution payments. Restitution orders that
fail to make the amount and other terms of the restitution
explicit are routinely stricken as vague or as an unauthorized
delegation to probation or correction officials of the court's
authority to order restitution.[78] As a federal appellate court
pointed out in one case involving a restitution order that
allowed a Georgia probation officer to fix the amount of
restitution, a procedure that allows the probation officer simply to accept the unchallenged statement of the victim without giving the offender prior notice and an opportunity to be
heard violates the offender's constitutionally protected right
to due process.[79]

Nevertheless, some states have authorized restitution orders that allow considerable latitude to probation officers or
to the parole commission to set the actual amount of restitution once a maximum or minimum amount has been fixed by

the court, or, where the offender is involved in a residential restitution center situation or a work-release program.[80]

How much proof must support the court's findings concerning the amount to be paid to the victim?

A finding of restitution in a certain amount will be upheld where there is any reasonable factual basis in the record for the amount of damages awarded.[81] Typically the record must include a finding concerning the extent of the victim's injury and that the injury was caused by the defendant; the burden is on the defendant to prove that he was only responsible for a lesser amount of injury.[82] Appellate courts are liberal in upholding orders awarding restitution to victims and have repeatedly held that the trial court is not held strictly to any technical limitation, even the usual requirement that damages be proved by a preponderance of the evidence.[83]

Who has the responsibility for insuring that restitution payments are actually received by the victim?

It varies from state to state. Many states place the burden of supervision of the payment of restitution on the court system itself, and in particular on the court clerk.[84] Other states assign responsibility to the offender's probation officer,[85] and some states make supervision of restitution payments the responsibility of the state's Department of Corrections.[86] In 1984, New York created county restitution authorities to coordinate and supervise restitution collections and to provide monthly accountings to the state.

In practice, does a defendant who is imprisoned have the opportunity to pay restitution while incarcerated?

No. There are currently no prison industry programs in the country where a prisoner can be employed for anything approaching normal wages.[87] In the early nineteenth century, prisoners worked for private employers under contracts with the state, but union opposition beginning in the latter part of the nineteenth century led to federal and state laws that severely restricted the commercial transaction of goods produced by prisoners.[88] In 1979, Congress passed the Prison Industry Enhancement under the Justice System Improvement Act that approves the potential development of prison industries in federal prisons but requires consultation with local unions and stipulates that inmate labor cannot displace any employed workers. In 1984, Congress amended the act to permit 20 pilot prison industry projects where prisoners would be paid full wages; between 5 and 20% of prisoners' earnings were earmarked for victim compensation funds. As part of the same legislation, federal grants were made available to states and cities to develop prison industry projects which would allow prisoners to pay restitution to victims.[89] Virtually the only current employment for prisoners is producing items such as mailbags or license plates for state or federal governments and there are severe statutory restrictions even on such production since relatively few prisoners are gainfully employed (and then only for token wages).

Is there any movement toward allowing prisoners to work outside of prisons to pay restitution orders?

Yes. Beginning with the Minnesota Restitution Center that was established in 1972, there has been a movement toward establishing special centers or shelters where prisoners who agree to provide restitution to victims or perform some community service can live or be supervised while working for private employers outside of prison.[90] At least 9 states have enacted legislation specifically authorizing the establishment of such programs.[91] Many such programs were established as experiments in the late 1970s with funds from the Federal Law Enforcement Assistance Administration. By 1979, there were over 30 programs in 20 different states providing monetary restitution to victims, another 21 programs where convicted persons provided restitution or performed community service, and another 30 programs that were oriented toward providing community service. Annual intake for these programs ranged from less than a hundred to several thousand prisoners.[92] When the LEAA ceased providing funding in 1981, many of these programs were restricted or abandoned.

How do restitution centers operate?

It varies from program to program.[93] Some deal only with prisoners who are paroled or on probation; others operate on referrals directly from the court as a form of pretrial diversion. Some are exclusively for felons, while others exclude persons convicted of felonies.

Some deal exclusively with adults, some with juveniles and others with a mixture. In some of the centers the offenders are required to reside at the center where they must return at the end of each day of private employment; others provide counseling and supervision but do not require on-site residence.

Most programs are affiliated either with state correction or public service agencies, county probation departments, or private community organizations.

The specifics of how these centers operate vary greatly; for example, the Minnesota Restitution Center (which was the first formal restitution program for incarcerated offenders, but has since closed) diverted property offenders after a few months in prison to a residential community correction center where the prisoners worked for private employers and performed community service.[94] In the Georgia restitution shelter program, parolees worked to provide financial restitution to victims and performed community service; participants in the program were required by the parole board to live at the restitution center for a specific period of time, to maintain a stable employment and to participate in a paid community service program after work on evenings or on weekends.[95]

Are victims involved in such programs?

It varies greatly from jurisdiction to jurisdiction. The victim involvement in the Georgia program, for example, is minimal (being limited to a receipt of restitution checks) and most programs discourage any active contact between victims and offenders. However, the Minnesota program had considerable success in directly involving victims with offenders in face-to-face negotiation over the extent of damages and development of a written agreement under which the offender would agree to pay the victim a certain amount of restitution. Currently a nonprofit community corrections organization, Prisoner and Community Together (PACT) operates a victim/offender reconciliation program in Elkhart County, Indiana, which arranges for face-to-face meetings between adult and juvenile offenders (primarily felony property offenders) and their victims to work out plans for restitution. In a small number of programs (such as the Pima County attorney's Adult Diversion Project in Tucson, Arizona), victim approval is a prerequisite for the use of restitution and victims can veto the admission of an offender into such a program (although it rarely happens).[96]

A few programs have also experimented with arranging for offenders (in appropriate cases) to perform services for the victims of their crimes; for instance, repairing vandalized property, but instances of such victim/offender contact are rare and only take place with the victim's consent.

Are such programs successful in obtaining restitution for victims?

It varies. A restitution program for juveniles established in 1975, by the Juvenile Court in Tulsa, Oklahoma, reported that victims (who averaged losses of $200) received on the average $90 from offenders admitted to the program.[97] The Georgia program in 1976 produced aggregate payments to victims of $62,500[98] and the Elkhart program reported that over 75 percent of the $21,775 in restitution agreed to in monetary contracts between victims and offenders in 1981 was paid.[99]

One commentator has observed (after studying a number of programs and interviewing administrators) that one reason for the failure of many programs to more effectively provide monetary restitution to victims is an institutional emphasis on the use of residential restitution centers as a means of diverting offenders from incarceration and saving the cost of imprisonment rather than on securing payments to victims.[100]

Do victims have the right to be notified of the court's initial order concerning restitution or subsequent modifications?

It depends on that state. Some states (such as New Mexico and South Dakota) specifically provide that the court clerk must send copies of the initial restitution order and any subsequent modifications to the victim.[101]

Can the offender request that the court reduce or otherwise modify the terms of an initial restitution order?

Yes. Offenders in most states have a specific statutory right to request a hearing on matters relating to restitution or to petition the court for modification of a restitution order; depending on the state, modification is permitted where the offender can show that there has been a change in his financial circumstances, that the order is producing undue hardship or that a modification would further the offender's rehabilitation.[102]

Must the ordered restitution be paid all at once?

No. Courts have discretion to order that restitution be paid in one lump sum in appropriate cases but more commonly defendants are ordered to make a series of payments to the victim.

Where the court's restitution order calls for a series of payments to the victim, is the offender in default of the restitution order if he fails to conform to the schedule established by the court?

Yes. [103]

What can a victim do if the offender fails to pay restitution as ordered?

It depends on the jurisdiction. In some states, the victim has a statutory right to request that the court conduct a hearing about restitution at any time during the period of the offender's probation; the victim can use this right to raise with the court the offender's nonpayment or default. [104] In jurisdictions without such an explicit statutory right, the victim is free to contact the judge by letter or telephone to bring to the court's attention the offender's failure to live up to restitution obligations. [105] Many states place responsibility for initiating restitution default proceedings on the prosecutor, [106] or on the entity that supervises the actual payment of restitution. [107]

Victim assistance organizations in many states (independent organizations as well as units operating out of the prosecutor's office) have set up procedures for assisting victims in documenting and bringing to the attention of the appropriate persons any default or nonpayment by the offender in connection with the restitution order. [108] Even where such assistance is not available, the victim is free to contact the prosecutor's office on his own, place the prosecutor on notice of the default and request that the prosecutor take action to enforce the restitution order. [109] Indeed, in some states, notification to the prosecuting attorney of any default or nonpayment of restitution is required by statute. [110]

Is the offender entitled to a hearing on a request that he be ordered to pay restitution?

It varies from jurisdiction to jurisdiction. Some states have statutes that specifically require notice to the defendant and a hearing to determine whether restitution should be ordered, the amount of restitution, what payments will be required, and how payment will be made. Under the federal procedure established by the Sentencing Reform Act of 1984, the defendant must be given notice that the court is considering imposition of a restitution order; the defendant and the government then have an opportunity to make written and oral submissions to the court and the court must state, for the record, the specific reasons for any restitution order.[111] Some states allow the court (or even correction or probation officials) to determine the amount and schedule of restitution without a prior hearing that gives the defendant an opportunity to be heard. In Arizona, New Jersey, and Washington, the courts are authorized to conduct hearings to determine restitution only if the record of the criminal trial does not contain sufficient information to support a finding as to the correct amount.[112]

Does the offender have any constitutional right to a hearing on restitution or to a jury trial on the amount of restitution to be ordered?

There is considerable uncertainty over the offender's constitutional rights in this area. Most courts faced with challenges to the constitutionality of restitution procedures have held that these procedures are not subject to the same protections (such as the right to a jury trial guaranteed by the Seventh Amendment) as civil suits because they are part of the sentencing phase of a criminal proceeding and therefore can be disposed of by a summary procedure.[113] A number of courts have rejected due process challenges to restitution procedures on the ground that offenders are permitted to choose restitution as an alternative to incarceration as a privilege, or act of grace; the offender has no right to escape imprisonment and thus the summary determination of his sentence—which may include restitution—does not deprive him of any right. It follows that since there is no deprivation of a right protected by the Constitution, there is no need for a notice or hearing required by the Fourteenth Amendment.[114]

However, many commentators have criticized this rationale for restitution procedures and have emphasized the need for the recognizing the offender's right to due process, including a full hearing and perhaps even a jury trial, on the grounds that his property, property rights and even liberty are significantly affected by a restitution order.[115] The Supreme Courts of Michigan and California have both criticized restitution orders where the judge ordered a particular amount of restitution based simply on his own belief or investigation of the damages suffered by the victim without requiring a hearing in open court, cross-examination of witnesses, appropriate pleading and discovery or even a jury trial on specific issues of liability and damages.[116]

In 1983, a federal district court held that the procedure established by the Victim Witness Protection Act for determining the amount of restitution was unconstitutional. Holding that it allowed determination of restitution without a jury trial, the usual rules of evidence or guarantees that the defendant was represented by an attorney, the court concluded that the act was so fundamentally unfair as to violate the defendant's Fifth Amendment right to due process; in part this unfairness resulted from the unfettered discretion it gave the trial judge to set damages virtually as he wished. Subsequent federal decisions have held that such sentences of restitution which have long been imposed (and do not deprive the defendant of his right to a criminal jury trial) do not violate the defendant's due process rights.[117]

Some judges have criticized as fundamentally unfair to the defendant any sentencing procedure that forces the offender to choose between restitution and incarceration; they argue that under such circumstances, any offender would feel compelled to consent to the requested restitution, even if he really believed the amount of damage to the victim to be excessive.[118] This has led at least one commentator to suggest a bifurcated hearing that would first determine the type of sentence to be imposed on the offender (incarceration versus probation) and second to assess the conditions of that sentence (such as restitution).[119]

In several states (including Kentucky, Missouri, and Tennessee), where a defendant objects to the extent of restitution or damage to the victim, there are currently statutes that require impaneling a jury to hear evidence and to determine the extent of damages and restitution to be ordered.[120]

Is the conduct of the victim to be considered in determining the amount of restitution awarded?

Yes. Where there is misconduct by the victim, courts will consider this in setting the amount of restitution to be paid by the offender.[121]

Where several codefendants in a criminal proceeding are responsible for all or part of the victim's loss, who is liable for the restitution payments?

As in a civil action, under these circumstances, criminal courts have made the codefendants jointly and severally liable so that each of them is responsible to pay back the full amount of the damage until the victim is completely compensated.[122]

How long after conviction or a guilty plea does the court set the amount and/or schedule for restitution?

It varies from jurisdiction to jurisdiction, but generally restitution must be ordered promptly or within a matter of weeks after the conviction.[123]

What happens to a restitution order if the offender appeals the judge's order?

Payment of restitution will usually be stayed pending the outcome of the appeal. Where an order of restitution has been stayed pending an appeal, a federal court can order a defendant to place the amount in escrow with the court or post a performance bond.[124] If the restitution order or conviction is overturned on appeal, the court may order the victim to return any restitution payments to the offender.[125]

If the defendant defaults on the ordered restitution payments, can he be imprisoned?

Yes. However, a showing that the default was intentional, in bad faith, or, at the very least, that it was unreasonable or reckless is usually required before a suspended sentence, probation, or parole will be revoked and the offender imprisoned.[126] In any revocation proceeding, it is an affirmative defense (which the defendant must show by a preponderance of the evidence) that he was unable to make the payments or that they constituted such a manifest hardship on him that the default was unintentional.[127] Where, one defendant who was employed failed to make $100 in monthly restitution payments and another defendant could not demonstrate that he had made a good faith effort to mortgage the house he had purchased with the proceeds of his welfare fraud, revocations have been upheld.[128]

Many cases have upheld the constitutionality of incarceration for failure to pay restitution.[129] However, where there was no showing of intentionality or bad faith, converting probation or a suspended sentence into a jail term has increasingly been found to violate the equal protection clause and/or the prohibition in a number of state constitutions against the use of the criminal process (and imprisonment) to force payment of a civil debt.[130] In 1983, the United States Supreme Court reversed the revocation of probation of an indigent probationer who despite repeated efforts was unable to find work or pay a $500 fine and $250 in restitution ordered by the court.[131] The court held that it was so fundamentally unfair to revoke probation under those circumstances (without any finding that the probationer was responsible for the failure or that alternative forms of punishment were inadequate) that such revocation violates the provisions of the Fourteenth Amendment. One federal district court also held in a 1983 case, that revocation of probation without a finding that the defendant failed to make a bona fide effort to pay restitution would violate the Eighth Amendment's prohibition against "excessive fines" and "cruel and unusual punishment."[132]

What happens if the court finds that the default was intentional and warrants incarceration?

It depends on the manner in which the case was originally processed. Where the defendant was not previously incarcerated probation will be revoked or the original suspended sentence will be activated.[133] Where the defendant is already in prison, he may be held in contempt of court and kept in prison until the debt is paid (usually for some maximum time period to be determined by dividing the total amount owed by a certain number of dollars per day).[134]

Where the offender is unable to pay the ordered restitution, what else can the sentencing court do?

In addition to imprisoning the defaulting offender, the sentencing court has a variety of options.[135] Where the offender can show that the ordered payment would produce serious hardship for him or his family or that his nonpayment is caused by an inability to pay, the court can revoke all or part of the restitution amount or any scheduled installment.[136] Courts can also temporarily suspend restitution or extend the payment schedule, often spreading out payments over the full probation period.[137] Where the offender was unable to pay restitution during the period of the initial sentence, courts have even increased the length of the sentence to allow the offender adequate time to make full restitution.[138] While some states do not limit the extent to which probation or a sentence can be extended to assure restitution, a number of states have strictly limited such extensions to the maximum statutory probation period,[139] or to a specified number of years beyond the original sentence or term of probation.[140] Federal law now requires that restitution be paid no later than the end of the probation period (if probation is ordered), five years after the end of the term of imprisonment (if there is no probation), or within five years after the date of sentencing.[141] Although extending the defendant's sentence or probation for failure to have sufficient financial means to pay restitution arguably raises the same problems of fundamental fairness and invidious discrimination in violation of the Fourteenth Amendment already discussed, challenges to such extensions on equal protection grounds have been rejected by courts in at least two cases.[142]

Increasingly in recent years, courts have also responded to nonpayment by the offender by converting the amount owed under the restitution order into a corresponding number of hours of unpaid community service (usually by dividing the amount owed by the prevailing minimum wage to arrive at the number of hours of service to be performed).[143] However, such a practice has the effect of depriving the victim of any possibility of obtaining restitution and also may violate the defendant's right to equal protection.[144]

Are there other practical methods used by courts to increase the likelihood that offenders will make the payments to victims dictated by restitution award?

Yes. Courts have used a variety of devices to increase the victim's practical leverage and the likelihood that restitution will be paid. In Texas, a sentencing judge can require the offender to send a letter to his employer authorizing payment by the employer of a certain portion of the offender's salary into court for payment of restitution.[145] Some states have statutes that authorize the victim to place a lien on the offender's assets (often from the time of arrest) and allow enforcement of the lien by execution against those assets.[146] Other states directly authorize the victim to levy execution against the offender's assets as if the victim were enforcing an unpaid civil judgment.[147] In some courts in New York, judges require the defendant to execute a confession of judgment as a condition of probation; this judgment is then enforceable against the defendant for the next twenty years.[148] In those same New York courts, judges sometimes stipulate that the convicted person use money posted by him to obtain a bail bond to immediately satisfy an order of restitution. As a means of assuring compliance with restitution orders, a Delaware pretrial diversion program involving mandatory restitution requires the offender to pledge his driver's license as a means of insuring compliance. To assist the victim in obtaining restitution, other states have required defendants to disclose the nature and location of assets, to post a cash bond to secure payment of restitution or authorize prosecutors to commence special attachment proceedings against the defendant's property.[149] One federal court took the extreme measure of requiring the defendant in a check-kiting scheme to execute documents immediately transferring to the victim all of the offender's assets and property.[150]

Is a court's order of restitution enforceable by the victim in the same way that a civil judgment against the offender is for damages?

In most jurisdictions, no. Ordinarily, at the end of a civil trial, where a court enters a judgment ordering a defendant to pay damages to another party, the party awarded the damages can use a variety of procedures (including attaching assets that belong to the defendant, garnishing wages payable to him by an employer or even executing on the defendant's property and selling it at auction) to enforce the judgment.[151] In most states, such a judgment can be enforced for years after it is entered; in New York, for example, a party has twenty years in which to enforce it.[152]

By contrast, an order of restitution ordinarily can be enforced only during the term of the sentence or probation and only through restitution payments supervised, collected and paid to the victim by a probation department, restitution program, court, or corrections department (depending on the jurisdiction). If the defendant fails to pay restitution, the victim's remedy is to seek revocation of the defendant's probation or parole; the victim himself is usually not entitled to levy on the defendant's assets.

However, a number of jurisdictions have now empowered courts to enter restitution orders that provide victims with the same rights as a civil judgment against the defendant. In Alabama and Delaware, for example, statutes have been enacted that permit courts to enter civil judgments of damages in favor of victims as part of a determination to enter an order of restitution.[153] The 1982 Federal Victim Witness Protection Act contains a restitution provision that specifically provides that restitution orders "may be enforced by the United States or a victim named in the order to receive the restitution in the same manner as a judgment in a civil action."[154] In addition, judges in Rochester, New York, and in other jurisdictions that have not specifically empowered the entry of civil judgments as part of restitution in a criminal case, have required criminal defendants to consent to a civil judgment of damages to be paid to the victim as a condition of probation, pretrial diversion, or parole.

Many advocates of the expanded use of restitution argue that judges have always been free to sentence defendants or order conditions of probation or parole without a jury. But this growing use of summary procedures in a criminal case to impose a civil judgment of damages on a defendant raises serious questions under the Seventh Amendment of the Constitution that guarantees defendants in civil trials the right to a trial by jury. One federal court in 1983, held that the 1982 Federal Victim Witness Protection Act was unconstitutional since it was in violation of the defendant's right to trial by jury in civil cases. The court also found that the statute left the judge with unfettered discretion in ordering the nature and amount of restitution and in allowing for such a determination without any ascertainable standards; according to the court, this was unfair to the defendant and violated due process. However, subsequent decisions by other federal courts have upheld the constitutionality of such restitution orders, pointing out that defendants' rights to a jury in criminal cases have always ended at trial, that judge-made sentences of restitution have long been part of the common law, and that the purpose of restitution (like imprisonment) is appropriate rehabilitation and punishment, not full monetary damages for a victim. The Supreme Court of Georgia upheld the constitutionality of a similar provision of Georgia's restitution statute, holding that there was no right to a jury trial since restitution was imposed as a penalty, not an obligation to pay civil damages.[155]

What is alternative sentencing?

It is the judicial use of conditions of probation, suspended sentences, or pretrial diversion that require the offender to perform community service, usually intended to impress on the offender the harm caused by his criminal act or to redress it. Thus, a Rochester judge has ordered a person guilty of property destruction and vandalism to help clean the city zoo and a San Francisco judge ordered a defendant guilty of embezzling between $1,000 and $4,000 from the government by falsifying overtime claims to spend four hours a day, five days a week for one year in the St. Anthony Dining Room, a facility operated by a Franciscan priest that provides free meals to the poor.[156] In Alameda County (Oakland), California, persons charged with drug, disorderly conduct, assault, theft, and burglary offenses can be diverted to community service; in 1975, 80 percent of such offenders completed community service.[157]

While the use of alternative sentencing varies greatly from jurisdiction to jurisdiction, judges are increasingly making use of it, and ordering sentences of community service alone or in connection with other sanctions (such as restitution to the victim or a fine). Since it has been said to "pay back" the community for damage done by the offender, some commentators consider it within the broad category of "restitution," and have argued that in crimes (such as drug offenses) it may be the only possible form of restitution.[158] Critics have argued that it does nothing to compensate the actual victim, that it is often used as a substitute for real restitution and that the arbitrary nature of the kind and amount of service ordered subjects the offender to a form of involuntary servitude.

A number of jurisdictions specifically empower judges to order community service as a sentence or condition of probation. As of 1979, more than fifty programs in different jurisdictions supervised offenders who were providing such service.[159] The 1982 Federal Victim Witness Protection Act specifically provides for offenders to perform community service (in lieu of monetary restitution to the victim) if the victim or his estate consents.[160]

When a criminal defendant is ordered to pay a fine, or forfeiture, are the proceeds used to provide restitution for victims?

No. Unlike a specific order of restitution, a fine or penalty is assessed by the court as part of the defendant's punishment, and not to compensate an individual victim.[161] Generally, such funds are added to the general fund of the state and are not used specifically to compensate victims. However, there are exceptions to this general rule;[162] for example in Arizona the court is allowed by statute to direct all or any portion of a fine as restitution to the victim.[163] In addition, in a number of states, special penalties (in the form of fixed fines or surcharges on other fines assessed) are used to fund the state's victim compensation program.[164]

Can a criminal defendant be required to pay restitution in addition to a fine?

Yes. In fact, in a number of jurisdictions, the courts are directed by statute to consider the effect of potential fines on the criminal defendant's ability to pay restitution and to give priority to providing restitution to the victim. To encourage restitution, the 1984 federal Sentencing Reform Act allows defendants who voluntarily make restitution to the victim to petition the court for a reduction in any unpaid fines equal to the amount of restitution which is paid.[165]

Can juveniles be ordered to pay restitution?

Yes. A number of states have enacted specific statutes that authorize orders of restitution for youthful offenders;[166] some make restitution mandatory or require that a juvenile offender obtain employment, if necessary, to allow him to make restitution. There are special mediation programs for juveniles (see Chapter VIII) many of which make restitution a necessary part of agreements that will allow the juvenile to avoid prosecution.

While the Federal Youth Corrections Act is silent on the question of whether the federal courts can authorize restitution in cases involving juvenile offenders, the courts have interpreted the sentencing and probation provisions of that statute broadly to allow restitution where it will promote the rehabilitation of the youthful offender, either as a condition of probation or as part of the defendant's sentence.[167]

The parents of a juvenile, in some states, may also be ordered to contribute to restitution. For example, the California Supreme Court upheld a restitution order which took into account the parents' financial resources which could be used to assist a juvenile offender in satisfying a restitution order and in Kentucky the parents of a juvenile offender can be ordered to post a $500 bond with the court which can be used to satisfy restitution orders.[168] However, in one Maryland case the court held that the state itself could not be considered a parent or ordered to pay restitution for the delinquent acts of a juvenile in the state's custody.[169]

Notes

1. Some states also use the term *reparation* to signify a type of repayment of losses paid a defendant in a criminal case, to the victim. *See, e.g.*, KY. REV. STAT. ANN. §431.200 (Bobbs-Merrill Supp. 1982) (reparation); Ala. Code §§15–22–29(b) (referring to reparation and restitution). Courts have suggested a variety of distinctions between these two terms. *See, e.g.*, *People v. Becker*, 349 Mich. 476, 484, 84 N.W.2d 833, 837 (1957) (reparation refers to compensation in damages; restitution involves the restoration of the thing taken or its value); *State v. Stalheim*, 275 Or. 683, 687–88, 552 P.2d 829, 832 (1976) (restitution involves the return of some object wrongfully obtained in committing a crime; reparation involves the repair, restoration, or compensation for resulting damages to personal property); *People v. Lofton*, 78 Misc.2d 202, 356 N.Y.S.2d 791 (Crim. Ct., N.Y. Co. 1974) (restoration consists of the return of all of the fruits of the offense; reparation refers only to the payment of an amount the defendant can afford). Increasingly, however, legislators are using the single term *restitution*—in the sense defined here—to describe compensation to victims by the criminal justice system. Harland, "Monetary Remedies for the Victims of Crime: Assessing the Role of the Criminal Courts," 30 *UCLA L. Rev.* 52, 64 (1982) ("Harland, Monetary Remedies").
2. *See* Harland, "Court-Ordered Community Service in Criminal Law: The Continuing Tyranny of Benevolence?" 29 *Buffalo L. Rev.* 425 (1980).
3. *Compare* A. Goldstein, "Defining the Role of the Victim in Criminal Prosecution," 52 *Miss. L. J.* 515, 532 (1982), *with* Bureau of Justice Statistics, United States Department of Justice, *Restitution to Victims of Personal and Household Crimes* (New York, 1980); ABA, *Victim/Witness Legislation; Consideration for Policymakers* (Washington, D.C.; ABA, Section of Criminal Justice; 1981), p. 18; *and* "Compensating the Victims of Crime," [hereafter "Victim/Witness Legislation"], 14 *Crim. L. Bull.* 203, 220–21 (1978).
4. M. Arnold, "Making the Criminal Pay Back His Victim," *National Observer*, p. 1 (Apr. 2, 1977); *Project Repay Yearly Report — 1981*; "Limits Increased for Restitution from Criminals," *N.Y. Times* B3 (July 20, 1983).
5. Exodus 22:1; Cyrus H. Gordon, *Hammurabi's Code: Quaint or Forward Looking?* (New York, 1960) p. 6.

6. S. Schafer, *Compensation and Restitution to Victims of Crime* 3 (2d ed. 1970) [hereafter "Compensation and Restitution"].

7. Ethelbert's code is set out in *The Laws of the Earliest English Kings* 5–9 (F.L. Attenborough, ed., 1963).

8. John Reeves, *History of the English Law* 14–17 (3d ed., 1814).

9. *Compensation and Restitution, supra* note 6, at 7; E. Jenks, *A Short History of English Law* 10–11 (1949).

10. J. Bentham, *Limits of Jurisprudence Defined* 298 (C. Everett, ed., 1945); O.W. Holmes, *The Common Law* 44 (1881); E. Ferri, *Crim. Sociology* 411–13 (J. Kelly, trans., 1917); Hall, "Interrelation of Criminal Law and Torts: I," 43 *Colum. L. Rev.* 753, 758–60 (1943).

11. Note, "Restitution and the Criminal Law," 39 *Colum. L. Rev.* 1185, 1198 nn. 65, 66 (1939).

12. *See, e.g.,* La. Code Crim. Proc. Ann. art. 895(8) (West Supp. 1982), adopting Model Penal Code Section 301.1 (Proposed Official Draft 1962).

13. Harland, *Monetary Remedies, supra* note 1, at 58 n.41.

14. *Id.;* Ariz. Rev. Stat. Ann. §§13–603(c)(1978); Iowa Code Ann. § 907.12(3) (West Supp. 1979).

15. *See, e.g.,* Kan. Stat. Ann. §22–2909 (1981); Oreg. Rev. Stat. § 135.891 (1981); Pa. Cons. Stat. Ann. R. Crim. P. Rule 182 (Purdon Supp. 1982); Tenn. Code Ann. §40–15–105(2) (1982); Okla. Stat. tit. 22, §991 c (1981); Ill. Ann. Stat. ch. 38, §1005–6–3.1 (Smith Hurd Supp. 1982–83).

16. *See, e.g.,* Md. Code. Ann. art. 27 §640(c) (1982); Alaska Stat. § 12.55.045 (1980).

17. This is the most common kind of restitution and is authorized in nearly all states.

18. U.S.C. §3651 (1970); Ala. Code. tit. 15, §22–52 (8) (1977); Alaska Stat. §12.55.100(a)(2) (1980); Ark. Stat. Ann. §41–1203(2)(h) (1977); Cal. Penal Code §1203.1 (West 1982); Conn. Gen. Stat. Ann. §53a–30(a)(4) (West 1972); Ga. Code Ann. §27–2711 (1978); Hawaii Rev. Stat. §706–624(2)(h) (1976); Ind. Code Ann. §35–7–2–1a(5) (Burns 1979); Ky. Rev. Stat. Ann. §533.030(2)(d) (Baldwin 1975); La. Code Crim. Proc. Ann. art. 895(A) (7) (West Supp. 1982); Me. Rev. Stat. Ann. tit. 17–A, §1204(2)(B) (Pamphlet 1982); Md. Ann. Code art. 27, §641(a)(1) (1982); Mich. Stat. Ann. §28.1133 (Callaghan Supp. 1982); Minn. Stat. Ann. §609.135(1) (West Supp. 1982); Neb. Rev. Stat. §§29–2219(2)(j) (1978), 29–2262(2)(j) (1979); Nev. Rev. Stat. § 176.185(3) (1981); N.J. Stat. Ann. §2C:45–1(b)(8) (West Pamphlet 1982); N. M. Stat. Ann. §31–20–6 (1981); N.Y. Penal Law § 65.10(2)(g) (Consol. Supp. 1982); N.C. Gen. Stat §§15A–1343(b)(6)(d), 15A–1343 (Supp. 1981); N.D. Cent. Code §12.1–32–07(2)(e) (1976); Ohio Rev. Code Ann. §2951.02(C) (Baldwin 1979); Okla. Stat. tit. 22, §991a(1)(a) (1981); Or. Rev. Stat. §137.106 (1981); Pa. Stat. Ann. tit. 18, §1106 (Purdon Supp. 1981); Tex. Crim. Proc. Code Ann. art. 42.12, §6(h) (Vernon Supp. 1982); Vt. Stat. Ann. tit. 28, §252(b)(5) (Supp. 1982–83); Va. Code §19.2–305 (Supp. 1982); Wash. Rev.

Code Ann. §9.95.210(2) (Supp. 1982); W. Va. Code §62–12–9 (1977); Ariz. Rev. Stat. Ann. §13–901(A), (F) (Supp. 1982–83); Colo. Rev. Stat. §16–11–204(2)(e) (1978); Ill. Ann. Stat. ch. 38, §1005–6–3(b) (9) (Smith-Hurd Supp. 1982–83); Kan. Stat. Ann. §21–4610(4) (1981); Utah Code Ann. §77–18–2(4) (Supp. 1981).

18. *See, e.g.,* Tex. Code Crim. Proc. Ann. art. 42.03 §5(b) (Vernon Supp. 1982); N.Y. Penal Law §60.27 (Supp. 1983); 18 U.S.C. § 3579(a) (1983).

19. *See, e.g.,* 18 U.S.C. §§3551, 3556; Minn. Stat. Ann. §299B.13 (West Supp. 1982) ("criminal acts"); Colo. Rev. Stat. §17–2–201(5) (C)(I) (Supp. 1981) ("criminal conduct"); N.J. Stat. Ann. §2C: 44–2 (1982) ("crime").

20. *See, e.g.,* S.D. Codified Laws Ann. §23A–28–3 (Supp. 1982) (excluding restitution for "petty offenses"); Md. Ann. Code. art. 27, §29 (1982) (burglary), 143(c) (bad checks); Tenn. Code Ann. § 40–20–116(a) (1982) (required sentence for stealing, receiving, or defrauding).

21. Ariz. Rev. Stat. Ann. §13–803(D) (Supp. 1981); S.D. Codified Laws Ann. §23A–28–2(3) (Supp. 1982). *See also People v. Prell,* 299 Ill. App. 130, 19 N.E.2d 637 (1939) (invalidating an order of restitution in connection with a conviction for willful and wanton driving).

22. Ark. Stat. Ann. §41–1203(2)(h) (1977); Kan. Stat. Ann. §21–4610(4) (1981); Neb. Rev. Stat. §29–2219(j) (1979); Utah Code Ann. § 77–18–1(4) (1982).

23. *People v. Grago,* 24 Misc.2d 739, 741, 204 N.Y.S.2d 774, 777 (Oneida Co. Sup. Ct. 1960).

23a. 18 U.S.C. §§3556, 3563.

24. *See, e.g.,* Me. Rev. Stat. Ann. tit. 17–A §§1322, 1324 (1982); *State v. Rose,* 45 Or. App. 879, 609 P.2d 875 (1980); *People v. Alexander,* 182 Cal. App.2d 281, 292, 6 Cal. Rptr. 153, 160 (1960); *U.S. v. Follette,* 32 F. Supp. 953 (E.D. Pa. 1940).

25. Iowa Code Ann. §907.12 (1)(a) (West 1979); S.D. Codified Laws Ann. §23A–28–2(1) (1979 & Supp. 1982).

26. N.C. Gen. Stat. §15A–1343(6)(d) (Supp. 1978); *Commonwealth v. Galloway,* 302 Pa. Super. 145, 448 A.2d 568 (1982); *People v. King,* 648 P.2d 173 (Colo. App. 1982).

27. 18 U.S.C. §3663(e)(1).

28. *See* Miss. Code Ann. §99–37–1(d) (Supp. 1982); N.M. Stat. Ann. § 31–17–1(A)(1) (1981); *State v. Barr,* 99 Wash.2d 75, 658 P.2d 1247 (1983); Me. Rev. Stat. Ann. Tit. 17–A, §§1322–1324 (1982) (authorizing payments to family members if they are dependents of the deceased victim). *People v. Pettit,* 88 Mich. App. 203, 276 N.W.2d 878 (1979).

29. 18 U.S.C. §3663(c).

30. *Compare State v. Armstrong,* 44 Or. App. 219, 605 P.2d 736 (1980); *Cuba v. State,* 362 So.2d 29, 31 (Fla. App. 1978); *State v. Horne,* 44 Or. App. 367, 606 P.2d 214 (1980) *with People v. Baker,*

39 Cal. App. 3d 550, 559–60, 113 Cal. Rptr. 248, 253–54 (1974) and *State v. Dillon*, 292 Or. App. 172, 637 P.2d 602 (1981). *Compare* ME. REV. STAT. ANN. tit. 17–A, §§1322, 1324 (1982).

31. *State v. Gerard*, 57 Wis.2d 611, 628, 205 N.W.2d 374, 382, *app. dismissed*, 414 U.S. 804 (1973); *State v. Barklind*, 12 Wash. App. 818, 532 P.2d 633 (1975); *State v. Rogers*, 251 N.W.2d 239 (Iowa 1977).

32. *See, e.g.*, ME. REV. STAT. ANN. TIT. 17–A §1325(2)(B) (1982). *People v. Heil*, 79 Mich. App. 739, 262 N.W.2d 895, 897 (1977).

33. *Gross v. U.S.*, 228 F.2d 612, 615 (8th Cir. 1956); *see generally State v. Barr*, 99 Wn. 2d 75, 658 P.2d 1247 (1983) (*en banc*); *Commonwealth v. Fuqua*, 267 Pa. Super. 504, 508–09, 407 A.2d 24, 25–6 (1979); *State v. Mottola*, 84 N.M. 414, 504 P.2d 22 (1972).

34. *See, e.g.*, ALASKA STAT. §12.55.100(a)(2) (1980); N.M. STAT. ANN. §§ 31–17–1(A)(4) (1978), 31–20–6(B) (Supp. 1983); ARIZ. REV. STAT. ANN. §13-603(c) (1978); S.C. CODE ANN. §17–25–125 (Supp. 1982); OR. REV. STAT. §137.103(3) (1981); *Heil, supra* note 32.

35. *See, e.g.*, ME. REV. STAT. tit. 17–A §1322(3) (1982); OKLA. STAT. tit. 22, §991(f)(3) (West Supp. 1981–82); IOWA CODE ANN. §907.12(1)(b) (West 1979); N.M. STAT. ANN. §31–17–1(A)(2) (1981); *Sprague v. State*, 590 P.2d 410, 415 (Alaska 1979).

36. 18 U.S.C. §3663(b).

37. *See, e.g.*, N.C. GEN. STAT. §15A–1343(b)(6), (d) (Supp. 1981). Cf. MISS. CODE ANN. §99–37–1(c) (Supp. 1982) (allowing for special damages recoverable in civil suits including lost property).

38. WASH REV. CODE ANN. §9A20.030(1) (Supp. 1982); *State v. Morgan*, 8 Wash. App. 189, 190, 504 P.2d 1195, 1196 (1973).

39. *State v. Sandifer*, 359 So.2d 990, 992 (La. 1979); *State v. Garner*, 115 Ariz. 579, 566 P.2d 1055 (1977).

40. *See State v. Gunderson*, 74 Wash.2d 226, 230, 444 P.2d 156, 159–60 (1968), *overruled on other grounds, State v. Gosby*, 85 Wash.2d 758, 539 P.2d 680, 686 (1975); WASH. REV. CODE ANN. § 9.95.210(2) (Supp. 1982).

41. *See, e.g.*, IOWA CODE ANN. §907.12(1)(b) (West 1979); N.M. STAT. ANN. §31–17–1(A)(2) (1981); OHIO REV. CODE ANN. §2929.02(D) (Baldwin Supp. 1979); S.D. CODIFIED LAWS ANN. §23A–28–2 (Supp. 1982).

42. *See, e.g.*, NEV. REV. STAT. §176.189(1) (1981); N.J. STAT. ANN. § 2C:43–2(b)(4) (1982); VA. CODE §19.2–305.1(B) (1983).

43. *See, e.g.*, IOWA CODE ANN. §907.12(3) (West Supp. 1979); S.C. CODE ANN. §§22–3–800 (Supp. 1981) (check fraud), 17–22–90(4) (pretrial diversion); TENN. CODE ANN. §40–20–116(a) (1982); N.D. CENT. CODE §12.48.1–03 (1976); DEL. CODE ANN. tit. 11, §4106(a) (Supp. 1982).

44. *See, e.g.*, 18 U.S.C. §§3553(c), 3663(a)(2); ARIZ. REV. STAT. ANN. §13–603(a) (1978); N.Y. PENAL LAW §60.27(1) (Supp. 1983).

45. *See, e.g.*, N.Y. PENAL LAW §60.27(1) (Supp. 1983); DEL. CODE ANN. tit. 11, §4106(a) (Supp. 1982).

46. F.R.Cr.P. Rule 32(c)(2).

47. *U.S. v. Welden*, 568 F. Supp. 516 (N.D. Ala. 1983).

48. *See, e.g.*, S.C. CODE ANN. §17–22–80 (Supp. 1982).

49. FLA. STAT. ANN. §921.143 (West Supp. 1982).

50. *State v. O'Connor*, 77 Wis.2d 261, 296, 252 N.W.2d 671, 686 (1977); OKLA. STAT. tit. 22, §991a(A)(1)(a) (1981).

51. *See, e.g.*, ARK. STAT. ANN. §46–117(c) (Supp. 1981); VA. CODE § 19.2–305.1(B) (1983).

52. *Commonwealth v. Williams*, 299 Pa. Super. 278, 445 A.2d 753 (1982); *People v. Knowles*, 92 Ill. App. 3d 537 (1980). *See also Huggett v. State*, 83 Wis.2d 790, 266 N.W.2d 403 (1978); *State v. Garner*, 115 Ariz. 579, 581, 566 P.2d 1055, 1057 (1977); *Lofton, supra* note 1.

53. *Coles v. State*, 290 Md. 296, 429 A.2d 1029 (1981); "Embezzler Agrees to Sell Home to Repay $73,000," *N.Y. Times*, (Mar. 1, 1984), B2.

54. *See, e.g.*, IOWA CODE ANN. §907.12(5) (West 1979); N.M. STAT. ANN. § 31–17–1(D) (1981); S.D. CODIFIED LAWS ANN. §23A–28–5 (1979); 18 U.S.C. §3664.

55. *State v. Garner*, 115 Ariz. 579, 582, 566 P.2d 1055, 1058 (Ct. App. 1977), but *compare State v. Benoit*, 131 Vt. 631, 635, 313 A.2d 387, 389 (1973) (a court must determine whether the defendant will be able to pay restitution).

56. *Compare* COLO. REV. STAT. §16–11–212(2) (1982) *with* N.D. CENT. CODE §12–48.1–03 (1976); WYO. STAT. ANN. §13–724(a) (1977).

57. *See, e.g.*, ARIZ. REV. STAT. ANN. §31–254(D)(2) (Pamphlet, 1982) (30 percent); LA. REV. STAT. ANN. §15:840.2(D)(2) (West, 1981) (30 percent); TENN. CODE ANN. §41–6–206 (1982) (20 percent maximum).

58. *See, e.g.*, S.C. CODE ANN. §17–22–40 (1982 Supp.).

59. *Commissioner of Motor Vehicles v. Lee*, 254 Md. 279, 287, 255 A.2d 44, 48 (1969) [superceded by Statute as stated in *Laurie v. State*, 29 Md. App. 609, 349 A.2d 276 (1975)]; *Stevens v. State*, 34 Md. App. 164, 172, 366 A.2d 414, 418 (1976).

60. UTAH CODE ANN. §76–3–201(3)(a) (Supp. 1981); FLA. STAT. ANN. §947.181(1) (West Supp. 1983).

61. *U.S. v. Buechler*, 557 F.2d 1002, 1008 (3d Cir. 1977); *U.S. v. Follette*, 32 F. Supp. 953 (E.D. Pa. 1940).

62. *Lofton, supra* note 52, at 202, 205, *People v. Grago*, 24 Misc.2d 739, 741, 204 N.Y.S.2d 774, 777 (Sup. Ct., Oneida Co. 1960); *People v. Funk*, 117 Misc. 778, 779–80, 193 N.Y.S. 302, 303 (Erie Co. Ct. 1921); *State v. Barnett*, 110 Vt. 221, 231–32, 3 A.2d 521, 525 (1939); *Thompson v. State*, 557 S.W.2d 521, 524–26 (Tex. Crim. App. 1977); *People v. Mahle*, 57 Ill.2d 279, 312 N.E.2d 267 (1974).

63. *See, e.g.*, *Follette, supra* note 61; *Funk, supra* note 62.

64. *Buechler, supra* note 61.

65. *See, e.g.*, *U.S. v. Taylor*, 305 F.2d 183, 187–88 (4th Cir. 1962), *cert. denied*, 371 U.S. 894 (1962); *State v. Eilts*, 23 Wash. App. 39, 596 P.2d 1050 (1979); *Bradley v. State*, 478 S.W.2d 527, 531 (Tex. Crim. App. 1972) (Roberts, J. concurring).

66. *Karrell v. U.S.*, 181 F.2d 981, 986–87 (9th Cir.), *cert. denied*, 340 U.S. 891 (1950).

67. Harland, *Monetary Remedies*, *supra* note 1, at 82–83.

68. *People v. Mahle*, 57 Ill. 2d 279, 312 N.E.2d 267 (1974). *See also State v. Scherr*, 9 Wis.2d 418, 423, 101 N.W.2d 77, 80 (1960).

69. *People v. Becker*, 349 Mich. 476, 84 N.W.2d 833, 838 (1957).

70. *Fresneda v. State*, 347 So.2d 1021, 1022 (Fla. 1977); *People v. Knowles*, 92 Ill. App.3d 537 (1980).

71. *See, e.g., Garski v. State*, 75 Wis.2d 62, 69–74, 248 N.W.2d 425, 430–31 (1977); *People v. James*, 25 Ill. App.3d 533, 323 N.E.2d 424 (1975); *State v. Gerard*, *supra* note 31; *but see, State v. Hawkins*, 656 P.2d 1264 (Ariz. App. 1983). *See generally, People v. Gallagher*, 55 Mich. App. 613, 620, 223 N.W.2d 92 (1974), *lv. denied*, 393 Mich. 766 (1974).

72. *U.S. v. Landay*, 513 F.2d 306 (5th Cir. 1975); *see also U.S. v. Buechler*, *supra* note 61, 557 F.2d at 1008 n.10 (3d Cir. 1977).

73. *Cooper v. State*, 356 So.2d 911, 912 (Fla. Dist. Ct. App. 1978), *reversed*, 377 So.2d 1153, *vacated*, 379 So.2d 201 (1980); *State v. Scherr*, 9 Wis.2d, 418, 101 N.W.2d 77 (1960).

74. *See, e.g., People v. Miller*, 256 Cal. App.2d 348, 64 Cal. Rptr. 20 (1967); *People v. Gallagher*, 55 Mich. App. 613, 618, 223 N.W.2d 92, 95 (1974); *People v. Dawes*, 132 Ill. App.2d 435, 436, 270 N.E.2d 214, 215 (1971), *aff'd*, 52 Ill. 2d 121, 284 N.E.2d 629 (1972).

75. *People v. Miller*, *supra* note 74, 256 Cal. App.2d at 356, 64 Cal. Rptr. at 25. *But see People v. Williams*, 247 Cal. App.2d 394, 55 Cal. Rptr. 550 (1966) (striking down a restitution order to a credit card company for outstanding charges when the defendant was convicted of assault with a deadly weapon upon a store owner who refused to accept the credit card; injury to the credit card company was merely collateral and too remote to justify restitution).

76. *Dawes*, *supra* note 74; *Gallagher*, *supra* note 74; *People v. Nawrocki*, 8 Mich. App. 225, 227, 154 N.W.2d 45, 46 (1967) (restitution was ordered in connection with all forged checks even though the conviction was limited to one check).

77. *People v. Lent*, 15 Cal.3d 481, 124 Cal. Rptr. 905, 541 P.2d 545 (1975).

78. *State v. Summers*, 60 Wash.2d 702, 375 P.2d 143 (1962); *People v. Julye*, 64 A.D.2d 614, 406 N.Y.S.2d 529 (1978); *People v. Frink*, 68 N.Y.S.2d 103 (Chenango Co. Ct. 1947); *U.S. v. Shelby*, 573 F.2d 971 (7th Cir.), *cert. denied*, 439 U.S. 841 (1978); *U.S. v. Mancuso*, 444 F.2d 691, 695 (5th Cir. 1971); *Shore v. Edmisten*, 290 N.C. 628, 638, 227 S.E.2d 553, 561 (1976); *State v. Calderilla*, 34 Or. App. 1007, 1010, 580 P.2d 578, 579 (1978); *People v. Good*, 287 Mich. 110, 282 N.W. 920 (1938); *Cox v. State*, 445 S.W.2d 200, 201 (Tex. Crim. App. 1969); *State v. Benoit*, 131 Vt. 631, 313 A.2d 387 (1973).

79. *Morgan v. Wofford*, 472 F.2d 822 (5th Cir. 1973).

80. FLA. STAT. ANN. §947.181(1) (West Supp. 1983); *People v. Marin,* 147 Cal. App.2d 625, 305 P.2d 659 (1957); *People v. Tidwell,* 33 Ill. App.3d 232, 338 N.E.2d 113 (1975).

81. *See, e.g.,* ARIZ. REV. STAT. ANN. §31–254(d)(1) (Supp. 1982–83); MD. ANN. CODE art. 27, §645M(a)(3) (1982); MISS. CODE ANN. §47–7–47(1), (4) (1981); Op. Tex. Att. Gen., No. MW–472 (May 18, 1982).

82. *See Commonwealth v. Seminko,* 297 Pa. Super. 418, 420–21, 443 A.2d 1192, 1193 (1982); *State v. Yost,* 654 P.2d 458, 461 (Kan. 1982); *People v. Sattler,* 20 Mich. App. 665, 174 N.W.2d 605 (1969); *State v. Harris,* 70 N.J. 586, 599, 362 A.2d 32, 38–39 (1976); OKLA. STAT. tit. 22, §991(a)(A)(1)(a) (1981).

83. *State v. Harris, supra* note 82; *People v. Miller, supra* note 74; *People v. Tidwell,* 33 Ill. App.3d 232, 237, 338 N.E.2d 113, 117 (1975).

84. *See, e.g.,* ARIZ. REV. STAT. ANN. §13–806(A) (West. Supp. 1982–8); FLA. STAT. ANN. §775.089(7) (West Supp. 1983); IND. CODE ANN. §35–83–2–2 (Burns Supp. 1983); IOWA CODE ANN. §907.12(4) (West 1979); N.M. STAT. ANN. §31–17–1(C) (1981); S.D. CODIFIED LAWS ANN. §23A–28–7 (1979); TEX. CODE CRIM. PROC. ANN. art. 42.03, §5(b) (West Supp. 1982); VA. CODE §19.2–305.1(c) (1983).

85. *See, e.g.,* CAL. PENAL CODE §1202.5(a)(2) (1982); COLO. REV. STAT. §16–11–212(2) (Supp. 1981); MASS. ANN. LAWS ch. 276, §92 (1980).

86. *See, e.g.,* OKLA. STAT. tit. 22 §991(a)(D) (West Supp. 1982–83); ARK. STAT. ANN. §46–117(c) (Supp. 1983); VT. STAT. ANN. tit. 13, 2578(c) (Supp. 1983).

87. Harland, *Monetary Remedies, supra* note 1, at 76, n.12 [quoting Chesney, Hudson, and McGlagen, "A New Look at Restitution: Recent Legislation, Programs and Research," 61 *Judicature* 348, 354 (1978)].

88. R. Meiners, *Victim Compensation,* Appendix A (Lexington Books, 1978).

89. 18 U.S.C. §4121–28. See also 18 U.S.C. §1761 and Justice Assistance Act of 1984 H.J. Res. 648, 98th Cong., 2d Sess., §501(a)(11) (October 4, 1984).

90. J. Hudson, B. Galloway, and S. Chesney, "When Criminals Repay Their Victims: A Survey of Restitution Programs," 60 *Judicature* 313 (February 1977) [hereafter "Hudson, *When Criminals Repay"*].

91. Harland, *Monetary Remedies, supra* note 1, at 77, n.155.

92. Harland, "A Survey of Restitution Programs," in Hudson, Galloway, and Novack, *National Assessment of Adult Restitution Programs: A Final Report,* Appendix A (Duluth, Minn.: U. of Minn. School of Social Development, 1980) [hereafter "Harland, *Survey of Programs"*].

93. *Id.*

94. Hudson, *When Criminals Repay, supra* note 90.

95. B. Reade, "How Restitution Works in Georgia," 60 *Judicature* 323 (1977) [hereafter "Reade, How Restitution Works"].

96. *See* Hudson, *When Criminals Repay, supra* note 90, at 320.

 97. B. Galaway et al., "Victims and Delinquents in the Tulsa Juvenile Court," *Federal Probation*, pp. 45–46.

 98. Reade, "How Restitution Works," *supra* note 95, at 327.

 99. ABA, *Dispute Resolution Programs: 1983 Directory*, p. 71.

100. Harland, "Goal Conflicts and Criminal Justice Innovation: A Case Study," *The Justice System Journal* 291 (1980).

101. N.M. Stat. Ann. §31–17–1(E) (1981); S.D. Codified Laws Ann. §23A–28–6 (1979).

102. *See* Iowa Code Ann. §907.12(7) (West 1979); Okla. Stat. tit. 22, §991(b) (1981); Fla. Stat. Ann. §§775.089 (5)(a)-(c), 775.089(3), 945.091(5)(b) (West Supp. 1983); Me. Rev. Stat. Ann. tit. 17-A §1328(1) (1982); Wash. Rev. Code. Ann. §7.68.120(3) (Supp. 1982).

103. *State v. Hudson*, 35 N.C. App. 378, 389, 241 S.E.2d 388, 389–90 (1978); N.J. Stat. Ann. §2C:46–1 (1982). *But see Campbell v. State*, 420 S.W.2d 715, 716–17 (Tex. Crim. App. 1967) (holding that the offender was not in default of a restitution order because the total amount could be paid "on or before" a specified date; nonpayment prior to that final date was not cause for revocation).

104. *See, e.g.*, N.M. Stat. Ann. §31–17(1)(f) (1981).

105. *Compare State v. Barnett*, 110 Vt. 221, 225, 3 A.2d 521, 522 (1939); Harland, *Criminal Restitution: The Views of Practitioners* (1981) (on file at the Criminal Justice Research Center, Albany).

106. *See, e.g.*, Ariz. Rev. Stat. Ann. §13–806(A) (West Supp. 1982–83); Miss. Code Ann. §99–37–7(1) (Supp. 1982); N.J. Stat. Ann. §2C:46–2(a) (1982); Okla. Stat. tit. 22, §991(b) (1981); Or. Rev. Stat. §161.685(1) (1981).

107. *See, e.g.*, N.J. Stat. Ann. §2C:46–2(a) (1982).

108. For example, the Victim Services Agency in New York City operates a very successful restitution program in connection with the Bronx and Brooklyn criminal courts. *See* R. Davis et al., "Administering Restitution Payments in Brooklyn and Bronx Criminal Courts: A Report on the Activities of the Victim Services Agency" (New York, 1980).

109. *U.S. v. Landy*, 53 F.2d 306, 307 (5th Cir. 1975) (emphasizing that the initiative for revocation proceeding came from the pressure that the victim exerted on the prosecutor).

110. *See, e.g.*, S.D. Codified Laws Ann. §23A–28–10 (1979).

111. *See, e.g.*, Md. Ann. Code art. 27, §641 (Supp. 1982); N.Y. Penal Law §60.27(2) (West Supp. 1982–83); 18 U.S.C. §3553(d).

112. Ariz. Rev. Stat. Ann. §§13–803(B), 13–901(H) (Supp. 1982–83); N.J. Stat. Ann. §2C:43–3(e) (1982); Wash. Rev. Code Ann. §9A.20.030(1) (West Supp. 1983–84).

113. *See, e.g.*, *State v. Harris*, 70 N.J. 586, 597, 362 A.2d 32, 37 (1976).

114. *See People v. Good*, 287 Mich. 110, 282 N.W. 920 (1938); *People v. Williams*, 57 Mich. App. 439, 442, 225 N.W.2d 798, 799 (1975); *People v. Heil*, 79 Mich. App. 739, 747, 262 N.W.2d 895, 899 (1977); *Commonwealth v. Walton*, 43 Pa. 588, 598 & n.15, 397 A.2d 1179, 1184 & n.15 (1979).

115. *Monetary Remedies, supra* note 1, at 94–108; Comment, "Rehabilitation of the Victims of Crime: An Overview," 21 *UCLA L. Rev.* 317, 325 n.36, 327 n.50 (1973).

116. *People v. Richards,* 17 Cal.3d 614, 620, 131 Cal. Rptr. 537, 541, 552 P.2d 97, 101, (1976); *People v. Becker,* 34 Mich. 476, 84 N.W.2d 833, 839 (1957).

117. *Compare U.S. v. Brown,* ____F.2d____(2d Cir. Sept. 7, 1984) *and U.S. v. Brown,* ____F. Supp.____ (E.D.Pa. July 10, 1984) *with U.S. v. Welden;* 568 F. Supp. 516 (N.D. Ala. 1983).

118. *State v. Sullivan,* 24 Or. App. 99, 544 P.2d 616, 619–20 (Schwab, C. J. dissenting); *State v. Barnett,* 110 Vt. 221, 235–36, 3 A.2d 521, 527 (1939) (Sherburne, J. dissenting).

119. Harland, *Monetary Remedies, supra* note 1, at 105–6.

120. KY. REV. STAT. ANN. §431.200 (Bobbs-Merrill Supp. 1982); MO. ANN. STAT. §§546.630, 640 (Vernon 1953); TENN. CODE ANN. §§40–20–116(a) and (b) (1982).

121. ME. REV. STAT. tit. 17–A §1325(1)(A) (pamphlet 1982). *Cf. Barnett, supra* note 105, 110 Vt. at 235–36, 3 A.2d at 527 (Sherburne, J. dissenting).

122. *See, e.g., State v. Bush,* 34 Wn. App. 121, 659 P.2d 1127 (1983) *(en banc); People v. Peterson,* 62 Mich. App. 258, 267–68, 233 N.W.2d 250, 255–56 (1975).

123. *See, e.g.,* N.M. STAT. ANN. §31–17–1(c) (1978); KY. REV. STAT. ANN. §431.200 (Bobbs-Merrill Supp. 1982) (90 days).

124. *See, e.g.,* Ariz. R. Crim. P. 31.6 (1956); F.R.CR. P. 38(e).

125. ME. REV. STAT. ANN. tit. 17–A, §1328(2) (1982).

126. *See, e.g.,* MISS. CODE ANN. §99–37–7(2) (Supp. 1982); OREG. REV. STAT. §161.685(2) (1981); IND. CODE ANN. §35–7–2–2(e) (Burns Supp. 1983). *See also* Harland, *Monetary Remedies supra* note 1, at 112 n.341.

127. *See, e.g., Cox v. State,* 445 S.W.2d 200, 202 (Tex. Crim. App. 1969) (Onion, J. concurring).

128. *State v. Blevins,* 54 N.C. App. 147 (1981); *Coles v. State,* 290 Md. 296, 429 A.2d 1029 (1981).

129. *State v. Yost,* 654 P.2d 458, 461 (Kan. 1982); *Maurier v. State,* 112 Ga. App. 297, 298, 144 S.E.2d 918, 919 (1965).

130. *Gerard, supra* note 31; *People v. Lemon,* 80 Mich. App. 737, 265 N.W.2d 31 (1978); *Gallagher, supra* note 74; *State v. Garner,* 115 Ariz. 579, 581, 566 P.2d 1055, 1057 (Ct. App. 1977).

131. *Bearden v. Georgia,* 103 S.Ct. 2064 (1983).

132. *Welden, supra* note 117.

133. *See, e.g.,* MD. ANN. CODE art. 27, §641(2)(b) (1982); CAL. PENAL CODE §120.2.5(a)(2)(b) (West 1982).

134. *See, e.g.,* ARIZ. REV. STAT. ANN. §13–806(C) (1978) (not more than 1 day per $10 or 30 days for a misdemeanor and 6 months for a felony); N.J. STAT. ANN. §2C:46–2(a) (West Pamphlet 1982) (not more than 1 day per $20 owed or 1 year).

135. *See, e.g.,* 18 U.S.C. §3565.

136. *See, e.g.*, OKLA. STAT. tit. 22 §991(b) (1981); ARIZ. REV. STAT. ANN. §13–806(D) (West Supp. 1982–83); IOWA CODE ANN. §907.12(4) (7) (West 1979); N.M. STAT. ANN. §31–17–1 (G) (1981); TEX. CRIM. PROC. ANN. art. 42.12, §8(c), art. 42.13, §6(c) (Vernon Supp. 1982).

137. *See, e.g.*, *People v. Baumgarten*, 13 Ill. App.3d 189, 192, 300 N.E.2d 561, 563 (1973) (temporarily suspending payments where there was a record of past payments and little likelihood that the defendent would commit another offense); *State v. Buelna*, 25 Ariz. App. 414, 417, 544 P.2d 238, 241 (1976).

138. *See, e.g.*, *U.S. v. Squillante*, 235 F.2d 46 (2d Cir. 1956); *People v. Holzapple*, 9 Ill.2d 22, 24, 136 N.E.2d 793, 794 (1956); *People v. Marks*, 340 Mich. 495, 498, 501, 65 N.W.2d 698, 700, 702 (1954); *U.S. v. Follette*, 32 F. Supp. 953 (E.D. Pa. 1940).

139. *See, e.g.*, IOWA CODE ANN. §907.12(8) (West 1979); S.D. CODIFIED LAWS ANN. §23A–28–8 (1979).

140. *See, e.g.*, ARIZ. REV. STAT. ANN. §13–902 (B) (1978) (3-year extension for felonies, 1 year for misdemeanors); ILL. ANN. STAT. ch. 38, §1005–5–6(d) (Smith-Hurd Supp. 1982–83) (2-year extension); N.Y. PENAL LAW §65.05(3) (Consol. 1977) (2-year extension).

141. 18 U.S.C. §3651.

142. *People v. Blackorby*, 41 Colo. App. 251, 253, 583 P.2d 949, 951 (1978). *Compare Huggett v. State*, 83 Wis.2d 790, 266 N.W.2d 403, (1978).

143. *See* Harland, "Court-Ordered Community Service in Criminal Law: A Continuing Tyranny of Benevolence," 29 *Buff. L. Rev.* 425 (1980). A number of states provide that the court may order a defendant, as a term of probation or suspended sentence, to per-form community services as an alternative to fines or restitution. *See, e.g.*, KAN. STAT. ANN. §21–4610(3) (1981).

144. Harland, *Monetary Remedies, supra* note 1, at 118.

145. TEX. CODE CRIM. PROC. ANN. art. 42.03, §5(b) (Vernon Supp. 1982).

146. *See, e.g.*, KY. REV. STAT. ANN. §431.200 (Supp. 1982); MO. ANN. STAT. §546.630, 640 (Vernon 1953). Harland, *Monetary Remedies, Supra* note 1, at n.363.

147. *See, e.g.*, ARIZ. REV. STAT. ANN. §13–806(E) (Supp. 1982).

148. *See, e.g.*, *People v. Thigpen*, 60 A.D.2d 860, 400 N.Y.S.2d 584 (1978).

149. DEL. CODE ANN. tit. 11, §4104(e–g) (Supp. 1982); *Panzavecchia v. Crockett*, 379 So.2d 1047 (Fla. App. 1980); HAWAII REV. STAT.; GA. CODE ANN. §17–14–13(c)(1982).

150. *U.S. v. Landay*, 513 F.2d 306 (5th Cir. 1975).

151. For a discussion of the methods for enforcing a civil judgment obtained by the victim, see chap. V.

152. N.Y.C.P.L.R. §211(b).

153. *See e.g.*, DEL. CODE ANN. tit. 11, §4105(e) (Supp. 1982); NEB. REV. STAT. §28–506 (1979).

154. 18 U.S.C. §3663(h).

155. *Compare U.S. v. Welden, supra* note 117 *with Canon v. State* 246 Ga. 754, 272 S.E.2d 709 (1980); *U.S. v. Brown,* ____F.2d____ (2d Cir. Sept. 7, 1984) *and U.S. v. Brown,* ____F. Supp.____ (E.D.Pa. July 10, 1984).

156. Hudson, *When Criminals Repay, supra* note 1, at 316–17 (subtitled, *How One Judge Uses Alternative Sentencing* by Francis McCarty).

157. N.Y. Crime Victims Board, *Restitution: State of the Art Survey,* pp. 36–37 (1981).

158. *U.S. v. Clovis Retail Liquor Dealers Trade Assn.,* 540 F.2d 1389, 1390 (10th Cir. 1976). *See also People v. Mandel,* 50 A.D.2d 907, 377 N.Y.S.2d 563, 564 (App. Div. 1975).

159. *See* note 144 *supra;* Harland, *Survey of Programs, supra* note 92.

160. 18 U.S.C. §336(b)(4).

161. *Commissioner of Motor Vehicles v. Lee, supra* note 59; *Thibedeau v. State,* 617 P.2d 759 (Alas. 1980).

162. *See, e.g.,* MD. ANN. CODE art. 26A §17 (Supp. 1982).

163. ARIZ. REV. STAT. ANN. §13–803(A) (Supp. 1982).

164. *See, e.g.,* CAL. GOVT. CODE §13967 (Supp. 1983); 9 OP. ATT. GEN. (Tenn.) 151, No. 91 (Nov. 13, 1977).

165. *See, e.g.,* 18 U.S.C. §3572; HAWAII REV. STAT. §704–641(3)(b) (1976); ILL. ANN. STAT. ch. 38 §1005–9–1(d)(2) (Supp. 1982). §3573(a)(2). *See also,* 18 U.S.C.

166. *See, e.g.,* KY. REV. STAT. §208.240 (Supp. 1982); *State v. Bush, supra* note 122; *In re D.G.W.,* 70 N.J. 488, 361 A.2d 513, 522 n.4 (1976).

167. 18 U.S.C. §§5005–5026. *U.S. v. Buechler,* 557 F.2d 1002, 1005–7 (3d Cir. 1977); *U.S. v. Hix,* 545 F.2d 1247, 1248 (9th Cir. 1976); *U.S. v. Durst,* 549 F.2d 799 (4th Cir. 1976) *aff'd Durst v. U.S.,* 434 U.S. 542 (1978). Similar reasoning has been used to justify the imposition of fines as a condition of probation for juvenile offenders under 18 U.S.C. §5010(a). *See, e.g., U.S. v. Oliver,* 546 F.2d 1096 (4th Cir. 1976).

168. *Charles S. v. Superior Court,* 187 Cal. Rptr. 144 (Sup. Ct. 1982); KY. REV. STAT. ANN. §208.235 (Bobbs-Merrill Supp. 1982).

169. *In re Arnold M.,* No. 96, September Term, 1983 (Md. App. February 8, 1984).

V

The Right to Bring Civil Actions for Damages Against the Criminal and Third Parties

Can a crime victim obtain a judgment from a civil court for damages caused by the crime?

Yes. In addition to awards from state compensation boards and restitution ordered by the criminal court, victims are entitled to bring actions in civil court seeking damages caused by the crime. Depending on the crime and the circumstances, the victim may be entitled to claim damages from the person who committed the crime; accessories and other persons who aided, abetted, or conspired with the criminal; and third parties who did not intentionally participate in the crime but whose negligence allowed the crime to occur. A victim may be entitled to assert one or more of a group of potential legal claims (or as they are sometimes called, causes of action) including such long-established common-law claims as battery, trespass, negligence, or breach of contract, as well as private claims for damages caused by a violation of a criminal statute.[1]

Can the victim initiate a suit for damages in civil court?

Yes. Unlike criminal proceedings, where the state initiates virtually all prosecutions, any party—including an injured victim—who can assert a claim recognized by the law for damages or other relief can commence a civil lawsuit.[2]

In which court should the victim bring his civil suit for damages?

The authors acknowledge their debt to the following articles on the recovery of damages by crime victims from third parties: F. Carrington, *Memorandum of Law: Third Party Litigation on Behalf of Crime Victims* (Virginia Beach, Va.: Crime Victims Legal Advocacy Institute, 1980), and D. Deacon, *Liability of Third Parties for the Criminal Acts of Others* (1982).

It depends on the jurisdiction and the circumstances. If the amount the victim is seeking in damages is minimal, the victim can take advantage of the simplified and expedited procedures available in small claims courts that consider civil actions for damages below a certain amount ($1,000 in many jurisdictions).[3] If the victim is asserting claims under a federal statute, has been injured as a result of a federal crime (often a crime involving or affecting interstate travel or commerce), or if the victim resides in a different state from all the defendants and his claims are in excess of $10,000, the victim may wish to assert his claims in the federal court where he resides, the defendant resides or where the crime occurred; whether he chooses to bring the action in federal court may well depend on the relative activity of the federal court's docket as compared to the local state court and whether the federal procedures are relatively advantageous.[4]

In most other cases, the victim's action would be brought in the state court that handles civil cases without regard to the amount in controversy for the state in which he or the defendants reside or where the crime occurred.

Does the victim need a lawyer to commence a civil action for damages?

It depends on the circumstances. Technically, a victim can bring an action *pro se* ("representing himself"), but the advisability of bringing an action without an attorney depends on the victim's claim; for example, the victim of minor property damage caused by vandalism could bring an action in many jurisdictions in a special court (often a small claims court) with simplified procedures specifically intended to allow persons to bring damage actions without a lawyer. Many cities have prepared materials describing the procedures for bringing small claims actions and the court clerks are often available to assist parties in pursuing such actions. Where the victim is seeking a large amount in damages (especially against a third-party defendant, such as a large corporation or governmental entity that is represented by skilled legal counsel) or has asserted a claim that raises complex or novel questions about a victim's right to damages, a lawyer is advisable in order to guide the victim through the complex procedures of a full-scale civil litigation, including trial and potential appeals.

Can a victim obtain free legal assistance in pursuing an action for damages?

No. Unlike criminals who are provided with free legal counsel to act as their defense lawyers in criminal prosecutions and often are provided with counsel, if they are unable to afford it, to assist them in defending against civil suits (including suits by victims) victims themselves are not ordinarily provided with free legal assistance. In fact, while the New York Legal Aid Society provides free legal assistance in a variety of circumstances to indigent parties seeking to bring civil lawsuits, as a practical matter, in almost all cases, it will not provide such assistance to indigent victims. First, the society perceives these suits as "fee-generating" (and not entitled to free representation); and second, since Legal Aid represents over eighty percent of the criminal defendants prosecuted in New York City, representing the victims would in most cases constitute an unethical conflict of interest with Legal Aid's role in defending criminals in criminal prosecutions and in civil lawsuits.

If the victim wishes the assistance of an attorney, he will have to engage one and enter into an agreement for the attorney's compensation. Attorneys involved in civil litigation often charge for their legal services on an hourly basis (sometimes in excess of two hundred dollars per hour for complex commercial litigation), but many attorneys will take on what they feel is a meritorious civil suit for damages in return for a contingency fee; that is, a promise that the victim will turn over a portion of any award of damages (often a third of the amount awarded to the victim) if the victim recovers. In certain rare cases, the court might also order the defendant to pay a victorious victim's attorney's fees. For other suggestions concerning representation of victims by attorneys, see Appendix C.

A. Suits Against Persons Who Commit the Crime

Why must the victim bring his own suit against the person who committed the crime for damages if the prosecutor has initiated criminal proceedings to redress the same crime?

There is really no explanation for this. When parties originally brought damage actions centuries ago in the king's court, a single action for "trespass" provided recovery for the victim as well as a fine or other punishment for the defendant for violating the "king's peace."[5] Until the early nineteenth century, victims privately paid for arrests and criminal prosecutions, and convictions typically allowed for repayment to the victim of his losses in money or services. At the beginning of the nineteenth century, there was even a common law doctrine called merger of felony that prohibited a victim from bringing a civil suit for damages where the conduct producing the injury could be criminally prosecuted as a felony.[6]

However, by the middle of the nineteenth century, criminal prosecutions were no longer commonly pursued privately, convicted defendants were sentenced to prison instead of performing service to victims and it became popular to think of criminal prosecutions as redressing a "public wrong" or a "wrong to society"; victims were left, when they could, to pursue damage actions in civil court to remedy the "private wrong" that they individually suffered as a result of the crime. By contrast, in France, a system has developed that allows victims to become "civil parties" to a criminal prosecution; after the court finds a defendant guilty of violating the criminal law, the victim's attorney is entitled to present evidence of damages suffered by the victim and to obtain a damage judgment against the defendant as part of the same proceeding.[7]

Are civil suits by victims against criminals common?

No. One study of Canadian victims indicated that only 1.8 percent recovered damages from the person who committed the crime.[8] However, there have been a number of recent well-publicized incidents where crime victims and their families sought substantial damages from their assailants including the following: (1) Two victims allegedly raped by the son of an official with the Ghana Mission to the United States (who was not criminally prosecuted because of diplomatic immunity) obtained judgments of $800,000 and $900,000 for physical and emotional injuries caused by the rapes. (2) A Maryland woman in 1976 received an award of $40,000 in compensatory damages and $325,000 in punitive damages against two men who had earlier pleaded guilty to rape and attempted rape charges. (3) The parents of a University of Virginia coed, stabbed to death in 1972, received a jury verdict of $15,746 against the alleged killer. (4) The families of three prison guards killed at San Quentin in 1971 during a prisoner's escape were awarded

$2.1 million against the convicts allegedly participating in the escape(s). One victim of attempted murder who suffered multiple stab wounds was awarded $8 million in 1982 by a Denver jury.[9] Numerous other suits have been filed against persons alleged to be guilty of criminal conduct in jurisdictions across the country.

Many of these suits are settled by agreements that obligate the criminal to pay a certain amount in damages to the victim or his family. In one case, for example, a suit brought by a 15-year-old rape victim was settled for $25,000; in another case, a convicted murderer agreed to pay the parents of his victim $100,000 in return for their agreement not to oppose his application for parole. While many of these agreements may be difficult to enforce, in some of these suits (including a case in Seattle in 1982, where a woman received $30,000 in the settlement of a case she brought against her father for alleged sexual abuse when she was a child and another Washington case where the victim received $15,000 from an alleged assailant in 1974), victims have actually received substantial payments from the persons they believe to have victimized them.[10]

However, in many cases, money damages are not the sole objective; as one rape victim made clear, her intent was not to collect money, but to have the opportunity, as part of her suit against her assailant, to express in civil court the outrage that she felt and to actually do "something about rape."[11] Such well-publicized suits (particularly where the victim actually obtains damages from the criminal) have encouraged other victims to pursue civil actions against criminals despite the obvious drawbacks.

What are the most significant obstacles to bringing a civil suit against the person who committed the crime?

There are a number of potentially significant problems facing any victim considering a civil suit against a criminal. First, ordinarily civil courts will only consider a suit and award a judgment of damages against a specific known defendant. Thus, if the victim does not know the identity of the perpetrator of the crime, he cannot commence a civil suit. Second, even if his identity is known, the criminal may be "judgment proof"; that is, he may have insufficient assets to satisfy any judgment for damages. Considering the time and expense involved in hiring an attorney and pursuing a civil case against an indigent defendant, a civil suit may well be financially impractical. Third, civil actions (which typically take years before they come to trial) will probably require the victim to "relive" the crime over and over again before and during the trial; typically, the victim will have to expose himself to questioning about the most intimate details of his own involvement in, and reaction to, the crime and will be required to maintain contact with the criminal (and preoccupation with the crime) for months and perhaps even years, after the conclusion of the criminal trial.

Nevertheless, a growing number of victims—motivated by a desire to see that "justice is done" and to make up for the powerlessness that they legitimately feel as a result of their victimization first by the criminal and then by the criminal justice system—have found compelling personal, moral, emotional, and psychological reasons for pursuing such civil actions. Victims are increasingly bringing such suits even where it is obvious that the criminal does not have the resources to satisfy a substantial judgment of damages. Such civil suits are now regularly being recommended by police or prosecutors if there are substantial reasons for not bringing a criminal prosecution and many commentators have argued that they represent a reasonable and practical means for allowing victims to express a deeply felt moral indignation.[12]

Are there advantages for a victim to bringing a civil action for damages as compared to seeking an award from a state compensation board or restitution?

Yes and no. A civil suit ordinarily takes years to come to trial, is impossible if the victim does not know the identity of the person or persons responsible for the crime (or whose negligence produced the crime), is impractical unless the defendant has enough assets to pay a civil judgment and may well require the expensive services of an attorney. By contrast, a victim can typically obtain a compensation award or an order requiring restitution without hiring an attorney within a few months of filing a claim or the commencement of a criminal prosecution; in the case of victims' compensation, the victim can receive money even if the identity of the criminal is unknown or if the criminal is indigent.

However, a civil judgment for damages has a number of significant advantages over the other methods for redressing the victim's injuries. In a civil action, a victim can seek damages for the full amount of her injuries or losses directly or indirectly due to the crime, including property damages and pain and suffering and can often obtain an additional award for punitive damages. By contrast, compensation awards are limited to a certain maximum amount, and virtually all states exclude compensation for pain and suffering and property damage; the amount of restitution is typically limited to what the defendant (given his financial capabilities) can actually pay without hardship. Victims who may be ineligible to obtain compensation awards (for example, because they are related to the criminal or because they are not financially needy) can obtain a civil judgment for damages. Victims who are ineligible to obtain restitution because they were indirectly injured by the crime or were victims of crimes for which the defendant was not charged or convicted can seek full recovery in a civil action. Civil actions have other advantages over restitution: a victim herself can initiate a civil action (and is not dependent on the prosecutor to bring a prosecution to obtain restitution); a victim can receive damages from third parties who assisted in the commission of the crime or whose negligence was responsible for its occurrence even if they were not charged in the criminal case; and unlike restitution that is limited to the period of sentencing or probation of the criminal, a civil judgment is usually enforceable for a long period of time and is not limited to enforcement by revocation of probation or parole.

Is a criminal prosecution or conviction of the defendant necessary before a victim can bring a civil suit?

No. In a criminal action, the prosecutor seeks to prove beyond a reasonable doubt that the defendant broke a specific criminal law; the only issue in the victim's civil case is whether the victim has shown by a preponderance of the evidence that the defendant caused the victim's injury and is legally responsible to pay damages. The two kinds of actions have different parties and are tried separately. The victim can claim damages in a civil action against someone the victim believes injured her regardless of whether a prosecutor has brought criminal charges or whether the defendant has been convicted of a crime.[13]

Can the victim sue a person acquitted in a criminal prosecution for damages caused by the same conduct that was at issue in the criminal case?

Yes. Unlike the Fifth Amendment prohibition against double jeopardy that prevents a defendant acquitted in a criminal proceeding from being tried again for the same conduct, acquittal in a criminal case does not bar a subsequent civil action involving the same defendant's conduct.[14]

Can the victim bring a civil damage action even if she has obtained a compensation award or restitution?

Yes. The right to bring a civil action for damages is not affected by whether a victim has received a compensation award; typically, state compensation statutes provide that evidence concerning compensation proceedings is not admissible in civil actions.[15] However, if the victim has received an award, the state may exercise its subrogation rights to become a party to the civil action and/or claim from the victim's recovery any amount already paid to the victim by the state in compensation for her injury.[16]

While the existence of a restitution order does not in itself prevent a civil action for damages, any amounts recovered by the victim under a restitution order must be deducted from any damages awarded to the victim in the civil action.[17]

Does the defendant have the right to insist that the trial of the victim's civil claim be delayed until after a pending criminal prosecution has concluded?

No. Courts have long allowed victims to bring civil damage actions while the criminal prosecution based on the same facts is still pending.[18] Courts in Delaware and New Jersey have specifically rejected the argument that failure to stay the victim's civil case pending the outcome of the criminal trial would violate the defendant's Fifth Amendment privilege against self-incrimination by forcing him to participate in discovery in the civil case that might incriminate him in the criminal proceedings.[19]

How long after the victimization can the victim wait before commencing a civil action against the person who committed the crime?

It depends on the civil claims being asserted and the jurisdiction. Every jurisdiction has "statutes of limitations" that limit the amount of time that can pass between an act creating an injury and the commencement of a civil action for damages; if the injured party attempts to commence an action after the time period prescribed by the appropriate statute of limitations, a court will dismiss the civil action. The exact amount of time varies from jurisdiction to jurisdiction and from claim to claim. In general, however, suits claiming damages caused by such intentional acts as assault, battery, and false imprisonment must be brought within a relatively short time after the commission of the tort; New York and California, for example, require that such actions be brought within one year of the commission of the acts that give rise to the civil claim.[20]

For many forms of street or residential crime, the identity of the criminal is not discovered until long after the crime has been committed. If the defendant is in hiding or has fled the jurisdiction, the statute of limitations may be tolled.[21] But short limitation periods often present a real obstacle to civil suits by crime victims. In many cases, victims prefer to wait until after a criminal investigation or prosecution has been concluded (and the defendant's guilt has been adjudged in a criminal context) before bringing a costly civil suit; since criminal prosecutions often conclude more than a year after the crime, a victim who waits for the criminal case to conclude to bring a civil action may well be barred by the statute of limitations. The inequity of this situation led the New York legislature in 1983, to amend its statutes of limitations for intentional torts (one year) and for wrongful death actions (two years) to explicitly provide that where a criminal action has been commenced in connection with the event or occurrence which formed the basis of a civil claim, the victim has one year from the termination of the criminal action in which to commence his civil action for damages, regardless of when the initial crime occurred.[22]

What is the procedure for bringing an action and obtaining a civil judgment of damages against the person who committed the crime?

It varies from jurisdiction to jurisdiction. However, there are a number of typical steps involved in bringing an action and obtaining a judgment.[23] As the party seeking the judgment (the "plaintiff"), the victim can initiate a civil action by preparing a brief statement of the legal claim for which he is seeking a remedy, the nature of the judgment he is seeking from the court (including, if known, the amount of damages), and a brief statement of the relevant facts; this legal document is called a complaint. The victim then must arrange for the service of the complaint on the perpetrator of the crime and any others from whom he is seeking damages (the "defendants"), usually by physically giving them a copy of the complaint along with a notice (a "summons") requiring them to respond to the allegations contained in the complaint within a certain short period of time (usually three weeks). Along with proof that the complaint has been served on the defendants, it is filed with the court; within a short time thereafter, the defendant submits an answer admitting or denying the allegations of the complaint and posing any defenses or counterclaims that the defendant might have.

In order to allow both the plaintiff and the defendant to prepare for trial, parties to civil actions are entitled to obtain answers to written questions ("interrogatories"), copies of relevant documents, physical examinations of the plaintiff (when he requests damages for physical injury) and even to question individual parties under oath. During the course of this process (called discovery), both the victim and the defendant are also permitted to obtain sworn testimony and other relevant evidence from third parties (including witnesses to the crime and the police) who may have information potentially relevant to the victim's civil claims. Such discovery is liberally allowed by the courts if the information sought has any relevance to the claims in the case and may take months, and often years, to complete.

Before, during, and after discovery, lawyers for one or both sides may make a variety of different kinds of motions for court orders permitting certain kinds of discovery, limiting discovery, dismissing plaintiff's claims (claims are only dismissed where the plaintiff would not be allowed to recover even if all the facts he alleged are assumed to be true) and for summary judgment deciding some or all of the legal issues in favor of a particular party (which is only awarded where the parties agree on the facts or where there is no genuine issue of fact to be decided at trial). Extensive use of discovery before trial, motions, and frequent adjournments make civil litigation extremely time-consuming; it frequently takes more than a year for cases to reach the trial stage.

After pretrial discovery and motions are concluded, the court places the victim's case on its trial calendar; trial calendars are so congested that in New York City, a case ready for trial in the New York County Supreme Court in 1984 would not actually be tried for fifteen months. In fact (as with criminal prosecutions), most civil cases do not go to trial; they are settled by a compromise agreement between the parties. If the case does go to trial, however, in civil cases involving amounts in excess of $20, the defendant has the right under the Seventh Amendment of the Constitution to a trial by jury. Although traditionally such cases were heard by 12 jurors, in many jurisdictions such cases are now heard by 6 jurors, and (with the agreement of both parties) a case may be heard by a judge sitting without a jury.

After opening arguments by attorneys representing the plaintiff and the defendant, the plaintiff will present his case; typically this includes the testimony of the victim and of witnesses, submission of evidence concerning the victim's damages and, where necessary, expert testimony on the defendant's liability or the damage suffered by the plaintiff. After the defendant presents his case, both sides present any rebuttal witnesses. Witnesses called by either side are subject to (sometimes extensive) cross-examination and documents may be challenged for relevance, reliability, or authenticity. After testimony is concluded and after summations by the attorneys, the jury is instructed on the law by the judge and retires to come to its verdict.

Unlike a successful criminal prosecution (which requires the prosecutor to prove the defendant guilty beyond a reasonable doubt), in order to recover a civil judgment against the defendant, a victim need only prove his claims against the defendant by a preponderance of the evidence; a preponderance of the evidence means proof that leads the jury (in many jurisdictions, simply a majority of the jury) to decide that the existence of the contested fact is more probable than its nonexistence.[24] After the jury's verdict, the judge will consider motions by both sides, which typically include motions by the losing party for a new trial (due to errors in prior rulings by the court) or for a judgment by the court in favor of the losing party notwithstanding the jury's verdict.

Either of the parties has the right to appeal the court's final judgment to an appellate court that has the power to overturn the trial court's judgment if, and only if, the trial court has made an error of law, or the jury's verdict is contrary to the evidence.

B. Types of Claims Against Persons Who Committed the Crime

What sort of common law claims can be made by victims to recover damages from the person who committed the crime?

It depends on the jurisdiction and the nature of the crime. The common law has long recognized the right of injured persons to bring civil actions to redress torts, civil wrongs (other than breach of contract) for which the court will provide a remedy in the form of damages. Although traditionally one tort— "trespass"—was the basis for all such actions for damages, any one of a number of torts currently recognized by the law may be the basis for a crime victim's damage action.

Generally speaking, a victim's complaint can include any of a group of so-called intentional torts that permit the court to award damages because the criminal intentionally disturbed or invaded the interests of the victim. In most jurisdictions, these include—

1. *battery* (intentional harmful or offensive "touching"; that is, painful, injurious, or undignified contact);

2. *assault* (intentional acts threatening the victim sufficient to cause fear of immediate harmful or offensive "touching");

3. *false imprisonment* (intentional confinement of the victim through physical force, threats, or barriers to a specific limited area);

4. *infliction of emotional distress* (extreme and outrageous conduct intended to cause severe emotional distress in the victim or his family);

5. *trespass to land* (intentional invasion of property in the possession of a victim);

6. *trespass* or *conversion of chattel* (intentional invasion of a victim's right to personal property, including interfering with its use, theft, or other dispossession, destruction, refusing to give up property wrongfully taken, or buying, receiving, selling, or disposing of stolen property).

Depending on the specific circumstances, victims of the same kind of crime could assert different kinds of civil claims.

A train passenger, for example, subjected to attempted intercourse by a railroad employee could maintain an action for assault, while a victim of a sexual advance who is constrained in her movement but not actually touched could bring an action for false imprisonment.[25] For that matter, a single crime could allow a victim to file a complaint containing a number of these claims. In a residential burglary, for example, where the criminal destroyed and/or stole the victim's property and physically detained and then attacked the victim, the victim might be entitled to assert claims based on all of these intentional torts.

If the victim himself has failed to take reasonable precaution for his own protection or is otherwise negligent in preventing his victimization, can he still recover damages from the person who committed the crime?

Yes. The victim's contributory negligence is no defense where his injuries were caused by the intentional criminal act of another.[26]

If two or more persons acted together to commit the crime, can the victim claim damages from each?

Yes. Where two persons act together (even by tacit understanding) to commit the crime that injures the victim, they are jointly liable to the victim for the resulting injury and they can be sued together or individually with each one liable for the full damages suffered by the victim.[27]

Can a victim assert a claim for damages against someone who does not actually participate in the crime but, before or after the crime is committed, assists the criminal?

Yes. In addition to the person who actually commits the crime, anyone who orders, directs, or permits the crime to occur or who gives the person who commits the crime assistance or encouragement is also liable for any damages suffered by the victim. This includes aiders and abettors as well as coconspirators.

Persons who "aid and abet" violations of the criminal law are themselves liable to the victim for damages if the victim can show (1) the existence of the criminal violation by the primary party; (2) knowledge of this violation on the part of the aider and abbetor; and (3) substantial assistance by the aider and abbetor in the achievement of the primary criminal violation.[28]

Although there is no separate tort of civil conspiracy, where two or more persons enter into a combination or agreement to cause damage to the victim or his property, and such damage results, all of the conspirators are liable for damages to the victim.[29] To prevail, the victim must show not only agreement but that an actual wrongful act was committed and that the victim was injured as a result. Each member of the conspiracy is equally liable for all of the damage done by all of the acts committed in pursuit of the original plan (even if each conspirator did not take an active part), and a person who joins the conspiracy at a later time may be liable for the previous acts of his coconspirators. Thus, for example, in one California case, a defendant who only assisted in disposing of some of the jewelry taken in a jewelry store robbery, was held liable for conversion of the total value of all the jewelry stolen; having conspired to help dispose of the stolen property, he was liable for the total amount taken even though he was not directly involved in the robbery itself.[30]

In addition to common law claims, are there criminal statutes that explicitly provide victims with the right to sue for damages in civil court when the statute is violated?

Yes. There are a variety of federal and state criminal statutes that explicitly create a private right to sue in civil court for damages caused by any violation of the statute. A description of all these statutes is beyond the scope of this book.

In general, private rights of action have been created where the criminal conduct prescribed by the statute is especially egregious, where it violates a strong social policy, or where there is some perceived need to encourage individuals to bring their own private damage actions as a supplemental means of enforcing the statute. The principal example of such legislation is the federal antitrust laws that make it a crime to engage in certain monopolistic practices; in order to further discourage monopolies and assist the government in its antitrust policies, persons and businesses injured by monopolistic practices in violation of the criminal statute are granted a private right to bring actions in civil court to recover three times the damages they actually suffered ("treble damages").[31] Other statutes create private rights of action with multiple damages for victims of crime under a variety of circumstances, most often where the victim sues to recover stolen property.[32]

In order to recover damages under these statutes, the

victim need only show that the defendant violated the explicit
provisions of the statutes and that this violation caused the
victim's injury; the violation of the criminal statute itself can
usually be demonstrated by introducing evidence of a criminal conviction or by other evidence that shows that it is more
probable than not that the defendant violated the criminal
statute.[33]

One such statute that has received an increasing amount of
attention in recent years and which allows certain crime
victims to recover multiple damages in appropriate cases is
the Racketeer Influenced and Corrupt Organizations Act
(RICO).

What is RICO?

In 1970, Congress enacted the Organized Crime Control
Act in response to corruption and to the financial drain on the
legitimate economy caused by organized crime. In order to
increase the effectiveness of law enforcement efforts directed
at organized crime, RICO makes it a federal crime to engage
in a variety of activities related to a "pattern of racketeering
activity" in connection with the operation of any "enterprise"
engaged in, or affecting, interstate commerce.[34] In addition
to strict criminal penalties (fines of up to $25,000 and impris-
onment for up to 20 years) the statute creates a number of
other remedies: for instance, allowing the government to
bring forfeiture proceedings, to dissolve or reorganize racketeering enterprises and to restrict future involvement in such
enterprises.[35] RICO also explicitly gives victims of racketeering the right to bring civil suits in federal court for damages
equal to three times their actual injury as well as providing
for them to recover any attorneys' fees spent on the litigation;
a number of states have enacted similar racketeering statutes
granting victims the right to sue for multiple damages.[36]

What conduct violates RICO?

RICO makes it a crime to (1) receive income (directly or
indirectly) from a pattern of racketeering activity and use or
invest that income in establishing or operating an enterprise
engaged in interstate commerce; (2) acquire or maintain an
interest or control of an enterprise through a pattern of
racketeering activity or collection of unlawful debt; (3) be
employed or associated with such an enterprise and conduct
or participate in the conduct of the enterprise's affairs through

a pattern of racketeering or collection of unlawful debt; or (4) conspire to do any of these things.[37]

When is a defendant guilty of collecting an unlawful debt or guilty of committing a pattern of racketeering activity?

Anyone who collects a debt incurred in connection with illegal gambling or loans that are usurious under state or federal law (provided the interest rate is at least twice the legal rate) is engaged in collecting an "unlawful debt."[38] Any person or organization that commits two or more crimes under the provisions of the RICO statute within a ten-year period (excluding time spent in prison) has engaged in a "pattern of racketeering activity."[39]

Among the many crimes ("predicate offenses") listed in the RICO statute are acts or threats involving murder, kidnapping, gambling, arson, robbery, bribery, extortion, and drugs that would constitute a state crime punishable by more than one year's imprisonment, as well as the following federal crimes:

1. counterfeiting;

2. embezzling;

3. receiving or transporting stolen property or property obtained by fraud interstate;

4. fraud using the United States mails or interstate telephone or telegraph communications;

5. obstruction of justice or of criminal investigations (including some intimidation of victims and witnesses);

6. bankruptcy fraud and securities fraud.[40]

The combination of this long list of predicate offenses and the broad language creating liability for involvement in a "pattern of racketeering activity" has led many critics to argue that the RICO statute is vague, that it does not give defendants sufficient notice of what is prohibited and therefore violates the defendants' rights to due process.

Is the statute restricted to individuals or enterprises associated with "organized crime"?

Probably not. The statute itself makes certain acts illegal, and never mentions "organized crime." While there is a disagreement between various courts on the issue, most courts that have faced this question have held that RICO applies to all enterprises and individuals who are guilty of the proscribed conduct whether or not there is a connection with organized crime.[41]

What constitutes an "enterprise" for RICO purposes?

The statute itself is extremely broad and states that an enterprise operated in violation of the statute could consist of an individual, a legal entity (such as a partnership or corporation), or even a group of individuals associated in fact without any legal relationship.[42] The Supreme Court has made it clear that the "enterprise" need not be a traditional business enterprise but can involve an association, the sole purpose of which is to commit certain criminal acts.[43] A number of courts have held that the commission of the crimes constituting the required "pattern of racketeering activity" can itself be considered the enterprise for RICO purposes and that no other separate criminal or other enterprise needs to exist. In one criminal case, for example, a court of appeals upheld RICO convictions involving a group of bettors and college basketball students whose "enterprise" consisted of their association during a particular basketball season to "fix" college basketball games (their "pattern of racketeering activity").[44] However, a number of other courts have required proof of the existence of a continuing enterprise apart from the specifically alleged "pattern of racketeering activity."[45]

When are victims entitled to recover damages under RICO and what sort of losses can be recovered?

Unlike some state-racketeering statutes that allow victims to recover any damages (presumably including personal injuries), RICO allows victims to bring treble damage actions only if they were injured in their business or property due to a violation of the statute's criminal provisions.[46] Thus, RICO does not generally allow victims to recover for personal injuries caused by crimes. A victim might claim that lost earnings or lost profits resulting from injury or disability due to crime are recoverable as injury to the victim's "business or property." However, at least one court has held that a victim of threats by a religious cult did not suffer a "commercial injury" and therefore was not entitled to bring an action pursuant to RICO.[47]

It is also not entirely clear which business and property

damages a victim might recover. Although the statute itself does not explicitly limit the kind of losses that can be recovered, a number of courts have narrowly interpreted this provision in order to prevent the statute from being used to recover treble damages in ordinary cases of business or securities fraud. Some courts have required that the injury suffered not result from the individual predicate criminal offenses but result, instead, from the entire pattern of racketeering activity (some courts have referred to this as the need to prove RICO injury).[48] Other courts have attempted to limit RICO's civil remedy to situations where the victim suffered a business loss due to unfair competition resulting from the defendant's racketeering activities.[49]

Is a criminal RICO conviction necessary before the victim can bring a civil action for damages?

Generally, the federal court of appeals for the Second Circuit (covering New York, Connecticut and Vermont), however, recently held that prior convictions for the predicate acts were a prerequisite to the maintenance of a civil RICO suit.[50] In other jurisdictions, if there has been no prior conviction, in order to recover damages, a victim will have to introduce evidence in the civil case proving that the defendant committed the predicate offenses for racketeering activity; the victim need not prove that the defendant is guilty beyond a reasonable doubt.[51]

Are prior criminal convictions for predicate offenses admissible in a civil action to establish the defendant's liability under RICO?

Yes. The statute itself explicitly provides that a federal RICO conviction estops the defendant from denying the essential allegation of the criminal offense in any subsequent civil action brought by the federal government.[52] However, where private victims have brought civil actions after a criminal conviction, courts in the subsequent civil action have held that such convictions are conclusive of liability, even when the prior convictions involved the predicate offenses making up the alleged "pattern of racketeering activity."[53]

When can persons associated with a racketeering enterprise be liable for damages under RICO?

Since it is a violation of the statute for anyone "employed

by, or associated with," an enterprise to conduct its activities "directly or indirectly" through a pattern of racketeering activity, technically anyone employed by any company or illegal association who is involved in the commission of two or more of the predicate offenses would be liable for damages.[54] Normally, conspirators are liable only for damage caused by the agreed on illegal objective of the conspiracy; under RICO, an individual who contributes to one form of criminal conduct could be liable for damages for injuries caused by the enterprise as a result of other crimes of which he had no knowledge.[55] Such an interpretation would be in line with the broad interpretation of the statute for criminal purposes to apply to "any person" who violates its explicit terms.[56] However, some courts have limited liability under RICO, holding that mere participation in the predicate offenses even in conjunction with a RICO enterprise is insufficient to support a civil claim for damages; to be liable, the defendant's participation ordinarily must be in the form of operation or management of the enterprise itself.[57] That the statute creates liability for those who merely participate in an uncertainly defined *enterprise* is yet another basis for the criticism that it is vague and violates defendants' Fifth-Amendment due process rights.

What are the advantages of bringing a RICO claim for damages?

Among other things, RICO (1) allows the victim to obtain treble damages and the cost of litigation (including his attorney's fees); (2) allows him to bring his action in federal court (which may have some procedural advantages or provide faster resolution of his claims); (3) may make persons associated with the enterprise liable for damages who would not otherwise be liable as conspirators; and (4) provides a means for obtaining damages for criminal acts that take place within ten years of the last act causing injury, provided the last act is within the usual statutes of limitations.

If there is no explicit private right of action, can a victim still claim damages for violation of a criminal statute based on an "implied" right of action?

It depends on the circumstances and the character of the criminal statute. There has long been a common law rule that a right for private recovery is to be recognized for every public wrong.[58] Relying on this rule, courts in virtually every jurisdiction have held that where a criminal statute is enacted for the protection of a particular class of persons, its violation may give rise to civil liability to an injured victim who is a member of that class.[59]

There is, however, wide disagreement in different jurisdictions about which kinds of statutes create private causes of action. While a number of states, for example, have allowed victims injured by cars whose drivers illegally left the keys in the ignition to recover damages from the owner of the stolen car, a number of jurisdictions (holding that the statute was only intended to prevent thefts) have refused to do so.[60] Relying on private causes of action implied from criminal statutes, a victim injured in an illegal boxing exhibition was permitted to recover damages from the promoter, and the victim of an intoxicated driver was permitted to recover from a roadhouse who sold liquor in violation of a statute making it a misdemeanor to serve alcoholic beverages to a drunkard or to an obviously intoxicated person.[61] In one such case the court held that a doctor's failure to report the injuries to a battered child, in violation of the criminal provisions of a child abuse-reporting statute, constituted negligence *per se*.[62]

The federal courts, on numerous occasions, have implied private causes of action for damages for persons injured by violations of federal statutes, regulations, and the Constitution.[63] Most frequently, such implied causes of action have been relied on by private parties who suffered losses in the purchase or sale of securities as a result of misrepresentations or omissions of material fact by securities sellers or by manipulation in violation of the federal securities laws or regulations thereunder.[64] However, the current trend in federal court is not to imply private rights of action from criminal statutes or regulations except under the following specific conditions: (1) where the victim is a member of the class for whose benefit the statute was enacted; (2) where there is indication that Congress intended to imply a private remedy or at least that it did not intend to deny one; (3) that a private damage action was consistent with the objective and scheme in enacting the statute; and (4) that it was appropriate to imply a federal remedy because the cause of action that the victim sought to enforce was not one traditionally available under state law.[65]

What must a victim prove in order to recover damages where the person guilty of the conduct that produced his injury or a third party has violated a criminal statute?

It varies widely depending on the statute and the jurisdiction. While defendants have been held strictly liable for any injury caused by conduct violating a few criminal statutes, in most cases, violations are considered "negligence per se"; that is, that the violation renders the defendant's conduct as "negligent" and that the victim can recover damages but still must show that this negligence caused his injury and that the defendant had no reasonable excuse for his conduct. In some jurisdictions, violation of the statute is only evidence of negligence that can be accepted or rejected by the jury.[66]

C. Recovery by the Victim's Estate or Family

Can a victim's family or estate recover damages if the victim's death was caused by a criminal act?

Yes. Under common law, there was no civil right of recovery for damages due to what was called wrongful death.[67] However, by statute, every state now provides for damage actions caused by "any wrongful act [or] neglect" that causes death, including intentional torts, such as crimes.[68]

The "wrongful death" statutes in most jurisdictions create a separate cause of action for the surviving relatives or heirs of the victim for injuries that they suffer as a result of the death of the victim; in such states, the victim's estate can assert its own separate claims for any losses suffered by the victim after the crime and prior to his death (such as medical expenses).[69] In some states, wrongful death statutes provide that any actions that the victim had at his death growing out of the injury survive him ("survival statutes") and that his estate may sue for the victim's injuries as well as losses (including lost future earnings) suffered by the estate as a result of the crime.[70]

What type of losses can a victim's estate or relatives recover under these wrongful death statutes?

It varies from jurisdiction to jurisdiction. In the minority of states that provide for the "survival" of claims the victim had at his death, his estate can recover such damages as medical expenses and loss of earnings from the time of the crime until death and even the loss of future economic benefits that may be calculated (depending on the jurisdiction) in terms of gross future earnings or net savings after expenses.[71]

In most jurisdictions, the surviving relatives or heirs are entitled to recover "pecuniary loss" suffered as a result of the victim's death, as well as any funeral expenses. *Pecuniary loss* is broadly defined to include loss by the relative of the victim's companionship, support, services, and contributions, including earnings (less living expenses) for the victim's remaining life expectancy, the replacement cost of homemaker's services, and even the cost of professional nursing care or counseling for family members that is required to replace the companionship that was provided by the victim.[72] In determining the amount of such losses, it is not relevant whether the spouse of the victim has remarried.[73] Nor does the age of the victim at the time of death prevent an award for pecuniary loss; courts have consistently allowed the family to recover pecuniary loss where the victim is a child (including contributions, earnings, and support that he might have provided to his family when he became an adult) as well as awards for pecuniary loss due to the death of elderly retired persons.[74]

There are, however, limits on what can be recovered under such statutes. While the victim's estate can recover for pain and suffering caused by the crime prior to death, the relatives cannot themselves bring a claim for their own pain, grief, loss of consortium (including sexual relations), or suffering.[75] While punitive damages are usually recoverable in those states that provide for the survival of the victim's own cause of action, they are not recoverable by the victim's relatives in most states.[76]

Where the victim is merely injured, can family members recover damages for losses that they may have suffered due to the victim's injuries?

It depends on the jurisdiction and the family relationship. Traditionally, common law provided for a limited recovery; husbands but not wives and parents but not children could recover for damages sustained by their relatives.[77] However, in recent years recovery by relatives for losses due to a victim's injury has been greatly liberalized.

The victim's spouse can recover damages for loss of consortium, "services" (broadly defined to include homemaking services, general usefulness, and contributions to the home) as well as actual expenses incurred in taking care of the victim.[78] Spouses of both sexes can now recover such damages.[79] However, there are some significant limitations on a spouse's ability to recover for loss of consortium; generally, it is only available where there has been a complete loss of companionship and/or intercourse for a specific period of time (as distinct from scarring or disfigurement that may only place a "strain" on the relationship) and it can only be recovered by the spouse of the victim if they were married at the time that the crime was committed.[80]

Parents of injured crime victims are also entitled to damages.[81] They can recover not only any medical expenses they incurred but also the economic value of any lost services or earnings the injured child would have provided. However, most courts have denied recovery by parents for loss of the child's society, comfort, or consortium.[82]

If the victim is a parent, in most states, the child has no right to recover damages for loss of support or parental affection, comfort, or consortium.[83]

Can members of the victim's family recover damages for emotional distress that they suffer as a result of the victimization?

As a general rule, courts have permitted family members to recover damages for emotional distress only if they were present at the scene of the crime and the defendant inflicted the emotional distress on the family member intentionally or recklessly.[84] Such recovery has been allowed, for example, where the wife of an assault victim witnessed the assault and where a child witnessed her mother's murder.[85]

California and a growing number of other states are now permitting family members present when the victim was injured to recover damages if their distress was foreseeable; that is, if the infliction of emotional distress was negligent, rather than reckless or intentional.[86] However, most states also stipulate that the negligent defendant expose the family member as well to an unreasonable risk of bodily injury or death (that the family member be in the so-called zone of danger) or that the force that injured the victim strikes the family member before they will permit a family member-observer to recover damages.[87]

Where victims have not been present at the scene of the crime, the courts have disallowed recovery for emotional distress. In one well-publicized case, for example, where the victim was bludgeoned to death in her parents' home by a former sweetheart but not discovered by her parents until after the attack, the court denied recovery, in part, because the parents were not present when the crime was committed.[88] Similarly, the parents of two young children who were sexually molested were denied recovery for emotional harm because they were not participants or even observers of the crime and any harm they suffered was not directly or intentionally inflicted.[89]

Obtaining Evidence, Securing Assets, and Proving Liability

If the crime was investigated by a grand jury prior to the victim's civil suit, can the victim obtain grand jury material during discovery in the civil case?

It depends on the jurisdiction and the circumstances. In cases brought by victims in federal court (and in jurisdictions that have adopted similar procedural rules), transcripts of testimony before a grand jury may be made available for copying and inspection upon the specific direction of the court in connection with the victim's civil case.[90] However, the United States Supreme Court has ruled that such testimony can only be made available in civil cases where the civil party seeking the transcript has a "particularized need" for obtaining that testimony.[91] This requirement can be satisfied if the victim can show that the grand jury transcript is needed to impeach a witness, refresh his recollection, test his credibility, or the like.[92] This right to inspect grand jury transcripts may be conditioned by the court on inspection taking place in the judge's chambers by the victim's attorney. Where the grand jury investigation is ongoing, the request for access to the transcripts will probably be denied.[93] Documents or exhibits presented to the grand jury are also discoverable by a victim in a civil suit but to obtain them the victim need only show that they are relevant to his claims.[94]

As part of discovery in his civil suit, can the victim obtain copies of reports prepared by the law enforcement officers investigating the crime?

It depends on the circumstances and the jurisdiction. Federal courts in numerous cases have allowed parties to obtain copies of reports of criminal investigations by the FBI and by local police departments where the reports being sought were relevant to the plaintiff's claims and the need for obtaining information contained in the reports outweighed any government interest in maintaining confidentiality.[95] In one Arizona case, for example, where the parents of a victim shot during a robbery by a person who was allegedly released from prison negligently, the court held that the family was entitled to all relevant information (including otherwise confidential reports to the parole board) which was reviewed by the board in making its decision to parole the killer.[96] Where there is a strong public policy requiring confidentiality (such as an ongoing criminal investigation or the need to protect the identity or methods of law enforcement agents), parts of the reports may be deleted or access to them may be denied altogether.[97]

If the criminal prosecution is still pending or if the defendant has not yet been charged with a crime, can he invoke his Fifth Amendment privilege against self-incrimination in civil proceedings brought by the victim?

Yes. The Fifth Amendment privilege against self-incrimination can be invoked in any action or proceeding, civil or criminal, and protects a party against any form of compulsion to testify, including any compulsion to produce incriminating documents. While this right is most commonly invoked by defendants in ongoing criminal prosecutions to prevent giving testimony or providing information that might incriminate them, it can also be invoked by the defendant in the civil suit brought by a crime victim or anyone else where the defendant has a reasonable belief that the specific information or testimony being sought might lead to a criminal indictment or conviction.[98] Where the defendant in the victim's suit has already been convicted of a crime or is otherwise immune from prosecution (for example, as a result of an immunity agreement with a prosecutor or because the statute of limitations on the crime has run), he cannot invoke his Fifth Amendment protection and can be compelled to provide testimony or relevant documents.

Even if there has been no prosecution and the defendant can invoke the Fifth Amendment or resists testifying or producing relevant documents, there are at least two important consequences for the defendant. First, a defendant cannot be held in contempt for failure to produce relevant documents or testimony if they would incriminate him.[99] Second, the constitutional privilege allows the defendant to deny the victim's claims, despite a refusal to explain that denial; thus, the privilege prevents courts from disallowing a defendant's answer denying liability even if the defendant refuses to provide evidence supporting his denial.[100]

However, there are some significant restrictions limiting the defendant's ability to invoke the Fifth Amendment in civil proceedings. First, it only protects against disclosures where there is a reasonable basis to believe that the information will actually be used in a criminal prosecution (or lead to other such evidence) and cannot be based on remote and speculative possibilities.[101] Second, if the defendant in the civil case takes the stand to testify on his own behalf, he cannot invoke the privilege against self-incrimination during cross-examination; a failure or refusal to testify or produce relevant books or papers once the privilege has been waived justifies striking the defendant's entire direct testimony (and with it, often the defendant's only factual defense).[102] Third, if the defendant legitimately and consistently invokes the privilege, he may, without explanation, deny the victim's allegations but cannot assert his own claims against the victim, assert affirmative defenses, or otherwise seek affirmative relief in court; as a result, where defendants have invoked the privilege, courts have repeatedly stricken the defendant's counterclaims and affirmative defenses.[103] While the defendant is free to invoke the privilege in a civil proceeding, doing so may well deprive him of any practical ability to put in evidence in his own defense and make summary judgment in favor of the victim virtually certain. Forcing the defendant to choose between self-incrimination and summary judgment in favor of the victim has been found not to violate the defendant's Fifth Amendment rights.[104]

If the defendant was acquitted in a criminal prosecution, can he introduce his acquittal as evidence in the victim's civil trial for damages?

No. Since the acquittal in the criminal case only represents a determination that the defendant's guilt was not established beyond a reasonable doubt, it is not admissible in a subsequent civil action to prove the defendant's general innocence or to prove any facts about his alleged conduct.[105]

If the defendant was convicted in a prior criminal prosecution, can his conviction be used as evidence in the victim's civil case?

Yes. Traditionally, a criminal conviction was not permitted

into evidence in a civil action for a number of technical reasons (including the potentially prejudicial influence that a judgment of another court might have on the jury in the civil case and the fear that the conviction of one person might be used in the civil trial against a third party).[106] However, over the past twenty-five years, there has been a growing tendency to admit a prior conviction for a serious criminal offense in a subsequent civil action and now, few, if any, courts adhere to the traditional rule.[107] The Federal Rules of Evidence, for example, allow the use of a felony conviction to prove any fact that was essential to sustain the conviction, even if the conviction itself is on appeal.[108]

In most jurisdictions, a criminal conviction can be admitted in a civil case as evidence of the character of the defendant's conduct but it is not conclusive or binding on the judge or jury in the civil trial.[109] In one Kentucky case, for example, the court held that a defendant's conviction for negligent homicide was admissible but not conclusive on whether the defendant was negligent for purposes of the personal injury action brought by the victim's estate.[110] However, in New York and a growing number of jurisdictions, a prior criminal conviction is admitted as conclusive proof of the underlying facts upon which the conviction rests and the defendant cannot challenge those proven facts in the civil proceeding.[111] In such jurisdictions, upon proof of a criminal conviction, the court will summarily hold the defendant to be liable to the victim and proceed with the trial only if there is a question as to the amount of damages incurred by the victim.[112]

Are all prior criminal convictions admissible?

No. Convictions are generally admissible where the prior criminal case necessarily decided an issue relevant to the civil proceeding and the defendant had a full and fair opportunity to contest that conviction.[113] As a result, in most jurisdictions, convictions for minor offenses (including traffic violations and some misdemeanors) are not admissible in civil damage actions or are denied preclusive effect because in prosecutions for minor offenses, the defendant may not have all of the rights normally available in a criminal prosecution and the minor penalties (such as a minimal fine for a traffic violation) do not encourage the defendant to actively or fully defend against such prosecutions.[114] One New York case, for example, refused to allow the victim to use the defendant's conviction by a city court for harassment as the basis for summary judgment in a civil suit for assault (despite testimony covering 100 trial transcript pages) on the ground that the defendant had limited rights in the city court criminal proceeding and was completely unaware that his conviction on a petty criminal "violation" might be used to conclusively establish liability in a damage suit seeking damages of $1.4 million.[115]

If the defendant in the criminal action pleads guilty or "nolo contendere," can this be introduced into the civil case as evidence of the defendant's liability?

Yes and no. In general, convictions based on guilty pleas are treated the same as convictions following a trial.[116] In those states where a conviction is not conclusive of liability, the defendant is free to introduce his own evidence justifying or explaining the plea.[117] Pleas of *nolo contendere* (which subjects the defendant to conviction without admitting guilt) are not admissible as evidence in a subsequent civil proceeding;[118] and a guilty plea that has later been withdrawn cannot be introduced as evidence in a subsequent civil case.[119]

As part of a victim's lawsuit, can a civil court, prior to judgment, order the defendant not to dispose of assets that might be needed to satisfy the victim's judgment?

It depends on the circumstances and the jurisdiction. Although the requirements vary from jurisdiction to jurisdiction, courts have a variety of means for preventing defendants in civil cases (including cases brought by victims) from disposing of assets that may be ultimately required to satisfy the victim's judgment.

One means for preventing the defendant from disposing of assets is prejudgment attachment. In New York, for example, an order of attachment (which has the effect of preventing the disposition of assets attached until dissolution of the attachment by the court) is available in any action for monetary damages where the defendant may attempt to frustrate enforcement of a judgment against him by assigning, disposing of, encumbering or secreting property or removing it from the state.[120] The family of the victim murdered by bestselling author Jack Abbott, as part of their civil action against Abbott for damages, obtained such a prejudgment order from a New York court attaching the royalties earned by Abbott's book, *In the Belly of the Beast*.[121] Before a victim can obtain such an order in New York, he must demonstrate that he has asserted a valid cause of action against the defendant, that it is probable that he will succeed on the merits of his action, and that the amount demanded from the defendant exceeds all known counterclaims against the victim.[122] The victim may also be required to post a bond to cover damages should the attachment later prove to have been unjustified. Such orders may also attach assets belonging to others (including family members) who the defendant might have transferred property to in order to prevent the victim from recovering his judgment.[123] Such attachment orders are also available on similar terms in the federal courts.[124]

Although the specific requirements vary somewhat from jurisdiction to jurisdiction, courts also have equitable powers to restrain or enjoin the defendant in a civil case from disposing of property or removing it from the jurisdiction until the victim's claims go to trial. Typically, the victim must be able to show that he probably will succeed on the merits of his claims, that if the requested order is not granted he will suffer irreparable injury (that is, injury that cannot be compensated in damages), and that the hardship he would suffer if the order is not granted would be greater than the hardship the defendant suffers if he is restrained from disposing of property.[125] In one case, an appellate court upheld an order enjoining a yacht owned by international financier Robert Vesco from departing Miami, Florida, while Vesco was a fugitive from justice in the United States and while a civil action was pending against him by a corporation he once controlled alleging numerous violations of federal securities laws.[126]

In most jurisdictions, such attachments and restraining orders may be available on very short notice without a hearing, but the constitutional right of the defendant to due process requires that within a short time the defendant be given an opportunity at a hearing to oppose the continuation of such attachment or injunctions.

Even where the defendant has succeeded in transferring assets to third parties to avoid a potential judgment in favor of the victim, the victim can assert a claim in his civil case against those third parties asking the court to set aside the conveyance of these assets as "fraudulent conveyances." The Uniform Fraudulent Conveyance Act provides that conveyances (1) that make a person insolvent; (2) that were made without fair payment by a person who believes he will incur debts beyond his ability to pay; or (3) made with an attempt to hinder, delay, or defraud present or future creditors (including the victim seeking damages) are "fraudulent" and the victim can seek an order from the court restraining the person who received the property from disposing of it or setting aside the conveyance or annulling the obligation.[127] Where such conveyances are to a member of the defendant's family, there is a particularly heavy burden on the defendant to prove that the property was transferred only after payment of a fair price.[128]

D. Obtaining Damages and Enforcing Judgments

Is there a maximum amount of damages that the victim can recover in a civil action?

No. However, recovery may be limited in some states, under some circumstances, to the amount that the victim (or his attorney) claims in damages in his complaint.[129]

What types of damages can be awarded to a victim?

In general, a victim can be awarded compensatory damages or punitive (sometimes called exemplary) damages. Compensatory damages are intended to compensate for injuries that the victim has suffered by restoring him, as nearly as possible, to his former position or giving him a monetary equivalent of what he has lost.[130] In most, but not all, states, where the defendant's conduct has been outrageous, oppressive, or malicious, the victim can also receive punitive damages that are intended to make an example of, and punish, the defendant.[131]

What kinds of losses can be recovered as compensatory damages?

It depends on the jurisdiction and the particular victim's claims. Victims can typically recover compensatory damages for the following kinds of losses or expenses incurred in connection with personal injuries due to a crime:

1. actual loss of wages or earnings;

2. projected loss of future earnings (reduced to present value);

3. costs of medical (including psychiatric) care;

4. monetary equivalent of physical pain and mental suffering (including loss of enjoyment, fright, nervousness, grief, humiliation, indignity, terror, and any future pain or anxiety) or disfigurement;

5. costs of any aggravation of a previously existing disease or injury;

6. costs of any subsequent disease or injury caused by the crime's effect on the victim.[132]

Damages for injury to, or loss of, property vary with the crime, the type of property, and the jurisdiction. In fraud cases, many jurisdictions allow the victim to recover the difference between the actual value of what he received and the value of what he was promised; other jurisdictions restrict him to recovery of his out-of-pocket loss (the difference between the value of what he gave up and what he received).[133] For injuries to personal property, victims typically can recover any loss in value of the property or the cost of repair plus any expenses caused by his inability to use the property for some period of time; if personal property has been destroyed, the usual measure of damages is the property's market value.[134] Where the victim's personal property has been stolen or otherwise converted, the victim is entitled to the value of the property (usually at the time of the theft) with interest; where stolen property is recovered, the victim is usually entitled to losses he suffered due to its temporary detention (for instance, rental value of substitute property or interest on the value of the property).[135] In cases involving injury to land or buildings, the victim is usually allowed to recover the difference between the market value of the property before and after the injury (although under some circumstances the victim can recover its normal rental value during that period, the cost of reasonable repairs to restore the property to its original condition, and even lost profits).[136]

Can victims recover their attorneys' fees in obtaining the judgment?
No. Typically, victims are entitled only to "costs" (fees charged by the court and certain other designated costs of litigation).[137] However, some statutes (such as RICO) specifically provide for the recovery of attorneys' fees.

Is the amount of damages awarded to the victim to be reduced by payments from other sources?

In general, no. Unlike, for example, victims' compensation awards, the amount that the victim receives is not reduced by insurance proceeds or other "collateral source" payments.[138] However, under most restitution statutes, the amount of damages awarded to the victim in a civil case is reduced by any amount received under a restitution order issued by the criminal court.[139]

What does the victim have to show in order to justify an award of punitive damages?

In general, intentional and deliberate conduct of an outrageous nature must be shown, usually along with evidence of actual malice on the part of the defendant (demonstrated by evidence concerning his motives or the outrageous nature of the act).[140] Punitive damages are intended to make an example of conduct of a criminal character, and have frequently been awarded in cases involving physical attacks, assaults, willful trespass, theft, or conversion of the victim's property.[141] As a general rule, the fact that the defendant has already been convicted of the crime, or is subject to potential criminal prosecution, does not violate the defendant's right to avoid double jeopardy or prevent the victim from seeking or obtaining punitive damages.[142] Nor will an award of punitive damages in favor of one victim prevent another victim of the same crime from also obtaining punitive damages against the defendant.[143] In about half the states a criminal conviction can be considered by the jury in determining how much, if any, punitive damages to award; in the other states, a conviction is not considered in any way relevant to the award of punitive damages.[144]

Can a jury verdict be set aside on appeal if the damages awarded to the victim are excessive or inadequate?

Yes, but the party attempting to overturn the verdict, as a general rule, is required to show that the amount awarded in damages is wholly unsupported by the evidence, so excessive as to be capricious or the result of passion, prejudice, or other factors not found in the evidence.[145] A trial court can set aside a verdict on similar grounds; it may also require the victim to give up a portion of what it considers to be an excessive award as a condition for denying a defendant's motion for a new trial *(remittitur)*, or require a defendant to pay more as a condition for denying a victim's motion for a new trial *(additur)*.[146] In one widely publicized case, the trial court upheld an award of damages to the singer Connie Francis for injuries and losses (including her inability to continue her singing career) which resulted from an assault in a motel room; rejecting the argument that the $2.5 million verdict was the result of "passion and prejudice," the court emphasized that the entertainer had lost earnings projected at between $5 and $11 million as well as suffering severe mental anguish and humiliation (although the court did use *remittitur* to reduce the award of damages to her husband for loss of her companionship and society from $150,000 to $25,000).[147]

If the victim obtains a judgment in a civil action, how can it be enforced?

It depends on the jurisdiction and the circumstances. In many cases, if the victim obtains a judgment for damages (and it is sustained on appeal) the defendant in the civil case will simply pay the judgment. If the defendant refuses to voluntarily pay, then there are a variety of means available for enforcing the judgment. Although the specific procedure varies considerably from state to state, a number of general alternatives are usually available to the victim.

A judgment for damages is usually directly enforceable against the defendant by obtaining a writ of execution from the court clerk that authorizes an appropriate official (typically a sheriff or marshall) to seize and appropriate a particular piece of personal or real property in the possession of the defendant or a certain monetary amount in damages.[148] The officer then seizes (or levies) on a sufficient amount of the defendant's property to satisfy the judgment within a certain limited period of time; money sufficient to satisfy the judgment is turned over to the victim and if the defendant's assets consist of property, the official will arrange for their sale at a public auction with the amount of the judgment paid to the victim and any excess proceeds being returned to the defendant.[149] Depending on the state, certain property (such as a future inheritance by the defendant) is not subject to levy and other property (including the defendant's home up to a particular amount, automobile, and property necessary for his job or profession) is exempt from execution.[150] Depending on the circumstances, where the defendant claims that his property is exempt from execution, due process may require a hearing before the property can be seized. There may be additional problems levying on property jointly owned by the defendant and someone else (including his spouse).[151]

In addition to executing a judgment against property in the defendant's possession, most states provide for a variety of other kinds of actions to assist in the satisfaction of a judgment including (1) an order allowing for examination of the defendant or third parties to determine the defendant's assets and moneys that are owed to him; (2) garnishment (attaching debts, including wages owed to the defendant by third parties); (3) suits directed at persons thought to be creditors of the defendants; and (4) suits to set aside fraudulent conveyances of property by the defendant to avoid payment of the victim's judgment.[152] In addition, depending on the state, there may be practical means of assisting in the enforcement of judgments; for instance, by obtaining a restitution order from the criminal court ordering the defendant to satisfy the victim's civil judgment.[153]

Where necessary, judgments of one state can be enforced against property in another state; although procedures vary, there is a trend toward allowing enforcement of such judgments in the same manner as a judgment of the state where the property is located.[154]

How long can a victim wait after the entry of a money judgment to obtain a writ and execute against the defendant's property?

It depends on the jurisdiction. While the time varies widely from state to state, most states allow judgment creditors long periods of time in which to enforce judgments so that they can take advantage of any improvement in the defendant's financial condition. Thus, for example, in California, a victim would have 10 years, and in New York 20 years to execute on a money judgment.[155] However, most states allow courts to extend this period beyond the usual limits where the victim can show that the delay in enforcement of the judgment was excusable and that he diligently attempted to locate and levy upon property owned by the defendant.[156]

If the defendant declares bankruptcy, is he still obligated to pay the victim's judgment?

Yes. Liability for willful or malicious injury to the victim is not dischargeable in bankruptcy.[157]

If the defendant prevails in the victim's civil case, can he use the judgment in the civil action to impeach a prior criminal conviction?

No.[158]

E. Claims Against Third Parties for Negligence in Allowing the Crime to Occur

What is negligence?

Negligence is a difficult concept even for lawyers and there is no simple definition. It is sometimes explained as doing something an ordinarily prudent or reasonable person would not have done under the circumstances or failing to do something a reasonably prudent person would have done.[159] Most commentators have emphasized that conduct is negligent if it unreasonably creates a great risk of danger or harm to others, thus falling below the standard established by law that requires each of us to conduct ourselves in a way that protects others from unreasonably great risks or harm.[160]

Ordinarily, the victim (or any other party to a civil action) can recover damages due to a defendant's negligence if he can demonstrate that—

1. the defendant had a duty to conform to a certain standard of conduct to protect others from unreasonable risks;

2. he failed to conform to that standard and breached his duty;

3. the breach actually caused the victim's injury;

4. there was a reasonably close link between the breach of duty and the resulting harm ("proximate cause");

5. the victim suffered actual injury or damage.[161]

Is a third party whose conduct fails to prevent a crime or otherwise protect the victim negligent and therefore liable for damages?

It depends on the facts and the jurisdiction. Traditionally courts did not recognize a general duty on the part of third parties to prevent anyone else from being victimized by crime.[162] In general, in deciding that a particular standard of conduct was reasonable (and any other conduct unreasonable) courts have looked at the risks involved in the conduct, its benefits or social utility, the practicality and relative costs of imposing a different standard of conduct, the foreseeability, probability, and potential severity of injury, the availability of alternative methods (and the costs of such methods), as well as general moral and ethical imperatives.[163] In the past, courts have shied away from imposing a duty to prevent crime or protect others from its consequences because of such factors as the inability to predict when, where, and how crime would occur, and the practical difficulties and costs in preventing crime. In addition, courts tended to see the criminal as an independent actor, beyond the reach or control of most third parties, whose clear guilt made him the one to bear sole liability for injury caused by his conduct.[164]

However, increasingly, courts in virtually every jurisdiction have been imposing a duty to prevent crime and to protect potential victims on a growing number of third parties. While there has not been a simple or clear general statement of the duties of third parties in this regard (and there still are many circumstances in which courts in particular jurisdictions have failed or refused to impose such liability on third parties), courts are now regularly holding that the prevalence of crime in modern society makes it a foreseeable risk in many everyday situations, that it is neither moral nor economical to require individual victims to bear the entire burden of the cost of crime, and that it is economically feasible and socially useful to make an increasing number of third parties liable for crimes that they could or should have foreseen and could or should have prevented. While the trend is very clearly in favor of allowing such suits, the rationale for permitting victims to recover against third parties varies from jurisdiction to jurisdiction and even from case to case. While denying a general duty to protect or prevent crime, some courts have carved out an exception where there was a "special relationship" between the defendant-third party and the victim or the criminal.[165] Other courts have permitted recovery emphasizing that the third party was in the best position to foresee or, as a practical matter, to prevent the victimization.[166] While no single approach to the question of a third party's duty under particular circumstances has emerged, one commentator has identified the following factors that consistently are referred to by courts dealing with such cases:

1. the degree of control that the third party has over the situation;

2. foreseeability;

3. the public's interest in safety from violent assault;

4. the victim's expectations and reliance on the defendant's protection;

5. the economic aspects of the relationship between the victim and the third party.[167]

If a third party's negligence is responsible for the commission of the crime, how much of the injury to the victim is the third party liable for?

All of it. Where the negligence of the third party and the intentional tort of the criminal independently contribute to the injury, the criminal and the third party are considered "successive tortfeasors" and the negligent third party is jointly and severally liable with the criminal for all of the injury to the victim.[168]

How long after the crime can a victim wait to sue a third party to recover damages caused by the crime?

It depends on the jurisdiction, the nature of the crime, and the third party being sued. Jurisdictions vary widely in the length of applicable statutes of limitations. In California, for example, if a victim or his family are seeking damages for personal injury or for wrongful death, there is a 1-year statute of limitations; if they are seeking damages for injury or conversion of real or personal property, fraud, or liability based on violation of a criminal statute, the statute of limitations is 3 years.[169] By contrast, in New York, there is a 3-year statute of limitations for actions to recover personal property, and damages for injury to real property and personal injury; a victim has 6 years to bring civil actions based on fraud or implied from a statute that does not contain its own statute of limitations.[170]

Where the third party is the state, a municipality, or a public employee, the defendant may be immune from a damage suit. But even if the governmental defendant can be sued for damages, there are typically special restrictions, including the requirement that a victim file a notice of claim within a short time of the injury and then commence an action within a certain time thereafter. New York (in addition to a 1-year statute of limitations specifically applicable to actions against sheriffs or other officers for the escape of a prisoner) requires the victim to give notice of any claim against a public corporation or political subdivision within 90 days after the crime (or after the appointment of an executor for the victim's estate) and commence any suit within 1 year thereafter (or 2 years thereafter for wrongful death actions).[171]

In California, a victim seeking damages for personal or property injuries caused by a governmental defendant must file a claim no later than 100 days after the crime; if the claim is rejected, the victim then has 6 months in which to commence an action for damages.[172]

In general, what sort of third-party defendants have been found negligent for failing to prevent the commission of a crime?

Courts in a number of jurisdictions have, under certain circumstances, allowed victims to recover damage awards from the following types of third-party defendants:

1. common carriers (such as trains, buses, airlines, and taxis);

2. innkeepers (hotels, restaurants, and motels);

3. landlords and others who own or operate residential or commerical property;

4. persons who own, control, or provide the instrumentality or means for committing the crime;

5. individuals and agencies (including police and other law enforcement officers) who voluntarily assume protection or are required by law to protect the victim;

6. prisons, hospitals, and others who are entrusted with the custody of dangerous persons who commit crimes after release or escape;

7. psychiatrists who treat someone who later commits a crime;

8. the criminal's employers;

9. victims' employers who fail to maintain a safe place to work;

10. schools and others with custody of minor victims;

11. parents of minors who commit crimes.

In recent years, victims and their families have received substantial awards from third parties, including the following:

1. an award of $800,000 to a victim's husband from a county government in the wrongful death of a victim stabbed by a burglar where the victim had been assured after calling 911 that help was on the way;[173]

2. an award of $186,000 from state parole officials to the family of a victim murdered during an armed robbery by a robber negligently released from prison;[174]

3. a $2.5 million jury verdict (later settled for $1.65 million) against a hotel chain to the singer Connie Francis as a result of inadequate door locks in a hotel room that allowed her to be victimized;[175]

4. a $415,000 award to a rape victim whose landlord negligently failed to secure the living room window;[176]

5. a $3 million award to a girl stabbed and mutilated by her father where the police negligently failed to arrest him for violating an order of protection barring such abuse;[177]

6. a $3 million award from a board of education to an eighteen-year-old girl raped in the stairwell of a junior high school by an older student with a history of sexual assault as a result of negligence in supervising the convicted rapist and protecting the girl;[178]

7. a $3,600 award from a supermarket chain to a victim in a parking lot mugging where the supermarket had negligently allowed six such muggings to take place within a four-month period;[179]

8. a $92,500 settlement payment from a tavern and radio station to the parents of a victim killed by an allegedly drunk driver who had been served beer at a party they sponsored.[179a]

Do common carriers have a duty to prevent passengers from being victimized by crime?
Yes. While third parties generally had no duty to prevent the commission of a crime, common carriers have long had a

duty to exercise "a high degree of care" to prevent passengers from suffering injuries.[180] The basis of the contractual relationship between the passenger and the common carrier has always been an agreement to provide safe transport in return for the price of a ticket. As a result of this "special duty" of common carriers, where their employees assaulted or otherwise injured passengers, the carriers have long been considered liable for the resulting injury.[181] Where the passenger was on the carrier or in its custody, common carriers have also been held liable for damages inflicted by nonemployees due to crime if they could have reasonably anticipated the attack to take place and did not intervene to protect the passenger.[182] A railroad company, for example, was found to owe a duty to a passenger waiting on a platform for a train to use reasonable care to protect the passenger from danger of a foreseeable criminal assault by tramps from a hobos' camp nearby.[183]

This duty to protect passengers existed not only on trains themselves but also on platforms and on other railroad premises.[184] In one recent case, an international airline was found absolutely liable under the Warsaw Convention for injuries suffered in a Greek airport as a result of a terrorist attack that took place while the victim was preparing to board the defendant's airplane.[185]

While privately owned common carriers have consistently been held to have such a duty to protect passengers and others on their premises, a recent Court of Appeals case in New York held that the municipally owned New York subway system (which has its own transit authority policemen) had no general duty to protect subway riders from victimization, in the absence of a "special relationship" between the police and a particular victim.[186]

If their guests are victimized, when are innkeepers liable?

It depends on the circumstances. Like common carriers, historically innkeepers have been expected to provide safe shelter for their guests. As a result, the proprietors of inns, hotels, motels, restaurants, and similar businesses have long been held to have a duty to protect their guests from injury, annoyance, or mistreatment.[187] Although some cases (comparing inns to common carriers) have held innkeepers to a "high degree of care," the prevailing view seems to be that innkeepers are not required to insure the safety of their guests but only to exercise reasonable care and precautions in making sure that their guests are not disturbed, injured, or otherwise victimized.[188]

Victims have been permitted to maintain actions against a hotel (1) where the victim was abducted from his room by intruders who had a key to his room and who were able to enter and exit the hotel (whose one security guard was home sick) with impunity through unguarded and unsupervised exits;[189] (2) where the victim was assaulted and raped in the interior hallway of a 300-room motel which (despite 30 criminal incidents during the prior 6 months) had no security system;[190] (3) where patrons were robbed and assaulted in their motel room, the motel had given out a pass key to their room, the supervisory employee was a 17 year old and the hotel maintained only one security guard who was apparently asleep at the time;[191] and (4) where victims attending a business convention were assaulted in a hotel parking lot by unknown assailants, the hotel had made no effort to determine the local crime situation, its security force failed to employ additional guards during the convention and no one patroled the aisles of the parking lot.[192]

Is the victim's own failure to take safety precautions relevant to the hotel's liability?

The cases are not consistent on this. Some courts have denied or reduced recovery to guests assaulted or burglarized in hotel rooms where there was evidence that they had left a window unlocked or failed to secure a door chain latch.[193]

Are negligent owners of restaurants or bars liable to crime victims?

Yes. Owners of restaurants and bars are liable to victims where, by using reasonable care, they or their employees could have discovered that the crimes were being committed or were about to be committed, or where they could have given the patron warning or have protected him by controlling the conduct of the person who committed the crime.[194] Typically, owners of restaurants and bars have been held liable where a patron was assaulted by someone who the defendant's employees knew was aggressive, dangerous, or prone to violence or where, prior to the assault, there were threats or arguments that put the defendant on notice of possible trouble and the defendant failed to intervene or call the police.[195] This liability can also extend to fights occurring outside of a bar or restaurant (even if the assailants were not customers) where the bar's employees failed to keep the assailants away or to call the police.[196] However, where the injury to the victim happened suddenly without warning (or is otherwise unforeseeable),[197] or where the victim himself provoked the assault or deliberately confronted the assailant, courts have refused to hold the third parties liable to the victim.[198]

Are bars or restaurants liable for crimes committed by persons intoxicated by liquor they serve?

It depends on the jurisdiction. The traditional common law rule—retained in some states—is that there is no action for damages based simply on injury or death following the sale of liquor to an ordinary man.[199] However, most jurisdictions have enacted statutes ("civil damage" or "dramshop" statutes) which make a seller of liquor liable to victims of crimes if the liquor was sold to the person while he was intoxicated, he committed the crime while intoxicated, and the intoxication was the proximate cause of the crime and the victim's injury.[200] Most states will not permit a victim to recover under such statutes if the victim bought drinks or otherwise facilitated the intoxication of the person who committed the crime.[201]

Even in many states that have not enacted statutes, liability has been found, as an exception to the general rule, where liquor was served to persons who were in such a condition as to be deprived of their willpower or responsibility for their behavior or who were habitual drunkards.[202]

However, in California, the threatened financial effect on establishments serving alcohol for all injuries in violation of such a statute, led the legislature to enact a statute making persons who serve liquor absolutely immune from liability (thus negating a prior decision of the California Supreme Court), except for serving liquor to intoxicated minors.[203]

Are persons who serve liquor to household guests or at private parties liable to victims?

No, in most states. Typically, social hosts are not liable under the dramshop acts. However, in a 1984 case, the New Jersey Supreme Court upheld the right of a victim hurt in a head-on collision with a drunk driver to recover damages from a private host who served the driver liquor and allowed him to drive away drunk.[204]

Can the victim sue a third party who provided a weapon, or other instrumentality that was used in committing the crime?

It depends on the jurisdiction and the circumstances. Traditionally there was no liability for negligently providing an instrument used in committing a crime. In some jurisdictions, this is changing; for example, some courts have upheld suits to recover damages from car owners who negligently left their keys in the ignition and were subsequently sued by victims injured by persons who stole the car.[205]

With respect to handguns, courts have differed on whether to impose a duty to the victim or the person or parties supplying the handgun. While a Florida court held the seller of a rifle to a person obviously acting erratically liable for the wrongful death of a victim shot by that rifle, a Kentucky court held that the importer of a handgun used to shoot a victim had no duty to protect the victim from criminal attack.[206] A New York court upheld an action seeking damages from a municipality brought by a woman wounded by her husband with a pistol that the police (knowing that the husband had no permit for the gun and that he had threatened the life of his wife and others) negligently returned to him.[207] In a 1983 case, a federal court in Louisiana permitted the mother of a murder victim to bring an action for damages against the manufacturer of the killer's handgun. The court held that marketing handguns to the public can be considered an "ultrahazardous activity" (similar to blasting with explosives or demolishing buildings) and that therefore the manufacturer (which went into this abnormally dangerous business) must be strictly liable for any damage caused by the guns it sells. A number of victims of shootings (including James Brady, presidential press secretary, and other victims of attempted presidential assassin John Hinckley, Jr., and the widow of a Chicago police officer killed by a .38 caliber pistol) have brought actions against handgun manufacturers on the ground that handguns are "inherently dangerous" and that manufacturers and distributors of such products are liable if they do not take adequate steps to assure that they do not find their way into the hands of psychologically disturbed persons or others likely to use them to kill or injure innocent victims.[208]

Are residential landlords liable to tenants, guests, or oth-

ers if they negligently allow a crime to occur on the premises?

Yes. Traditionally, the landlord had no duty to prevent his tenants, or anyone else, from being victimized by crime. In the rural society that produced common law, the tenant took full possession of any leased premises, and most tenants were as skillful in living on and working the land as their landlords. In modern urban society, the realities are very different: crime is an everyday occurrence, tenants are likely to lease and control one of a number of apartment units with entrances and exits and all common areas being controlled by the landlord, and a tenant may be completely unaware of the risk of crime in his building. Over the last fifteen years, the landlord/tenant law has undergone major changes in this regard, and most jurisdictions now explicitly recognize a duty by the landlord to prevent foreseeable risks, provide reasonable protection and security for tenants and use reasonable care in protecting persons lawfully on the premises from criminal attack.

The first major case recognizing a landlord's obligation to protect tenants from criminal activities of third parties was the decision by a federal appellate court in Washington, D.C., in *Kline v. 1500 Massachusetts Avenue Apartment Corp.*[209] In that case a tenant of a 600-unit apartment building in a high crime area was assaulted and robbed in the common hallway of the building. When the tenant moved in there was a doorman and the entrances to the building were locked or guarded; by the time of the assault, there was no longer a doorman and entrances were commonly left unlocked or open. During the months prior to the assault, there was an increasing number of assaults, larcenies, and robberies perpetrated against tenants in the common hallways of the building. The court found that under the circumstances where the landlord had received notice of repeated criminal assaults, these crimes occurred in hallways exclusively under his control and he had every reason to believe that the crimes would happen again, he had a duty to take steps to minimize the risk to tenants. In addition, the court found that there was an implied contract between the landlord and tenant to provide those protection measures within his reasonable capacity; that is, the measures that were in effect when the tenant began her tenancy. Because the landlord allowed the security to deteriorate he had breached a contract with the victim.

Numerous cases in a number of jurisdictions have followed

the reasoning adopted by the court in *Kline* and found violations of duties to protect tenants if a landlord failed to—

1. provide safe, secure, or adequate lights, locks, doors, or windows;[210]

2. secure vacant floors or apartments that housed vandals who preyed on tenants;[211]

3. maintain the use (once employed) of doormen, managers, or other guards, or was negligent in using or supervising them;[212]

4. exercise reasonable care in hiring janitors, superintendents, or other employees who victimized tenants;[213]

5. warn tenants of a foreseeable risk of crime or misrepresented to security measures;[214]

6. adopt improved security procedures or surveillance where crime had become so rampant in the neighborhood or so common in the building that the landlord was on notice that he should have adopted better security measures.[215]

Under such circumstances, courts in a number of states, in addition to finding negligence on the part of the landlord, have ruled that failure to provide adequate security breaches an implied or explicit "warranty of habitability" in the tenant's lease.[216]

Some courts have denied recovery where the victim failed to show the prevalence of criminal activity in the area, where there was insufficient proof that the landlord's negligence explicitly caused the victimization, or the court could conclude that the victimization might have occurred even if security services had been at full strength.[217] Other cases have denied recovery where the crime was sudden and unpredictable, such as one case where an assailant threw aluminum paint from a roof of an apartment building onto a tenant.[218] Courts (New Jersey, New York, and Illinois) have also been hesitant, at least under some circumstances, to impose a duty to protect on the government for publicly owned housing projects; one such case denied recovery for a nine-year-old girl who was raped in a housing project and thrown off a fourteen-story building when the project had a history of rampant crime and inadequate patrols by housing authority police.[219] The court held that the authority was immune from suit because it was acting in its "governmental" function in supplying police patrols and not as a "proprietor" of residential buildings.

Are proprietors of businesses and owners of commercial buildings liable for crimes that occur on the premises to customers, commercial tenants, or others?

Yes. Although the acceptance of such liability is not universal, the general rule now appears to be that anyone who holds premises open to the public for business purposes is liable for injuries that occur on the premises due to crimes if he fails to use reasonable care to discover the crime or the likelihood that it will occur or give adequate warning to the visitors or otherwise protect them.[220] In deciding whether to hold the landlord or proprietor of the business liable for negligence, courts have considered such factors as—

1. the prevalence of crime in the area;

2. the frequency with which crimes have previously been committed on the premises;

3. whether the victim was given any warning concerning the foreseeability of the occurrence of a crime;

4. the character and supervision of guards and other security personnel;

5. the quality of security systems in the building;

6. the safety (including lighting) of any parking areas.[221]

Where recovery has been denied, it has often been because the court considered a criminal act to be sudden and unpreventable or because there was no history of prior crimes on the premises or in the area.[222] However, there is a growing trend toward holding those in control of business premises liable even if there was no history of prior crime. The Michigan Supreme Court, for example, held the owner of a professional office building liable for injury caused when a patient of a mental health clinic tenant attacked a victim in a building with no history of crimes; despite the low probability of an attack based on past history, the great potential harm to victims required that the landlord take reasonable steps to prevent injury, including issuing warnings to visitors and other personnel of the potential danger.[223] In a case that comes very close to imposing strict liability on the owner of business premises, a rape victim was permitted to bring an action for damages against the operator of a hotel where the victim was attacked by a male assailant in a women's restroom. Although there was no evidence that the hotel was in a high crime area, that any violent crimes had taken place on the premises (or any criminal activity in the area of the restroom), the court held that "common experience" dictates that "rape can occur anywhere" and that in exercising proper care under the circumstances, the victim could recover if she could show that the hotel could have improved security by increasing its security force, placing a television monitor in the lobby or locking the restrooms in order to keep out potential molestors.[224]

If, during the course of a robbery, a proprietor of a business or someone on the scene takes an action that provokes the robber to shoot, assault, or otherwise injure a victim, is that proprietor liable for damages to the victim?

It depends on the circumstances. Courts have held that there may be liability for conduct that incites, encourages, or otherwise induces a criminal to assault, shoot, or otherwise injure those at the scene but determining whether there is liability for resistance to an armed robber will depend on the particular circumstances, a careful calculation of the benefits, and utility of resistance versus the risks to others and whether there was any less dangerous alternative course of action.[225] In general, courts have denied third-party liability under these circumstances. In one Illinois case, for example, the owner of a currency exchange was found to have no duty to honor the demands of a criminal, even where the robber threatened to kill a customer if the owner did not comply with his demands for money.[226] It is also clear that the proprietor of a business being robbed is not liable where the victim himself attempts to confront or restrain the robber.[227]

Are employers liable for the criminal acts of their employees?

It depends on the jurisdiction and the circumstances. Traditionally, employers were liable only for the actions of their employees within the proper scope of their employment; thus victims could not sue employers for injuries due to, for example, shootings or sexual advances, because such activity was not within the proper scope of the assailant's employment.[228] This rule has been used to deny recovery even in some recent cases (including one case in which a court refused to recognize that an employer could be liable for negligently hiring a security guard who raped a victim even if the victim had retained the company to protect her).[229] On the other hand, certain employers, such as common carriers, are universally agreed to have a duty to protect certain victims (their passengers) from injury, death, and even annoyance caused by their employees.[230]

Although decisions in different jurisdictions are not entirely consistent, there is a clear trend in favor of allowing victims to recover from employers whose negligence in hiring or supervising their employees resulted in victimization (whatever the scope of the employee's proper employment). Thus, victims and their families were permitted to bring actions against the operators of a resort hotel for a sexual attack allegedly committed on a guest's fifteen-year-old daughter by a hotel employee where there was alleged negligence in supervision, and against a furniture store owner who negligently allowed a truckdriver to hire a teenage helper at random off the street where the helper subsequently stole the victim's wallet while moving his furniture.[231]

Many of the cases permitting victims to recover against employers involve situations where the employer negligently failed to ascertain that the employee had a prior criminal record (particularly in situations where the employee would be working unsupervised in the victim's home).[232] However, some courts have held that employers may satisfy this duty of investigation by a routine inquiry and have denied recovery where the employee's criminal record was out of state (and therefore would not have been uncovered in a routine inquiry), or if the prior criminal record was for a crime different from the crime for which the victim is suing for damages (for instance, if the civil case involves victimization for arson or rape and the prior conviction was for theft).[233] In addition, some states have enacted statutes expunging criminal records or making them unavailable to prospective employers; under such circumstances it is unlikely that employers could be held negligent for being unaware of an employee's prior criminal record.[234]

If the victimization occurs on, or in connection with, the

victim's job, can the victim recover damages for injury caused by the employer's negligence?

Yes. Employers have a duty to their employees to provide a safe place to work. This duty extends to taking reasonable precautions to prevent an employee from being victimized, including adopting appropriate security provisions and warning of any foreseeable dangers of victimization. The United States Supreme Court, for example, upheld a young female employee's right to sue her employer for injuries suffered as a result of a criminal assault, where as part of her job, she was required to work at night in an isolated and unguarded building.[235] Similarly, an Arizona court upheld the right of a store clerk to recover damages from his employer after he was shot by a robber while working alone after midnight on the grounds that the employer failed to provide a reasonably safe place to work and breached a promise that the employee would not have to work alone at night.[236]

But this view of an employer's duty to his employee is not universal: other cases have held that the owner of a cab owed no duty to protect his driver from crime that might have been prevented by installing a bullet-proof shield and that a corporation had no duty to transfer an employee who was threatened and eventually kidnapped.[237]

In some cases, victims have been denied recovery where the nature of the employee's work was such that the employee had knowledge of the risk of victimization and by assuming that risk was responsible for his own injury.[238] Under many circumstances, victimized employees may also be entitled to workmen's compensation.[239]

Are there circumstances under which third parties voluntarily assume a duty to protect the victim?

Yes. In addition to the situations where police voluntarily assume a duty to informants, or to other persons who they know to be threatened, there are a variety of circumstances under which third parties have been found to have, by their own promise or affirmative action, explicitly or implicitly assumed a duty to protect a person who was subsequently victimized. Often such a promise is an explicit or implicit part of a contract between the victim and some other party for employment, tenancy, or other services. In numerous cases, for example, where employees were hired during a strike on the express condition that they be provided with protection from strikers, the employers have been found liable for damages suffered by the employee at the hands of strikers.[240] Where a landlord assumed the obligation of providing a lobby attendant, the victim of an attempted murder (who had previously been threatened and who relied for protection on the lobby attendant) was permitted to bring an action against the landlord for negligence in allowing the attendant to be absent at the time. Similarly, where a security company provided burglar alarm service under contract with the victim's employer and negligently sounded a supposedly silent alarm that caused the intruder to harm the victim, it was liable to the victim for damages.[241]

In these and similar cases, in addition to recovering for the third parties' negligence, victims have also successfully recovered for the third parties' breach of a contractual obligation to provide promised protection or security.[242] However, before a victim can recover for breach of contract, the terms of the contract must clearly include an intent to provide protection to the victim. Thus, in one case, a court dismissed a victim's action for the failure of uniformed guards at his place of work to prevent him from being shot by an intruder where the guards were hired to protect the company's facilities and not the victim. In another case, a court dismissed a damage action against a tour operator on the ground that the victim's payment for a trip to Rome did not contractually obligate the defendant to warn him of the possibility of street crime or to prevent him from being victimized.[243]

Where children are victimized, are courts likely to find that third parties have a duty to protect the victims from crime?

Yes. Given the relative helplessness of children and the fact that adults are far more likely to foresee the occurrence of crime than a child victim, there is a clear trend toward holding that schools, camps, and others who are entrusted with the custody of children, have a duty to protect the child and that negligent failure to take steps to prevent the victimization makes the third party liable to the victim or to the victim's family for damages. New York courts have sustained actions leading to a $3 million damage judgment where an 18-year-old girl was raped in a school by an older student with a history of sexual assaults because of the board of education's negligent failure to supervise the convicted rapist or protect the girl, and in a case where a child was injured in a schoolyard by snowballs thrown by other children where there was no adult supervision.[244] Similarly, a sexually abused child was permitted to maintain an action against the child's mother for her alleged failure to take affirmative steps to prevent the child from being molested by the mother's boyfriend; as the person with custody of the child, the court imposed a duty of protection on her mother.[245] One California case even went so far as to hold that a doctor was liable for damages suffered by a victim of child abuse if he had examined the child, negligently failed to diagnose the child's bruises as resulting from "battered child syndrome" and returned the child to her parents for further abuse.[246]

Can a victim recover damages from the police for failing to provide him with protection against crime?

In general, no. Courts have consistently taken the position that the police are not insurers of the safety of the public; there is no requirement, for instance, that policemen be posted wherever a crime might occur. In large part, this has been justified by a refusal to interfere with decisions traditionally made by the executive or legislature about how and where to allocate public resources and available police.[247] The traditional rule has been that municipalities and police officers are liable only for misfeasance (illegal or improper performance of an act or duty) and not for simple nonfeasance (failure to do anything). As a result, victims cannot recover for a simple failure of the police to provide protection or to enforce the laws.[248] This is true even in jurisdictions with statutes generally instructing the police to prevent crime or to protect citizens; such statutes are only intended to benefit the public in general and not any particular victim. In a number of cases, for example, police have been held to have no duty to arrest intoxicated motorists who later killed or injured victims.[249]

Even where a particular victim has specifically requested police assistance for protection, the simple failure to provide this protection usually has been found not to create a valid claim by the victim for damages. Thus, in a case where after being repeatedly threatened by a former suitor, a woman called the police and the suitor threw lye in her face when the police failed to appear, the court held that there was no obligation to provide protection.[250] This lack of duty to provide protection to particular victims is sometimes contained in statutes that "immunize" police departments from such suits by victims.[251]

This absence of a duty to provide protection has even been applied by some courts to hold that police patrols employed by a state or municipality in public housing projects or in publicly owned transit systems have no duty to prevent crimes, even where private owners of railroads or housing might have been found to have a duty to provide protection.[252]

Are there exceptional situations when the police are held liable for damages for failure to protect the victim?

Yes. Where the police have undertaken a "special duty" to protect a particular individual (either by promise, by statutory directive, or as an implication from the circumstances), they can be found liable for damages if they are negligent in performing that duty. Although there is no generally accepted definition of when the police have such a special duty and the cases are not entirely consistent, victims have been allowed to recover damages in a number of jurisdictions when—

1. the victim was an informer, undercover agent, or provided services in assisting the police to identify or apprehend a criminal;[253]

2. during civil disturbances or riots, the police specifically promised to protect property from looting;[254]

3. the victim or his property were taken into custody by the police and left unprotected from subsequent victimization;[255]

4. specific officers promised to protect victims from specific assailants, or warn them of the presence of persons who previously victimized or threatened them;[256]

5. there was a court order (such as an order of protection in domestic abuse cases) directing the police to provide protection for a particular victim;[257]

6. the police undertook guard duties that otherwise would have been performed by private individuals;[258]

7. in some jurisdictions, the police took an assailant or his weapon into custody and then released him, when it was foreseeable he would commit a crime;[259]

8. a statute or regulation required the police to take certain steps to protect victims or prevent certain crimes (for example, where a domestic violence statute mandated arrests for violations of orders of protection).[260]

In one recent New York case, for example, where a victim was killed after calling the police on a special 911 emergency assistance number and being assured that help was on the way, and where the police operator negligently took down the wrong address and there was no follow-up to determine where the telephone call came from, the court held that the victim's stabbing death at the hands of a burglar was due to a breach by the police of the "special duty" that it had assumed by assuring the victim to stay put and wait for help to arrive.[261] Although there seems to be a trend toward recognizing a broader category of special duty by police officers, the cases are not entirely consistent and, at times, the doctrine is overly restrictive and unfairly applied to prohibit certain victims from recovering damages. In one case, for example, the California Supreme Court denied a victim of multiple stabbings the right to recover damages from police officers who had the laundromat where she was stabbed under surveillance at the time; because there was no "special relationship" between the officers and the assailant or the victim, there was no liability.[262] Another case (in the District of Columbia) grew out of an incident where two men broke into a house occupied by three women, attacked one of the women and the other two telephoned the police. The police answered the call, knocked on the door and then left; when the two women who had telephoned tried to attract the attention of the departing police, they were discovered by the intruders and repeatedly raped. The court found a special duty to the two women who telephoned the police and allowed them to maintain an action for damages; because the third woman had not telephoned the police or received any specific assurance of protection, there was no "special relationship" and her claim for damages was dismissed.[263]

Where a prisoner is negligently paroled or otherwise released from prison, can a victim of his subsequent crime recover damages from the state or members of the parole board?

It depends on the jurisdiction and the circumstances.

Historically, governments, including state and federal corrections agencies and officials, were absolutely immune from damage suits by their citizens. Within the last half century, the federal government, states, and municipalities have, for at least some purposes, waived their immunity from suit. In most jurisdictions (including suits against the federal government), there are statutes or court decisions that retain immunity for actions or decisions that require the use of an official's "discretion"; where the injury resulted from negligence in operational (or "ministerial") acts, the victim or other injured party can recover damages for the government's negligence.[264] Courts and legislatures have retained this immunity to encourage officials to freely exercise discretion without fear of subsequent retaliatory suits for damages. Such immunity (called discretionary immunity or quasi-judicial immunity) has been available to parole boards and to others who make the decision to release prisoners.[265] In addition, in some states, such as California, there are statutes that specifically confer blanket immunity on both the parole board and its employees in any suits brought by victims injured by the release of a prisoner.[266]

Thus, in most jurisdictions, both the parole board and its members, even where negligent, cannot be sued for damages caused by a released prisoner. However, in some jurisdictions and under some circumstances, courts have indicated that parole boards can be held liable to victims. The Arizona Supreme Court, for example, has abolished absolute immunity for parole board members, holding that the parents of a victim killed during a robbery could recover damages for the parole board's gross negligence in releasing a prisoner who had completed only a third of a sentence for armed robbery where there was a prior record of two burglaries, a parole violation, and eight psychiatric reports that described him as extremely dangerous.[267] Recovery may also depend on the type of release and who authorized it. A New York court, for example, ruled that since a prisoner's temporary release was authorized by a "temporary release committee" (and not by the parole board) there was no absolute immunity from suit.[268] The court held that since prison authorities had taken custody of the prisoner, the temporary release committee had a duty to make inquiries to determine whether there was a history of violent behavior that would make the prisoner a foreseeable risk to the public; if the committee failed to exercise reasonable care in making the inquiry, it was negligent and could be liable for damages.

Critics of this developing liability have argued, however, that the parole decision is, under the best of circumstances, a difficult one, that imposing civil liability will stifle the board's independence in making decisions and that boards will deny appropriate releases rather than incur possible liability for a mistake.

Does a parole decision that produces a subsequent victimization violate the victim's constitutional right to be free of governmental deprivation of life or property without due process of law?

No. The Supreme Court has expressly refused to find that the action of a parole board in California in releasing a prisoner who subsequently attacked a victim violated the victim's due process rights. The Court held that the victim's injury was caused by the released convict and not by "state action" of the parole board and then observed that since the attack took place five months after the release, the attack was too remote a consequence of the board's actions to hold its members liable for damages to the victim.[269] In the same case, the Court rejected the victim's claim that the California statute absolutely immunizing the parole board from liability for damages deprived victims of the right to recover damages in violation of the victims' due process rights and upheld immunity as rationally related to the purpose of encouraging parole board discretion.

Can parole or probation officials be held liable for damages caused by negligence in supervising a released prisoner?

Yes. Even in jurisdictions (such as California) that absolutely immunize officials for damages caused by the actual decision to parole, there can and has been liability for negligence in supervising or controlling a paroled or probationed prisoner for failing to prevent him from victimizing others. Unlike the actual decision to parole, in such cases, the officials making the actual placement or supervising the parolee are engaged in only "ministerial" or "operational" activities, do not have absolute immunity and are liable for negligence.[270] Courts in New York, California, and the District of Columbia, for example, have held parole officials liable for placing parolees in work situations that were inappropriate given the parolee's prior violent history or for failing to fully inform or warn the persons who employed the parolee of his record or tendencies.[271]

Are mental hospitals that negligently release patients who subsequently commit crimes liable to victims for damages?

It depends on the circumstances and the jurisdiction. In general, awards of damages to victims for release of mental patients are rare. In most jurisdictions, state hospitals and supervisory personnel are immune to suits where, in the exercise of their discretion, they release a patient; in some states (such as California) there are statutes that make mental hospitals and their employees absolutely immune from damage suits.[272]

Even where hospitals and their employees are not immune from damage suits, courts have been reluctant to impose liability on mental hospitals or doctors, usually citing the difficulty of determining when a patient is "cured" or when further violence is foreseeable, and the right of the patient to be released into the general community and returned to a useful life as soon as possible.[273] As a result, in most states, a mere error in judgment on the part of the releasing physician is not sufficient to produce liability; the victim must show that the release violated generally accepted medical and psychiatric standards routinely followed in such situations.[274] Some courts have imposed a stricter standard, requiring hospitals and their staffs to carefully consider the possibility of violence on the patient's part after he leaves the hospital and to take whatever reasonable steps are necessary to prevent such violence.[275]

Typically the cases where victims have been allowed to recover from a hospital or its staff, involved gross negligence in the releasing decision; for instance, releasing a patient with known homicidal or violent tendencies or basing the determination to release the patient on an incomplete or inaccurate record.[276] In one such case, the court placed a person convicted of abducting a young girl from a girl's school in a psychiatric institute. The hospital released him to an outpatient facility without obtaining the required approval by the court and he abducted and killed another girl from the same school; the court allowed the victim's family to bring a damage action against the hospital.[277]

Are prison officials whose negligence allowed a prisoner to escape liable for damages committed by the escaped prisoner?

It depends on the jurisdiction and the circumstances. Some jurisdictions (such as California) have made public entities and public employees immune from suits to recover damages caused by escaped prisoners.[278] Other states (such as Utah) have taken the position that decisions to place prisoners in work release or minimum security programs from which they thereafter escaped were "discretionary" and therefore immune from suit.[279]

However, there appears to be a trend toward limiting such immunity and allowing victims of crimes committed by escaped prisoners to recover damages. In one Nevada case, for example, a woman allegedly raped by a prisoner who escaped from a minimum security facility was permitted to bring a negligence action against the state where the prisoner had escaped through unlocked prison gates. The court explicitly refused to find immunity and rejected the idea that operations in prison facilities are discretionary or otherwise immune from negligence suits.[280] In one striking case, the family of a victim killed during the course of an armed robbery received $186,000 from the state of Washington where the alleged killer was a prisoner (with a record of 40 felony convictions and 17 escape attempts) who escaped from an unauthorized program instituted by the warden called Take a Lifer to Dinner after leaving prison accompanied only by the prison baker.[281]

Where the crime committed by an escaped prisoner was not foreseeable based on the prisoner's past record or where the victim was injured by an escaped prisoner's negligence (specifically where a victim was struck by an automobile stolen by an escaping prisoner), courts have denied recovery on the ground that the negligence producing the escape was not the proximate cause of such unforeseeable results.[282]

Is a psychiatrist or therapist liable for failure to warn or protect the victim if his patient threatens to harm a specific victim?

Yes. In the leading case on psychiatrist liability to crime victims, *Tarasoff v. Regents of University of California*, a therapist's patient told him that the patient was going to murder a former girlfriend when she returned from abroad.[283] Although the therapist suggested confinement, he was overruled by other doctors at a university hospital; no one warned the patient's girlfriend and he murdered her. The California Supreme Court held that when a therapist determines (or pursuant to the standards of his profession should determine) that his patient presents a serious danger of violence to others, he has a duty to exercise reasonable care to protect the foreseeable victim from damages and that the therapist in this case was negligent in violating this duty by failing to warn the victim. Following *Tarasoff,* victims of crimes committed by psychologically or emotionally disturbed persons brought a number of similar cases. In one such action, a woman whose former boyfriend was in treatment in a university clinic was awarded $10.3 million in damages as a result of the university's failure to warn her of danger and the boyfriend's subsequent conduct in allegedly throwing sulfuric acid on her. In another case, the court allowed the parents of a girl allegedly murdered by a former next-door neighbor to bring an action where the murderer related to his therapist specific fantasies about the victim, including attacking her with a knife.[284] While generalized threats do not create liability, a threat against a specific identifiable victim has been held to trigger the therapist's duty to warn.[285] In such actions, the usual psychotherapist-patient privilege does not apply and the victim is permitted to obtain copies of any psychiatric records concerning the person who committed the crime that may be in the possession of the therapist.[286] Critics have expressed concern about the effects of such liability on the relations between patients and therapists generally, and specifically about the potential intrusion of the courts on the patient's privacy.

Can the victim recover damages from the parents of a minor who committed a crime?

It depends on the jurisdiction and the circumstances. Actions for negligence against parents have been upheld where there were allegations that (1) they failed to control a child's destructive behavior in their presence; (2) they allowed the child to play with dynamite caps or loaded firearms; (3) a child known to have previously caused fires was allowed access to matches; and (4) parents failed to warn a babysitter of the violent tendencies of their four-year-old child.[287]

At common law, parents who were not themselves negligent were not "vicariously" liable for damage caused by their children. However, a number of states have enacted statutes that now make parents liable, under some circumstances, for damages caused by the criminal activity of their children up to a maximum amount. In California, for example, a parent is liable for up to ten thousand dollars in damages caused by any willful misconduct by a child.[288]

If the victim himself is guilty of conduct that helps produce his own victimization or injury, can he still recover damages for third-party negligence?

It depends on the circumstances and the jurisdiction. The traditional common law rule was that the party who contributed to his own injuries by failing to take reasonable precautions for his own protection ("contributory negligence") or who recognized and understood the risk or danger he confronted and voluntarily chose to encounter it ("assumption of risk") was not permitted to recover damages even if they were initially caused by another's negligence.[289] The result of this was to absolutely bar a victim from recovering for damages from a third party when, for example, the victim robbed or assaulted in his own hotel room contributed to the victimization by failing to lock a window or door.[290]

However, a majority of states no longer allow the victim's own negligence to absolutely bar recovery. Most states, by statute or court decision, have adopted "comparative negligence." Where the victim herself is negligent, the jury determines how much of the damages were actually caused by the victim's own negligence and then reduces or eliminates an award against a negligent defendant accordingly.[291] In the majority of these states, the victim will receive no damage if her negligence equals or exceeds that of the third-party defendant; in the remaining comparative negligence states, the victim is entitled to recover for any proportion of his damages caused by the third-party defendant, even if the victim's own negligence exceeded that of the third-party defendant.[292]

Can a victim obtain punitive damages from a third-party defendant?

No. Since punitive damages are only available where the defendant is guilty of outrageous or malicious conduct, courts have routinely refused to permit victims to recover punitive damages from third parties whose negligence, however extreme, allowed the crime to occur.[293]

Can the victim recover from his insurance company for losses caused by crimes?

Yes. Many forms of commonly purchased insurance also protect the insured from losses due to crime. Automobile insurance companies, for example, reimburse a victim if a victim's car or property within the car is stolen; homeowner's or tenant's insurance commonly insures structures and personal property from damage by arson, riots, vandalism, and theft; and medical insurance, disability insurance and other forms of insurance commonly provided by employers will allow victims of personal injury to recover at least some medical and hospital expenses and sometimes part of the victim's lost salary due to inability to work.[294]

In urban areas where there is a high risk of crime and residential insurance is not otherwise available, tenants and homeowners can obtain affordable crime insurance for their residences from the Federal Crime Insurance Program. As of 1982, this program was available to residents of 27 states, the District of Columbia, Puerto Rico, and the Virgin Islands. It requires that the insured maintain certain simple protective devices (including a "dead bolt" lock), and the policy protects against burglary, damage to the home caused during a burglary or robbery, and theft of personal property by violence or threat of violence inside or outside of the home. Information can be obtained by writing to: Federal Crime Insurance, P.O. Box 41033, Bethesda, MD 20814, or calling toll-free, 800–638–8780. Comparable state-run crime indemnity programs are available to residents in such states as New Jersey and Indiana.

In addition, a variety of specialized forms of crime insurance are also available. In 1981, with a great deal of fanfare, two insurance companies announced plans to sell violent crime insurance that would provide mugging victims with up to $2,000 for medical expenses, $1,000 for property loss, $2,000 for rehabilitation, and some amount for mental anguish, as well as $150 per week for 13 weeks if the victim was unable to work, and $3,000 in death benefits to the victim's family; however, these policies have been criticized for being too limited in the risk that they insure, and expensive and inferior in their protection to that provided by conventional medical or life insurance.[295] Private insurance companies offer stores and businesses a variety of insurance against business-related crimes, including (1) mercantile open-stock policies (which reimburse losses by burglary or robbery); (2) a store owner's burglary and robbery policy (insuring against robbery of money, securities, and merchandise both within and outside the premises, including losses due to kidnapping, burglary, and thefts from a night depository or messenger); and (3) a broad-form storekeeper's endorsement (which insures against employee dishonesty, loss of money, and securities inside and outside the premises, merchandise burglary, counterfeit paper, and depositers' forgery as well as vandalism, burglary, or robbery). [296] In high crime areas, crime insurance for small businesses insuring against loss due to burglary, robbery, or theft from a night depository or safe is available from the Federal Crime Insurance Program.

What is the procedure for recovering under such an insurance policy?

Although the specifics vary with the insurer, in general, the victim prepares an inventory of his allowable expenses, damages, or lost property (including doctor's bills, receipts for lost property, and descriptions of items lost or damaged). These are submitted to the insurance company (which usually also requires a copy of the police report filed in connection with the crime) and the insurance company's adjustor verifies the claim and offers an amount (less than the amount claimed by the victim) in settlement. Settlements in property cases are typically based on the present value of lost property (not the original or replacement value) and limited in the type of doctors and other expenses that are reimbursed. Most policies also contain a deductible (often $100) with respect to lost and damaged property as well as certain maximum amounts that can be claimed in connection with certain losses. If the victim brings a civil action and obtains a judgment, insurance policies typically contain subrogation provisions that allow the insurance company to recover the amount paid to the victim from any judgment or to bring its own damage action against persons who caused the loss.

If the victim fails to recover damages caused by the crime and does not obtain reimbursement from insurance, can he deduct the unreimbursed loss from his income for federal income tax purposes?

It depends on who the victim is and the amount of the loss. Beginning in 1983, individual victims can deduct unreimbursed property losses due to theft or criminal casualty but only if they exceed 10 percent of the victim's adjusted gross income plus $100. The victim may also deduct medical expenses due to personal injury caused by the crime but only those unreimbursed medical expenses that exceed 5 percent of the victim's adjusted gross income. Businesses that suffer losses due to crime can deduct as business losses the entire amount of the unreimbursed losses from their reported income.[297]

Notes

1. For a discussion of victims' rights to recover damages from criminals and from third parties, *see generally* F. Carrington, *Memorandum of Law: Third Party Litigation on Behalf of Crime Victims* (Virginia Beach, Va.: Crime Victims Legal Advocacy Institute, 1980) (available from Crime Victims Legal Advocacy Institute, 210 Laskin Rd., Suite 9, Virginia Beach, VA 23451) [hereafter "Memorandum"]; D. Deacon, *Liability of Third Parties for the Criminal Acts of Others* (1982); Carrington, "Victims' Rights Litigation: A Wave of the Future?" 11 *U. Rich. L. Rev.* 447 (1977) [hereafter "Victims' Rights"]; Note, "California's Approach to Third Party Liability for Criminal Violence," 13 *Loyola L.A.L. Rev.* 535 (1980); Note, "Negligence Liability for the Criminal Acts of Another," 15 *J. Marsh. L. Rev.* 459 (1982) [hereafter "Negligence Liability"]; and the following annotations: 46 A.L.R. 3d 1084 (failure to provide police protection); 10 A.L.R. 3d 619 (private person's duty to prevent criminal attacks); 70 A.L.R. 2d 621 (innkeepers' liability for criminal attacks); 38 A.L.R. 3d 699 (negligent release of mental patients); 93 A.L.R. 3d 999 (liability for assaults on patrons); 43 A.L.R. 3d 331 (liability of landlords for criminal injuries); 83 A.L.R. 3d 1201 (therapists' liability for patient's criminal acts).
2. *See, e.g.,* F.R.C.P. Rules 3, 4, 17.
3. *See, e.g.,* N.Y.C. Civ. Act Act §§1801–1814 (up to $1,500 in damages).
4. 28 U.S.C. §§1332, 1391.
5. W. Prosser, *Law of Torts,* §2 n.17 (4th ed. 1971).
6. *Koenig v. Nott,* 2 Hilt. 323, 8 Abb. Prac. 384 (1859).
7. For a description of the French system, *see* P. Campbell, "A Comparative Study of Victim Compensation Procedures in France and the United States: A Modest Proposal," 3 *Hastings Intl. and Comp. L. Rev.* 321 (1979).
8. A. Linden, "Victims of Crime and Tort Law," in Hudson and Galloway, eds., *Considering the Victim: Readings in Restitution and Victim Compensation* 243 (Ontario, Canada: Charles C. Thomas 1975) (4.8 percent of the victims surveyed attempted to collect damages from their attackers; only 1.8 percent succeeded).

9. "Getting Even Suits Crime Victims," *Chicago Sunday Sun Times*, June 19, 1983, at 10 (Living); Carrington, *Victims' Rights, supra* note 1; "Getting Status and Getting Even," *Time*, Feb. 7, 1983, at 40.

10. "Rape Redress," *Time*, Aug. 25, 1980, at 59; M. Galante, "Son's Killer Agrees to Pay Parents Not to Bar Parole," *Natl. Law Journal*, Apr. 2, 1984, at 4; "Dad Pays $30 G in Sex Abuse," *N.Y. Daily News*, Apr. 22, 1982, at 8; *Dept. of Labor v. Dillon*, 28 Wash. App. 853, 855, 626 P.2d 1004 (1981).

11. *Washington Post*, Feb. 1, 1976, §B, at 1, col. 6.

12. *See, e.g.*, C. LeGrand and F. Leonard, "Civil Suits for Sexual Assault: Compensating Rape Victims," 8 *Women's L. F.* 479 (1979); Comment: "The Civil Action for Rape: A Viable Alternative for the Rape Victim?" 1978 *S. Ill. U. L. J.* 399 (1978).

13. *See, e.g., City of New York v. Carolla*, 48 Misc. 2d 140, 264 N.Y.S.2d 408 (Civ. Ct., N.Y.C. 1965); Miss. Code Ann. §99–37–17 (1978).

14. *See, e.g., U.S. v. Rubin*, 243 F.2d 900 (7th Cir. 1957); *Murray and Sorenson, Inc. v. U.S.*, 207 F.2d 119 (1st Cir. 1953); *Beckett v. Dept. of Social and Health Services*, 87 Wash.2d 184, 550 P.2d 529 (1978).

15. *See, e.g., Braithewaite v. Christy*, 301 F.2d 196 (2d Cir. 1981).

16. *See, e.g.*, N.Y. Exec. Law §634 (McKinney's 1984–84). For a discussion of a state's subrogation rights as a result of compensation awards, *see* pp. 200–202, *supra*.

17. *See, e.g.*, N.Y. Penal Law §60.27, 603(6); Wisc. Stat. Ann. §973.09(7) (Supp. 1983–84) (requiring a separate hearing to determine the amount of the set-off).

18. *See, e.g., Poston v. Home Insurance Co. of New York*, 191 S.C. 314, 4 S.E.2d 261 (1939); *State v. Schauenberg*, 197 Iowa 445, 197 N.W. 295 (Iowa 1924).

19. *Insurance Co. of North America v. Steigler*, 300 A.2d 16 (Del. Super. 1972); *National Freight, Inc. v. Ostroff*, 133 N.J. Super. 554, 337 A.2d 647 (1975).

20. N.Y.C.P.L.R. §215(3); Cal. Code Civ. Prac. § 340 (3).

21. *See, e.g.*, N.Y.C.P.L.R.§ 207 (tolling statute due to absence from the state or due to the use of a false name).

22. N.Y.C.P.L.R. §15(8); N.Y.E.P.T.L. §5–4.1(2).

23. *See, e.g.*, F.R.C.P. Rules 3–16, 26–63.

24. C. T. McCormick, *Law of Evidence*, at §319 (1954).

25. *See, e.g., Berger v. Southern Pacific Co.*, 144 Cal. App.2d 1, 300 P.2d 170 (1956); LeGrand and Leonard, "Civil Suits for Sexual Assault: Compensating Rape Victims," 8 *Golden Gate U.L. Rev.* 479, 494 (1979).

26. Rest.2d, Torts §481; *Bartosh v. Banning*, 251 Cal. App.2d 378, 385, 59 Cal. Rptr. 382 (1967).

27. Prosser, *supra* note 5, at §§46–47.

28. *See IIT v. Cornfeld*, 619 F.2d 909, 922–28 (2d Cir. 1980); *Rolf v. Blyth, Eastman Dillon and Co.*, 570 F.2d 38, 47–48 (2d Cir.), *cert. denied*, 439 U.S. 1039 (1978); *Schwartz v. Schwartz*, 81 Misc.2d 177, 365 N.Y.S.2d 584 (Civ. Ct., N.Y.C. 1974), *modified on other grounds*, 82 Misc.2d 51, 365 N.Y.S.2d 589 (1st Dep't 1975).

29. *Chase Manhattan Bank of North America v. Perla*, 65 A.D.2d 207, 411 N.Y.S.2d 66 (4th Dept. 1978); *Neblett v. Elliott*, 46 C.A.2d 294, 302, 115 P.2d 872 (1941).

30. *Rosefield v. Rosefield*, 221 C.A.2d 431, 435, 34 Cal. Rptr. 479 (1963); *Corris v. White*, 29 A.D.2d 470, 289 N.Y.S.2d 371 (4th Dept. 1968); *Devries v. Brumbach*, 53 C.2d 643, 2 Cal. Rptr. 746, 349 P.2d 532 (1960). *See also* 20 N.Y. Jur. 2d 3–35 ("Conspiracy-Civil Aspects").

31. 15 U.S.C. §15.

32. *See, e.g.*, CAL. AGRIC. CODE §21844 (West Supp. 1984) (theft of cattle); CAL. PENAL CODE §496 (West Supp. 1984) (stolen property); CONN. GEN. STAT. ANN. §52–564, –565 (West Supp. 1982) (stolen property; forgery and counterfeiting); W. VA. CODE §61–3–50 (1977) (bootleg recording); S.C. CODE ANN. §32–1–10 (Law Coop. 1976)(recovery of gambling losses).

33. *See, e.g.*, *U.S. v. Cappetto*, 502 F.2d 1351 (7th Cir. 1974), *cert. denied*, 420 U.S. 925 (1975) (RICO).

34. 18 U.S.C. §1962.

35. *Id.* at §1964(a).

36. *Id.* at (c). A number of states have enacted similar racketeering statutes. *See, e.g.*, ARIZ. REV. STAT. ANN. §13–2314 (West Supp. 1982–83); FLA. STAT. ANN. §895.03, .05 (8) (West Supp. 1982).

37. *Id.* at §1962.

38. *Id.* at §1961(6).

39. *Id.* at (5).

40. *Id.* at §1961.

41. *See, e.g.*, *Moss v. Morgan Stanley, Inc.*, 719 F.2d 5 (2d Cir. 1983); *Schacht v. Brown*, 711 F.2d 1343 (7th Cir. 1983); *Bennett v. Berg*, 685 F.2d 1053, 1063 (1982), *aff'd en banc*, 710 F.2d 1361 (8th Cir. 1983); *Crocker National Bank v. Rockwell Int. Corp.*, 555 F. Supp. 47 (N.D. Cal. 1982). *See also* 116 Cong. Rec. 35, 204 (1970); 116 Cong. Rec. 35, 343–46 (1970). *But see Adair v. Hunt Intl. Resources Corp.* 526 F. Supp. 736–48 (N.D. Ill. 1981); *Hokama v. E. F. Hutton and Co.*, 566 F. Supp. 636 (C.D. Cal. 1983); *Noland v. Gurley*, 566 F. Supp. 210 (D. Colo. 1983).

42. 18 U.S.C. §1961(4).

43. *U.S. v. Turkette*, 452 U.S. 576 (1981).

44. *U.S. v. Mazzei*, 700 F.2d 85 (2d Cir.), *cert. denied*, 163 S.Ct. 2124 (1983). *See also Moss v. Morgan Stanley, Inc., supra* note 41; *U.S. v. Bajaric*, 706 F.2d 42 (2d Cir. 1983) ("the enterprise was, in effect, no more than the sum of the predicate racketeering acts").

45. *See, e.g.*, *Bennett v. Berg, supra* note 41; *U.S. v. Computer Sciences Corp.*, 689 F.2d 1181, 1190 (4th Cir. 1982); *Bays v. Hunter*

Savings Assn., 539 F. Supp. 1020, 1024 (S.D. Ohio 1982); *Van Schaick v. Church of Scientology of California, Inc.*, 535 F. Supp. 1125, 1136 (D. Mass. 1982).

46. Compare 18 U.S.C. §1964(c) *with* FLA. STAT. ANN. §895.05.

47. *Van Schaick v. Church of Scientology of California, Inc. supra* note 45. *But see* cases construing RICO's damage provisions liberally. *Slattery v. Costello*, F. Supp. (D.D.C. 1983); *Cenco v. Seidman & Seidman*, 686 F.2d 449, 457 (7th Cir. 1982).

48. *See, e.g., Moss v. Morgan Stanley, Inc.*, *supra* note 41. *Bankers Trust Co. v. Feldesman*, 566 F. Supp. 1235 (S.D.N.Y. 1983), *aff'd*, Dkt. No. 83–7636, slip.op. 5607 (2d Cir. July 26, 1984); *Harper v. New Japan Securities Int'., Inc.*, 545 F. Supp. 1002, 1007 (C.D. Cal. 1982); *Landmark Savings and Loan v. Rhoades*, 527 F. Supp. 206, 208 (C.D. Mich. 1981).

49. *North Barrington Development, Inc. v. Fanslow*, 547 F. Supp. 207, 211 (N.D. Ill. 1980).

50. Compare Moss, *supra* note 41 at n. 15 (and cases cited in that footnote) *with Sedima, S.P.R.L. v. Imrex Co.*, Dkt. No. 83–7965, slip op. 5535 (2d Cir. July 25, 1984).

51. *Cappetto, supra* note 33.

52. 18 U.S.C. §1964(d).

53. *See, e.g., Anderson v. Janovich*, 543 F. Supp. 1124, 1127–32 (W.D. Wash. 1982); *State Farm Fire and Casualty Co. v. Estate of Caton*, 540 F. Supp. 673, 675 (N.D. Ind. 1982). *Municipality of Anchorage v. Hitachi Cable, Ltd.*, 547 F. Supp. 633, 644 (D.Alas. 1982).

54. 18 U.S.C. §1962(c).

55. *See, e.g., U.S. v. Elliott*, 571 F.2d 880 (5th Cir. 1978).

56. *U.S. v. Campanale*, 518 F.2d 352, 363 (9th Cir. 1975), *cert. denied*, 423 U.S. 1050 (1976).

57. *See, e.g., Bennett v. Berg*, 710 F.2d 1361, 1364 (8th Cir. 1983).

58. *Prosser, supra* note 5, at §36.

59. *See, e.g., Rest.2d Torts*, §874A; 4 Witkin, *Summary of California Law*, §7.

60. Compare Ney v. Yellow Cab Co., 2 Ill.2d 74, 117 N.E.2d 74 (1954); *Zinck v. Whelan*, 120 N.J. Super. 432, 294 A.2d 727 (1972); *Garbo v. Walker*, 129 N.E.2d 537, 57 Ohio Op. 363 (1955) *with Galbraith v. Levin*, 323 Mass. 255, 81 N.E.2d 560 (1948) *and Frank v. Ralston*, 145 F. Supp. 294 (W.D. Ky. 1956), *aff'd*, 248 F.2d 541 (6th Cir. 1957).

61. *Hudson v. Craft*, 33 C.2d 654, 660, 204 P.2d 1 (1949); *Vesel v. Segar*, 5 C.3d 153, 95 Cal. Rptr. 623, 486 P.2d 151 (1971) [overruled by CAL. B. & P. C. §25602(c)].

62. *Landeros v. Flood*, 17 C.3d 399, 131 Cal. Rptr. 69, 551 P.2d 389 (1976).

63. *See, e.g., Texas and Pacific Railway Co. v. Rigsby*, 241 U.S. 33, 39 (1916); *Wyandotte Transportation Co. v. U.S.*, 389 U.S. 191, 201–2 (1967); *Bivens v. 6 Unknown Named Agents*, 403 U.S. 388 (1971);

Cannon v. University of Chicago, 441 U.S. 677 (1979); *Carlson v. Greene*, 446 U.S. 14, 19–20 (1980).

64. *See J. I. Case Co. v. Borak*, 377 U.S. 426, 432 (1964).

65. *Cort v. Ash*, 422 U.S. 66, 78 (1975).

66. *Compare Hardaway v. Consolidated Paper Co.*, 366 Mich. 190, 114 N.W.2d 236 (1962) *with New Amsterdam Casualty Co. v. Novick Transfer Co.*, 274 F.2d 916 (4th Cir. 1960) (Maryland Law). *See* discussion in Prosser, *supra* note 5, at §36.

67. *Baker v. Bolton*, 1 Camp. 493 (1808).

68. Prosser, *supra* note 5, at §127. *See, e.g.*, N.Y.E.P.T.L. 5:4–1 *et seq.*

69. *Id.*

70. *See, e.g.*, WASH. REV. CODE. ANN. §4.20.046 (Supp. 84–85).

71. Prosser, *supra* note 5, at §127; *Warner v. McCaughan*, 460 P.2d 272 (Wash. 1969); *Balmer v. Dilley*, 81 Wash.2d, 367, 502 P.2d 456 (1977).

72. *See, e.g.*, *Wardlow v. City of Keokuk*, 190 N.W.2d 439 (Iowa 1971); *Green v. Bittner*, 424 A.2d 210 (N.J. 1980); *Sea Land Services, Inc. v. Gaudet*, 414 U.S. 573 (1974) (admiralty); *Krouse v. Graham*, 19 C.3d 59 (1977).

73. *Cavallaro v. Michelin Tire Corp.*, 96 C.A.3d 95 (1979); *Groesbeck v. Napier*, 275 N.W.2d 388 (Iowa 1979).

74. *Bartlett v. Hanover*, 9 Wash. App. 614, 513 P.2d 844, 848 (1973); *Mitchell v. Buchheit*, 559 S.W.2d 528 (Mo. 1977); *Bond v. United Railroads*, 159 Cal. 270, 276 (1911); 81 A.L.R.2d 949.

75. *Compare McGale v. Metropolitan Transportation Authority*, 429 N.Y.S.2d 418 (1980); *Albarren v. City of New York*, 437 N.Y.S.2d 4 (1981) *with Krouse v. Graham, supra* note 72.

76. *See Kern v. Kogan*, 93 N.J. Super. 459, 226 A.2d 186 (1967); *Tarasoff v. Regents*, 17 Cal.3d 425, 551 P.2d 334, 131 Cal. Rptr. 14 (1976); *Robert v. Ford Motor Co.*, 73 A.D.2d 1025 (3d Dep't 1980), *appeal dismissed*, 49 N.Y.2d 1047 (1980).

77. Prosser, *supra* note 5, at §125.

78. *Id; Shreve v. Faris*, 144 W. Va. 819, 111 S.E.2d 169 (1959); *Manders v. Pulice*, 102 Ill. App.2d 468, 242 N.E.2d 617 (1968); *Norton v. U.S.*, 110 F. Supp. 94 (N.D. Fla. 1953); *Edminster v. Thorp*, 101 C.A.2d 756, 759, 226 P.2d 373 (1951).

79. *Id.*

80. *Park v. Standard Chem. Way Co.*, 60 Cal.3d 47, 50 (1976); *Sawyer v. Bailey*, 413 A.2d 165 (Me. 1980); *Tong v. Jocson*, 76 Ca.3d 603 (1977).

81. *Baxter v. Superior Court*, 19 Cal.3d 461 (1977).

82. *Id; Hair v. Monterey*, 45 Cal.3d 538 (1975).

83. *Suter v. Leonard*, 45 Cal.3d 744 (1975); *Borer v. American Airlines*, 19 Cal.3d 441 (1977). *But see Weitl v. Moes*, 311 N.W.2d 259 (Iowa 1981) (allowing recovery for loss of parental consortium).

84. Rest.2d Torts §46(2)(a); *Grimsby v. Samson*, 530 P.2d 291 (Wash. 1975).

85. *Watson v. Dilts*, 116 Iowa 249, 89 N.W. 1068 (1902); *Mahnke v. Moore*, 197 Md. 61, 77 A.2d 923 (1951).

86. *See, e.g., Dillon v. Legg*, 68 Cal.2d 728 (1968).

87. *See, e.g., Bobsun v. Sanperi*, N.Y.2d (1984); *National Car Rental System, Inc. v. Bostic*, 423 So.2d 915 (Fla. App. 1982), *pet. for rev. denied*, 436 So.2d 97, 99 (Fla. 1983).

88. *Garland v. Herrin*, 724 F.2d 16 (2d Cir. 1983).

89. *Lauver v. Cornelius*, 85 A.D.2d 866, 446 N.Y.S.2d 456 (3d Dept. 1981); *Markowitz v. Fein*, 30 A.D.2d 515, 290 N.Y.S.2d 128 (1st Dept. 1968).

90. F.R.C.P. Rule 6(e).

91. *Pittsburgh Plate Glass Co. v. U.S.*, 360 U.S. 395 (1959); *U.S. v. Proctor and Gamble Co.*, 356 U.S. 677 (1958); *Baker v. U.S. Steel Corp.*, 492 F.2d 1074, 1079 (2d Cir. 1974).

92. *U.S. v. Proctor and Gamble Co.*, *supra* note 91, 356 U.S. at 683; *Texas v. U.S. Steel Corp.*, 546 F.2d 626, 631 (Fifth Cir. 1977).

93. *Baker v. U.S. Steel Corp.*, *supra* note 92; *Founding Church of Scientology of Washington v. Kelley*, 77 F.R.D. 378 (D.D.C. 1977).

94. F.R.C.P. Rule 26; *U.S. v. Interstate Dress Carriers, Inc.*, 280 F.2d 52, 54 (2d Cir. 1960); *U.S. v. Saks and Co.*, 426 F. Supp. 812, 814 (S.D.N.Y. 1976); *Mallinckrodt Chemical Works v. Goldman, Sachs and Co.*, 58 F.R.D. 348, 352–54 (S.D.N.Y. 1973); *Davis v. Romney*, 55 F.R.D. 337, 340–42 (E.D. Pa. 1972).

95. F.R.C.P. 26(b); *Gaison v. Scott*, 59 F.R.D. 347 (D. Haw. 1973); *Wood v. Breier*, 54 F.R.D. 7 (E.D. Wis. 1972); *Frakenhauser v. Rizzo*, 59 F.R.D. 339 (E.D. Pa. 1973).

96. *Grimm v. Arizona Bd. of Pardons and Paroles*, 564 P.2d 1227 (Ariz. 1977).

97. *See Founding Church of Scientology of Washington v. Kelley*, *supra* note 93; *Gaison v. Scott*, *supra* note 95, 59 F.R.D., at 352–53.

98. *Kastigar v. U.S.*, 406 U.S. 441 (1972); *Banca v. Town of Phillipsburger*, 436 A.2d 944, 181 N.J. Super. 109 (1981); *Andresen v. Bar Assn., of Montgomery County, Md.*, 305 A.2d 845, 269 Md. 313, *cert. denied*, 414 U.S. 1065 (1973).

99. *See, e.g., LeBlanc v. Spector*, 378 F. Supp. 310 (D. Conn. 1974).

100. *Abramowitz v. Voletsky*, 262 N.Y.S.2d 991 (Sup. Ct., Kings Co. 1965); *Barbato v. Tuosto*, 38 Misc.2d 823, 238 N.Y.S.2d 1000 (Sup. Ct., Monroe Co. 1963); *McKelvey v. Freeport Housing Authority*, 29 Misc.2d 140, 220 N.Y.S.2d 628 (Sup. Ct., Nassau Co. 1961).

101. *Kastigar v. U.S.*, 406 U.S. 441, 444; *Zicarelli v. New Jersey State Commission*, 406 U.S. 472, 478 (1972).

102. *Brown v. U.S.*, 356 U.S. 148 (1958); *Berner v. Schlesinger*, 11 Misc.2d 1024, 178 N.Y.S.2d 135 (Sup. Ct., N.Y. Co. 1957), *aff'd*, 6 A.2d 781, 175 N.Y.S.2d 579 (1st Dep't 1958); *Annest v. Annest*, 49 Wash.2d 62, 298 P.2d 483 (1956); *Meyer v. Second Judicial District Court*, 591 P.2d 259 (Nev. 1979).

103. *See, e.g., Nuckols v. Nuckols*, 189 So.2d 832 (Fla. App. 1966); *Levine v. Bornstein*, 13 Misc.2d 161, 174 N.Y.S.2d 574 (Sup. Ct.

1958), *aff'd*, 7 A.D.2d 995, 183 N.Y.S.2d 868, *aff'd*, 6 N.Y.2d 892, 190 N.Y.S.2d 702, 160 N.E.2d 921 (1959); *Zaczek v. Zaczek*, 20 A.D.2d 902, 249 N.Y.S.2d 490 (2d Dep't 1964).

104. *See Clark v. Lutcher*, 77 F.R.D. 415 (M.D. Pa. 1977); *U.S. Trust Co. v. Herriott*, 407 N.E.2d 381 (Mass. App. 1980); *Berner v. Schlesinger, supra* note 102.

105. *See, e.g., Zurek v. Woodbury*, 446 F. Supp. 1149 (N.D. Ill. 1978); *Herndon v. City of Ithaca*, 43 A.D.2d 634, 349 N.Y.S.2d 227 (1973); *Massey v. Meurer*, 25 A.D.2d 729, 268 N.Y.S.2d 735 (1966); *Morrissey v. Powell*, 304 Mass. 268, 23 N.E.2d 411 (1939).

106. 5 Wigmore, *Evidence* §1671(a).

107. McCormick, *supra* note 24, at §318.

108. F.R.E. Rule 803(22).

109. *See, e.g., Asato v. Furtado*, 474 P.2d 288, 293 (Haw. 1970).

110. *Weichhand v. Garlinger*, 447 S.W.2d 606 (Ky. 1969).

111. *See, e.g., S. T. Grand, Inc. v. City of New York*, 32 N.Y.2d 300, 344 N.Y.S.2d 938, 298 N.E.2d 105 (1973); *Cumberland Pharmacy v. Blum*, 69 A.D.2d 903, 415 N.Y.S.2d 898 (1979); *U.S. Fidelity and Guaranty Co. v. Moore*, 306 F. Supp. 1088, 1094–95 (N.D. Miss. 1969).

112. *See, e.g., Read v. Sacco*, 49 A.D.2d 471, 375 N.Y.S.2d 371 (1975); *McMillan v. Williams*, 455 N.Y.S.2d 523 (Sup. Ct., N.Y. Co. 1982); *Zurich Insurance Co. v. Buono, N.Y.L.J*, p. 6, col. 4 (Mar. 27, 1984), (Sup. Ct. N.Y. Co.).

113. *See, e.g., S. T. Grand, Inc. v. City of New York, supra Asato v. Furtado, supra* note 109.

114. *See, e.g.,* NEW YORK VEH. and TRAF. LAW §155; NEW YORK CITY CIVIL COURT ACT §1808; *Haynes v. Rollins*, 434 P.2d 234 (Okl. 1967); *Loughner v. Schmelzer*, 421 Pa. 283, 218 A.2d 768 (1966); Rest.2d Judgments §68.1, subd. [c] and comment d.

115. *Gilberg v. Barbieri*, 53 N.Y.S.2d 285, 441 N.Y.S.2d 49, 423 N.E.2d 807 (1981).

116. *Cumberland Pharmacy v. Blum, supra* note 111.

117. *Kickasola v. Jim Wallace Oil Co.*, 144 Ga. App. 758, 242 S.E.2d 483 (1978), *cert. denied*, 436 U.S. 921 (1979).

118. F.R.E. Rule 410; *Neuner v. Clinkenbeard*, 466 F. Supp. 54 (W.D. Okla. 1978); *Warren County School Dist. v. Carlson*, 418 A.2d 810 (Pa. Cmwlth. 1980).

119. *See, e.g.,* F.R.E. Rule 410; *U.S. v. Albano*, 414 F. Supp., 67 (S.D.N.Y. 1976).

120. CPLR §6201; *McDonnell and Co. v. Sarlie*, 21 A.D.2d 767, 250 N.Y.S.2d 672 (1st Dept. 1964).

121. *N.Y. Times*, Apr. 6, 1982, at B 1, 6.

122. C.P.L.R. 6212(a).

123. *See, e.g., Maro Hosiery Corp. v. Hann*, 59 A.D.2d 674, 398 N.Y.S.2d 433 (1st Dep't 1977).

124. F.R.C.P. Rule 64.

125. *See, e.g., Sonesta International Hotels Corp. v. Wellington Associates*, 483 F.2d 247, 250 (2d Cir. 1973).

126. *International Controls Corp. v. Vesco*, 490 F.2d 1334, 1353–55 (2d Cir. 1974).

127. *See, e.g.*, N.Y. Debtor and Creditor Law §§273, 275, 276, 279; *American Surety Co. v. Conner*, 251 N.Y. 1, 166 N.E.2d 783 (1929); *In re Luftman*, 245 F. Supp. 723, 725 (S.D.N.Y. 1965).

128. *Orbach v. Pappa*, 482 F. Supp. 117 (S.D.N.Y. 1979).

129. *Becker v. S.P.V. Construction Co.*, 27 Ca.3d 489, 494, 612 P.2d 915, 165 Cal. Rptr. 825 (1979) (default). *But see* F.R.C.P. 54(c); Cal. Code Civ. Prac. §580; *Riggs, Ferris and Geer v. Lillibridge*, 316 F.2d 60 (2d Cir. 1963).

130. Rest.2d Torts §§902–06, 911.

131. *Id.* at §908.

132. *Id.* at 913A, 924, 926; 4 Witkin, *supra* note 59, at §883–90.

133. *Id.* at §549.

134. *Id.* at §§927, 928.

135. *Id.* at §§927, 931.

136. *Id.* at §929.

137. *Id.* at §914.

138. *Id.* at §920A; *Helfend v. Southern California Rapid Transit Dist.*, 2 Cal.3d 1, 6 (1970).

140. *See, e.g., Davis v. Hearst*, 160 Cal. 143 (1911).

141. *See, e.g., Livesey v. Stock*, 208 Cal. 315, 321 (1929) (assault with a deadly weapon); *Bergevin v. Morger*, 130 C.A.2d 590, 593 (1955) (unprovoked kicking attack); *Fletcher v. Western Nat. Life Ins. Co.*, 10 C.A.3d 376, 404 (1970) (intentional infliction of emotional distress); *Taylor v. Wright*, 69 C.A.2d 371, 384 (1945); *Donnell v. Bisso Brothers*, 10 C.A.3d 38, 44 (1970) (bulldozed victim's property); *Haigler v. Donnelly*, 18 Cal.2d 674, 681 (1941) (conversion of money).

142. *See, e.g., Roshak v. Leathers*, 277 Or. 207, 560 P.2d 275 (1977); *Gray v. Janicki*, 118 Vt. 49, 99 A.2d 707 (1953); *King v. Nixon*, 207 F.2d 41 (D.C. Cir. 1953); *Pendeleton v. Davis*, 46 N.C. 98 (1853). *But see Nicolson's Mobile Home Sales, Inc. v. Schramm*, 164 Ind. App.598, 330 N.E.2d 785 (1975).

143. *Lemer v. Boise Cascade Inc.*, 107 C.A.3d 1, 8, 165 Cal. Rep. 555 (1980).

144. *Compare Browand v. Scott Lumber Co.*, 125 Cal. App.2d 68, 269 P.2d 891 (1954) *with Gray v. Janicki*, 118 Vt. 49, 99 A.2d 707 (1953).

145. *Blackmon v. Kirven*, 170 S.C. 190, 192 (1933); *Zibbell v. Southern Pacific Co.*, 160 Cal. 237, 255 (1911).

146. Rest.2d, Torts §901; Cal. Code Civ. Prac. §657(5).

147. *Garzilli v. Howard Johnson Motor Lodge, Inc.*, 419 F. Supp. 1210 (E.D.N.Y. 1976).

148. *See, e.g.*, Cal. Code Civ. Prac. §681 *et seq.*; N.Y.C.P.L.R. §5101–5107, 5201–5210, 5221–5240, 5250–5252.

149. *See, e.g.*, Cal. Code Civ. Prac. §§699.53(a), 701.520, 701.570(d), 701.810–830. N.Y.C.P.L.R. §§5102, 5103, 5201–3, 5232–36.

150. *See, e.g., Anglo-California National Bank v. Kidd*, 58 Cal.2d 651, 655 (1943); N.Y.C.P.L.R. §§5205–6.

151. *Schoenfeld v. Norberg*, 11 C.A.3d 755 (1970).

152. *See, e.g.*, 5 Witkin, *California Procedure*, §§123–207.

153. *State v. Sampson*, 203 Neb. 786, 280 N.W.2d 81 (1979); *People v. Marks*, 340 Mich. 495, 65 N.W.2d 698 (1954); *U.S. v. Landay*, 513 F.2d 306 (5th Cir. 1975).

154. *See, e.g.*, N.Y.C.P.L.R. §§5401–08.

155. Cal. C.C.P. 681; N.Y.C.P.L.R. §211(b); ILL. REV. STAT. ch. 77 §6.

156. *See, e.g.*, CAL. CODE CIV. PRAC. §683.110–220; *Butcher v. Brouwer*, 21 C.2d 354, 357 (1942); ILL. REV. STAT. ch. 83, §24(b) (1977).

157. 11 U.S.C. §523(a)(6).

158. *State v. Johnson*, 96 Idaho 727, 536 P.2d 295 (1975). *But see Bowling v. State* — Md. App. — (1983).

159. *See, e.g., Fouch v. Werner*, 99 C.A. 557, 564, 279 P. 183 (1929).

160. Prosser, *supra* note 5 at §31, at 145; Rest. 2d, Torts §282.

161. *Id.* at §30, at 143.

162. *See, e.g., id.* at §§33, 56; Rest. 2d, Torts §§315, 448.

163. *See, e.g., U.S. v. Carroll Towing Co.*, 159 F.2d 169 (2d Cir. 1947); *Raymond v. Paradise, Unified School District of Butte County*, 218 C.A.2d 1, 8, 31 Cal. Rep. 847 (1963); Rest.2d Torts §291.

164. Prosser, *supra* note 5, §33, at 173.

165. *See, e.g., Tarasoff v. Regents, supra* note 76, at 435; Rest.2d, Torts §315.

166. *See, e.g., Kline v. 1500 Mass. Ave. Corp.*, 439 F.2d 477, 481 (D.C. Cir. 1970); *Neering v. Illinois Cent R.R. Co.*, 383 Ill. 366, 50 N.E.2d 497 (1943).

167. *See, e.g.*, "Negligence," *supra* note 1, at 466.

168. Rest.2d, Torts §§875, 879; 4 Witkin, *Summary of California Law*, §§34, 35 (8th ed., 1974).

169. 2 Witkin, *California Procedure* §§308–348.

170. N.Y.C.P.L.R. §§213, 214.

171. *Id.* at §215; N.Y. Gen. Mun. L. §50-e.

172. CAL. GOVT. C. §911.2, 913.

173. *DeLong v. County of Erie*, 60 N.Y.2d 296, 469 N.Y.S. 2d 611 (1983).

174. *Grimm, supra* note 96.

175. *Garzilli, supra* note 147.

176. *Daily News*, June 2, 1983, at 39, col.1.

177. *N.Y. Times*, Apr. 24, 1983, at 46, col. 3.

178. *Id.*

179. *Newsweek*, Aug. 16, 1982, at 63.

179a. "Tavern Pays Parents of Driver's Victim," *N.Y. Times* (Sept. 13, 1984) A 18, cl. 6.

180. *See, e.g., Kline v. Santa Barbara Consolidated Ry. Co.*, 150 C. 741, 745, 90 P. 125 (1907).

181. *See, e.g., Barad v. New York Rapid Transit Corp.*, 162 Misc. 458, 295 N.Y.S. 901 (Mun. Ct., N.Y.Co. 1937).

182. *See, e.g., Tickner v. Rochester-Genesee Regional Transportation*

Authority, 87 Misc.2d 703, 386 N.Y.S.2d 622 (Sup. Ct., Monroe Co. 1976).

183. *Neering v. Illinois Cent. R. Co.*, *supra* note 166.

184. *See, e.g., Bardavid v. New York City Transit Authority*, 82 A.D.2d 776, 440 N.Y.S.2d 648 (1981).

185. *See Day v. Trans-World Airlines, Inc.*, 528 F.2d 31 (2d Cir. 1975), *cert. denied*, 429 U.S. 890 (1976).

186. *Weiner v. Transportation Authority*, 55 N.Y.2d 175, 440 N.Y.S.2d 141, 433 N.E.2d 124 (1982).

187. *Fortney v. Hotel Rancroft, Inc.*, 5 Ill. App.2d 327, 125 N.E.2d 544 (1955); 70 A.L.R.2d 621.

188. *Compare Fortney v. Hotel Rancroft, Inc.*, *supra* note 187 *with McKee v. Sheraton-Russell, Inc.*, 268 F.2d 669 (2d Cir. 1959) and *Tobin v. Slutsky*, 506 F.2d 1097 (2d Cir. 1974); *Phillips Petroleum Co. v. Dorn*, 292 So.2d 429 (Fla. App., Dist. 4, 1974).

189. *Margreiter v. New Hotel Monteleone, Inc.*, 640 F.2d 508 (5th Cir. 1981).

190. *Orlando Executive Park, Inc. v. P.D.R.*, 402 So.2d 442 (Fla. App. Dist. 5, 1981), *petition denied*, 411 So.2d 384 (Fla. 1981).

191. *Kraaz v. La Quinta Motor Inns, Inc.*, 396 So.2d 455 (La. App. 1981).

192. *Walkoviak v. Hilton Hotels Corp.*, 580 S.W.2d 623 (Tex. Civ. App. 14th Dist. 1979). For other cases holding innkeepers liable, *see also Peters v. Holiday Inns, Inc.*, 89 Wis.2d 115, 278 N.W.2d 208 (1979); *Kiefel v. Las Vegas Hacienda, Inc.*, 404 F.2d 1163 (7th Cir.) *cert. denied*, 395 U.S. 908 (1969); *Jeness v. Sheraton-Cadillac Properties, Inc.*, 48 Mich. App. 723, 211 N.W.2d 106; *Dean v. Hotel Greenwich Corp.*, 21 Misc.2d 702, 193 N.Y.S.2d 712 (Sup. Ct., N.Y. Co. 1959).

193. *Compare Rosier v. Gainesville Inns Ass., Inc.*, 347 So.2d 1100 (Fla. App. Dist. 1 1977) *with Orlando Executive Park, Inc. v. P.D.R.*, *supra* note 190. *Compare Moskowitz v. M.I.T.*, Index No. 14786–79 (N.Y. Sup. Ct.) in *New York State Jury Verdict Review and Analysis*, Vol. 1, no. 1 at 5, 6 (Oct. 1983).

194. *See Weihert v. Piccone*, 273 Wisc. 448, 78 N.W.2d 757 (1956).

195. *See, e.g., Winn v. Holmes*, 143 Cal. App.2d 501, 299 P.2d 994 (1956); *Shank v. Riker Restaurants Associates, Inc.*, 28 Misc.2d 835, 216 N.Y.S.2d 118 (Sup. Ct. N.Y. Co.), *aff'd* 15 App. Div.2d 458, 222 N.Y.S.2d 683 (1961); *Kimple v. Foster*, 205 Kan. 415, 469 P.2d 281 (1970); *Nevin v. Carlasco*, 365 P.2d 637 (Mont. 1961); *Kane v. Fields Corner Grille, Inc.*, 171 N.E.2d 287 (Mass. 1961); *Manuel v. Weitzman*, 23 Mich. App. 96, 178 N.W.2d 121, *modified*, 386 Mich. 157, 191 N.W.2d 474 (1971); *Miller v. Staton*, 58 Wash.2d 879, 365 P.2d 333 (1961); *Manzanares v. Playhouse Corp.*, 25 Wash. App. 905, 611 P.2d 797 (1980).

196. *Quinn v. Winkel's, Inc.*, 279 N.W.2d 65 (Minn. 1979).

197. *Devine v. McLain*, 306 N.W.2d 827 (Minn. 1981); *Babrab, Inc. v. Allen*, 408 So.2d 610 (Fla. App. Dist. 4 1981); *Munn v. Hardee's*

Food Systems, Inc., 266 S.E.2d 414 (S.C. 1980); *Kipp v. Wong*, 517 P.2d 897 (Mont. 1974); *Filas v. Daher*, 218 N.W.2d 467 (Minn. 1974); *Weihert v. Piccone, supra* note 194.

198. *See, e.g., Romero v. Kendricks*, 74 N.M. 24, 390 P.2d 269 (1964); *Archer v. Burton*, 91 Mich. App. 57, 282 N.W.2d 833 (1979); *Radko v. Carpenter*, 281 Or. 671, 576 P.2d 365 (1978).

199. *See, e.g., Pierce v. Lopez*, 16 Ariz. App. 54, 490 P.2d 1182 (1972); *Hull v. Rund*, 374 P.2d 351 (Colo. 1962); *Shelby v. Keck*, 85 Wash.2d 911, 541 P.2d 365 (1975).

200. *See, e.g., Brown v. Iaconelli*, 26 Misc.2d 194, 206 N.Y.S.2d 669 (Mun. Ct., Kings Co. 1960); *Ross v. Roberta Bar & Grill, Inc.*, 83 App. Div.2d 550, 441 N.Y.S.2d 23 (2d Dept. 1981).

201. *See, e.g., Latsis v. Walsh*, 28 Ill. App.2d 91, 170 N.E.2d 633 (1960).

202. *See, e.g., Hull, supra* note 199; *Mason v. Roberts*, 33 Ohio St.2d 29, 62 Ohio Ops.2d 346, 294 N.E.2d 884 (1973).

203. Cal. B. & P. C. 25602(c).

204. *Compare Gabrielle v. Craft*, 75 A.D.2d 939, 428 N.Y.S.2d 84 (1980) *with Kelly v. Gwinell*, — N.J. — (1984).

205. *See, e.g., Zinck v. Whelan*, 120 N.J. Super. 432, 294 A.2d 727 (1972); *Enders v. Apcoa, Inc.*, 55 Cal. App.3d 897, 127 Cal. Rptr. 751 (1976).

206. *Compare Angell v. F. Avanzini Lumber Co.*, 363 So.2d 571 (Fla. App., Dist. 2, 1978) *with Bennet v. Cincinnati Checker Cab Co.*, 353 F. Supp. 1206 (E.D. Ky. 1973).

207. *Benway v. City of Watertown*, 1 A.D.2d 465, 151 N.Y.S.2d 485 (4th Dep't 1956).

208. *Richman v. Charter Arms Corp.*, 571 F. Supp. 192 (E.D. La. 1983); "Suits Target Handgun Makers," *Nat. L. J.*, at 1 (Nov. 29, 1982); "Getting Even Suits Crime Victims," *Chicago Sunday Sun Times*, June 19, 1983, at 10 (Living).

209. *Kline v. 1500 Massachusetts Ave. Apartment Corp., supra* note 166. *See also* 43 A.L.R.3d 331.

210. *Johnston v. Harris*, 387 Mich. 569, 198 N.W.2d 409 (1972); *Trentacost v. Brussel*, 82 N.J. 214, 412 A.2d 436 (1980); *Dick v. Great South Bay Co.*, 106 Misc.2d 686, 435 N.Y.S.2d 240; *Spar v. Obwoya*, 369 A.2d 173 (D.C. App. 1977).

211. *Phillips v. Chicago Housing Authority*, 91 Ill. App.3d 544, 414 N.E.2d 1133 (1980); *Stribling v. Chicago Housing Authority*, 340 N.E.2d 47, 34 Ill. App.3d 551 (1975).

212. *Cross v. Chicago Housing Authority*, 74 Ill. App.3d 921, 393 N.E.2d 580 (1979); *Holley v. Mt. Zion Terrace Apartments, Inc.*, 382 So.2d 98 (Fla. App. Dist. 3, 1980); *Secretary of Housing and Urban Development v. Layfield*, 88 Cal. App.3d Supp. 28, 152 Cal. Rptr. 342 (1978); *Ramsay v. Morrissette*, 252 A.2d 509 (D.C. App. 1969).

213. *See, e.g., Thahill Realty Co. v. Martin*, 88 Misc.2d 520, 388 N.Y.S.2d 823 (Civ. Ct., Queens Co. 1976).

214. *O'Hara v. Western Seven Trees Corp.*, 75 Cal. App.3d 798, 142 Cal. Rptr. 47 (1977).

215. *See, e.g., Sherman v. Concourse Realty Corp.*, 47 App. Div.2d 134, 365 N.Y.S.2d 239 (2d Dept. 1975); *Trentacost, supra* note 210.

216. *Layfield, supra* note 212; *Brownstein v. Edison*, 103 Misc.2d 316, 425 N.Y.S.2d 773 (Sup. Ct., Kings Co. 1980); *Trentacost, supra* note 215.

217. *See, e.g., 7735 Hollywood Blvd. Ventures v. Superior Court*, 116 Cal App.3d 901, 172 Cal. Rptr. 528 (2d Dist. 1981); *Flood v. Wisconsin Real Estate Investment Trust, Inc.*, 497 F. Supp. 320 (D. Kan. 1980); *Gant v. Flint-Goodridge Hospital*, 359 So.2d 279 (La. App. 1978), *cert. denied*, 362 So.2d 581 (La. Sup. Ct. 1978).

218. *Gulf Reston, Inc. v. Rogers*, 215 Va. 155, 207 S.E.2d 841 (1974).

219. *Bass v. City of New York*, 38 A.D.2d 407, 330 N.Y.S.2d 569 (2d Dept. 1972); *Pippin v. Chicago Housing Authority*, 78 Ill.2d 204, 399 N.E.2d 596 (1979); *Goldberg v. Housing Authority of the City of Newark*, 38 N.J. 578, 186 A.2d 291 (1962).

220. Rest.2d, Torts §344; 93 A.L.R.3d 999. *See also*, M. Brazyler, *The Duty to Provide Adequate Protection: Landowners' Liability for Failure to Protect Patrons from Criminal Attack*, 21 ARIZ. L. REV. 727 (1979).

221. *Picco v. Ford's Diner, Inc.*, 113 N.J. Super. 465, 274 A.2d 301 (1971); *Kraustrunk v. Chicago Housing Auth.*, 95 Ill. App.3d 529, 420 N.E.2d 429 (1981); *Winn-Dixie Stores, Inc. v. Johnstoneaux*, 395 So.2d 599 (Fla. App. Dist. 3, 1981), *petition denied*, 402 So.2d 614 (Fla. 1981); *Foster v. Winston-Salem Joint Venture*, 274 S.E.2d 265 (N.C. App. 1981); *Nallan v. Helmsley-Spear, Inc.*, 50 N.Y.2d 507, 429 N.Y.S.2d 606, 407 N.E.2d 451 (1980).

222. *See, e.g., Rogers v. Jones*, 56 Cal. App.3d 346, 128 Cal. Rptr. 404 (1976); *Hewett v. First National Bank*, 155 Ga. App. 773, 272 S.E.2d 744 (1980); *Cornpropst v. Sloan*, 528 S.W.2d 188 (Tenn. 1975).

223. *Samson v. Saginaw Professional Building, Inc.*, 393 Mich. 393 (1975).

224. *Virginia D. v. Madesco Investment Corp.*, 648 S.W.2d 881 (Mo. 1983). *See also Oppenheimer v. Chase Manhattan Bank*,—N.Y.S.2d— (Civ. Ct. N.Y.Co. 1984) (robbery at automatic teller).

225. *See, e.g., Genovay v. Fox*, 50 N.J. Super. 538, 143 A.2d 229, *reversed on other grounds*, 29 N.J. 436, 149 A.2d 212 (1958); *Helms v. Harris*, 281 S.W.2d 770 (Tex. Civ. App. 1955).

226. *Boyd v. Ricine Currency Exchange, Inc.*, 56 Ill.2d 95, 306 N.E.2d 39 (1973); *Adkins v. Ashland Supermarkets, Inc.*, 569 S.W.2d 698 (Ky. App. 1978); *Roberts v. Tiny Tim Thrifty Check*, 367 So.W.2d 64 (La. App. 1979).

227. *See, e.g., Cook v. Safeway Stores, Inc.*, 354 A.2d 507 (D.C. App. 1976); *Boss v. Prince's Drive-Ins*, 401 S.W.2d 140 (Tex. Civ. App. 1966).

228. *See, e.g., Cary v. Hotel Rueger, Inc.*, 195 Va. 980, 81 S.E.2d 421 (1954); *Dantos v. Community Theatres Co.*, 90 Ga. App. 195, 82 S.E.2d 260 (1954).

229. *Rabon v. Guardsmark, Inc.*, 571 F.2d 1277 (4th Cir. 1978).

230. *Rydberg v. Mitchell*, 87 F. Supp. 639 (D. Alaska 1949); *Berger v. Southern Pacific Co.*, *supra* note 25.

231. *Tobin v. Slutsky*, 506 F.2d 1097 (2d Cir. 1974); *Weiss v. Furniture in the Raw*, 62 Misc.2d 283, 306 N.Y.S.2d 253 (Civ. Ct. Queens Co. 1969).

232. *See, e.g.*, *Thahill Realty v. Martin*, *supra* note 213; *Kendall v. Gore Properties*, 236 F.2d 673 (D.C. Cir. 1956); *Komine v. Booker*, Civ. No. 2805 (Haw.2d Cir. Ct.) (Wailuku, Maui) (1978). *See also* "13 Million Dollars in Rape-Murder," *Chicago Sun-Times*, Jan. 24, 1975, p. 1, col. 1.

233. *See, e.g.*, *Mays v. Pico Finance Co.*, 339 So.2d 382 (La. App. 1976); *Lou-Con, Inc. v. Gulf Building Services, Inc.*, 287 So.2d 192 (La. App. 1973) *writ refused*, 290 So.2d 899 (La. 1974); *Stevens v. Lankard*, 25 N.Y.2d 640, 306 N.Y.S.2d 257 (1969).

234. *Hersh v. Kentfield Builders, Inc.*, 385 Mich. 410, 189 N.W.2d 286 (1971). *See, e.g.*, ILL. REV. STAT., ch. 38, §§206–7 (1973); CONN. GEN. STAT. §§54–90 (Supp. 1976).

235. *Lillie v. Thompson*, 332 U.S. 459 (1947). *See also Sapp v. City of Tallahassee*, 348 So.2d 363 (Fla. App. 1st Dist. 1977).

236. *Circle K Corp. v. Rosenthal*, 118 Ariz. 63, 574 P.2d 856 (1978). *But see Larrabee v. Marine Midland Bank-Central*, 55 A.D.2d 1018, 391 N.Y.S.2d 214 (4th Dept. 1977); *Dwyer v. Erie Investment Co.*, 138 N.J. Super. 93, 350 A.2d 268 (1975).

237. *Hosein v. Checker Taxi Co.*, 95 Ill. App.3d 150, 419 N.E.2d 568 (1981); *Curtis v. Beatrice Foods Co.*, 481 F. Supp. 1275 (S.D.N.Y. 1980).

238. *Smith v. Officers and Directors of Kart-N-Karry, Inc.*, 346 So.2d 313 (La. App. 1977).

239. *Warner v. State*, 54 N.Y.2d 143, 448 N.Y.S.2d 78 (1981).

240. *Kansas O. & G. Ry. Co. of Texas v. Pike*, 264 S.W. 593 (1924).

241. *Nallan v. Helmsley Spear*, *supra* note 221; *Nieves v. Holmes Protection Service*, 446 N.Y.S.2d 865 (Sup. Ct. 1981); *Crossland v. New York City Transit Authority*, *N.Y.L.J.*, at 13, col. 3 (Sup. Ct., Kings Co., Jan. 19, 1984).

242. *See, e.g.*, *McKee*, *supra* note 188.

243. *Bernal v. Pinkerton's, Inc.*, 52 A.D.2d 760, 382 N.Y.S.2d 769 (1976); *Taylor v. Trans-World Airlines, Inc.*, 56 Ohio App.2d 117 (1977).

244. "Jury Awards $3 Million Dollars to Girl Raped in Stairwell of School," *N.Y. Times*, Apr. 24, 1983, at 46, col. 4; *Cioffi v. Bd. of Education*, 27 App. Div.2d 826, 278 N.Y.S.2d 249 (1967).

245. *State v. Walden*, 293 S.E.2d 780 (N.C. 1982).

246. *Landeros v. Flood*, *supra* note 62.

247. *See, e.g.*, *De Long v. County of Erie*, *supra* note 173.

248. *See, e.g.*, *Simpson's Food Fair v. Evansville*, 272 N.E.2d 871 (Ind. App., 1971); *Massengill v. Yuma County*, 104 Ariz. 518, 456 P.2d 376 (1969). *See also* 46 A.L.R.3d 1084. One exception to this general rule is the long-established liability of municipalities to

provide protection of life and property during riots; in some jurisdictions Riot Acts even create a presumption of municipal liability for riot damage. *See Mayor and City Council of Baltimore v. Silver*, 263 Md. 439, 283 A.2d 788 (1971).

249. *See, e.g., Massengill v. Yuma County, supra* note 248; *Evett v. Inverness*, 224 So.2d 365 (Fla. App. 1969), *cert. dismissed*, 232 So.2d 18 (Fla. 1970); *Evers v. Westerberg*, 38 App. Div.2d 751, 329 N.Y.S.2d 615 (2d Div. 1972).

250. *Riss v. City of New York*, 27 App. Div.2d 217, 278 N.Y.S.2d 110, *aff'd*, 22 N.Y.2d 579, 293 N.Y.S.2d 897, 240 N.E.2d 860 (1967); "City is Cleared in Exorcism Death of Baby by Scalding," *N.Y. Post*, June 14, 1982, at 3.

251. *See, e.g., Stone v. State*, 106 Cal. App.3d 924, 165 Cal. Rptr. 339 (3d Dist. 1980); *Bruttomesso v. Las Vegas Metropolitan Police Dept.*, 591 P.2d 254 (Nev. 1979).

252. *See, e.g., Goldberg v. Housing Authority of City of Newark, supra* note 219; *Weiner v. Metropolitan Transportation Authority, supra* note 186.

253. *See, e.g., Christy v. City of Baton Rouge*, 282 So.2d 724 (La. App.), *application denied*, 284 So.2d 776 (La. 1973); *Estate of Tanasijevich v. Hammond*, 383 N.E.2d 1081 (Ind. App. 1978); *Swanner v. U.S.*, 309 F. Supp. 1183 (M.D. Ala. 1970); *Schuster v. City of New York*, 5 N.Y.2d 75, 180 N.Y.S.2d 265, 154 N.E.2d 534 (1958); *Gardner v. Chicago Ridge*, 71 Ill. App.2d 373, 219 N.E.2d 147 (1966).

254. *Bloom v. City of New York*, 78 Misc.2d 1077, 357 N.Y.S.2d 979 (Sup. Ct., N.Y. Co. 1974); *Silverman v. City of Fort Wayne*, 357 N.E.2d 285 (Ind. App. 1976).

255. *Susser v. New York*, 97 Misc.2d 984, 413 N.Y.S.2d 83 (Civ. Ct., N.Y. Co. 1979); *Parvi v. City of Kingston*, 41 N.Y.2d 553, 394 N.Y.S.2d 161, 362 N.E.2d 960 (1977).

256. *See, e.g., Fair v. U.S.*, 234 F.2d 288 (5th Cir. 1956); *Zibbon v. Town of Cheektowaga*, 382 N.Y.S.2d 152, 51 A.D.2d 448 (4th Dept. 1976).

257. *Baker v. New York*, 25 App. Div.2d 770, 269 N.Y.S.2d 515 (2d Dept. 1966); *Sorichetti v. City of New York*, 95 Misc.2d 451, 408 N.Y.S.2d 219 (Sup. Ct., Bronx Co. 1978).

258. *Florence v. Goldberg*, 44 N.Y.2d 189, 404 N.Y.S.2d 583, 375 N.E.2d 763 (1978).

259. *See, e.g., Mentillo v. City of Auburn*, 2 Misc.2d 818, 150 N.Y.S.2d 94 (Sup. Ct., Cayuga Co. 1956); *Benway v. Watertown, supra* note 207.

260. *Nearing v. Weaver*, 295 Or. 702, 670 P.2d 137 (1983).

261. *DeLong v. County of Erie, supra* note 173.

262. *Davidson v. City of Westminister*, 32 Cal.3d 197 (1982).

263. *Warren v. Dist. of Columbia* (C.A. 79–6).

264. *See, e.g.*, 28 U.S.C. §2680(a); *Santangelo v. State*, 103 Misc.2d 578, 426 N.Y.S.2d 931 (Ct. Cl. 1980). *See generally* Note, "Holding

Governments Strictly Liable for the Release of Dangerous Parolees," 55 *N.Y.U.L.Rev.* 907 (1980).

265. *See e.g., Pate v. Alabama Board of Pardons and Paroles,* 409 F. Supp. 478 (M.D. Ala. 1976); *Siess v. McConnell,* 74 Mich. App. 613, 255 N.W.2d 2 (1977); *Burg v. State,* 147 N.J. Super. 316, 371 A.2d 308 (1977).

266. *See, e.g.,* CAL. GOVT. CODE §845.8(a).

267. *Grimm v. Arizona Bd. of Pardons and Paroles, supra* note 96. *See also Estate of Armstrong v. Pennsylvania Bd. of Probation and Parole,* 46 Pa. Cmwlth. 33, 405 A.2d 1099 (1979).

268. *Santangelo v. State, supra* note 264.

269. *Martinez v. California,* 444 U.S. 277 (1980).

270. *See, also, Patricia J. v. Rio Linda Union School District,* 132 Cal. Rptr. 211 (1976); *Reiser v. District of Columbia, supra; Robilotto v. State,* 104 Misc.2d 713, 429 N.Y.S.2d 362 (Ct. Cl. 1980).

271. *Goergen v. State,* 18 Misc.2d 1085, 196 N.Y.S.2d 455 (Ct. Cl. 1959); *Reiser v. Dist. of Columbia,* 563 F.2d 462, 479 (D.C. Cir. 1977); *Johnson v. State,* 69 Cal.2d 782, 447 P.2d 352, 73 Cal. Rptr. 240 (1968).

272. *Hernandez v. State,* 11 Cal.App.3d 895, 90 Cal. Rptr. 205 (1970).

273. *Id.; Milano v. State,* 44 Misc.2d 290, 253 N.Y.S.2d 662 (Ct. Cl. 1964).

274. *Ellis v. U.S.,* 484 F. Supp. 4 (D.S.C. 1978); *Hernandez v. State, supra* note 272; *Schwenk v. State,* 250 Misc. 407, 129 N.Y.S.2d 92, *appeal dismissed,* 131 N.Y.S.2d 455 (3d Dept. 1953).

275. *Leverett v. State,* 61 Ohio App.2d 35, 15 Ohio Ops.3d 62, 399 N.E.2d 106 (1978); *Eanes v. U.S.,* 407 F.2d 823 (4th Cir. 1969); *Durflinger v. Artiles,*—F.2d—(10th. Cir. 1984).

276. *See, e.g., Underwood v. U.S.,* 356 F.2d 92 (5th Cir. 1966); *Fair v. U.S.,* 234 F.2d 288 (5th Cir. 1956); *Williams v. U.S.,* 450 F. Supp. 1040 (D.S.D. 1978); *Estate of Mathes v. Ireland,* 419 N.E.2d 782 (Ind. App. 1981); *Hicks v. U.S.,* 357 F. Supp. 434 (D.D.C.), *aff'd,* 511 F.2d 407 (D.C. Cir. 1975); *Homere v. State,* 370 N.Y.S.2d 246 (3d Dept. 1975).

277. *Semler v. Psychiatric Institute,* 538 F.2d 121 (4th Cir.), *cert. denied,* 429 U.S. 827 (1976).

278. *See County of Sacramento v. Superior Court of Sacramento County,* 8 Cal.3d 479, 105 Cal. Rptr. 374, 503 P.2d 1382 (1973).

279. *Epting v. State,* 546 P.2d 242 (Utah 1976).

280. *State v. Silva,* 86 Nev. 911, 478 P.2d 591 (1971). *See also Webb v. State,* 91 So.2d 156 (La. App. 1956); *Geiger v. State,* 242 So.2d 606 (La. App. 1970).

281. *Taylor v. State of Washington,* No. 211–130 (Sup. Ct., Pierce Co. Wsh. Sept. 10, 1973), cited in *Memorandum, supra* note 1, at 16.

282. *See, e.g., Williams v. State,* 308 N.Y. 548, 127 N.E.2d 545 (1955); *Green v. State,* 91 So.2d 153 (La. App. 1956); *West Virginia v. Fidelity and Casualty Co.,* 263 F. Supp. 88 (S.D.W. Va. 1967).

283. *Tarasoff v. Regents of University of California, supra* note 76.

284. *Moskowitz v. MIT,* 14786/79 (Sup. Ct., N.Y. Co.); *McIntosh v. Milano,* 168 N.J. Super. 466, 403 A.2d 500 (1979). *See also Lipari v. Sears, Roebuck and Co.,* 497 F. Supp. 185 (D. Nev. 1980). *See also* "Forcing the Therapists to Pay," *N.L.J.,* Jan. 17, 1983, at 1, c. 1.

285. *Thompson v. County of Alameda,* 27 Cal.3d 741, 614 P.2d 728, 167 Cal. Rptr. 70 (1980).

286. *Mavroudis v. Superior Court,* 102 Cal. App.3d 594, 162 Cal. Rptr. 724 (1st Dist. 1980). *See generally* B. Ennis & R. Emery, *The Rights of Mental Patients* (New York: Avon Books, 1978 revised ed.).

287. *Johnson v. Glidden,* 76 N.W. 933 (S.D. 1898); *Kuhns v. Brugger,* 135 A.2d 395 (Pa. 1957); *Ellis v. D'Angelo,* 116 Cal. App.2d 310 (1953). *See also Rausch v. McVeigh,* 105 Misc.2d 163, 431 N.Y.S.2d 887 (1980); *Hugler v. Rose,* 451 N.Y.S.2d 478 (1982).

288. Cal. Civ. Code §1714.1. *See also* Ill. Rev. Stat. ch. 70 §51 *et seq.*; Cal. Veh. Code §§17708–17709.

289. Rest.2d, Torts §463, 467.

290. *See, e.g., Rosier v. Gainesville Inns Ass., Inc., supra* note 193.

291. *See, e.g., Liv. Yellow Cab Co.,* 13 Cal.3d 804 (1975).

292. *See* Prosser, *supra* note 5, at §67.

293. *See, e.g., Tarasoff v. Regents of University of California, supra; Garzilli v. Howard Johnson Motor Lodge, Inc., supra* note 283. *But see Industrial Park Businessmen's Club, Inc. v. Buck,* 252 Ark. 513, 479 S.W.2d 842 (1972).

294. *See* "Home Insurance Basics," "Auto Insurance Basics," and "Tenants Insurance Basics," (available from the Insurance Information Institute, 110 Williams St., New York, N.Y.).

295. "Insurance Companies' New Policy May Ease a Mugger's Conscience," *The Wall Street Journal,* at 1. Sept. 28, 1981; "Crime Victim Policy Comes Under Attack," *The National Underwriter,* (Sept. 25, 1981), at 2.

296. "Crime Coverage Provisions and Their Endorsements," *The Professional Agent,* Dec. 1980, at 14.

297. 26 U.S.C. §§165 (c); 213; 165.

VI

The Right to Share in the Profits from the Criminal's Depiction of the Crime

Do victims have any special right to share in profits from books, movies, or television shows based on the criminal's "story" of the crime?

Yes. At least twenty-two states and the federal government have enacted special statutes (often called Son of Sam statutes) which require writers, journalists, publishers, or filmmakers who contract with an accused or convicted person for rights to his "version" of the crime to turn any payments over to an escrow fund operated by the state; these funds are then available to satisfy victims' judgments against the criminal.[1] In states without such statutes, by attachment or otherwise, a victim may be able to prevent the criminal defendant from disposing of the proceeds from sales of his version of the crime, if those proceeds may be necessary to satisfy the victim's judgment against him.

How do these special Son of Sam statutes work?

Although they vary from state to state, these statutes require that anyone who contracts with a person accused or convicted of a crime must provide the state with a copy of this contract. Where the state determines that he is being paid for his depiction of the crime or his thoughts or feelings about it, any payment due to the accused or convicted person is escrowed by the state for a certain period of time. If during that time, the person has been convicted of the crime and the victim begins a civil action for damages against him, any judgment the victim receives can be satisfied out of the funds being held by the state in escrow. Depending on the jurisdiction and the circumstances, the escrow funds may also be used to pay the accused or convicted person's attorneys' fees or other expenses. Any remaining funds may be paid to the criminal or (in some jurisdictions) revert to the government.

However, critics have argued that these statutes are largely symbolic (few crimes produce best-selling books), that they violate equal protection by treating the proceeds of book contracts different from other assets, and that they "chill" the criminal's exercise of free speech in violation of the First Amendment.

Why are these statutes called Son of Sam statutes?

During the summer of 1977, New York City was the scene of a series of random shootings of young couples committed by an unknown assailant (the so-called .44 caliber killer) who identified himself in notes to the media as the Son of Sam. There was speculation at the time that the killer's "story" could be sold to a publisher for at least $200,000. Outraged, Senator Emmanuel R. Gold introduced the first Son of Sam statute in the New York legislature stating at the time that

> [I]t is abhorrent to one's sense of justice and decency that an individual, such as the .44 caliber killer, can expect to receive large sums of money for his story once he is captured, while 5 people are dead and other people were injured as a result of his conduct. This [statute] would make it clear that in all criminal situations, the victim must be more important than the criminal.[2]

At least twenty-one other states have adopted comparable or identical statutes escrowing funds where a notorious criminal sells his story to the media. In 1984, Congress amended the federal criminal code to include a provision allowing a judge (in the interests of justice or where a restitution order requires it) to issue an order requiring a defendant to forfeit all or part of the proceeds of any sale of his "story."[3]

Are large payments to a criminal for his "story" common?

No. However, a small number of criminals who have committed especially gruesome or notorious crimes have received fees of hundreds of thousands of dollars for their "stories." Notorious criminals who have received substantial royalties for the rights to describe their crimes include—

1. Susan Atkins, a member of the Manson family who received almost $200,000 for an interview describing her role in the Sharon Tate murder;

2. James Earl Ray, the convicted murderer of Martin Luther King, Jr., who received in excess of $40,000 in royalties for his story;

3. John Wojtowicz, who received in excess of $40,000 for the rights to depict the bank robbery he committed in 1972, which was the basis for the film *Dog Day Afternoon;*

4. Jack Abbott, who received $500,000 or more in connection with his best-selling novel *In the Belly of the Beast*, his autobiographical depiction of his life in prison including crimes that he committed there, and the rights to his life story;

5. David Berkowitz, the "Son of Sam" killer, who actually received $250,000 for his story.[4]

While such payments are made to very few criminals and Son of Sam laws will not assist the vast majority of victims in recovering damages, the very notoriety of the crimes that do attract such large payments make Son of Sam laws important symbols to some people that criminals will not be permitted to profit from their crimes.

How often have the Son of Sam statutes actually been used to escrow funds for victims?

Not very often. In New York, from 1977 to 1983, payments to only seven criminals (including Berkowitz and Wojtowicz) have been escrowed under New York's Son of Sam statute. As a result of lengthy delays in the victims' civil trials against these criminals, only one victim (a victim of Wojtowicz's bank robbery) has actually received a distribution of such funds.[5]

Do these laws apply to every person who commits a crime or only to persons who commit certain kinds of crimes?

It varies with the state. While New York's statute applies to any person guilty of "a crime in the state," statutes in other states (such as Alabama and Arizona) are limited to persons who have committed felonies. The federal statute applies only to federal offenses resulting in physical harm to an individual.[6]

Do these laws apply to contracts with persons accused of crimes or only to convicted criminals?

Although the states vary in establishing the point in the criminal proceedings at which the statute becomes operative with respect to particular criminals, typically they apply to persons who have been indicted, or accused of a crime, in addition to persons already convicted. However, the federal statute requires actual conviction before the proceeds are forfeited.[7]

What happens to the fund if the person accused of the crime is acquitted?

Virtually all of the statutes specifically require that upon dismissal of charges or acquittal of the accused, funds in the escrow account are to be immediately paid to the accused person.

Which agency administers the escrow fund?

It varies from state to state. In New York, for example, it is the responsibility of the Crime Victims Board while in Alabama, the escrow fund is maintained by the Board of Adjustment and in South Carolina, it is maintained by the courts. Under the federal statute the Attorney General escrows the proceeds as part of the federal Crime Victims Fund.[8]

What sort of contracts for rights to the criminal's "story" are covered by these statutes?

Virtually all contracts. The statutory language is extremely broad and applies to contracts with "every person, firm, corporation . . . or other legal entity" and the criminal or his "representative or assignee" with respect to his feelings or emotions about the crime or a reenactment in "a movie, book, magazine article, tape recording, phonograph record, radio or television presentation, [or] live entertainment of any kind."[9] It is encumbent upon anyone entering into such a contract to provide the state with a copy of the contract, thus assisting the state in determining whether the contract is covered by the statute.[10]

How does the state determine whether a contractual payment is to be escrowed? Is the accused or convicted person entitled to a hearing in connection with that determination?

The procedure for determining whether a particular payment is to be escrowed varies from state to state but the criminal is probably entitled to a hearing. New York's Son of Sam law (and the laws in other states patterned after it) do not provide for any specific procedure for determining whether a particular payment should be escrowed. However, New York's Crime Victims Board has adopted regulations[11] governing determinations under the Son of Sam law that provide that, after a review of any submitted contracts, the board will issue a proposed determination and/or administrative order. The accused, the contracting parties, and any known victims are given written notice that the proposed determination will become final in thirty days unless a hearing is requested. If a hearing is requested, a board member conducts the hearing, and a written record of the hearing is maintained. The board member files a report with the board, which then issues a final decision. Either the victim or the criminal can request a rehearing (upon a showing of good cause) or a court review of the board's decision. In cases where the chairman of the board determines that a substantial danger exists that the criminal defendant will attempt to conceal, waste, or dispose of the funds or remove them from the state, the chairman is also empowered to make an emergency determination escrowing funds until a hearing and final determination.

Florida by statute provides for an automatic lien on any contractual payments for a criminal's story.[12] The state then is obligated to commence a court proceeding to perfect the lien before it can take possession of the payments. During that proceeding the criminal and any contracting parties would have notice and an opportunity to be heard on the applicability of the statute to the particular payment at issue.

Under the federal statute, funds are only escrowed after the United States Attorney makes a specific motion (with prior notice to all interested parties, including the defendant and any victims) for a court order of special forfeiture. It is up to the judge to decide whether all or a portion of the funds are to be escrowed. If a restitution order requires forfeiture, it is mandatory. If not, it is up to the court to decide whether "the interests of justice" require forfeiture.[13]

Is such a hearing prior to escrowing the funds necessary?

Probably. The United States Supreme Court has repeatedly held that government action to attach or escrow funds or other property without notice or without a prompt opportunity to be heard, violates the Fourteenth Amendment's guarantee of due process.[14] Focusing on the absence of specific hearing requirements in a number of Son of Sam statutes, several commentators have indicated that escrowing funds to be paid to a criminal without a hearing would violate the accused or convicted person's due process rights.[15] However, in those states (such as New York and Florida) that have administrative or court proceedings providing specific notice to the criminal defendant and contracting parties as well as an opportunity for a hearing and judicial review, there would seem to be no violation of the defendant's or any contracting party's right to due process.

Can the criminal defendant transfer rights to his story to his attorney or to other third parties in order to avoid application of the statute?

No. Virtually all of the states have specifically provided that any attempt by the accused or his attorney to create a dummy corporation or to otherwise transfer rights to his story in order to defeat the statute "shall be null and void as against [the] public policy" of the state. The federal statute specifically provides that funds received by the defendant or "a transferee" can be subject to forfeiture.[16]

In addition, the ABA Code of Professional Responsibility specifically provides that a lawyer shall not enter into any arrangement or understanding with a client by which he acquires an interest in publication rights with respect to the subject matter of his employment.[17] The blatant conflict of interest that occurs when a lawyer is attempting to represent a client and also to prepare his own version of the notorious case in which he is involved has led courts to remove attorneys who have entered into such retainer agreements or hold, on appeal, that such agreements deprive the criminal defendant of a fair trial.[18]

What is the penalty if the contracting party fails to turn over to the state funds to be paid to the criminal for his "story"?

It depends on the state. The New York federal statute and most of the states that have enacted Son of Sam statutes provide no explicit penalty for parties who contract with criminals and who fail to comply with the payment requirement. One commentator has suggested that despite the lack of a specific penalty, under such statutes, the purchaser of the rights will be liable to the state in damages for the funds paid to the criminal that should have been turned over to the state.[19] Arizona makes such a sanction explicit; the publisher is responsible to the State Industrial Commission for all funds paid to or received by the criminal.[20]

Several states also provide for criminal penalties. Alabama makes the contracting party's failure to turn over the funds a felony punishable by imprisonment for a period of up to ten years plus a fine equal to the net proceeds earned from the reenactment of the crime,[21] Georgia makes the contracting party guilty of a separate misdemeanor for each day he violates the statute, and Illinois makes failure to pay the funds to the state a business offense punishable by a fine of no less than $5,000.[22]

Does the state have any obligation to notify victims of the existence of the escrow fund?

Yes. In New York, the state is required to advertise the existence of the fund in a newspaper of general circulation once every six months for five years from the date it receives the funds.[23] In Alabama, the state is required to notify all known victims (or their families) and provide a list of the names of criminals for whom money is being held in escrow to each of the state's probate judges to be made available for public inspection. The federal statute requires publication of the details of the forfeiture within 30 days after imposition of a forfeiture order.[24]

Which victims are entitled to satisfy judgments from the escrow fund?

Typically, the statutes define victims broadly to include any person who suffers personal, physical, mental, or emotional injury, or pecuniary loss as a direct result of the crime. The federal statute is apparently limited to individual victims who suffered physical harm from the crime.[25]

Is the victim of a particular crime entitled to satisfy a judgment only from funds paid for the depiction of the particular crime in which he was involved, or can a victim also satisfy his judgment from funds obtained from that criminal's depiction of other crimes involving other victims?

This is not entirely clear. In New York, in 1982, Jack

Abbott was convicted of manslaughter in the stabbing death of a waiter and aspiring actor, Richard Adan, while on parole. Pointing out that the widely publicized murder had substantially enhanced the sales of Abbott's book, attorneys for Adan's family argued that since the purpose of the Son of Sam law was to prevent criminals from profiting from their crimes, the royalties from Abbott's book and any sale of the rights to his life story (even the right to depict events prior to the Adan killing) should be escrowed under New York's Son of Sam law.[26] However, this argument would appear to directly conflict with the specific language of New York's Son of Sam law: it applies only to a person accused or convicted of "a crime," to the reenactment or depiction of "such crime" and specifically defines the victim as someone who suffers loss "as a direct result of the crime."

In construing the statute, one New York court explained the victim's right to share in the proceeds of the contract by saying that it is the depicted victimization that is really responsible for the fee paid to the criminal. Relying on this language, commentators have argued that only victims of the crime that produced the royalty payments should be entitled to satisfy judgments from the funds paid for that depiction.[27]

How can the victim obtain funds from the escrow account?

Typically two things must happen: the criminal must be convicted and the victim must obtain a civil judgment against him for damages. Under the federal statute, a federal court civil judgment gives the victim an absolute right to obtain escrowed funds; a state court judgment can only be enforced against escrowed funds if a federal court decides it is "in the interests of justice" to do so.

Is there a certain time limit before which the victim must obtain this civil judgment?

No. But typically states must close the escrow account five years after it is established unless a victim's civil action is then pending.[28] Thus, while the victim need not obtain a judgment within five years, in most states he must commence his lawsuit for damages against the criminal within five years of the establishment of the escrow account.

When is a criminal defendant considered convicted for purposes of the statute?

Typically, a defendant has been "convicted" (1) where there is a judgment of guilt; (2) where the defendant is found not guilty by reason of insanity; (3) where there has been a guilty plea; or (4) where, as a result of plea bargaining and/or pretrial diversion, the defendant has "voluntarily and intelligently admitted the commission of a crime for which [he] is not prosecuted."[29] However, where the defendant, due to insanity, has been found to lack the capacity to understand a trial or assist in his own defense, the agency maintaining the escrow is authorized to commence a proceeding before a state's civil court to determine the disposition of the escrow fund.[30]

Where the victim obtains a civil judgment against the criminal defendant, is the victim entitled to the entire amount of the escrow fund?

Probably not. If there are multiple victims with judgments totaling more than the amount of the escrow fund, the victim will not be entitled to satisfy his entire judgment. Statutes in Georgia and Illinois explicitly allow all victims of the crime to recover damages from the fund and if it is insufficient to satisfy all claims, the victims are to share in the fund proportionately.[31] While New York's statute has no such provision, it has been interpreted by the courts to allow for proportionate recovery where there are multiple victims.[32]

Even if there is only one victim and he has obtained a judgment equal to or greater than the escrow fund, depending on the jurisdiction, there may be other creditors who have priority over payment of the victim's judgment. In New York, for example, any amounts authorized by the court for payment of the criminal defendant's lawyer or by the Crime Victims Board in connection with the sale of the story must be satisfied before the victim obtains funds from the escrow account.[33] In addition, the Crime Victims Board is entitled to collect any amounts paid to the victim as victim's compensation (as long as they do not exceed half of the net amount of the civil judgment obtained by the victim) before the victim's judgment is satisfied.[34] Then the victim's judgment is satisfied, and any remaining funds are paid first to other judgment creditors of the criminal defendant and then (if any funds are left) to the convicted person himself.

In Florida, by contrast, payments received by the state are to be divided as follows: twenty-five percent of the total is to be paid to dependents of the convicted felon, and victims are entitled to damages determined by the court up to twenty-five percent of the total. Funds are then used to pay court costs, trial expenses (including reasonable per diem payments for the state's prosecutors) and the per capita cost of the defendant's imprisonment; the remainder of the fund (if any) is to be paid to the convicted felon on release.[35]

Under what circumstances can funds in escrow be used to pay the criminal defendant's attorney's fees or other expenses?

It varies from state to state. In New York, the criminal defendant's attorney can make an application to the court for payment of attorneys' fees incurred in the criminal process and the Crime Victims Board, at its discretion, can pay agent's fees, attorneys' fees, and other expenses necessary to secure the sale of the rights, as long as the total of all these expenses does not exceed a fifth of the amount in the escrow account.[36] Virtually all of the statutes have similar provisions for the payment of attorneys' fees but Alaska limits payment of the defendant's legal fees to situations where the defendant otherwise has insufficient assets of his own to pay legal fees. The federal statute allows a federal court to order up to 20% of the escrowed funds to be paid for attorney's fees arising from the offense if it is "in the interests of justice" to do so.[37]

Some commentators have criticized the use of escrow funds to pay attorneys' fees on the ground that the indigent criminal defendant would be provided with counsel at the public's expense in any case and that in some situations, such funds might be used to pay the defendant's legal fees in a civil action brought by the victim.[38] It is perhaps for these very reasons that Alabama's statute contains no provision for payment of the convicted or accused person's legal fees.

What happens to the funds remaining in the escrow account if the defendant is convicted but his crime is victimless, if no victim obtains a civil judgment against him, or if the total of the judgments obtained by the victim is less than the total amount in the escrow fund?

It depends on the state. New York's Son of Sam statute explicitly provides that money remaining in the escrow fund five years after its establishment (if no civil action is pending and if other creditors have been paid) is to be paid to the criminal.[39] However, in Arizona and Alabama, at the end of five years, if there are no victim's claims pending and if there are residual funds in escrow, the funds revert to the state. Under the federal statute it is up to the judge to determine what should be done with all or any part of the escrowed funds at the end of five years; the court specifically has the power to order that all or any part of the funds can be retained in the Crime Victims Fund and be used to pay victims' compensation and for victims' assistance. [40] '

Can the defendant avoid a Son of Sam statute by simply delaying sale of his story until after the statute of limitations has run for the victim to bring a civil action?

In most states, no. Typically the statutes of limitations applicable to civil actions for intentional injury caused by crime are short, often three years or less. [41] However, as enacted in all of the states (except for Idaho, Illinois, Texas, and Georgia) the Son of Sam law specifically provides that the period (usually five years) within which the victim must begin a civil action does not run "until an escrow account has been established." [42] In one New York case, growing out of the 1972 bank robbery depicted in *Dog Day Afternoon,* a victim who had been held hostage sued to recover a share of the $43,000 placed in escrow in December 1977. Refusing to dismiss the victim's civil suit on the ground that the one-year statute of limitations applicable to assault and false imprisonment had run, a New York appellate court held that the statute created a new *in rem* cause of action (that is, an action to determine ownership of the escrow fund). This allowed the victim to pursue a civil claim within five years after the establishment of the escrow fund (even if the fund was created years after the crime) as long as the claim was satisfied only out of the proceeds in the escrow fund and did not create a personal liability on the part of the criminal. [43] Emphasizing the harm to the victim if he was unable to satisfy a judgment from this escrow fund, the court held that the legislature could authorize such a limited revival of the victim's cause of action for damages where the one-year statute of limitations had initially run without violating the criminal defendant's due process rights under the federal or state constitution. As interpreted by the New York court, this revival of the victim's claims (for the limited purposes of recovering a judgment to be satisfied from the escrow fund) has the advantage of allowing the person victimized by an indigent criminal defendant to wait until after the defendant receives a substantial payment for his story before bringing what could otherwise be a costly and unnecessary civil suit against the defendant who could not otherwise satisfy any judgment the victim obtains.

Does the state's action in escrowing the proceeds of the criminal's story violate the First Amendment?

Probably not. A number of commentators (including civil liberties organizations) have argued that Son of Sam laws abridge important First Amendment rights of accused or convicted persons by temporarily or permanently preventing them from receiving royalties and thus discouraging them from telling their story. Burdening publishers and others who contract with criminals with the significant procedural requirements of these statutes is also said to "chill" their exercise of their right to publish such stories. Others have stated that these laws violate the First Amendment by depriving the accused or convicted person of the funds and resources necessary to communicate his "story" and by preventing the public from hearing the accused or convicted person's own version of what happened and therefore violating the public's "right to know."[44] In making these arguments, critics have relied on a number of Supreme Court decisions in other areas that have stricken statutes that chilled the exercise of speech (by creating financial disincentives or otherwise) or that abridge the public's right to know.[45]

However, no court has invalidated a Son of Sam law on First Amendment grounds. The U.S. Supreme Court has repeatedly held that legislation can have the effect of interfering with free expression if it is otherwise constitutional, furthers a substantial governmental interest, was not intended to suppress free expression and if there is no less burdensome means of achieving the desired governmental end.[46] Commentators have observed that the purpose of these statutes is to ease the crime victim's ability to recover damages caused by the crime and not to prevent the criminal from telling his story. One commentator has argued that such laws actually encourage publication of the criminal's story because the use of the proceeds to pay victims removes some of the moral stigma and negative publicity that might otherwise result from entering into such contracts.[47] As a practical matter, such statutes have not deterred either criminals or publishers from publishing such stories (including the story of the Son of Sam killer himself, David Berkowitz); substantial incentives for the criminal to tell his story (such as the payment of legal fees and possible recovery of any residual sums after victims have satisfied their judgments) still exist in states that have enacted these laws. These considerations—along with the public policy interest in preventing criminals from profiting from their crimes, encouraging respect for the criminal justice system and the law, and deterring persons who might otherwise be lured by notions of profiting from criminal notoriety—and the incidental effect Son of Sam laws have on the free exercise of expression—have led most commentators to conclude that these laws do not violate the First Amendment.[48]

Have there been other constitutional challenges to these laws?

Yes. Convicted persons have challenged Son of Sam statutes on the grounds that they are vague (and therefore violate due process) and that they violate the convicted person's and buyer's right to contract. The New York courts have rejected each of these arguments.[49]

Although no court has adopted this argument, critics have also suggested that these statutes violate equal protection by creating a class of defendants whose property is more easily subject to attachment by the state.

What rights to share in profits do victims have with respect to the criminal's depiction of the crime in states that have not enacted Son of Sam laws?

Even in jurisdictions without Son of Sam laws, victims who have commenced a civil action for damages against the criminal can, under some circumstances, prevent the criminal or others from dissipating the proceeds of any contract for the criminal's story.[50] Most states have statutes that specifically authorize the court (as part of the civil lawsuit) to attach all or part of a defendant's assets, usually upon a showing that the defendant is likely to dissipate, conceal, or assign those assets in order to avoid satisfying a judgment in the civil action and that the assets are necessary to satisfy the expected judgment. In many states, such prejudgment attachment can be ordered by a judge without a hearing (where the victim can show necessity for immediate relief) provided that the attachment is confirmed by the court within a short time thereafter and where the defendant has been given notice and an opportunity to be heard concerning the attachment. A New York judge ordered just such a prejudgment attachment of Jack Abbott's royalties from *In the Belly of the Beast* in the civil suit brought by the family of his murder victim specifically so that funds would be available to satisfy any eventual judgment against Abbott.[51]

Even where attachment statutes may not be applicable, courts have a general equitable power to enjoin parties to civil lawsuits from dissipating assets until after a trial where the victim can show that he is likely to obtain a judgment for damages against the accused or convicted person and will be irreparably injured if the payment for the defendant's story is dissipated, concealed, assigned, or that the defendant or his assets are likely to leave the jurisdiction.

In addition, a victim (particularly one who has already obtained a judgment against the accused) may have the statutory right to set aside conveyances made by the criminal for inadequate consideration and that were meant simply to defraud creditors, such as the victim. Even if the transfer was made for adequate consideration, a victim who has obtained a judgment against a criminal may be given a limited priority over other transferees.

Notes

1. States that have enacted such statutes include FLA. STAT. ANN. §944.512 (Supp. 1983); IND. CODE ANN. §16–7–3.7 (Burns 1979); OHIO REV. CODE ANN. §2743.81 (Baldwin 1982); OKLA. STAT. tit. 22, §17 (1981); PA. STAT. ANN. tit. 71, §180–7.18 (Purdon Supp. 1982); MONT. CODE ANN. §53–9–104(e) (1983); IOWA CODE ANN. §910.15 (Supp. 1983); ALA. CODE §§41–9–80 to –83 (Supp. 1981); ALASKA STAT. §18.67.165 (Supp. 1980); ARIZ. REV. STAT. ANN. §13–4202 (1978); GA. CODE ANN. § 17–14–30 (1982) IDAHO CODE §19–5301 (1979); Criminal Victims' Escrow Account Act §3, ILL. ANN. STAT. ch. 70, §403 (Smith-Hurd Supp. 1981); KY. REV. STAT. §346.165 (Supp. 1980); MASS. GEN. LAWS ANN. ch. 258A, §8 (West Supp. 1981); MINN. STAT. ANN. § 299B.17 (West Supp. 1981); NEB. REV. STAT. §81–1835 (Supp. 1980); N.Y. EXEC. LAW §632–a (McKinney Supp. 1980); S.C. CODE §§ 15–59–40 to –50 (Supp. 1980); TENN. CODE ANN. §§29–13–201 to –208 (1980); TEX. REV. CIV. STAT. ANN. art. 8309–1, §§16–18 (Vernon Supp. 1980); WASH. REV. CODE ANN. §7.68.200 (Supp. 1981). For the federal version of the Son of Sam statute see 18 U.S.C. §3671.

Detailed analyses of these statutes (which greatly assisted the authors in preparing this chapter) can be found in P. Hudson, "Statutes that Prevent Enrichment of Criminals at the Expense of Crime Victims" [reprinted in *Pepperdine U. L. Rev.* (1984)] [hereafter "Hudson article"]; Note, "In Cold Type: Statutory Approaches to the Offender as Author," 71 *J. Crim. L. & C.* 255 (1980) [hereafter "Cold Type article"]; Note, "Alabama's Anti-Profit Statute: A Recent Trend in Victim Compensation," 33 *Ala. L. Rev.* 109 (1981) [hereafter "Anti-Profit article"].

2. N.Y. LEGIS. ANN., 1977, p. 267.

3. 18 U.S.C. §§3671, 3672.

4. See "Selling a Client's Story," *Time*, Jan. 19, 1970 at 62; *Ray v. Rose*, 535 F.2d 966, 971 (6th Cir.), *cert. denied*, 429 U.S. 1026 (1976). *Barrett v. Wojtowicz*, 94 Misc.2d 379, 404 N.Y.S.2d 829 (1978), *aff'd*, 66 A.D.2d 604, 414 N.Y.S.2d 350 (1979); D. Margolick, "Abbott Case Exploring Issue of Profit from Crime," *N.Y. Times*, Apr. 6, 1982, at B1; 6 [hereafter "*Times* article"].

5. Hudson article *supra* note 1, at 37 ns. 140, 141; *Times* article *supra* note 3, at B6.

6. Compare New York Exec. Law §632–a(1) with ALA. CODE §41–9–80 (1982), ARIZ. REV. STAT. ANN. §13–4201(1) (1978) and 18 U.S.C. §3671(a).

7. *See, e.g.*, N.Y. EXEC. LAW §632–a(1) (convicted or accused); ALA. CODE §41–9–80 (1982) (indicted or convicted). *But see* 18 U.S.C. §3671(a).

8. *See* N.Y. EXEC. LAW §632–a; ALA. CODE §41–9–80 (1982); (Supp. 1981); S.C. CODE §§15–59–60 (Supp. 1983).

9. N.Y. EXEC. LAW §632–a.

10. *Id.* at (1).

11. Title 9, N.Y.C. R&R Subtitle M (Crime Victims Board) §526.

12. FLA. STAT. §944.512 (Supp. 1983).

13. 18 U.S.C. §3671.

14. *See, e.g., Fuentes v. Shevin*, 407 U.S. 67 (1972); *N. Georgia Finishing, Inc. v. Di-Chem., Inc.*, 419 U.S. 601 (1975); *Mitchell v. W. T. Grant Co.*, 416 U.S. 600 (1974).

15. *Cold Type* article *supra* note 1, at 271–73; Anti-Profit article *supra* note 1, at 135–39.

16. *See, e.g.*, N.Y. EXEC. LAW §632–a(9). Texas is the only state that has enacted a statute without this provision. *See also*, 18 U.S.C. §3671(a).

17. ABA CODE OF PROFESSIONAL RESPONSIBILITY, D.R. 5–104(B).

18. *Maxwell v. Superior Court of Los Angeles County*, 101 Cal. App. 736, 161 Cal. Rptr. 849 (1980); *People v. Corona*, 80 Cal. App.3d 684, 145 Cal. Rptr. 894 (1978). *But see Ray v. Rose*, 535 F.2d 966 (6th Cir.), *cert. denied*, 429 U.S. 1026 (1976) (requiring a showing of actual prejudice before finding a denial of effective counsel due to potential conflict).

19. *Cold Type* article *supra* note 1, at 264 n.82.

20. ARIZ. REV. STAT. §13–4202 (L) (1979).

21. ALA. CODE §41–9–80 (1982).

22. GA. CODE ANN. §17–14–32 (1982); ILL. ANN. (S)TAT. ch. 70, §409 (Smith-Hurd Supp. 1983–84).

23. New York Exec. Law §632–a(2).

24. Ala. Code §41–9–81 (1982); 18 U.S.C. §3672.

25. *See, e.g.,* N.Y. Exec. Law §632–a(10)(a). *But see* 18 U.S.C. §3671(d).

26. *Times* article *supra* note 3, at B6.

27. *Barrett v. Wojtowicz,* 66 A.D.2d 604, 615, 414 N.Y.S.2d 350, 357 (2d Dept. 1979); *Cold Type* article *supra* note 1, at 258 n.24; Anti-Profit article *supra* note 1, at 113 n.19.

28. *See, e.g.,* N.Y. Exec. Law §632–a(1). *But see* Ill. Ann. Stat. ch. 70, §403 (Smith-Hurd Supp. 1983–84) (two-year requirement); Mass. Gen. Laws ch. 258A §8 (West Supp. 1984-85) (3-year requirement).

29. N.Y. Exec. Law §632–a(10) (b), 5.

30. *Id.* at (6).

31. *See* Ga. Code Ann. §17–14–31(h)(1982); Ill. Ann. Stat. ch. 70, §408 (Smith-Hurd Supp. 1983–84).

32. *Barrett, supra* note 27.

33. N.Y. Exec. Law §632–a(11)(a).

34. *Id.* at (b).

35. Fla. Stat. §944.512 (Supp. 1983).

36. N.Y. Exec. Law §632–a(8).

37. Alaska Stat. §18.67.165 (d) (1981); 18 U.S.C. §3671(c)(1).

38. *Cold Type* article *supra* note 1, at 259; Anti-Profit article *supra* note 1, at 120.

39. N.Y. Exec. Law §632–a. Similar provisions are to be found in a number of other states (including Kentucky, Texas, and Washington).

40. Ala. Code §41–9–82 (1982); Ariz. Rev. Stat. Ann. §13–4202(D)–(E) (1979); 18 U.S.C. §3671(c)(2).

41. *See, e.g.,* N.Y. C.P.L.R. §§214, 215.

42. *See, e.g.,* Ala. Code §41–9–83 (1982).

43. *Barrett, supra* note 27, at 609–11, 353–55.

44. *See Cold Type* and Anti-Profit articles *supra* note 1; Note, "Criminals Turned Authors: Victims' Rights vs. Freedom of Speech," 54 *Ind. L.J.* 443 (1979).

45. *See, e.g., Grosgean v. American Press Co.,* 297 U.S. 233 (1936); *Buckley v. Valeo,* 424 U.S. 1 (1976); *Kleindienst v. Mandel,* 408 U.S. 753, 762–63 (1972); *Procunier v. Martinez,* 416 U.S. 396 (1974).

46. *U.S. v. O'Brien,* 391 U.S. 367 (1968).

47. Hudson article *supra* note 1, at 42.

48. *See, e.g.,* Hudson and *Cold Type* articles *supra* note 1.

49. *In re Johnsen,* 103 Misc. 2d 823 (Sup. Ct., Kings Co. 1979) (rejecting the argument that the statute is unconstitutionally vague); *Agron v. Crime Victims' Compensation Board, N.Y.L.J.* p. 1, 6 (Sup. Ct., N.Y. Co., Mar. 27, 1981) (the statute is not unconstitutional as an impairment of the obligations of contracts).

50. For a discussion of the victims' use of prejudgment attachment in civil suits against criminals, injunctions against the dissipation of assets, and actions to set aside fraudulent conveyances, *see* chap. V.

51. *Times* article *supra* note 3 at B6.

VII

The Right to Be Free of Victim or Witness Intimidation

What is victim or witness intimidation?

Generally speaking, intimidation is the use of threats or actual physical force to influence a person's testimony or prevent or dissuade him from cooperating in the prosecution of criminal cases by withholding or destroying evidence, evading a subpoena, failing to appear at a trial, or failing to report crimes to the appropriate law enforcement officers.[1]

In practice, intimidation can take many forms. It can involve an express threat by a person who committed a crime (or his family, friend, or associates) to "get" a victim or witness if he goes to the police or cooperates in a prosecution, or it may be more subtle (for instance, friends and neighbors urge the victim to get revenge instead of going to the police). Many victims "feel" intimidated without any specific threats and generally fear retribution from some source if they become involved in the criminal justice system.

Is such intimidation widespread?

A study conducted in 1976 found that 28 percent of all witnesses who refused to cooperate in the prosecution of crimes did so due to "fear of reprisal."[2] Another study conducted by the Victim Services Agency (VSA) in New York City of 295 victims involved in criminal prosecutions in the Brooklyn criminal courts indicated that at some point 21 percent of them had been threatened by the defendant, and 5 percent by the defendant's family or friends. From this sur-

The authors wish to express their thanks to Demetra McBride for her valuable assistance in the preparation of this chapter.

281

vey the VSA concluded that as many as 7,500 victims are threatened each year in the Brooklyn criminal courts.[3]

Naturally, it is imposaible to say how many victims and witnesses fail to report crimes because of fear of retaliation but the most recent statistics prepared by the National Institute of Justice show that only a third of all crimes are actually reported to the police.[4]

What should a victim do if he is intimidated?

It depends on the circumstances. If the intimidation is intended to prevent the victim from coming forward to report a crime or from providing information to law enforcement officers, the victim should report the incident to the police or to the local prosecutor's office. If a criminal prosecution is already pending and if the intimidation is aimed at preventing the victim from testifying, the victim should report any intimidation to the prosecutor in charge of the case.

What can the police and prosecutor do about intimidation?

It depends on the circumstances. In many cases, persons intimidating the victim may be guilty of one or more of a number of criminal offenses; in these cases, the prosecutor can commence a criminal proceeding against the persons who initiated the intimidation. If the intimidating conduct takes place in or near the courtroom itself during the trial or pretrial proceedings, the judge can initiate contempt proceedings against the intimidating parties. In addition, there are a variety of practical measures employed by judges, police, prosecutors, and victim assistance organizations that can prevent intimidation or threats or ease the victims' fear of reprisal.

Is intimidation a crime?

In general, yes. If the intimidation or retaliation takes the form of physical violence or restraints, it can be prosecuted as murder, kidnapping, assault, or as other similar felonies. However, intimidation and retaliation often take the form of threatening or menacing activity intended to pressure or worry the victim or witness without actually inflicting physical injury. In virtually every jurisdiction there are statutes that make such nonviolent but deliberately offensive conduct a crime. In New York, for example, any conduct intended to alarm or seriously annoy a person (including threatening physical violence, using abusive language and physically following another person) constitutes harassment (a violation) and subjects the offender to a fine; the use of physical menace to instill fear of imminent serious physical injury (menacing) is a misdemeanor; and threats intended to change a person's actions through instilling fear of personal injury, property damage, or some other harm to health, reputation, or career, constitutes coercion (usually a misdemeanor).[5] Depending on where the activity takes place, the intimidation could also be prosecuted as loitering or criminal trespass.

Use of harassment, coercion, and similar statutes to prevent intimidation does create two substantial problems. First, such statutes usually stipulate that the prosecutor prove that the defendant intended to harass or coerce the victim or witness; such cases are sometimes very difficult to prove. Second, many critics have argued that such statutes do not clearly provide defendants with sufficient notice of the kinds of acts that are proscribed. Since such statutes are vague and have the potential for being used to prosecute lawful activity, it has been argued that they violate the defendant's right to due process.

Are there statutes that generally make it a crime to prevent witnesses from cooperating with law enforcement agencies or testifying at trials?

Yes. There are federal statutes and statutes in every state that generally make it a crime to intimidate witnesses in order to disrupt a pending criminal investigation or proceeding. Anyone who corruptly, by threats or by force, endeavors to influence, intimidate, or impede any witness in a federal proceeding, or who injures a witness or his property in retaliation for his cooperation, has long been liable to prosecution under the federal "obstruction of justice" statute; convictions carry sentences up to five years in prison.[6] The statute applies to threatening letters and verbal threats (even where no force is actually used) as well as to "endeavors"; that is, unsuccessful attempts to intimidate.[7] Courts have liberally interpreted its application to include witnesses before grand juries and other federal proceedings and investigations as well as at actual criminal trials;[8] intimidations or retaliation can also be prosecuted as "obstruction of justice" if it takes place long after the conclusion of the criminal trial.[9]

There are also state "obstruction of justice" or similar statutes that apply to witnesses in state criminal proceedings.

New York's "witness tampering" statute, for example, makes it a misdemeanor to induce a witness in a state criminal proceeding to avoid testifying or to use fraud or false statements to affect his testimony; where the intimidation takes the form of threats or actual physical violence it can be prosecuted as a felony.[10]

Do these traditional "obstruction of justice" and similar statutes apply to all victim and witness intimidation or retaliation?

No. Typically such statutes are intended only to prevent the obstruction of pending proceedings. Unless the victim is already under subpoena to appear as a witness or is reasonably likely to be called as a witness, the intimidation does not constitute "obstruction of justice"; as a result, it is not traditionally "obstruction of justice" to intimidate a victim or witness to prevent him from reporting a crime.[11] In addition, some of these statutes only authorize prosecution where the person doing the intimidating knows that the victim or witness is about to be called in the proceeding.[12]

Are prosecutions for intimidation common?

It depends on the nature of the intimidating conduct and the jurisdiction. If the victim is killed, kidnapped, or seriously assaulted to prevent him from testifying (particularly in well-publicized cases), the intimidation will probably be vigorously prosecuted under the appropriate murder, kidnapping, or criminal assault statutes.[13]

Unfortunately most intimidation or retaliation is not so visible or highly publicized. Typically it involves threats or menacing that fall short of physical violence. The defendant in one rape case, for example, sat at tables in the restaurant where the victim worked as a waitress every day, eight hours a day until she withdrew the charges against him.[14] Another rape victim was so unsettled by the periodic appearance of the defendant in the lobby of her apartment building (despite a court order requiring him to stay away from her) that she quit her job, moved out of her apartment and bought a mobile home that she moved frequently in order to evade further intimidation.[15] No charges were filed against the defendants in either of these cases for crimes related to their intimidation of the victims.

In fact, during one six-month period in 1978, the district

attorney's office in Los Angeles County filed only 5 witness intimidation cases. Two were dismissed, 2 resulted in convictions followed by probation and the third was jailed on a misdemeanor count. Of 20,000 persons in California's adult correctional system at that time, only 11 were serving time for violation of the state's felony witness intimidation law.[16]

Why are there so few prosecutions for intimidation?

There are a number of reasons. First, many prosecutors have the perception that except in organized crime cases, threats of violence against victims or witnesses are rarely carried out; limited in the number of prosecutions they can bring or cases they can investigate, prosecutors and police typically choose to use their limited resources to investigate or prosecute more "serious" crimes and generally ignore threats that they feel are unlikely to be carried out. This attitude may explain the experience of one witness to a brutal assault and attempted murder who was repeatedly threatened by the criminal defendant (who even told the witness that there was a "contract" on the witness's life). When the witness reported the threats to the prosecutor handling the assault and attempted murder case, he was told that the prosecutor could do nothing until the defendant "tried something" (that is, until the witness is actually attacked).[17] Second, the penalties for such crimes as menacing, coercion, and harassment are very limited; besides reenforcing the perception of the police and prosecutors that such crimes are not "serious," many prosecutors feel that if the defendant is already facing a substantial sentence for the prosecuted offense, nothing is to be gained by adding charges of menacing, coercion, or harassment (which, themselves, may be very difficult to prove).

In the past five years there have been changes in the laws of certain jurisdictions that make it easier to bring prosecutions for intimidation; these new laws have contributed to a new perception on the part of police, prosecutors, and the general public that intimidation is a serious crime.

Which jurisdictions have enacted these new intimidation laws?

As of 1983, five states—Pennsylvania, Rhode Island, Delaware, California, and Wisconsin[18]—and the federal government[19] have enacted statutes, or broadened previous "obstruction of justice" statutes, explicitly to make it a felony under many circumstances to intimidate victims or potential witnesses, whether or not there is a pending proceeding.

What prompted these changes?

In 1979, the American Bar Association's Criminal Justice Section held two days of public hearings that highlighted the impact of victim and witness intimidation on the criminal justice system and resulted in a series of recommendations for legislatures, law enforcement agencies, prosecutors, the courts, and others for alleviating intimidation. Among these recommendations was that states adopt a Model Statute concerning the Intimidation of Witnesses and Victims. This Model Statute was approved by the ABA's policy-making House of Delegates in August 1980. The Model Statute has been enacted in five states and is presently pending in the legislatures of others.

In 1982, a federal bill proposed by Senators John Heinz and Paul Laxalt was enacted by the United States Congress as the Victim and Witness Protection Act of 1982. In enacting this legislation Congress specifically found:

> Under current law, law enforcement agencies must have cooperation from a victim of crime and yet neither the agencies nor the legal system can offer adequate protection or assistance when the victim, as a result of such cooperation, is threatened or intimidated."[20]

What conduct does the ABA Model Statute proscribe?

In essence, it makes it a crime to intentionally intimidate or attempt to intimidate victims or witnesses from reporting crimes, cooperating with authorities or testifying.

Does it cover victims of all crimes?

Yes. It prohibits the intimidation of victims of "*any* crime as defined under the laws of [the enacting state] or any other state or of the United States," even if the crime was only attempted.[21]

Which witnesses are covered by the Model Statute?

There is a broad definition of witness as anyone with knowledge of facts relating to any crime, who has testified, who has reported a crime to any law enforcement officer or who has been subpoenaed by a court in any state or of the United States. The statute also covers intimidation of anyone who "would be believed by any reasonable person" to be a witness.[22]

When is a person guilty of intimidation under the Model Statute?

Every person is guilty of intimidation who knowingly and with an intent to annoy or injure or interfere with the orderly administration of justice, prevents or dissuades any witness or victim from giving testimony or from (1) reporting the victimization to law enforcement officers, probation authorities, or judges; (2) causing a complaint or probation or parole violation from being made and prosecuted; or (3) arresting any person in connection with such a victimization. The same kind of interference with a person acting on behalf of a victim is also prohibited.[23]

Because of the broad category of acts proscribed by the Model Statute, defendants' attorneys can be expected to argue that it is vague and that it violates due process.

Is it a defense that the attempted intimidation failed and that the victim or witness did actually cooperate with law enforcement personnel or testify?

No. Conduct is prohibited "without regard to success or failure," even if no one was physically injured or actually intimidated.[24]

What is the punishment for such intimidation?

The conduct described constitutes a misdemeanor.[25] However, this conduct becomes a felony when it (1) is accompanied by an express or implied threat of force or violence against person or property; (2) is an act in furtherance of a conspiracy; (3) is committed by a person who has been previously convicted of intimidation; or (4) is committed for pecuniary gain.[26]

What forms of intimidation are crimes under federal law?

Under the Victim and Witness Protection Act of 1982, three different types of tampering with a witness/victim or informant are prohibited.

1. It is a felony to use physical force, threats, or fraudulent or misleading conduct to influence testimony in an official

proceeding; to cause the person to withhold testimony or evidence; to evade a subpoena or fail to appear before an official proceeding; or to hinder, delay, or prevent the report of an offense to a federal law enforcement officer or judge.

2. It is a misdemeanor to intentionally harass a person in order to hinder or dissuade him from (a) attending an official proceeding; (b) reporting a crime or parole violation to a federal official or judge; (c) arresting a person in connection with a federal offense; or (d) commencing or assisting in a criminal prosecution or parole or probation revocation proceeding.

3. The federal act also makes it a felony to "retaliate" against a witness, victim, or informant who has attended, testified, or supplied documents to an official federal proceeding or who has made a report of a federal offense or violation of a probation or parole by knowingly causing or threatening bodily injury or damage to another person's property.[27]

Does the federal act cover intimidations involving both federal and state crimes?

No. The federal statute is explicitly limited to intimidation that prevents participation in federal proceedings or reports to federal law enforcement officers or investigators.[28]

Does this mean that a person is only guilty of intimidation if he knew that there was a pending federal proceeding or that a report of a crime was to be made specifically to a federal officer?

No. While cases under the general federal obstruction of justice statute usually require such specific knowledge and intent of *federal* involvement, the 1982 act explicitly provides that no "state of mind" need be proved with respect to the fact that there was a pending federal proceeding or that a report was to be made to a federal officer; that is, the offender need not know that a federal violation or federal officer was involved.[29]

What happens if the person accused of "tampering" or "retaliation" claims he was only attempting to persuade the victim to tell the truth?

The federal act explicitly places the burden on the person accused of intimidation to prove "by a preponderance of the evidence" that the intimidating conduct consisted "*solely* of lawful conduct" and that his "*sole* intention was to encourage, induce, or cause the other person to testify truthfully."

However, since the Sixth Amendment protects the defendant's right to adequately prepare a defense, it is questionable whether placing this burden on the defendant or his lawyer is constitutional.

Will the police provide adequate protection for victims against intimidation?

During its hearings on victim and witness intimidation, the ABA Criminal Justice Section found that (1) actual intimidation is common; (2) there has been little systematic law enforcement response; and (3) the police do not have adequate resources to deal with the problem. As a result, in order to encourage victim or witness cooperation, police often promised increased patrols or extra protection even when they knew nothing further can be done to protect the witness.[30]

Is this fair to victims?

No. Although false promises of protection would appear to be common practice among police and prosecutors in many jurisdictions, the statutory "bills of rights" for crime victims and witnesses enacted in a number of states including Washington, Wisconsin, Rhode Island, Nebraska, and Oklahoma recognize a right to receive protection from harm and threats of harm resulting from the cooperation of law enforcement officers and prosecutors and guarantee witnesses and victims the right to receive information as to the actual level of protection available.[31]

Similarly, one of the guidelines for federal law enforcement officials adopted by the attorney general in July 1983, under the Federal Victim Witness Protection Act states that "a victim or witness should routinely receive information on steps that law enforcement officers and attorneys for the government can take to protect victims and witnesses from intimidation."[32]

Even in jurisdictions where there is no statutory right to such information or protection, victim and witness assistance programs can provide detailed information about available means to protect against intimidation and the actual level of protection being provided in specific cases.

Whether or not there is a statutory guarantee or informal mechanism for obtaining accurate information about levels of protection, prosecutors or law enforcement officers who falsely or negligently promise special protection and fail to provide it have assumed a "special duty" to the victim or witness requesting protection and are liable for any damages for injury that results from their failure to provide the promised protection.[33]

In practice, what means besides criminal prosecution for intimidation are ordinarily employed to protect a victim or witness from intimidation?

Methods for preventing intimidation or for protecting witnesses and victims vary from jurisdiction to jurisdiction. Practices to combat intimidation include the following:

1. special victim/witness intimidation units in law enforcement agencies or in prosecutors' offices with experience in dealing with victim and witness fears and marshaling available resources for protection against intimidation or threats;

2. twenty-four hour "hotline" (which is provided in many jurisdictions by victim/witness assistance programs) where a victim can report instances of intimidation or threats and receive immediate support, assistance, or information;

3. installation, upon request, of recording devices for phone calls and phone traces that can be used to discover the source of telephone threats to victims or witnesses;

4. although round-the-clock protection or surveillance is impossible in all but the most unusual cases, police can and do meet serious threats and intimidation by increasing the number and nature of police patrols in a victim or witness's neighborhood;

5. in some jurisdictions local victim and witness assistance programs can provide secure transportation for threatened victims or witnesses to and from work or the courthouse;

6. where warranted, in extremely serious cases of intimidation, some jurisdictions can arrange for a victim or witness to be temporarily or permanently relocated (with mail stop, phone disconnect, and forward services). Obviously, this is only used in the most extreme situations, most commonly to move victims or witnesses in public housing projects from one project (where the persons responsible for the intimidation lived) to another project.[34]

What is the federal witness protection program?

Under the Organized Crime Control Act of 1970 and the Witness Security Reform Act of 1984, the United States Attorney General is authorized to provide relocation and other protection for certain witnesses, potential witnesses and their families. In practice this has meant relocating witnesses and their families and providing them with new identities, the documents to support these new identities, as well as housing, employment, medical services, and other social services.[35]

Which victim/witnesses are eligible for the program?

The victim must be a witness or potential witness for a federal or state prosecutor in an investigation or trial involving organized crime or another serious offense. The Attorney General must make a determination that the victim is likely to be the object of a violent crime as a result of his participation in the trial or investigation. Relocation and protection can also be provided for the witness's immediate family or a person closely associated with the witness if they are also in danger.

Before admitting a potential witness to the program, the Attorney General must make a written assessment of each potential witness including his suitability for relocation, the need for his testimony, any criminal background and whether relocation would threaten anyone else's safety. Since many of the witnesses admitted to the program are themselves organized crime figures, the 1984 Act specifically bars admission of any witness where the risk of danger to the public, including potential harm to innocent victims, outweighs the need for the person's testimony. Candidates for the program are screened and approved by the federal prosecutor or assistant attorney general in charge of the proceeding and are admitted only where there is a specific case in progress; where the life of the witness or his family is in immediate jeopardy; and where it is to the advantage of the federal government to provide the protection for the witness and/or his family. Every witness admitted to the program must enter into a memorandum of understanding in which he agrees to cooperate with the prosecution, not to commit any crime, take all necessary steps to avoid detection, comply with all legal obligations (including parole, probation, and child custody obligations) and keep program officials informed of his whereabouts.[36]

What effect will acceptance in the program have on the victim's daily life?

Unlike local relocation programs within the same community, the federal witness protection program deliberately severs all of the victim or witness's ties with his previous life (including business, employment, and family relationships) and relocates him to an entirely new residence (usually hundreds of miles away). As a condition of the program, the victim or the witness must agree to stay away from the "danger area" (that is, his former residence) or to do anything that would reveal his current location or identity; failure to strictly abide by this condition can result in termination of federal protection and participation in the program.[37]

The completeness with which ties to the victim/witness's former life are severed (including family ties) has produced a number of suits by family members of persons accepted into the witness protection program aimed at forcing the government to permit at least some continuing contact. In one recent case, a federal appellate court ruled that a divorced father, whose children had been accepted into the federal witness protection program with their mother (his former wife), had the right to bring an action for deprivation of his civil liberties where the government's operation of the program effectively terminated all of his contact with his children without prior notice, without an opportunity to be heard, or without a determination that protection of the victim/witness could be accomplished by less drastic means. Recognizing the seriousness of this problem, Congress included in the 1984 Act specific provisions for protecting child custody and visitation rights under these circumstances (including disclosure by protected witnesses of the existence of competing custody or visitation rights, a promise to abide by the rights of others and a procedure for mediating or arbitrating changes in custody or visitation decrees).[38]

Can the person arrested for committing a crime be released on bail even where there have been threats or intimidation of the victim or witnesses?

It depends on the jurisdiction. The accused has a constitutional right to a hearing to determine whether he may be released on bail.[39]

The standard for determining whether a criminal defendant should be released from jail on bail prior to his trial vary from state to state, but traditionally, the primary (and in some states, the sole) standard was whether the accused was likely to flee the jurisdiction or would appear for trial. Thus, in many jurisdictions the effect of the crime on the victim, his views on pretrial release, and whether or not there has been any threats or intimidation directed against victims or witnesses has not been considered relevant in the decision whether to release the accused on bail.

However, a number of jurisdictions have recently departed from this traditional lack of concern for the effect pretrial release will have on the victim or witnesses.

What are these recent developments?

A number of states now consider the effect of pretrial release on victims or witnesses along with the traditional test of whether the accused will appear for trial.

In approving the criminal justice initiative containing the Victims' Bill of Rights in 1982, for example, California enacted a provision that basically changed the weight that judges give to these criteria in establishing bail and tip the balance strongly in favor of the victim. The California initiative amended the state constitution to add the following provision:

> In setting, reducing, or denying bail, the judge or magistrates will take into consideration the *protection of the public*, the seriousness of the offense charged, the previous criminal record of the defendant, and the probability of his or her appearing at the trial or hearing of the case. *Public safety shall be the primary consideration.* . . . When a judge or magistrate grants or denies bail or release on a person's own recognizance, the reasons for that decision shall be stated in the record and included in the Court's minutes. [emphasis added]

In 1984, Congress amended the federal bail law to provide that criminal defendants were not to be released on bail alone if the judge determines that such release will endanger the safety of any other person or the community. In such cases it permits the court to condition release on measures that will protect victims and witnesses (for example, by ordering the defendant to avoid all contact with victims or potential witnesses) or to deny release altogether. The court or the prosecutor can request a hearing for an order denying release if there is a serious risk of actual or attempted obstruction of justice or threats, intimidation or injury to a prospective witness. In order to detain a defendant, the proof that no combination of release conditions will assure the safety of victims or witness must be clear and convincing.[40]

Some commentators have argued that criminal defendants have a constitutional right to bail and that they can be detained before trial only if the court determines that they will not appear for trial; under this view of the Constitution, pretrial detention solely intended to prevent the defendant (who has not yet been tried) from committing a subsequent crime violates his Fourteenth and Eighth Amendment rights.

Is intimidation by an accused person released on bail grounds for revocation of bail?

Yes. In those states that consider the interest of the victim in granting bail, a change in circumstances evidenced by new instances of intimidation would seem to be grounds for reconsideration and (after a hearing) revocation of bail. In those states that have enacted the ABA Model Statute, there is an explicit statutory provision that makes the absence of intimidation a condition of pretrial release; any willful violation of this condition is subject to sanction, including revocation of pretrial release and/or forfeiture of bail and issuance of a bench warrant for the defendant's arrest. Under the 1984 federal Bail Reform Act, violation of release conditions barring victim or witness intimidation or of the federal obstruction of justice or victim/witness protection laws are grounds for revocation of release as well as prosecution for contempt. Any sentence for an offense (such as obstruction of justice or intimidation) committed while on release must be served consecutively (i.e. in addition) to the sentence the defendant receives for the crime with which he was initially charged.[41]

Can anything be done to prevent intimidation of victims or witnesses in the courtroom or during trial?

Yes. During its hearing on victim and witness intimidation, the ABA Criminal Justice Section found that intimidation of witnesses by the defendant (or his family members or friends) in or around the courtroom during trial is a common problem. To prevent the opportunity for such intimidation, guidelines for federal courts and for many state courts require that they maintain separate, secure waiting areas for victims and witnesses away from the place where the defendant waits.[42] In addition, victim/witness programs often provide "escorts" for victims and witnesses to accompany them to and throughout the courthouse.

Can the trial judge do anything to prevent intimidation?

Yes. The trial judge has the power to issue a variety of different orders that can reduce or prohibit victim or witness intimidation.

Where the judge believes that a victim or witness's safety would be threatened by disclosure of her name or address (which normally can be obtained by the defendant's attorney), the court can order that they not be disclosed to the defendant or to his attorney.[43] In considering whether to grant such orders, courts will ordinarily also consider the defendant's need to obtain this information in order to prepare an adequate defense. If the judge detects intimidating conduct in or around his courtroom, he has the power to reprimand or censure the persons he believes to be guilty of the conduct or to order them removed from the courtroom.[44] In serious cases of intimidation in the courtroom, judges have the power to commence criminal proceedings against the guilty party for contempt of court.

What kind of conduct constitutes criminal contempt?

A person can be found guilty of criminal contempt for any willful or malicious misbehavior intended to interfere with the dignity or propriety or the administration of justice.[45] The same kinds of intimidating conduct that violate obstruction of justice statutes can also constitute criminal contempt.[46] However, unlike an obstruction of justice, intimidation only constitutes criminal contempt if it takes place in the "presence" of the court. Cases dealing with this presence requirement have come to very different conclusions. (1) Some limit contempt to conduct during the actual court session in the judge's courtroom. (2) Others allow contempt to reach conduct anywhere in the courthouse. (3) Under some circumstances, contempt has reached conduct outside the courthouse. (4) In some cases, whether intimidation constituted contempt or not, the case turned on whether the court was in session or had adjourned.[47]

Where the court determines that intimidation constitutes

criminal contempt, a separate proceeding can be commenced and if the defendant is found guilty of criminal contempt resulting from intimidation, he can be fined, imprisoned, or both.[48] In many jurisdictions, where the penalty for contempt is six months' imprisonment or less, such contempt proceedings are tried summarily by the judge without a jury.[49] Critics have argued that summary imprisonment without trial by jury even for six months or less violates the defendants' right to a jury.

In such situations, the court has the choice whether to proceed with a trial for criminal contempt or to allow the prosecutor to bring a separate action for obstruction of justice, and the court may commence a criminal contempt proceeding even if the intimidating conduct could be indictable as a separate criminal offense.[50]

Does a prosecution for criminal contempt or obstruction of justice foreclose prosecution of the intimidating conduct as a separate crime?

No. A person guilty of a physical attack on a victim or witness in court can be prosecuted under a criminal contempt statute and then can be prosecuted again for criminal assault. Since the same act can constitute two separate offenses, trial of the defendant on both offenses does not violate the constitutional prohibition against double jeopardy.[51]

Can a judge order the defendant or some other person believed to be guilty of intimidation to stay away from the victim or witness?

Yes. Judges have the power under a variety of statutes as well as general equitable powers to order defendants and other persons whom the judge believes to be guilty of intimidation to stay away from the victim or witness.

When the defendant is arraigned, for example, the judge can make it a condition of his pretrial release that he not have any contact with the victim or witnesses, or even stipulate that he stay away from the victim's neighborhood.[52] Similarly, in nearly every state, a victim of domestic violence can obtain a protection order (or restraining order) from the court that forbids the abuser from continuing abusive behavior (including intimidation or retaliation for commencing a criminal proceeding) and in appropriate circumstances will order the abuser to leave the victim alone or to move out of the victim's residence, even if the title or lease to the premises is in the abuser's name. In many jurisdictions an order of protection may be available to a victim of actual or threatened assault or harassment even if the victim is not related to, or does not reside with, the offender. In many jurisdictions, victims can also obtain a peace bond that requires the person guilty of the harassment to deposit a certain amount of money with the court; if he continues to harass or intimidate the victim, the amount is forfeited. These means of protecting victims (which are more often used in domestic violence cases) are discussed at length in chapter X.

For a period in the 1970s, the New York City criminal courts issued admonishment forms, which were used in cases where the criminal defendant had obtained pretrial release or had been discharged after a guilty plea and the judge felt it was necessary to admonish the defendant to stay away from the victim. The forms acted as a record of the court's order and documented the intimidation. Now that victims in New York are eligible for orders of protection (even if they are not related to the offender or in the same household) use of such orders has replaced the admonishment forms in New York but such a procedure may well be useful to victims and prosecutors in other jurisdictions that have not enacted broad protection order statutes.

Where intimidation comes from persons other than the criminal defendant, judges have broad equitable powers to issue injunctions (after a full hearing or submission of affidavits) in situations of intentional harassment where the victim or witness is threatened with irreparable injury restricting the activities of the person accused of the intimidation or simply enjoining him from further intimidation.[53]

In addition, in the states that have enacted the ABA Model Statute, judges sitting in criminal trials can issue orders enjoining the defendant or other persons to cease intimidation, to keep a prescribed geographic distance from the witness or victim or to have no communication with the witness or victim except through an attorney, after a showing (which can be based on a statement by the prosecutor) that intimidation has occurred or is likely to occur. Such orders can be issued with or without a hearing. In addition, the statute gives the judge explicit authority to order a particular law enforcement agency within the jurisdiction to provide protection for a victim or witness.[54]

The Federal Victim Witness Protection Act of 1982 provides United States district judges with specific authority upon application by the United States attorney to issue, without a hearing or notice to the defendant, a temporary order restraining intimidating or retaliatory conduct that violates the provisions of the act.[55] Such an order will remain in effect for ten days unless the person restrained moves to dissolve the order. Similarly, after a hearing, a judge can enter such an order that will remain in effect for three years and is renewable upon application by the United States attorney. An application for an order can be made in the context of an existing criminal trial or can be the basis of a separate civil action brought against an individual other than the criminal defendant.

If a person subject to any of these orders prohibiting contact with, or intimidation of, a victim violates the specific terms of the order, the trial judge can make a finding of contempt summarily (without a hearing or a jury trial) and fine anyone found violating the order, or (in extreme cases) order such a person to be imprisoned until he complies with the order.[56]

Notes

1. *ABA Model Statute: Intimidation of Witnesses and Victims* §§1–4 (reprinted in ABA, Victim Witness Assistance Project, *Victim/Witness Legislation: Considerations for Policymakers* (Washington, D.C.: ABA; 1981, pp. 33–35) [hereafter "ABA Model Statute"]; 18 U.S.C. §1512.

2. ABA, *Reducing Victim/Witness Intimidation: A Package*, p. 2 [hereafter "ABA Package"].

3. E. Connick, "Witness Intimidation: An Examination of the Criminal Justice System's Response to the Problem" (New York: Victim Services Agency, 1982).

4. *See* A. Paez, *Criminal Victimization in the U.S.* (Washington, D.C.: Bureau of Justice Statistics, Mar. 1983) (N.C.J.–87577).

5. N.Y. PENAL LAW §§240.25, .30; 120.15.

6. 18 U.S.C. §1503.

7. *Id.*

8. *See, e.g., U.S. v. Walasek*, 527 F.2d 676, 678 (3d Cir. 1975); *U.S. v. Pendergast*, 35 F. Supp. 593 (W.D. Mo. 1940).

9. *U.S. v. Verra*, 203 F. Supp. 87, 89 (S.D.N.Y. 1962) (assaulted several weeks after the verdict); *U.S. v. Woodmasee*, 354 F.2d 235 (2d Cir. 1965) (assaulted after release from prison).

10. N.Y. PENAL LAW §§215.10–.13. *See also* N.Y. PENAL LAW §§100 (criminal solicitation), 135.60, .65 (coercion).

11. *See, e.g., Walker v. U.S.*, 93 F.2d 792, 795 (8th Cir. 1938); *Kloss v. U.S.*, 77 F.2d 462, 464 (8th Cir. 1935).

12. *See, e.g.*, N.Y. PENAL LAW §§215.10, .11.

13. *See, e.g.*, "CBS Murder Mastermind Found Guilty," *N.Y. Post*, June 1, 1984, at 7.

14. Testimony of A. Petromelis, N.Y. Legislative Joint Public Hearings on Victim and Witness Intimidation, New York City, May 10, 1984 [hereafter "Intimidation Hearings"].

15. Testimony of Rev. Howard Velzy, *Intimidation Hearings, supra* note 14.

16. *ABA Package, supra* note 2, at 3.

17. Testimony of "John Doe," *Intimidation Hearings, supra* note 14.

18. WISC. STAT. ANN. 940.41 *et seq.*; 18 PA. C.S.A. §4951 *et seq.*; R.I. GEN. LAWS ANN. §§11–32–4 *et seq.*; 11 DEL. CODE ANN. §3531; CAL. PENAL LAW §136.1 *et seq.* Since each of these states has enacted the ABA Model Statute verbatim, all references to basic provisions of the statute will be to the section numbers used by the ABA Model Statute.

19. 18 U.S.C. §1512 *et seq.*

20. *Id.* (annotation); 96 STAT. 1248 §2(a)(4).

21. ABA Model Statute §1(c). *But see* WISC. STAT. ANN. §940.41(2) that applies only to offenses and crimes under Wisconsin's own penal law.

22. ABA Model Statute §1(b). Wisconsin limits its protection of subpoenaed witnesses to witnesses who have been served with a subpoena issued under Wisconsin law.

23. ABA Model Statute §2.

24. *Id.* at §4.

25. *Id.* at §2.

26. *Id.* at §3.

27. 18 U.S.C. §§1512, 1513.

28. *Id.* at §1515(1).

29. *Id.* at §1512(e).

30. *ABA Package, supra* note 2, at 13.

31. *See, e.g.*, WASH. REV. CODE ANN. §7.69.030(3) (Supp. 1982); WIS. REV. STAT. §950.04 (4).

32. See 33 Cr.L.Rptr. 3329 (1983) (Justice Department Guidelines on the Treatment of Victims and Witnesses).

33. *See, e.g., Swanner v. U.S.*, 39 F. Supp. 1183 (D. Ala. 1970); *Schuster v. New York*, 5 N.Y.2d 75, 180 N.Y.S.2d 265, 154 N.E.2d 534 (1958).

34. NOVA, *Campaign for Victims Rights*, p. 58 (1983).

35. 18 U.S.C. §§3481; 3521 to 3528.

36. 18 U.S.C. §§3521(a)(1),(c),(d)(2); Justice Department Order OBD 2110.2 (Jan. 10, 1975) at 1–3.

37. *U.S. v. Franz*, 707 F.2d 582, 590–91 (D.C. Cir. 1983).

38. *Id.* See also *Ruffalo v. Civiletti*, 539 F. Supp. 949 (W.D. Mo. 1982), *aff'd*, 702 F.2d 710 (8th Cir. 1983); *Grossman v. U.S.*, 80 Civ. 5589 (S.D.N.Y. dismissed without prejudice, Mar. 23, 1982).

39. U.S. Const. amend. 8.

40. Calif. Const. art. I, §28(e); 18 U.S.C. §§3141–3143.

41. ABA Model Statute §7; 18 U.S.C. §3145.

42. *See, e.g.*, ABA Package *supra* note 2, at 26–27. *See also* notes 31 and 32 *supra*.

43. *McGrath v. Vinzant*, 528 F.2d 681 (1st Cir. 1976); *People v. Benjamin*, 52 C.A.3d (5th Dist. 1975); ILL. REV. STAT. ch. 110A §412(i) (Supp. 1983). Cf. CONN. GEN. STAT. §54–86 (d) (victim of sex assault); ME. REV. STAT. ANN. tit. 30 §508 (1979) (minor victim of a sexual offense).

44. ABA Package, *supra* note 2, at 23.

45. 18 U.S.C. §401. State court judges have similar contempt powers to punish intimidation. *See, e.g.*, *Anderson v. Williard*, 180 S.E.2d 410, 413 (N.C. App. 1971); *Herring v. State*, 165 Va. 254, 140 S.E. 491 (1927). *See generally*, N. Dorsen & L. Friedman, *Disorder in the Court*, ch. 6 (Pantheon, 1973).

46. *U.S. v. Essex*, 407 F.2d 214 (6th Cir. 1969); *U.S. v. Walasek*, 527 F.2d 676 (3d Cir. 1970); *U.S. v. Howard*, 569 F.2d 1331 (5th Cir. 1978); *U.S. v. Harris*, 558 F.2d 366 (7th Cir. 1977); *In re Carr*, 436 F. Supp. 493 (N.D. Ohio 1977).

47. *See Ex Parte Savin*, 131 U.S. 150 (1889) (the judge's presence includes courtrooms and all supplemental rooms utilized by courts or witnesses); *In re Carr*, 436 F. Supp. 493 (N.D. Ohio 1977) ("presence" included conduct in the court, or witness room and ladies room); *Woody v. State*, 572 P.2d 241 (Okla. Crim. App. 1977) (any part of court building or where court has business); *Shoemaker v. K-Mart, Inc.*, 204 F. Supp. 260 (1968) (a corridor is not "in presence" of court); *but see Farese v. U.S.*, 209 F.2d 312 (1st Cir. 1954).

48. *See In re Stewart*, 571 F.2d 958, 964–66 (5th Cir. 1978).

49. *See U.S. v. Essex*, *supra* note 46; *Osborne v. Purdome*, 244 S.W.2d 1005 (Mo. 1951).

50. *U.S. v. Fidanian*, 465 F.2d 755 (5th Cir. 1972).

51. *U.S. v. Rollerson*, 449 F.2d 1000 (D.C. Cir. 1971).

52. *See, e.g.*, Ariz. R. Crim. P. Rule 7.3(b) (1982); 18 U.S.C. §3146.

53. Cf. *Gallela v. Onassis*, 487 F.2d 986 (2d Cir. 1973).

54. ABA Model Statute §5.

55. 18 U.S.C. §1514.

56. *See, e.g.*, *People v. Barasch*, 21 Ill. 2d. 407, 173 N.E.2d 417 (1961).

VIII

The Right to Resolve Disputes Outside the Traditional Justice System

Is criminal or civil court adjudication the victim's best means for redressing injuries or losses caused by crimes?

In many cases it is not. There are a number of drawbacks to court adjudication. First, involvement with the civil or criminal courts may result in long delays before any final judgment. It often takes four years or more for courts in cities such as Boston, Chicago, and Philadelphia to process personal injury cases,[1] and in many major cities months pass between the filing of a criminal complaint and trial.

In addition to these delays, there is the high cost of resorting to the courts due to legal fees, lost wages resulting from conferences with attorneys and attendance at court sessions. Where the victim knows the accused (especially where they have an ongoing personal or business relationship), there are also strong pressures not to "drag him into a lawsuit" that may take years to resolve or result in a criminal record. Consequently, in one study, 87 percent of all criminal cases involving a prior relationship were dropped due to the victim's decision not to continue cooperating with the prosecution (by contrast, dismissal for lack of victim cooperation happened in only 29 percent of cases involving strangers).[2]

Last, and perhaps most important, are the practical limitations of court adjudication. Ordinarily, courts are limited to determining whether the accused is guilty of, or liable for, a

The authors would like to express their gratitude to Daniel McGillis of Harvard Law School for his assistance in preparing this chapter and for the use of material contained in the articles on mediation identified in the footnotes to this chapter that Professor McGillis authored or coauthored.

particular incident (for instance, a theft or assault), but that incident may be no more than one manifestation of an ongoing dispute or conflict. One study in New York City found that in 56 percent of all felony arrests involving actual or threatened personal injury the victim had a prior relationship with the defendant.[3] Such disputes are often the result of what both parties consider reciprocal offenses committed by the other party or of other complex issues requiring compromise on both sides. These disputes may not be suited to court adjudication where the only issue is responsibility for a single incident on a "winner takes all" basis.

Traditionally such disputes were resolved by segments of the community that conciliated or mediated the dispute between the parties. The justice of the peace, the school, the religious institution, the extended family group, the politician, and the policeman on the beat all assisted in the resolution of minor disputes. But with increasing urbanization, mobility, and a decline in traditional values and institutions, the sense of community and respect for community order has substantially reduced conflict resolution outside of the court system. In other countries, where traditional values and community cohesiveness remain strong, the resort to courts to resolve such disputes is far less than it is in the United States. Americans, for example, are a hundred times more likely to resort to civil court suits to resolve disputes as are the residents of Norway and Finland, and countries such as China have a long history of resolving most civil disputes by extrajudicial mediation involving neighbors or representatives of the local community.[4]

Do victims interested in ending criminal conduct or getting compensation for injuries have any alternative to bringing a criminal or civil action?

Yes. Victim and perpetrator can informally settle a dispute involving arguably criminal conduct; they can resort to a variety of specialized conciliation or mediation boards restricted to a certain ethnic or religious group or business; or they can seek a resolution before one of the growing number of dispute resolution centers and neighborhood justice centers that handle (often on referral from the criminal courts) a broad range of civil and criminal disputes generally growing out of an ongoing relationship between the parties.

Is it legal for the victim and perpetrator to voluntarily agree on compensation or redress for the victim?

Yes. If the victim knows the person guilty of the criminal conduct, victims can (and often do) negotiate a settlement by which the victim is compensated for injury or is assured that the criminal conduct will not be repeated. This is a common resolution of disputes involving relatively minor crimes or injury to the victim.

Such a settlement (which can be written or oral) usually involves compromise. The parties communicate about the nature and purpose of the guilty conduct and the victim's perceived loss; eventually they come to some kind of agreement mutually acceptable to both parties. Often this negotiation ("conciliation") will involve a "go-between." The settlement itself can involve payment to the victim by return or repair of the victim's property or an agreement on guidelines for future conduct or relations between the parties.

Such negotiation is particularly likely to occur where there is an ongoing relationship between the parties (for instance, husband-wife, purchaser-supplier, landlord-tenant, or neighbors) because this ongoing relationship carries with it a built-in capacity for each side to impose sanctions for any future breach of the agreement.[5]

Can the victim use threats of criminal prosecution to pressure the perpetrator into returning stolen property or otherwise compensating the victim?

It depends on the circumstances. In most states, it is a crime known as compounding if a victim who has been directly injured as a result of a felony agrees with the criminal that the victim will not prosecute on the condition that stolen goods be returned or that the victim be compensated or otherwise rewarded.[6] However, in some states, it is an affirmative defense to the crime of compounding that the amount received by the victim constituted restitution and did not exceed what the victim lost as a result of crime.[7] Other states have enacted statutory exemptions for informal agreements by merchants not to press charges in exchange for restitution where the crime involved passing bad checks or the fraudulent use of credit cards.

As a practical matter, prosecution for violation of compounding statutes is extremely rare and informal agreements to return property in exchange for an agreement not to prose-

cute are commonly entered into between shoplifters and
storeowners or thieves and insurance companies. In fact,
after the victim and the perpetrator enter into such an agreement for restitution, in some states, this agreement can be
used by the criminal as an affirmative defense to any prosecution brought against him for the crime that produced the
agreement.[8]

However, the courts have strongly disapproved practices
such as the arrest of a shoplifter until he agrees to reimburse
a storeowner where police detention is deliberately used as
pressure to induce the defendant into an informal settlement.[9]

**If the victim herself cannot threaten criminal prosecution
in order to get compensation, can her attorney threaten to
present criminal charges in order to pressure the accused
for reimbursement or some other civil settlement?**

No. It is unethical for an attorney to threaten criminal
prosecution solely to obtain an advantage in a civil matter.[10]

**For victims of crimes resulting from ongoing disputes who
cannot by themselves negotiate a settlement with the other
parties, is there any forum (other than the courts) for assistance in resolving the dispute?**

Yes. In many urban jurisdictions there have long been
forums for specific groups or specific problems that would
allow a victim to meet with the other party to the dispute
and, with the organized help of other community members,
come to some compromise. Members of the Jewish community in New York City, for example, have long presented
disputes (at the rate of a thousand a year) to the Jewish
Conciliation Board; a panel made up of a lawyer, a rabbi, and
a community member meet with the disputants to resolve
disputes (some involving potentially criminal conduct) relating to marital, business, family, and religious matters. Similar
techniques for resolving disputes also exist in certain Chinese-
American communities.[11]

Consumers victimized by business fraud have long had
access to facilities for mediation provided by local Better
Business bureaus or special projects, such as the Automobile
Consumer Action programs.[12] Frequently, such programs find
that their involvement representing the victim (even before
actual mediation) results in an informal settlement.

Similarly, businessmen and corporations frequently agree

to mediate or arbitrate business disputes (some of which involve potential criminal liability for fraud or for violation of government regulations) before panels of professional arbitrators or before mediators supplied by the American Arbitration Association (AAA); the AAA currently has hundreds of professionals available to sit on arbitration panels and arbitrates commercial claims through twenty-four regional offices in cities across the United States.

Beyond the specialized forums, are there forums in which average victims of minor crimes, such as assault, theft, or larceny can resolve their disputes?

Yes. There are now alternative dispute resolution centers that provide mediation or arbitration for a broad range of minor criminal and civil disputes in more than 30 states.[13] The first such programs were started in 1969 by prosecutors who saw the need to improve the method in which minor criminal cases are resolved. In that year, the Philadelphia district attorney, the American Arbitration Association, and the Municipal Court instituted the Philadelphia Municipal Court Arbitration Court Tribunal that gave disputants in minor criminal matters the option of proceeding in court or resorting to binding arbitration. At the same time, the Columbus, Ohio, Night Prosecutor's Program was begun; this program (which uses law students as mediators) now handles over 20,000 cases per year. By the late 1970s, dispute resolution programs had developed in such cities as Miami, Rochester, Boston, New York City, and San Francisco.[14] Although the number of dispute resolution programs is constantly increasing, as of 1983, there were approximately 180 such programs nationally which are listed (along with their addresses) in Appendix D.

What are the reasons for this rapid recent growth in alternative dispute resolution centers?

The new centers (1) provide increased access to justice through prompt hearings and through elimination of the usual legal costs; (2) increase the efficiency of the legal system by allowing the courts to concentrate on serious cases not suited to mediation; (3) improve the resolution of ongoing disputes by eliminating the usual courtroom restrictions on evidence, trial time, and the limitation of proceedings to exploration of a particular dispute (rather than the underlying problem); and

(4) provide benefits for the community through increased involvement in the resolution of disputes that affect the community, training of citizens involved in the process as mediators and, ultimately, a reduction in community tensions.[15]

Who sponsors these dispute resolution programs?

There are a variety of sponsors. Programs are sponsored by—

1. the local courts;

2. prosecutors' offices (Columbus program);

3. county governments (the Portland, Oregon, program);

4. community groups (such as the San Francisco Community Board program and the Los Angeles Neighborhood Justice Center);

5. religious groups (Christian Conciliation Service in Albuquerque, New Mexico, and Seattle, Washington);

6. universities (University of Massachusetts Mediation Program);

7. private organizations with ties to the local justice system (such as the Rochester program operated by the American Arbitration Association and the mediation centers operated by New York City's Victim Services Agency).[16]

Often the character and operation of programs will differ greatly depending on the program's sponsorship and objectives. Most of the programs are sponsored by, or have strong ties to, the existing criminal justice system. They regularly receive referrals of criminal matters that the police, prosecutors, or courts have determined can be more effectively or appropriately handled by mediation. Thus, the goals and procedures of such programs reflect the need to process these referred matters, obtain a satisfactory resolution or return them for prosecution to the criminal justice system. In New York City, for example, the strong ties between privately run mediation centers and the courts are reflected by the fact that most victims who attempt to file complaints in the criminal court are directed to see a representative of a mediation program before the court will even consider a citizen initiated criminal complaint.

By contrast, a number of programs (including the San

Francisco Community Board program and the Fair Haven, Connecticut, program are community-based organizations, with active outreach programs) and promotion. Most of the disputes considered by these programs involve such life-style conflicts as misunderstandings between roommates, neighbors, or landlords and tenants. The San Francisco program operates 6 separate boards serving 19 communities in San Francisco and the program makes every effort to assure that the 3 to 5 panelists hearing a particular dispute are residents of, or knowledgeable about, the particular neighborhood in which the dispute occurred.

Although sponsorship and operation of dispute resolution programs have primarily been local, the federal government and several states have also made efforts to encourage the development of alternative dispute resolution programs. In 1977, the federal government provided funding for three model experimental neighborhood justice centers in Atlanta, Kansas City, and Los Angeles and, in 1980, Congress enacted the Dispute Resolution Act, establishing a national clearinghouse for research and information on dispute processing programs that was also intended to provide support for experimental dispute resolution programs.[17] As of 1984, however, the federal government had failed to provide funding for programs under the Dispute Resolution Act.

Prior to 1983, lawmakers in 12 states had considered enacting legislation dealing with alternative dispute resolution centers.[18] Minnesota, North Carolina, and Connecticut have each appropriated funds for model dispute resolution programs.[19] But the most comprehensive program for state-funded alternate dispute resolution has been created in New York which, in 1981, enacted the Dispute Resolution Act establishing a statewide network of community dispute resolution centers to be supervised by New York's Office of Court Administration with a funding of $3.5 million over the first 3 years.[20] By May of 1983, 21 dispute resolution centers were in operation in New York, during the 6-month period from April 1 through September 1982, they processed 21,000 cases referred by, or diverted from, the New York criminal courts.[21] Florida (which has considered legislation since 1979 to establish a comprehensive statewide dispute resolution program) has also developed centers with ties to the courts in a number of its judicial circuits.[22]

What types of disputes are handled by these centers?

It depends on the center. Most will process a broad variety of civil and minor criminal matters with the primary requirement being that the individuals involved in the dispute have an ongoing relationship; typically, they are members of the same family, neighbors, or have a landlord/tenant or employer/employee relationship. But there may be other restrictions. Many will not handle disputes where the victim has been physically injured; for example, dispute resolution centers operated under New York's Community Dispute Resolution Center program are barred from accepting any disputes that involve felony indictments, violent felonies, drug offenses, second felonies, or where one of the disputants is named in a pending criminal case (even if it involves an unrelated matter).[23] A small number of programs (such as the center that operated in conjunction with the Brooklyn criminal courts in the late 1970s) have successfully mediated disputes involving serious felonies such as rape, robbery, burglary, and kidnapping, and reported that such disputes could be successfully resolved in mediation while similar cases (involving felonies between parties with ongoing relationships) were usually dismissed by the criminal court due to failure to prosecute.[24]

While some programs process primarily civil disputes (St. Petersburg/Clearwater), others process primarily or exclusively criminal disputes (Boston Urban Court and Jacksonville). The types of complaint resolved by the programs also vary, with some handling primarily harassment, minor assault, or domestic disputes (Rochester Community Dispute Services and Victim Services Agency's Brooklyn Mediation Center), while others primarily deal with property questions, such as claims involving "bad checks" (Columbus Night Prosecutor's Office).[25]

How do victims bring their disputes before dispute resolution centers?

It depends on the program. All of the programs will accept disputes from victims who walk in off the street, as long as they satisfy the programs' requirements. In about twenty percent of the programs (including such community-based programs as the San Francisco Community Board Program and Fair Haven (Connecticut) Community Mediation program) the majority of the disputes are brought in by victims who have learned of the programs from their outreach efforts.

However, in most programs, the majority of disputes are referred by the criminal justice system itself. In the Boston Urban Court Program, for example, well over half of all the disputes are referred by judges in the district court after a criminal complaint has been filed and after the defendant has been arrainged. Judges will adjourn further hearings in the criminal case for ninety days to allow the parties (in appropriate cases) to mediate their dispute. The Columbus program receives most of its cases from referrals by the city prosecutor's office that screens misdemeanor complaints and refers appropriate cases to the Night Prosecutor program for mediation. Other programs (such as the Miami, Tucson, and New York programs) also receive direct referrals before actual prosecution from police precincts or from criminal courts.[26]

Is there a fee?

No. Ordinarily access to these programs is free; in some programs, there may be a nominal fee that is waived if the victim is indigent.[27]

What guarantee is there that the person accused of the crime will participate in the dispute resolution?

It depends on the program. In some programs (such as the San Francisco program) participation by all parties is strictly voluntary. In others, where the dispute was referred by the prosecutor's office, the judge, or a court clerk, if the accused fails to participate in the mediation or arbitration, the pending criminal case can be reactivated or the prosecutor (if he hasn't already done so) may file criminal charges based on the victim's complaint; this is sometimes made explicit by letters sent to the person accused of the crime.

What techniques are used to resolve the disputes?

It depends on the program. In a number of programs after the victim reports the dispute and requests resolution, the programs will contact the offender, notify him of the victim's complaint and attempt to elicit a preliminary response; programs in Miami and Albuquerque report that many, if not most, of the disputes they handle can be resolved at this stage by concilation orchestrated by the program without the need for a hearing.[28]

Where conciliation fails, programs will schedule hearings involving both the victim and the offender but the nature of the hearings vary from program to program. Because participation in the dispute resolution process is purely voluntary, one commentator has argued that there is no constitutional requirement of a particular kind of notice or hearing and no need to satisfy the due process clause of the Fourteenth Amendment.[29]

Some of the programs (such as the San Francisco, Miami, and Boston programs) employ mediation. In such programs, the victim and the other party meet with a professional mediator, air their differences and attempt to come to some kind of agreement (voluntarily and mutually arrived at) which will compensate the victim for past injury and/or produce an agreement about future conduct.

Other programs (such as the IMCR's Dispute Resolution Center in New York City and the Rochester program) include the option of binding arbitration. Typically such programs first attempt to resolve disputes through mediation; only if mediation fails will the arbitrator(s) impose a binding agreement upon the parties. The frequency with which an arbitrated solution is imposed depends on the program; one New York City project reported that only five of its cases reached arbitration while in Rochester, some 40 percent of the cases resulted in an imposed settlement.[30]

How soon after referral are disputes usually heard?
Most projects hold hearings within 7 to 10 days after referral.[30]

Who are the hearing officers who mediate or arbitrate these disputes?
It varies from program to program. While representative community members are used as hearing officers in some programs (such as San Francisco and Boston), law students act as mediators in the Columbus, Ohio, program, psychologists and social workers act as mediators in Miami, and lawyers are hearing officers in the Orlando program.

Before such individuals actually serve as hearing officers, they receive special training, although the amount and nature of the training varies. By statute, mediators in New York Community Dispute Resolution centers are required to have at least 25 hours of training.

What are mediation hearings like?
Some use a panel of mediators (up to 5 in San Francisco)

while others use single mediators. Some projects usually hold brief hearings (30 to 45 minutes in Miami) while others have hearings that last nearly 2 hours (for instance, Boston). Virtually all projects, as a matter of policy, are prepared to hear disputes for as long as is necessary to reach an agreement (or to decide that no agreement can be reached).

Typically, such hearings begin with a statement by the complainant and then a response from the person accused of the crime. If no agreement can be worked out by face-to-face confrontation, most of the programs will use "caucuses," where hearing officers meet privately with each side to discuss issues and to determine potential "bottom line" settlements before continuing joint discussions. By allowing each side to air its grievances, the hope is that there can be greater communication and understanding and some agreement about past transgressions and future conduct.

Are these hearings limited to the specific incident that brought the dispute to the program?

No. Within the time constraints available, hearing officers are trained to deal with the history and underlying problems that may have produced the incident initially at issue. Thus, in a case of assault, the mediation may involve a detailed description of the history of the neighborhood dispute, the feelings of both sides, and the nature of the continuing confrontation between parties that produced the particular assault at issue. In such a case, mediation (which can produce an agreement on the underlying issues and not just compensation for a particular incident of assault) may be far superior to traditional court adjudication.[31]

Do most hearings produce an agreed upon resolution?

Yes. A 1977 survey of four programs indicated that 90 percent of the hearings produced agreements; a similar survey of 1,500 disputes in Florida in 1978, found agreements in 80 percent of the disputes that had hearings.[32]

Does such a hearing conform with the parties' constitutional rights?

Probably. Although no cases have clearly faced the issue, dispute resolution (particularly where it results from a referral from the state criminal courts or involves a program operated, authorized, or sponsored by a state or local government) potentially implicates a number of constitutionally protected rights, including the right to a jury trial in civil cases (Seventh Amendment), the right to be represented by counsel and to be supplied with counsel if a party is indigent (Sixth and Fourteenth Amendments), and the right to be free from deprivation of property without due process of law (Fourteenth Amendment). Commentators have argued that such programs do not violate the parties' constitutional rights, since—

1. they are not in the nature of a criminal prosecution;

2. participation is purely voluntary (and therefore the participants have waived any constitutional rights and the procedure does not result from state action);

3. dispute programs—which provide both parties with an opportunity to be heard, sufficient notice of the hearing to make the opportunity meaningful, and an impartial hearing officer—satisfy due process;

4. resolutions in mediations are the result of voluntary agreements between the parties and no one is forced to give up property or alter conduct;

5. the preservation of common law right to trial by jury guaranteed by the Seventh Amendment is not static but can embrace such innovations in the common law as alternative forums for dispute resolution.[33]

In fact, the director of the San Francisco Community Board program has argued that alternative dispute resolution programs are protected by the Ninth and Tenth Amendments as activities of individuals and of states not subject to federal regulation without a compelling interest.[34]

Should the victim be represented by an attorney before or during the hearing of the dispute?
Probably not. All of the programs encourage direct dialogue between the victim and the offender, without the intercession of a lawyer. Most allow attorneys to attend the hearing but strongly discourage them from speaking; some prohibit either party from being represented by attorneys during most hearings. The exception is in domestic disputes where, in many programs, attorneys (particularly where divorce is at issue) do participate in hearings along with the parties.

What if mediation fails to produce any agreed on resolutions?

It depends on the program. In those programs (such as the IMCR New York City programs and the Rochester program) which have arbitration, the hearing officer can impose an agreement on both sides. In programs where the dispute was initially referred by the court or law enforcement officers, the dispute is usually referred back to the criminal justice system for processing. In other programs, where the parties to the dispute cannot agree, the dispute simply continues.

Where the dispute is resolved, is there a written agreement signed by the parties?

Yes. Although a few programs (such as the Columbus program) do not use signed resolutions, most do have the parties sign a resolution but in many of these programs (such as the Boston, San Francisco, Atlanta, and Tucson programs) the written agreements are not binding. In the Rochester program, by contrast, the parties are asked to sign a written agreement stipulating that it is fully enforceable in the courts.

Are there limits to what the parties can agree to in order to resolve a dispute?

Generally, no. In fact, such agreements often involve detailed guidelines for future conduct or forms of restitution for past damage or injury that would not ordinarily be found in a court order. An assault growing out of a blocked driveway, for example, produced a resolution between two neighbors that detailed future parking procedures for their cars.[35] Although agreements for restitution or damages may be equally creative, participants in the New York Community Dispute Resolution Program are limited to monetary awards of a thousand dollars or less.[36]

How are agreements enforced?

It varies. In the IMCR Dispute Resolution Centers in New York City and in the Rochester program, all agreements (whether mediated or arbitrated) are written up as arbitration awards. State law typically provides that such awards can be enforced in civil courts by making a motion to "confirm" the award.[37] After confirmation (and such awards are to be confirmed unless they are tainted by fraud or the arbitrator grossly abused his discretion) the victim can obtain a judgment against the respondent in the dispute and, if necessary, execute on assets to satisfy that judgment, or obtain a finding by the court that the other party is guilty of contempt for failure to live up to agreements regarding future conduct. To assist in the enforcement of awards, some programs even provide copies of the final agreement to the court referring the dispute.

In practice, however, few awards are enforced in court since warnings by the project staff or threats of lawsuits have usually produced compliance or satisfaction of the original award, and if the alleged violation of the agreed upon resolution involves a serious criminal act, staff members typically refer the victim to criminal court to file a new charge or revive the original complaint rather than going to a civil court to enforce the agreement.

If a victim is dissatisfied with the results of a hearing can he appeal or ask for a rehearing?

Yes. Most programs provide for rehearings or appeals but these are very rare.

Do parties actually live up to these resolutions?

Yes. A 1977 survey indicated that in three programs where statistics were available (Boston, Columbus, and New York City) less than 15 percent of the resolutions that came out of mediation or arbitration were violated and less than 5 percent were returned to the court system for enforcement of agreements or otherwise.[38] Other studies in Florida and Dorchester, Massachusetts, showed that even months after the hearing, about half of the victims felt the agreement was holding up or that the dispute was resolved.

Do the dispute resolution programs follow-up on these resolutions to ascertain whether they have been satisfied?

Yes. Most of the programs check back with disputants at some time between 2 weeks and 60 days after the hearing. In some of these programs, if there has been a breakdown in the resolution, the program will assist the victim in preparing (or reviving) a criminal claim or in making a motion in civil court to confirm and enforce the award.

Are statements or disclosures made during the course of such dispute resolution confidential?

It depends. In programs such as the San Francisco Community Board program, where all disputes (except domestic disputes) are resolved in public, there is no promise or expectation of confidentiality. However, in most programs, the hearings as well as discussions between parties and mediators are held in private and a variety of legal and practical means are used to maintain their confidentiality. In New York, all memorandums, work product, or case files of mediators as well as communication related to the subject matter of the mediation or that involve mediators, the parties, or witnesses is confidential and cannot be used by either party in subsequent civil or criminal cases.[39] Florida has enacted a similar statute for its juvenile arbitration program; confidentiality statutes have been proposed in California, Colorado, and Oklahoma and are under discussion in a number of other states.[40]

In jurisdictions where there is no special statutory protection for communication involved in mediation or arbitration, other devices may be used to preserve confidentiality. Most jurisdictions have statutes or rules of evidence that make all or part of such communications (as offers in settlement and compromise) privileged and not therefore discoverable in subsequent civil litigation.[41] In one Florida case (where there was no blanket privilege for communication involving mediation), the court refused to allow discovery of statements made in a hearing as part of the St. Petersburg/Clearwater Citizens' Dispute Settlement program on the grounds that such communications involved compromises or settlement and therefore were not admissible in subsequent civil litigation.[42] In other jurisdictions, programs (such as the one in Suffolk County, New York) have negotiated agreements with local prosecutors' offices that information gathered by mediators will not be demanded in related criminal cases or have adopted practical procedures (such as limitation of dispute records to a three-by-five card or swearing mediators to confidentiality and instructing them to destroy all notes (Dorchester, Massachusetts program) to ensure confidentiality.

Is alternative dispute resolution available for crimes involving juveniles?

Yes. Some of the dispute resolution centers (such as the San Francisco Community Board program) routinely process a high proportion of disputes involving juveniles. In addition, there are a number of programs that deal exclusively with juvenile offenders.[43] There are dispute centers in Richmond, Virginia; Cleveland, Ohio; and New York City (Bronx) which mediate disputes involving juvenile offenders, often requiring the participation of the offender's family in the resolution of the dispute. Three counties in Delaware; 17 cities in Florida; Akron, Ohio; and Anarundel County, Maryland, operate programs that defer the prosecution of juvenile offenders for harassment, property destruction, assault, and similar misdemeanors pending a mediated or arbitrated settlement. Such mediation or arbitration often produces a written agreement by the juvenile offender to apologize to victims, provide restitution, or to perform community services; if no agreement is reached within a certain amount of time (usually 90 days), the matter is referred back to the family court or juvenile court for prosecution. The Children's Aid Society PINS Mediation Project also offers mediation (in the boroughs of New York City) as an alternative to family court for juvenile status offenders and their families.

There are also a number of programs designed to develop alternative sentences (often including restitution to the victim) for juvenile offenders who admit their guilt. One program in 19 counties in New Jersey (authorized by the New Jersey Supreme Court) processes over 14,000 deliquents a year who have been referred for sentencing by the courts. These conference committees recommend sentences but if the juvenile refuses to agree to them, he is referred back to the courts for more traditional sentencing. Similar programs (explicitly authorized by Washington's Juvenile Code) operate in Seattle and other Washington cities. In some cities (such as Denver) there are student juries or youth courts that provide sentencing for juvenile delinquents by their peers. Although such innovations have obvious advantages, they are not without potential problems, including the legal incapacity of many juveniles to enter into binding arbitrated or mediated agreements and the issue of whether a juvenile's consent to participate in such proceedings under the circumstances can be considered informed or voluntary.[44]

Notes

1. E. Johnson, V. Kantor, and E. Shwartz, *Outside the Courts: A Survey of Diversion Alternatives in Civil Cases* (Denver: National Center for State Courts, 1977), p.2.

2. Vera Institute of Justice, *Felony Arrests: Their Prosecution and Disposition in New York City's Courts* (New York: Vera Institute of Justice, 1977).

3. *Id.* at 19.

4. D. McGillis and J. Mullen, *Neighborhood Justice Centers: An Analysis of Potential Models* (Washington, D.C.: National Institute of Law Enforcement and Criminal Justice, 1977), pp. 1, 2, 10–11 [hereafter "McGillis, *Neighborhood Justice Centers*"].

5. *Id.*; M. Galanter, "Why the 'Haves' Come Out Ahead: Speculations on the Limit of Legal Change," 9 *Law and Society Rev.* 95, 128 (1974).

6. *See, e.g.,* IOWA CODE ANN. §720.1 (West 1979); *Rieman v. Morrison,* 264 Ill. 279, 106 N.E. 215, 217 (1914). *See also* 4 W. Blackstone, *Commentaries* 133 (discussing the historical origins of compounding as the common-law crime of "theft bote," stealing the fine that should go to the king).

7. *See, e.g.,* S.D. COD. LAWS ANN. §22–11–11 (1979); UTAH CODE ANN. §76–8–308(2) (1978).

8. *See People v. Korn,* 217 Mich. 170, 177, 185 N.W. 817, 819 (1921). *But see* ALASKA STAT. §12.45.130 (1980) (requiring official approval); LA. REV. STAT. ANN. §21.24 (1979) (requiring continued prosecution).

9. *See, e.g., Falco, Inc. v. Bates,* 30 Ill. App.3d 570, 572, 334 N.E.2d 169, 171 (1975); *People v. Anonymous,* 56 Misc.2d 792, 290 N.Y.S.2d 507 (Nassau Co., Sup. Ct. 1968).

10. ABA *Code of Professional Responsibility,* Disciplinary Rule 7–105(a).

11. J. Yaffe, *So Sue Me! The Story of a Community Court* (New York: Saturday Review Press, 1972); L. W. Doo, "Dispute Settlement in Chinese-American Communities," 21 *American J. Comparative Law,* 650 (1973).

12. For a list of such programs across the country, see McGillis, *Neighborhood Justice Centers, supra* note 4, at 12–13.

13. A list of the names and addresses of these programs is contained in Appendix D. This list is taken from ABA, Special Committee on Alternative Dispute Resolution, *Dispute Resolution Program 1983 Directory* (Washington, D.C.: ABA 1983) [hereafter "ABA Program Directory"].

14. D. McGillis, *Minor Dispute Processing: A Review of Recent Developments,* in R. Tomasic and M. Feeley, *Neighborhood Justice* (New York: Longman, 1982) p. 63 [hereafter McGillis, *Minor Dispute Processing*].

15. D. McGillis, "The Quiet [R]Evolution in American Dispute Settlement," *Harv. L. School Bulletin* (Spring 1980), at 21 [hereafter "McGillis, *The Quiet Revolution*"].

16. *See* the *ABA Program Directory* for individual program affiliations.

17. 28 U.S.C. Appendix (pamphlet 1983), 94 Stat. 17 (1980).

18. For descriptions of the operations of the federally funded model programs, see R. Cook, et al., *Neighborhood Justice Center Field*

Test: Executive Summary of Final Evaluation Report (U.S. Department of Justice, 1980).

18. ABA Special Committee on Alternative Means of Dispute Resolution, *State Legislation on Dispute Resolution* (June 1982) [hereafter "*State Legislation*"].

19. MINN. REV. STAT. ch. 494 (1981); Conn. Public Act No. 82–383 (1982); *State Legislation*, p. 27.

20. N.Y. JUDICIARY LAW, Art. 21–A.

21. *The New York Mediator Newsletter*, vol. 2 no. 2, (May 1983) p. 1.

22. M. Bridenback, *The Citizen Dispute Settlement Process in Florida: A Comprehensive Assessment* (Aug. 1980) [hereafter "Bridenback, *Florida Mediation*"].

23. N.Y. JUDICIARY LAW 849–b(4)(f).

24. Vera Institute of Justice: *Mediation and Arbitration as an Alternative to Prosecution in Felony Arrest Cases* (New York, 1980); R. Davis, "Mediation: The Brooklyn Experiment," in R. Tomasic and M. Feeley, eds., *Neighborhood Justice: Assessment of an Emerging Idea* (New York: Longman, 1982), pp. 154–70.

25. For detailed breakdowns of the types of disputes handled by various programs across the country, consult the listing for particular programs in the *ABA Program Directory*.

26. McGillis, *Neighborhood Justice Centers, supra* note 4, at 139–40.

27. *See, e.g.*, N.Y. JUDICIARY LAW §849–b (4)c.

28. ABA, *Alternative Dispute Resolution: Who's in Charge of Mediation* (Washington, D.C., 1982), pp. 45–51; T. Weigand, *Assisting the Victim: A Report on Efforts to Strengthen the Position of the Victim in the American System of Criminal Justice* (Germany: Max Planck Institute, July 1981), p. 34.

29. P. Rice, "Due Process," *The Mooter*, vol. 2, no. 4 (reprinted in P. Wahrhaftig, ed., *The Citizen Dispute Resolution Organizers Handbook* (Pittsburgh: Grassroots Alternative Dispute Resolution Clearing House, 1979), p. 66; Rice, "Mediation and Arbitration as a Civil Alternative to the Criminal Justice System—An Overview and Legal Analysis," 29 *Amer. U. L. Rev.* 17, 46–47 [hereafter "Rice, Mediation and Arbitration"].

30. McGillis, *Minor Dispute Processing, supra* note 14, at 71.

31. For descriptions of mediations involving (1) a neighborhood dispute over a blocked driveway, see McGillis, *The Quiet Revolution*, pp. 22–24; (2) a conflict between a Hispanic tenant and an Anglo landlord; and (3) a dispute between a noisy tavern and its neighbors see (San Francisco) *Community Board Newsletter*, vol. IV, no. 2 (Apr./May 1983), pp. 7, 8.

32. *See* McGillis, *Neighborhood Justice Centers, supra* note 4; Bridenback, *Florida Mediation, supra* note 22, at 10.

33. *See* Rice, *Mediation and Arbitration, supra* note 29; J. Stanley, "Minor Dispute Resolution," 68 *ABAJ* 62, 64 (1982).

34. (San Francisco) *Community Board Newsletter*, vol. IV, no. 3 (June/July 1983), p. 21.

35. *See* McGillis, *The Quiet Revolution, supra* note 15, at 22–24.

36. N.Y. JUDICIARY LAW §849–b(4)(e).

37. *See, e.g.*, N.Y. C.P.L.R. art. 75.

38. McGillis, *Neighborhood Justice Centers, supra* note 4, at 142.

39. N.Y. JUDICIARY LAW §849–b(6).

40. FLA. STAT. §39.334(4) (West Supp. 1983). *See also State Legislation supra* note 18.

41. *See, e.g.*, F.R.E. Rule 408.

42. *Francis v. Allen*, Civ. No. 78–0008–46 (Pinellas) (Mar. 10, 1978).

43. For a general description of the operation of juvenile alternative dispute resolution programs and a list of their addresses, see E. Vorenberg, *A State of the Art Survey of Dispute Resolution Programs Involving Juveniles* (Washington, D.C.: ABA, Special Committee on Alternative Means of Dispute Resolution, July, 1982).

44. *Id.*

IX

The Rights of Elderly Crime Victims

Do elderly crime victims have special rights?

Yes. In addition to the rights generally available to victims of crime, there are programs in many jurisdictions that provide special services to elderly Americans who have been victimized or who are likely to be victimized. Statutes that provide for restitution or create publicly funded compensation programs for victims in several states contain special provisions that apply to elderly victims seeking compensation or restitution. In addition, a number of states have adopted or are considering legislation that enhances the punishment of those who victimize the elderly and/or make it a criminal offense to abuse, neglect, or exploit the elderly or to fail to report such abuse.

Is this because the elderly are victimized more frequently than the average American?

No. Although over two million people above the age of sixty-five were victims of crime in a recent year, the elderly, taken as a group, are victimized significantly less frequently than the rest of the population.[1] In 1977, for example, the average American was five times as likely to be the victim of a violent crime (including robbery, rape, assault, or simple theft) and twice as likely to be the victim of a burglary than

The authors gratefully acknowledge their debt in preparing this chapter to two excellent works on the victimization of the elderly: Victoria Jaycox, Lawrence J. Center, and Edward F. Ansello, *Effective Responses to the Crime Problem of Older Americans: A Handbook* (Washington, D.C.: National Council of Senior Citizens, 1982); and James Bergman, "Elder Abuse Reporting Laws: Protection or Paternalism" (1982) (unpublished).

an elderly American.[2] That the elderly are less frequently targets of crime is apparently the result of certain characteristics of their life-style; that is, many elderly Americans spend a large proportion of their time (for health and financial reasons) in the relative safety of their homes and, in most states, forty percent or more of the elderly population lives in relatively safe rural areas.[3] The special emphasis that has been placed on preventing the elderly from being victimized and assisting them is not the result of the overall frequency of crime against them, but of the impact it has on the elderly and on specific groups of elderly Americans.

What is this special impact?

First, victimization surveys show that older persons are victimized disproportionately for certain crimes; for example, while older victims are less frequently victims of robberies, over half of the robberies involving persons over sixty-five result in injury to the victim. Similarly, although generally less likely to be the victim of theft, older women are victims of purse snatching more often than any other age group.[4] The elderly are particularly susceptible to a variety of types of consumer fraud and con games (including fraudulent home repair schemes, land sales, door-to-door sales, and mail fraud), because of age-related physical handicaps, depression, lower educational levels, or fear of aging and death.[5]

Certain subgroups are victimized more frequently than the average elderly person; for example, while the rate of purse snatching for all elderly Americans is high, the rate of personal larceny with contact (purse snatching and pickpocketing) among elderly blacks is 5 *times* the frequency of that among elderly whites.[6] Of the elderly who live in cities, 60 percent (or 1/3 of all elderly Americans) live in inner-city areas.[7] These inner-city elderly are victimized at a significantly higher rate than the average American. A survey of victimization in 8 American cities in 1975, showed that in 4 of the cities surveyed (Newark, Cleveland, Atlanta, and Denver), the elderly were more frequently victims of robbery with injury than younger residents.[8] In a 13-city study conducted in 1974, elderly residents of San Francisco were shown to be 13 times more likely to be victimized by purse snatching than the national average of elderly Americans: in nearby Oakland, the elderly were 6 times as likely as the national average to be injured in a robbery.[9] A New York City survey of more than 1,500 people over the age of 60 residing in the inner city revealed that 41 percent had been recently victimized by crime.[10]

Most important, the vulnerability of the elderly to crime, the resulting impact on their lives, and their fear of crime have produced a concern that is not directly proportionate to the statistical rate of their victimization. Since many elderly are dependent on small fixed incomes for their support, they are ill equipped to deal with the losses (personal injury or damage to property) which accompany victimization. Studies show that the financial loss suffered by the elderly due to crime (as a percentage of their monthly income) is significantly higher than that of younger crime victims; in one study in Kansas City, the financial loss for elderly victims averaged 23 percent of the victim's entire month's income and entirely wiped out the monthly incomes of those below the poverty line.[11]

The loss of particular pieces of property essential to the elderly person's life (for instance, a wheelchair or in some situations, a television) can drastically affect the person's life; with fixed income and fixed needs, such property may be impossible to replace. Moreover, the elderly are physically vulnerable to attack: they are less able to defend themselves, they are more likely to suffer from physical ailments that decrease their mobility and they are more fragile and more easily hurt. When the elderly do need medical care, the cost constitutes a much larger proportion of their income than for any other age group of victims. For elderly victims—who may have low self-esteem, who may have lost the support of loved ones, and who are physically ailing—the shock of victimization can be extreme, often resulting in paranoia, dependency, or other psychological crises.

Thus, despite their statistically low rate of victimization, it is hardly surprising that polls and surveys of the elderly have repeatedly ranked crime as their most important concern, ahead of such concerns as health care or lack of money.[12]

What special services are available to the elderly to help prevent crime or reduce their fear?

Police departments, law enforcement agencies, and community groups (often groups consisting of the elderly themselves) offer a variety of services and programs. In general, these programs seek to educate and assist the elderly in reducing the opportunity for criminals to victimize them on the streets and at home.[13]

Typically, local police departments will provide written materials to elderly persons upon request with a variety of tips for avoiding crime. The public will be alerted to the existence of these materials (and to the availability of police officers willing to speak to groups of elderly citizens on crime prevention) by community-wide media campaigns, including public service announcements and advertisements on buses and subways. In order to highlight its efforts, New York City has sponsored a Senior Citizens Crime Prevention Week (with workshops and meetings of citizens' task forces) and Milwaukee has sponsored a Crime Prevention Fair that publicized the services of a dozen crime-related volunteer and government programs.

Efforts aimed at reducing *street crime* against the elderly have included—

1. distribution of free or inexpensive whistles or Freon air horns to elderly persons, which can be carried in a pocket and can alert people in the area that a crime is being committed;

2. programs (such as the one in Wilmington, Delaware) which encouraged potential victims of purse snatching to sew special pockets on the inside of their coats to hold cash or important cards;

3. implementation of a Direct Deposit Program in 1972, sponsored by the United States Department of the Treasury that encouraged elderly persons who received government pensions, V.A. benefits, Social Security benefits, and SSI (Supplemental Security Income) to allow the federal government to automatically deposit these funds into personal savings or checking accounts, eliminating theft of government checks and diminishing the risk of being mugged on the way to or from the bank;

4. establishment of escort services (such as the federally funded program in Washington, D.C., for senior citizens living in a high crime area) which provide for the elderly person to be accompanied by a volunteer escort to the store, to the doctor, or to some other local destination to reduce the chances that the elderly person will be victimized;

5. establishment of "safe corridors" where volunteers are posted along certain main shopping corridors during specific hours and days of the week to keep an eye on elderly persons doing shopping and thus deter crime;

6. organization of senior citizen volunteer corps (such as the ones organized in Tucson, Arizona; Washington, D.C., Huntington, West Virginia; and Du Val County, Florida) to patrol neighborhood streets;

7. use of special police teams (such as the one organized in Brooklyn) to act as decoys on buses frequented by the elderly.

Organizations in many communities also sponsor programs intended to reduce *residential crime*.

1. Police—and, in some communities, such as St. Petersburg, Florida, and Phoenix, senior citizens' groups—offer free security surveys that will assess a house or apartment's vulnerability to burglary and make recommendations for making it more secure, including such inexpensive measures as cutting down shrubbery (in which a burglar might hide) and leaving lights on in particular locations.

2. Police and other groups (such as senior citizen posses in Phoenix) publicize and assist elderly persons in participating in Operation Identification (ID) whereby a potential victim marks valuable items of property with a personal ID number using special engraving devices made available at no charge—notices indicating that the property has been marked prove to be deterrents to burglars (who often find marked property to be difficult to sell).

3. Otherwise expensive security hardware such as locks and peepholes are made available to elderly persons or installed free or for little cost by such organizations as the New York City Aging Agency; a senior citizens' group in St. Louis, Missouri; and the Las Vegas Retired Senior Volunteer Program.

4. Government funding has paid for the installation of "buddy buzzers" in the Bronx, in units of retirement apartment buildings, that allow residents who are victimized or who otherwise need help to push a button that sounds a buzzer in a neighbor's apartment.

5. In one especially ambitious program—"Senior Power" in

Akron, Ohio—11,000 elderly residents were recruited to tip off the police to suspicious activities in their neighborhood— the result was a 15-percent decline in burglary against senior citizens.

There are also a variety of community action programs designed to deter crime in a particular locale. In 1977, one study found that there were over 800 citizen patrols operating in the United States (most with small budgets and volunteer staffs) which patroled a particular neighborhood (by foot or in a car) or a particular building or apartment complex; these patrols reported suspicious activities to the police (often by citizens band radio) and provided such additional services as escorting tenants to and from their apartments. In some neighborhoods or on certain blocks, residents have been organized (without actually patrolling the area) to report suspicious activity to other neighbors or the police.[14]

Once an elderly person has been victimized, can he expect any special treatment from the police?

Yes. A number of police departments (including those in New York City and Cleveland) have established special "senior citizen units" which deal with crimes against older persons. These units have been specially trained in dealing with such physical and practical problems of elderly victims as failing hearing, immobility, and low tolerance for stress. In addition, in some cities, such as Chicago, there are training programs for all police recruits which are designed to dispel stereotypes about older people and sensitize policemen to the special needs of the elderly.[15]

Is special counseling available to elderly crime victims?

Yes. In Denver, for example, a state-sponsored, visiting nurse program makes house calls on elderly victims; these specially trained nurses provide crisis counseling for elderly victims and referral to other social service agencies. In communities like Los Angeles, senior citizen centers operate their own victim assistance programs and have provided counseling to older crime victims. A number of programs have adopted peer counseling. In these projects, such as the Victim Assistance Program for Older Adults in Tampa, Florida, the staff consists of neighborhood workers (all over the age of fifty-five) trained in crisis intervention counseling and referral;

the volunteer staff interviews senior victims in the immediate neighborhood, provides crisis counseling and makes referrals for more intensive counseling and other services when necessary.

Is special assistance available to elderly victims who have been physically injured or disabled?

Yes.[16] Every state has an office on aging and there are more than 660 local area or city agencies on aging throughout the United States. These agencies fund, or have contacts with, a variety of programs that provide assistance to injured or disabled elderly crime victims. Most provide homemaker services (at a minimal cost) for older persons who are ill or who are otherwise unable to move around due to injury. Such agencies may also make food available for the elderly victim who is too sick to leave his own apartment, usually through a program called Meals on Wheels. One victim assistance project in Los Angeles collected contributions of canned food from local merchants and distributed it to victims who could not afford food or who were unable to shop for themselves. A number of community programs provide companionship for the injured elderly crime victim, either by arranging for regular visitors or through a program where a particular individual contacts the victim by phone once or twice a week and makes sure that all of the victim's needs have been met. A federally financed program in Washington, D.C., obtained permission from the government and from local banks to pick up food stamps for elderly persons unable to leave their apartment, and to deposit or to withdraw money from banks and perform other tasks that immobility prevented them from performing for themselves.

Do any of the state crime victim compensation programs specially process claims by elderly victims?

Yes. The programs in both New York and New Jersey have established special units to assist elderly victims in the processing of their claims for compensation.

Are the compensation programs' restrictions on eligibility and benefits different for elderly victims?

Yes. In addition, in a number of states, the standards for eligibility for elderly victims are more liberal than those for crime victims in general. In Virginia, for example, elderly victims are exempt from the minimum loss requirement or hundred-dollar deductible applicable to claims by other crime victims.[17]

Several programs also provide elderly victims with greater benefits than they make available to victims in general. While compensation for property loss or transportation expenses is generally prohibited, New York, for example, has enacted a provision that allows for compensation of up to two hundred and fifty dollars to elderly victims for loss of "essential personal property," (for instance, wheelchairs, hearing aids, and in appropriate cases, television sets) and for transportation expenses due to court appearances.[18] Legislation proposed in Ohio goes even further: elderly victims would be compensated not only for damage or loss to essential property, but also for any loss of their ability to function as well as pain and suffering.[19]

Is special emergency financial assistance available to elderly crime victims?

Yes.[20] In addition to the state compensation programs' emergency awards, churches, synagogues, and charities often provide small gifts or loans to elderly crime victims. There are also emergency cash funds for elderly crime victims maintained by municipal programs in such cities as New York, Pasadena, and Las Vegas. In New York City, for example, the Victim Services Agency will provide "dignity money" for older victims as a gift, loan, or a voucher payment without requiring the victim to demonstrate financial hardship.

Is domestic victimization of the elderly a crime?

Yes. With the growing concern for domestic victimization in general, there have been numerous reports of domestic victimization of the elderly by persons in the family or household where they live. The dependency and inability of many elderly Americans to function on their own has made some of them targets of long-term physical, psychological, and material or financial abuse or neglect by the very people (often family members) upon whom they are dependent. Depending on the specific circumstances such abuse may constitute assault, kidnapping, attempted murder, or some other traditionally recognized crime. But, in over thirty states there is legislation that allows elderly victims related to the abuser or living in the same household to file for an order of protection prohibiting further abuse; in some states (such as Ohio) there are statutes that make domestic victimization of the elderly household member a separate criminal offense[21] (see chapter X). In some states, there are substantial additional penalties for criminal conduct that has the effect of abusing or neglecting the elderly. In Nevada, for example, a person who causes an older person to suffer unjustifiable physical pain or mental suffering as a result of abuse is guilty of a gross misdemeanor, but if there is substantial bodily or mental harm, the offender is subject to imprisonment for not less than one year and as many as six years.[22]

Is there any legal requirement to report such domestic victimization of the elderly?

Yes. In at least 35 states it is a crime for certain persons (usually including health professionals) to fail to report instances of abuse or neglect of the elderly.[23]

Is abuse of the elderly a serious problem?

Yes. Although the need to provide guardianship services for elderly Americans with infirmities (primarily those who live alone) had long been recognized, it was only after congressional hearings and after the publication of four separate studies in 1979 that abuse of the elderly by relatives or by other persons upon whom they were dependent was "discovered" as a serious problem.[24] Although 12 states had created protective service programs for the elderly that included some mandatory reporting provisions prior to 1979, more than 20 states enacted mandatory reporting laws (many also providing protective services for elderly victims for the first time) between 1979 and 1983.[25]

What kinds of abuse are to be reported?

It depends on the state; some of the states require that abuse be reported where an elderly person has been subject to neglect or exploitation.[26] Others (such as Florida) require that abuse, maltreatment, or exploitation be reported only if the victim suffers some infirmity of aging (such as brain damage or physical, mental, or emotional dysfunctioning).[27]

As for what constitutes *abuse* itself, at least one state provides no definition at all,[28] and others define *abuse* as: the infliction of physical pain, injury, or mental anguish; willful deprivation by a caretaker or by another person of services necessary to maintain mental or physical health; and even self-neglect.[29] Three states (Massachusetts, New York, and Washington) limit the mandatory reporting requirements to the abuse of elderly residents of nursing homes or of other long-term care facilities.[30]

Typically, such statutes require that a report be made within a short period of time after discovery of the abuse or neglect to the local or state agency dealing with the welfare of the aged or to the police department.[31] If the neglect or abuse involves a government agency, then the report is to be made to an agency other than the one suspected of abuse.

Who is required to report such abuse?

It varies. Some states (including Rhode Island and Texas) make it a crime for any person who has reasonable cause to believe that there has been abuse, neglect, or exploitation to fail to report it.[32] Most states, however, limit the requirement of reporting to medical personnel, community service workers and certain other designated persons who treat or have regular contact with elderly persons.[33]

What is the penalty for failing to report instances of abuse or neglect of the elderly?

It varies, but typically failure to report abuse or neglect in violation of the statute constitutes a misdemeanor and subjects the offender to a fine.[34] To encourage reports, where a person erroneously reports abuse in good faith, many states grant the person making the report immunity from any civil or criminal liability.[35]

What happens after a law enforcement officer or a state agency receives the report of elder abuse?

It varies from state to state. Some states require report of the abuse but make no provision for a follow-up or for providing any services to the victim.[36] Other states (such as Minnesota, Texas, Rhode Island, and Vermont) mandate not only reporting but also investigation of cases and authorize the appropriate state agency to respond by utilizing its existing services (although many such agencies have little or no funding).[37]

Still other states have enacted protective service laws which, in response to reports of abuse, give them broad powers over the elderly victim including the right to evaluate a victim's needs for protective services; the right of law enforcement officers to enter the victim's home; the right to consult with neighbors and family members who know the victim; and even allow state agencies to involuntarily transfer the victim to state facilities.[38] The Alabama protective services statute, for example, provides that the relevant state agency can determine that the victim needs protective services even if the victim refuses them and can make an application to a court for placement of the victim in a foster home, nursing home, or other similar facility against his will without a hearing (although a hearing must be held within the subsequent thirty days).[39]

Although many of these protective services statutes state that they were enacted with the intent that the services provided should be the least restrictive on the victim's life, some commentators have argued that the use of mandatory reporting statutes together with broad powers to protect the victim (even against his will) will interfere with the elderly victim's life without giving him the prior notice or opportunity to be heard guaranteed by due process. The fear is that such unbridled state power will produce interventions that hurt the victim more than they help.[40]

Does the fact that a victim is elderly affect the prosecution or sentencing of the crime?

Yes, in a variety of different ways. The victim's age is often a factor in such discretionary judgments as whether to prosecute a crime and how a judge sentences a convicted criminal defendant. For example, in Ohio, the fact that the victim is over 65 or disabled is to be considered a factor against probation of the defendant.[41] A number of other states have proposed legislation that enhances punishment where the victim is elderly.[42] Some states (including Connecticut, Massachusetts, Wisconsin, Virginia, and Nevada) have proposed or enacted legislation that makes a particular crime against an elderly victim a separate offense, which may be prosecuted in addition to any other offenses that the defendant has committed.[43] In Rhode Island, for example, an assault and battery upon a person over the age of 60 that causes bodily injury is, in itself, a separate felony punishable by up to 5 years in prison.[44] Other states have enhanced sentencing for crimes against the elderly: in Nevada conviction of any of a number of crimes involving victims 65 or older carries a mandatory additional prison term (equal to the term prescribed by statute for the underlying crime); in Louisiana crimes against the elderly bring a mandatory 5-year additional prison term with no parole (even if the criminal defendant was unaware of the victim's age); in California, probation, parole, or suspended sentences are denied to perpetrators of certain serious crimes against handicapped victims or victims over 60; and in Hawaii judges have been given discretion to sentence defendants in such cases to an extended indeterminate term up to life imprisonment for certain crimes where the elderly or handicapped victim suffers serious personal injury.[45]

Other states have proposed or enacted legislation that makes the advanced age of a victim a factor to be considered in ordering a criminal defendant to pay restitution.[46]

Does enhanced punishment for crimes involving elderly victims violate the criminal defendant's constitutional rights?

Courts have differed on this. California's sentencing statute was upheld by an appellate court against claims that it mandated discriminatory sentencing and, under some circumstances, would permit a court to enhance the defendant's sentence even if the defendant did not know the victim's age.[47] The court concluded that classification of sentences by a victim's age (rather than by any class of defendants) did not constitute discrimination in violation of the equal protection clause and that parole (which is a privilege) could be denied due to the victim's age even if the defendant did not know the victim was over 60. By contrast, a sharply divided Louisiana Supreme Court ruled that Louisiana's sentencing statute for crime against the elderly was unconstitutional as excessive and cruel and unusual punishment because it would require a minimum five-year prison sentence (with no maximum permissible sentence) for even such a simple battery as purse snatching.[48]

What can elderly victims do about consumer fraud and con games?

The elderly consumer can avoid such common door-to-door or mail frauds as—

1. home repair and improvement schemes;

2. medical quackery;

3. insurance fraud;

4. hearing aid sales;

5. land sales schemes;

6. fraudulent funeral practices—.

by being skeptical of promises that are "too good to be true," be requesting all representations and promises in writing, by asking for references and checking the reputation of the company selling the good or service (for example, by contacting the appropriate Better Business Bureau), by comparison shopping (by checking the price of the offered property or service with others offering similar property or services), and by keeping careful records of all moneys paid in connection with such schemes.

If the elderly person has been victimized, she can commence a civil suit for fraud or breech of contract seeking damages against the company or salesman; if the amount lost is small, such an action can be brought easily and quickly without a lawyer in small claims court. In addition, the victim should report this crime (as all other crimes) to the police, but also to city or state agencies specializing in consumer fraud; often such agencies can bring pressure on companies to make refunds where appropriate and can take actions that will prevent others from being so victimized.

There are also a number of state and federal statutes that give victims of consumer frauds special rights. In 1979, for example, regulations promulgated by the Federal Trade Commission (FTC) stipulated that hearing aid dealers must offer a trial period for customers to decide whether the device they have bought is right for them.[49] Thus, any special purchases by the elderly are absolutely cancelable within seven days. Similarly, the FTC has issued a Cooling Off Period Door-to-Door Sales regulation for purchases in the home exceeding twenty-five dollars. The salesperson is obligated to give the purchaser a written contract and notice of cancellation forms and the customer has three days in which to cancel the contract by completing and mailing the forms.[50] Where the elderly person believes that the misrepresentation has been made by a reputable business, he can contact the local Better Business Bureau or a trade association (such as a funeral directors' association in cases of purchase of funeral services) which can contact the company making the sale and arrange for a full or partial refund.

Notes

1. A. Paez, *Criminal Victimization in the U.S.*, (Washington, D.C.: Bureau of Justice Statistics, March 1983) (N.C.J.–87577).
2. V. Jaycox, L. Center, and E. Ansello, *Effective Responses to the Problem of Older Americans: A Handbook*, p. 37 (Washington, D.C.: National Council of Senior Citizens, 1982) [hereafter "Jaycox"]. See also, the ACLU handbook, R.N. Brown, *The Rights of Older Persons* (New York: Avon Books, 1979).
3. *See, e.g.*, A. S. Harbert and C. W. Wilkinson, "Growing Old in Rural America," *Aging*, Jan. 1979.
4. Jaycox *supra* note 1, at 39, 41.
5. *See* Robert N. Butler, *Why Survive? Being Old in America* (New York: Harper, 1975).
6. Jaycox *supra* note 1, at 43.
7. National Council on Aging, *Fact Book on Aging: A Profile of America's Older Population* (Washington, D.C.: NCOA, 1978).
8. U.S. Department of Justice, Law Enforcement Assistance Administration, *Criminal Victimization in Eight American Cities* (Washington, D.C.: Government Printing Office, 1975).
9. Jaycox, *supra* note 1, at 44.
10. U.S., Congress, House, Select Committee on Aging, Subcommittee on Housing and Consumer Interests, *In Search of Security: A National Perspective on Elderly Crime Victimization*, 95 Cong. 1st Sess., cmm. pub. no. 95–87 (Washington, D.C.: Government Printing Office, 1977).
11. U.S., Congress, House, Select Committee on Aging, *Research into Crimes against the Elderly, Pt. II*, Joint Hearings before House Subcommittee on Domestic and International Scientific Planning, Analysis and Cooperation and Subcommittee on Housing and Consumer Interest, Feb. 1, 1978 (Washington, D.C.: Government Printing Office, 1978); Midwest Research Institute, *Crimes Against the Aging: Patterns and Prevention* (Kansas City, Mo.: MRI, 1977).
12. L. Harris et al, *The Myth and Reality of Aging in America* (Washington, D.C.: National Council on the Aging, 1975).
13. Jaycox, *supra* note 1, at 76–79, 115–45, 181–87 (describing programs listed in the text).
14. *Id.* at 115, 116 (describing programs listed in the text).
15. *Id.* at 89, 218 (describing programs listed in the text).
16. *Id.* at 215, 217 (describing programs listed in the text).
17. VA. CODE §19.2–368.11 (1983).
18. N.Y. EXEC. LAW §631(8) (allowing elderly victims to recover the loss of essential property up to $250 plus transportation expenses).

19. Ohio S.B. 92 (1982).
20. Jaycox, *supra* note 1, at 214 (describing programs listed in the text).
21. L. Lerman and F. Livingston, "State Legislation on Domestic Violence," *Response*, vol. 6, no. 5 (Sept./Oct. 1983).
22. Nev. Rev. Stat. §200.5099 (1982).
23. Karen J. Meyers and James A. Bergman, *An Analysis of the Laws Concerning Elder Abuse in Massachusetts and Other States* (Boston: Legal Research and Services for the Elderly, 1979).
24. J. Bergman, "Elder Abuse Reporting Laws: Protection or Paternalism" (1982), pp. 38–42 [hereafter "Bergman"].
25. *Id.* at 45–47, 55.
26. *See, e.g.,* Nev. Rev. Stat. §200.5093 (1982).
27. Fla. Stat. Ann. tit. 29 §410.106, .102 (West 1983).
28. Okla. Stat. tit. 43A §804(A)(1980).
29. *See, e.g.,* Ala. Code §38–9–2(6) (Supp. 1983); Conn. Gen. Stat. ch. 814 §46a–14(4) (West 1984).
30. N.Y. Pub. Health Law §2803–d (1980); Mass. Gen. Laws Ann. ch. 111, §72f–72I (1983); Wash. Rev. Code §§70.124.010 to 70.124.090 (1981).
31. Nev. Rev. Stat. §200.5093(1)(1982).
32. R.I. Gen. Laws §42–66–8 (Supp. 1983); Tex. Hum. Res. Code, 48.036 (Vernon 1984).
33. Nev. Rev. Stat. ch. 200 §2–11 (1981).
34. *See, e.g.,* Vt. Stat. Ann. tit. 18 §1152(d) (1982); Nev. Rev. Stat.§ 200.5096 (1981).
35. *See, e.g.,* Nev. Rev. Stat. §200.5096 (1981).
36. Bergman, *supra* note 24, at 56.
37. *See, e.g.,* Vt. Stat. Ann. tit. 18 §1154 (1982).
38. *See, e.g.,* Fla. Stat. Ann. tit. 29 §410.104 (West 1983); Okla. Stat. tit. 43A §805–07 (1980).
39. Ala. Code §38–9–5 (Supp. 1983).
40. Bergman *supra* note 24, at 30–60.
41. Ohio Rev. Code Ann. §2951.02(D)(4) (Baldwin 1979).
42. *See* C. Schafer, *Summary of 1982 State Legislation Re: Crime Victims and Non-Criminal Matters with Particular Emphasis on Older Persons* (Washington, D.C.: American Association of Retired Persons, Oct. 1982) [hereafter "Schafer"].
43. *Id.;* Conn. Gen. Stat. Ann. §53a–59a (West 1983).
44. R.I. Gen. Laws §11–5–10 (1981).
45. Nev. Rev. Stat. §193.169 (1981); La. Stat. Ann. §14:50.1 (West 1983); Cal. Penal Code § 1203.09 (West Supp. 1984); Hawaii Rev. Stat. §§706–661, –662 (5) (1983 Supp.).
46. *See* Schafer, *supra* note 42; Ohio Rev. Code Ann. §2929.11 (D) (Baldwin 1979).
47. *People v. Peace,* 166 Cal. Rptr. 202, 107 Cal. App. 3d 996 (1980).
48. *State v. Goode,* 380 So. 2d 1361 (1980).
49. Jaycox *supra* note 1, at 151–70.
50. *Id.;* 16 C.F.R. 233 (1982).

X

The Rights of Domestic Violence Victims

What is domestic violence?
As used here, domestic violence includes three separate but related types of crimes: spouse abuse, child abuse, and elderly abuse. In each of these categories the abuser and the victim share a common family or household and because the crimes take place largely in private, they were not the focus of public attention until recently. Victims of each of these types of abuse have benefited from recent legislation and from court decisions creating new, or expanding old, rights.

What is spouse abuse?
Spouse abuse (also referred to as marital abuse or wife battering) is usually used to describe serious or repeated injury caused by a person who is married to, cohabitates with, or is involved with the victim in an intimate sexual relationship.[1]

Is spouse abuse a serious problem?
Yes. Nearly 6 million victims are abused by their spouses

The authors acknowledge that most of the information contained in this chapter was taken from Lisa Lerman and Franci Livingston, "State Legislation on Domestic Violence," *Response*, vol. 6, no. 5 (Sept./Oct. 1983). A copy of this study that contains a comprehensive state-by-state analysis can be obtained from the Center for Women Policy Studies, 2000 P St. N.W., Suite 508, Washington, DC 20036. In addition, Ms. Lerman and Ms. Livingston kindly provided invaluable advice and criticism of a draft of this chapter. The authors also acknowledge their debt to material contained in A. Boyland and N. Taub, *Adult Domestic Violence: Constitutional Legislative and Equitable Issues* (Legal Services Corp. Research Institute, 1981) and ABA, *Recommendations for Improving Legal Intervention in Intra-Family Child Abuse Cases* (Washington, D.C.: ABA National Legal Resource Center for Advocacy & Prevention, 1982).

each year, and crime surveys indicate that in 40 percent of all homicides involving women victims the murderer is the victim's spouse, relative, or social partner.[2] During one nine-month period in 1979, the police department in Cleveland received approximately 15,000 domestic violence calls, and nationally, police officers, spend a third of their time responding to domestic violence calls.[3]

Are the victims of spouse abuse limited to married women?

No. In one study of battered women who received hospital treatment 73 percent of the victims were single, divorced, or separated;[4] other studies have found that a lesser (although still substantial) proportion of abuse victims are unmarried.[5]

Do spouse abuse victims have any special rights?

Yes. While spouse abuse victims have always had remedies, in recent years, many states have enacted legislation creating or expanding the rights of spouse abuse victims. Many of the statutes are listed by state in Appendix E. Among other things, these new statutes

1. broaden the power of courts in civil actions to provide protection for abuse victims;

2. make it an independent crime to abuse a spouse;

3. give police new powers to make arrests in spouse abuse cases;

4. require police and courts to assist victims in bringing spouse abuse prosecutions; and

5. make provisions for counseling, shelter, and other services to spouse abuse victims.[6]

Unfortunately in many jurisdictions there is a substantial discrepancy between the powers conferred on police and prosecutors by the new laws and actual practice. In far too many law enforcement agencies there is continuing resistance to vigorous prosecution and punishment of spouse abuse.

Can the victim obtain an order from the court (without commencing criminal proceedings) which will provide her with some sort of protection against further abuse?

Yes. In divorce or domestic relations cases, courts have

long had the power to issue orders enjoining further abuse until the divorce is final. Such injunctions are still available in divorce proceedings, but forty-three states and the District of Columbia have enacted legislation that also allows battered women to obtain civil protection orders without filing for separation or divorce.[7] As one commentator has observed, "A protection order (also called a temporary restraining order or temporary injunction) is an injunction designed to prevent violence by one member of a household against another." Depending on the state's law, the court can require the abuser to—

1. move out of the residence shared with the victim;

2. refrain from abuse or contact with the victim;

3. enter a counseling program;

4. pay support of the victim and/or minor children in her custody;

5. pay the victim restitution (for medical expenses, lost wages, moving expenses, or property damage caused by the abuse), and/or attorneys' fees or court costs.[8]

What sort of conduct toward the victim can the court prohibit in an order of protection?

It depends on the state. All states with protection order legislation allow courts to enjoin actual physical abuse of the victim, most allow prohibition of threats of abuse or efforts to molest or disturb the peace of the victim, and many authorize orders prohibiting the abuser from generally having contact with the victim or placing restraints on the victim's personal liberty.[9] Some states have even enacted abuse statutes that confer on the court broad powers to issue any orders "necessary" or "appropriate" to reduce or eliminate the likelihood of violence or abuse.[10] Many statutes specifically allow courts to exclude the abuser from the victim's place of employment or business, from the victim's school, from a shelter where she has gone for protection, and from the victim's home, whether or not she lives with the abuser.[11]

If the victim and the abuser share the same residence, can the protection order bar the abuser from the shared residence?

Yes. In forty-one states, spouse abuse statutes allow courts to issue orders evicting the abuser or granting the victim exclusive use of the residence. Twenty-one states specifically allow for eviction of the abuser even if the residence is in the abuser's name, although some of these states limit such eviction to cases where there is a legal obligation to support the victim or children, where the abuser is married to the victim, or where they jointly own or lease the residence.[12]

In cases where eviction of the abuser is impossible or inappropriate, fourteen states also authorize courts to order the abuser to provide alternative housing for the victim and any minor children.[13]

If the abuser owns all or part of the residence, does such an order destroy his property interest?

No. Many abuse acts explicitly protect the abuser's title to real property.[14] In fact, the New Hampshire statute also provides for the abuser (accompanied by a policeman) to be allowed to enter the residence to remove his personal property.[15] In one case, an alleged abuser challenged the constitutionality of the Pennsylvania abuse statute on the ground that an eviction order obtained without notice to the abuser barring him from his family's jointly owned residence violated the abuser's constitutional rights by depriving him of property without due process.[16] Observing that the exclusion was for a limited period of time, that the abuser's title to the real property was not affected by the order, and that it was a legitimate exercise of the state's police power to protect abused spouses and children, the court upheld the statute and found no unconstitutional taking of the abuser's property.

Can the court order the abuser to undergo counseling as part of a protection order?

Yes. Twenty-three states specifically allow the court to include a provision for counseling in a protection order. Some of these states permit courts to require the abuser to attend counseling, while other statutes only permit the court to recommend counseling.[17] However, some also allow for counseling for the victim.[18] Ordinarily the parties must arrange for payment of the cost of this counseling themselves, but where the abuser is indigent, some statutes specifically provide for the county to assume the costs of counseling.[19]

Can protection orders limit the abuser's contact with his own children?

Yes. In thirty-three states, courts are explicitly empowered to grant temporary custody of minor children to the victim and to limit the abuser's visitation rights as part of a protection order.[20] Illinois, for example, also directs the court to consider in determining custody whether the best interests of the child require a temporary award of custody to the victim as a result of physical violence directed at, or witnessed by, the child.[21] Although the abuser is allowed reasonable visitation rights, some states authorize courts to restrict or even to eliminate such rights under appropriate circumstances. California, for example, specifically allows the court to restrict visitation by the abuser to situations where a third person is present, and Illinois allows for the complete denial of visitation rights where it would "endanger seriously the child's physical, mental, moral, or emotional health."[22]

Can the court order the abuser to pay for the support of the victim or minor children?

Yes. In twenty-eight states, there are specific provisions for court-ordered temporary support, but typically such provisions may limit support to persons (such as a legally married spouse or natural child) who the abuser already has an independent legal obligation to support.[23]

If the abuse has caused personal injury or monetary damage to the victim, can restitution be ordered as part of the protection order?

It depends on the jurisdiction. At least nine jurisdictions (Alaska, California, Illinois, Maine, Massachusetts, Mississippi, New Hampshire, New Jersey, and New York) specifically allow protection orders to include provisions for restitution. The losses for which restitution can be ordered vary from state to state. While New York limits restitution to medical expenses, California permits such additional costs as psychological care and temporary housing. New Jersey (in addition to lost earnings, out-of-pocket expenses, and moving expenses) also permits awards for pain and suffering and even punitive damages.[24]

Can protection orders limit the abuser's use or sale of personal property such as furniture or automobiles?

Yes. At least ten states provide for orders restricting the use, possession, or control of personal property (such as furniture and automobiles) and at least nine states specifically allow for orders prohibiting the abuser from disposing of certain personal property being used by the victim.[25]

Can the court order either party to pay court costs or attorneys' fees incurred in connection with the petition for the order?

Yes. Most statutes allow for a court order awarding costs or attorneys' fees to one party of the other, but the statutes vary concerning the court's authority to enter such orders. Most states provide for the abuser to pay the victim's costs and fees if an order is obtained.[26] But a number of states permit such awards to either party at the discretion of the court.[27]

How can a victim obtain a protection order?

Although the specific procedure varies from jurisdiction to jurisdiction, typically a victim must file a petition with a designated court containing facts sufficient to justify issuing a protection order. A hearing date (usually within two weeks of filing) is indicated in the petition or set by the court. The abuser must be served with a copy of the petition and notified of the hearing date. A judge or magistrate (sitting without a jury) then holds a hearing (at which both parties have an opportunity to testify) and determines whether there is sufficient basis for issuing a protection order. It is useful but not necessary for a victim to be represented by a lawyer when she files a petition, and there are clinics in some cities that may assist the victim in this regard. In some jurisdictions, the court clerks or victims' assistance units in the prosecutor's office may also be available to provide assistance in filing the petition.[28]

What if the abuser fails to appear at this hearing?

If, after being notified of the hearing date, he fails to appear, the abuser waives any right to a hearing and an order can be obtained on the basis of the victim's own testimony.[29]

What must the victim demonstrate at the hearing in order to obtain a protection order?

The requirements vary from jurisdiction to jurisdiction. In general, courts will issue protection orders where a preponderance of the evidence shows that abuse has been threatened, attempted, or already occurred. Many also allow issuance of a protection order if it can be proven that a child was sexually abused.[30]

Where the mistreatment of the victim has been more psychological than physical, can the victim obtain a protection order?

It depends on the jurisdiction. In a few states (such as California) there are specific provisions for protection orders based on a showing of harassment, emotional distress, or psychological abuse.[31] Such statutes make protection orders available to victims kept prisoners by abusers, who have had property destroyed, or whose homes have been broken into. Such relief may also be available in a jurisdiction such as the District of Columbia whose definition of abuse includes any act committed against an eligible party that would be punishable as a crime; in such a jurisdiction, protection orders can be issued for assaults, as well as for burglary, harassment, or destruction of property.[32]

Even where a reference to harassment or psychological abuse is not explicit in a statute, it may be the basis for relief. The North Dakota Supreme Court, for example, has interpreted North Dakota's abuse statute (which explicitly defined abuse as including physical harm, bodily injury, assault, or threats thereof) to be broadly applicable to "all forms of abuse, including mental harm."[33]

Is the victim's right to relief affected by her own use of force to defend herself?

Probably not. The Maine statute specifically provides that the victim's right to relief "shall not be affected by the [victim's] use of reasonable force and response to abuse by the [abuser]." The abuse laws in Tennessee and Illinois contain similar provisions.[34] In other jurisdictions, judges, at their discretion, can be expected to take into account the reasons for any use of force by a victim in considering the victim's petition, even where such provisions are not explicit parts of the law.

If a victim needs a protection order quickly, can she obtain one prior to a hearing?

Yes. Virtually all states that have enacted protection order legislation permit the victim to apply for a temporary protection order that will usually be issued by a judge without a hearing within days, or even within hours of the victim's request. Many states require that courts give priority to such applications and review them on the day they are filed or on the next court day.[35] Although the procedure varies from state to state, typically if the victim can show an immediate need for relief (often an immediate danger of further abuse), the judge can issue the order *ex parte;* that is, without notifying the abuser or giving him an opportunity to be heard.[36] In many jurisdictions, such *ex parte* orders are the norm.

However, as compared to protection orders issued after a hearing, the nature and duration of such temporary orders is limited. In some states, judges cannot include provisions relating to visitation or attorneys' fees in a temporary protection order.[37] Even more important, these temporary orders are of limited duration and typically last only for a specific number of days or until a hearing can be held on the victim's application for an ordinary protection order.[38] However, in Arizona, the District of Columbia, and Pennsylvania, the burden is on the abuser to request a hearing; if he fails to request a hearing, the temporary protection order continues in effect.[39]

If the need for emergency relief occurs at night, on weekends, or at other times when the court that would ordinarily hear an application for a temporary order is closed, thirteen states have specifically provided that the victim can obtain an emergency protection order from a local magistrate or from other courts; typically, these emergency orders only stay in effect until the court that normally considers applications for temporary protection orders reopens.[40]

Why is a hearing required, with the abuser present, so quickly after the entry of a temporary order?

The Supreme Court has repeatedly held that it violates a person's right to due process for a court to severely restrict his conduct or his access or use of property without notice or a hearing.[41] The requirement of a hearing (with prior notice to the abuser) within a short period of time after the entry of a temporary *ex parte* order is intended to guarantee the abuser's right to due process. The Missouri Supreme Court rejected just such a due process challenge to the *ex parte* eviction procedure in the Missouri Adult Abuse Act.[42] After considering the abuser's interest in remaining in the shared residence, the government's interest in prompt protection of the victim and the risk of erroneous deprivation because of the *ex parte* procedure, the court found that a temporary eviction order was "a reasonable means to achieve the state's legitimate goal of preventing domestic violence" and that the act provided procedural safeguards since (1) the deprivation was temporary; (2) an *ex parte* order could only be issued upon a showing of "immediate and present danger of abuse" to the victim; and (3) the abuser had the opportunity within days of the eviction to present his objections at a hearing on the application for a full protection order. Trial courts in Pennsylvania and Ohio have also upheld such *ex parte* relief from due process challenges.[43]

How long will a full protection order stay in effect?

It varies greatly from jurisdiction to jurisdiction. In most of the jurisdictions that allow orders of protection, the order can stay in effect for up to a year.[44] However, in Kentucky, there is no maximum duration of such an order, while in West Virginia, the maximum duration of a protection order is one month.[45] In addition, in a number of states, the commencement or conclusion of a divorce or separation proceeding terminates protection orders.[46] Nineteen states explicitly provide for the renewal of protection orders upon their expiration for an additional term at the court's discretion.[47]

Does the victim have to be married to the abuser in order to be entitled to an order for protection?

In most states, no. A few states (such as Arizona and Florida) limit protection to current or former spouses.[48] In all of the other states that permit courts to order protection orders, victims with other kind of family relationships to the abuser and even some nonrelated victims can also apply for protection orders.

What other family members besides spouses are entitled to protection orders?

It depends on the state. Two thirds of the states that have protection order legislation also permit orders to be issued protecting minor children of the victim or of the abuser.[49] More than half of the statutes include parents of the parties.[50] Two thirds of the states also make provisions for protection of other family members (such as stepchildren) or include a general category of victims related by "consanguinity or affinity" (that is, by blood or by marriage). A number of states require that these related persons reside with the abuser in order to be eligible for a protection order.[51]

Where the victim is part of an unmarried couple can she obtain a protection order?

In most states. However, despite the frequency of abuse involving unmarried couples and persons who are involved in a relationship but live apart, some states do not allow such victims to seek protection orders or limit their availability.[52]

About half the states provide protection orders to unrelated household members or to persons who "cohabit" with the abuser.[53]

A number of states provide protection to victims "living as spouses," but generally do not define this phrase.[54] One commentator has suggested that this phrase should be interpreted in light of the state's requirements for common-law marriage (usually consummation, cohabitation, and public holding out as being married).[55] Other commentators have taken a more liberal view and have suggested that this phrase makes protection order laws broadly applicable to all unmarried couples.[56] One Pennsylvania court (in dictum) interpreted Pennsylvania's abuse statute (which referred to persons "living together as spouses") as covering any unmarried persons living together.[57] By contrast, some states (such as Wisconsin) explicitly restrict coverage of persons "living as spouses" to opposite sex relationships where there are minor children in common.[58]

If the victim divorced the abuser or left him and was subsequently abused, is she eligible for a protection order?

It depends on the state. Most states allow victims of abuse by their former spouses to bring an action for a protection order.[59] At least eleven states allow persons formerly "living as spouses" with the abuser to bring such actions, and at least sixteen states allow former household members or persons of the opposite sex who live together "as if married" to bring such petitions.[60] However, some of these states may have additional restrictions on eligibility, such as Kansas's requirement that both of the parties (at the time of the petition) have legal access to the residence they formerly shared.[61]

Is the victim ineligible to obtain a petition if she has left the residence to avoid abuse?

No. Most of the statutes explicitly state that the victim's eligibility for an order of protection is not affected when the victim leaves the residence to avoid abuse.[62] Nor is the victim's decision to leave the marital residence to escape abuse grounds for denying her temporary child custody.[63]

Can a spouse file for a protection order if there is already a pending divorce or separation proceeding?

Yes. In most states a petition for a protection order can be filed regardless of any other action (including a divorce or separation proceeding) pending between the parties. However, a number of states specifically provide that an abuse act protection order may not be sought by a spouse who is party to a pending divorce action.[64]

Can a petition for a protection order be filed by a parent on behalf of a child who is abused?

It depends on the state. About half of the states that allow for protection orders permit parents to file for a petition on behalf of a minor who has been victimized or even to allow other adult members of the household to file petitions for minors. In one North Dakota case, the court specifically held that the daughter of a man who allegedly had sexually abused her three sisters, could petition for a protection order not only on her own behalf but on behalf of a sister who had also been victimized but who had not personally requested or consented to the order, and in a New York case, the court allowed a pregnant victim to file for a protection order on behalf of her unborn child.[65]

Is the victim required to use a lawyer to file the petition for a protection order?

No. Most of the state statutes specifically provide that the victim can file for a petition without an attorney and a number of these states also require that the court prepare petition forms that are usable by lay people.[66]

Various jurisdictions have adopted a number of other procedures to make it easier for victims to obtain protection orders. In 11 states, abuse acts require the court clerk to assist the victim in filing a petition.[67] In a number of jurisdictions, courts are prohibited from charging fees for the filing of protection order petitions or are limited to only minimal fees (typically under $30) which can be waived if the victim is indigent.[68] Similarly, once an order of protection is issued, about half of the states provide for copies to be given to the victim free (or for a $1 charge).[69] Other courts waive for protection orders the usual requirement of posting a bond or monetary undertaking to cover potential damage caused by wrongful issuance of injunctive order.[70] Service of the order on the abuser by the police is also provided by a number of states, at little or no cost to the victim.[71]

Although these procedures assist only one party to the proceeding—the victim—they have been upheld against constitutional challenges by abusers. In one case, a Minnesota court upheld a provision requiring clerks to assist battered women in filling out protection order petition forms, as a reasonable court rule and as a legitimate attempt to protect spouse abuse victims.[72] The court specifically rejected the defendant's arguments that this provision violated the constitutional guarantee of separation of powers or created a biased court.

Besides the victim, who receives copies of the court's protection order?

It depends on the state. Virtually all of the states mandate that a copy of the order be given to the abuser, but while some of the states provide for the court to issue the order directly to the abuser, others require that the victim arrange for service of the order on the abuser (although such service may be performed for the victim by the police).[73] In some states, where the abuser has actual notice of the order, it is not necessary for him to receive a copy to be held liable for violation of that order.[74]

In addition, a number of states also require the court to send a copy of the protection order to the local police (although in some states, this is only at the victim's request).[75]

Is there a penalty if the abuser violates an order of protection?

Yes, although the nature of the penalty varies from jurisdiction to jurisdiction.

In 31 states an abuser who violates an order of protection is guilty of contempt of court.[76] While some of these statutes explicitly state that violation will be treated as "civil contempt,"[77] some states have statutes that seem to indicate that the abuser can be prosecuted for criminal contempt.[78] However, most states fail to explicitly state whether the contempt proceeding will be for civil or criminal contempt, although many provide upon violation of the order for imprisonment (up to a year) and/or a fine (up to $2,000).[79]

In some states (such as California), which provide defendants in civil contempt proceedings with the same rights as defendants in criminal contempt trials, this distinction may not be important.[80] But in many jurisdictions, civil contempt defendants may be found guilty based on a preponderance of the evidence (unlike criminal contempt defendants they do not have to be found guilty beyond a reasonable doubt) and may have other procedural disadvantages. The effect of this ambiguity in most states was made clear by one 1978 Pennsylvania case.[81] In that case, the trial court determined that there had been no violation of the order of protection and no contempt. When the victim attempted to appeal, the appellate court held that the finding of contempt was "criminal" in nature and "indistinguishable from ordinary criminal convictions," that the abuser had a constitutional protection against double jeopardy, and that therefore the appellate court was unable to reverse or even review the lower court's findings that there was no violation. Thereafter, the Pennsylvania legislature amended the Abuse Act to specifically provide that violation of protection orders constituted "indirect criminal contempt," but also stated that the abuser had no right to a jury trial.[82]

In 19 states, in addition to other potential criminal violations and contempt, an abuser who violates a protection order may be prosecuted for a misdemeanor offense.[83] In order to constitute a misdemeanor, however, the violation typically must be committed with knowledge of the existence of the protection order.[84] Twelve states allow for prosecution either for a misdemeanor or for contempt.[85] Sixteen of the states allowing prosecution have specified jail terms of 6 months or more for violation of a protection order and fines of $500 or more instead of, or in addition to, a jail sentence; however, actual imprisonment in such cases is "relatively rare."[86]

Where there has been a violation of an order of protection through assault or through some other criminal activity, is the victim forced to choose between a criminal prosecution

for the assault and a prosecution for a violation of the protection order?

No. In one Pennsylvania domestic violence case, the court explicitly held that a finding of indirect criminal contempt did not preclude prosecution on other criminal charges growing out of violation for the protection order, including assault, trespass, and rape.[87]

Can the abuser prevent his spouse from testifying against him at a criminal trial for abuse or violation of a protection order?

No. In cases involving spouse abuse, most states no longer allow this adverse testimonial privilege in criminal or civil cases. Traditionally, there was a marital testimonial privilege at common law (intended to protect and preserve family peace and harmony) which allowed the defendant in a criminal proceeding to disqualify his spouse as a witness against him. However, in 1980, the United States Supreme Court held that the defendant cannot prevent adverse testimony from his or her spouse in federal criminal proceedings and noted the trend (in most states) to abolish this marital privilege against adverse testimony in criminal proceedings.[88]

In states where there are no statutes providing for issuance of an order of protection, are there any circumstances under which courts are permitted to issue comparable orders providing for support, temporary custody, or prohibiting abuse?

Yes. Idaho, New Mexico, and Washington make no special provision for orders of protection but in these and in most other states injunctions prohibiting abuse were and still are available as part of divorce, separation, or other domestic relations proceedings. Orders comparable to a protection order evicting an abuser from the marital residence are usually available in such actions, but the victim may have to demonstrate an immediate necessity to protect the safety of person or property or that such relief is necessary to prevent an adverse effect on the victim's children.[89] Some states have suggested that no showing of imminent actual physical injury is necessary in such cases as long as there is a severe threat to the victim's mental health or that of the victim's children.[90]

Even where there is no matrimonial proceeding pending, courts have the general equitable power to issue injunctions ordering an abuser to stop conduct that harasses, molests, assaults, or humiliates the victim.[91]

If there is no protection order in effect, is spouse abuse a crime?

Yes. While every state has criminal laws that could be applied to spouse abuse, traditionally police and prosecutors did not treat it as a criminal matter; only recently has spouse abuse itself been categorized as a separate criminal offense.

To encourage the prosecution of abusers, eleven states have made spouse abuse a separate offense. Some of these states also make abuse of a former spouse a crime. In five of these states (under some circumstances), spouse abuse is a felony; in the others it is a misdemeanor. Although such criminal laws reduce the burden of proof required to obtain a conviction, create more severe punishments for abusers, and have the effect of making it more likely that abusers are prosecuted and arrested, an appellate court upheld California's spouse abuse law as a reasonable response to a serious problem and found that it did not unreasonably discriminate against abusers or violate equal protection.[92]

The specific definition of the crime, the required relationship between the victim and the abuser, and the severity of the punishment varies from state to state. California, for example, makes it a felony to subject spouses or cohabitants of the opposite sex to willful "corporal" injury resulting in a traumatic condition: convicted abusers can be sentenced to up to four years' imprisonment.[93] By contrast, Arkansas's statute is limited to "wife beating" or "assault on wife" and is punishable as a misdemeanor or felony depending on the seriousness of the injury.[94] In Rhode Island, domestic assault is punishable by imprisonment of up to one year or a fine up to five hundred dollars or both and the victim need only reside in the same household. In Tennessee, assault and battery against a spouse is a misdemeanor (unless aggravated by use of a weapon), and in Ohio, physical harm to a family or household member is a felony only if the abuser has already been previously convicted of domestic violence.[95]

What can a court do to prevent further abuse by a defendant released on bail prior to trial?

It depends on the state. Six states specifically allow the judge to deny pretrial release to an accused spouse abuser if such release would create the threat of bodily harm to another person.[96] Some fifteen states (such as Ohio, North Carolina, Massachusetts, and New York) allow the criminal court to place conditions on pretrial release or issue a protection order barring the defendant from having contact with the victim, making threats, or removing property prior to trial.[97]

Can the criminal court order restitution to the victim if the defendant is convicted of, or admits to, spouse abuse?

It depends on the state. In Massachusetts and New Hampshire there are specific restitution provisions applicable to persons convicted of spouse abuse.[98] In other states, general statutes relating to pretrial diversion, probation, or sentencing may also permit the criminal court to order the defendant to pay restitution to the victim.[99]

In cases where the defendant is guilty of the crime of spouse abuse or of violating a protection order, do courts have punishment options other than imprisonment?

Yes. Seven states have statutes that specifically create diversion, deferred prosecution, or special supervision programs for persons guilty of spouse abuse and/or violation of protection orders.[100] Although the courts and prosecutors have discretion in admitting abusers and the specific requirements vary from state to state, typically such programs are available to abusers (1) who admit their guilt; (2) who waive their right to a speedy trial; (3) who have not previously been admitted to a diversion program; and (4) who do not have a prior criminal conviction for domestic abuse or another serious crime. In return for an agreement to defer prosecution for a certain period of time, the abuser agrees to participate in a program (usually involving periodic reports to the court or a social agency, counseling, and strict adherence to any orders of protection); if the abuser successfully completes the program, in some states the prosecution against him is permanently dismissed and his arrest record is expunged. Arizona's program is unusual in requiring the consent of the victim before the abuser is placed in a diversion program, although other states (such as Ohio) will request information from the victim that is included in the presentencing report prepared for the judge.[101]

A number of states also allow criminal courts (independent of any organized diversion program) to order defendants who were convicted or entered guilty pleas in domestic violence cases to undergo counseling as a condition of probation or any suspended sentence; some make counseling a mandatory condition of probation or a suspended sentence in such cases.[102] However, in states without such statutes, it still may be within the discretion of the court to order counseling or other appropriate rehabilitation, or to stipulate that the defendant have no further contact with the victim, as conditions of probation or suspended sentences.[103]

Can the victim choose to initiate a criminal prosecution and also seek a civil protection order?

Yes, in most states. The laws in three quarters of the states that authorize protection orders explicitly permit victims to seek protection orders in addition to any pending or contemplated criminal action.[104] However, as a practical matter, most prosecutors remain reluctant to file criminal actions against abusers; in such jurisdictions the victim's only practical course may well be to seek a protection order. One exception is New York where victims must choose between criminal prosecution or civil protection; this requirement has been upheld against constitutional challenges that it was vague and that it violated due process and equal protection. In 1978, New York did liberalize this requirement by allowing victims seventy-two hours after commencement of a proceeding in either family court or criminal court in which to change their minds.[105]

What can the victim do, short of commencing a civil suit or criminal prosecution, to prevent future abuse?

Depending on the jurisdiction, there may be a number of other options open to spouse abuse victims.

In some jurisdictions (such as Westchester County, New York), at the request of the victim, the prosecutor may send the abuser a warning letter informing him that a complaint has been received and that he may be guilty of illegal conduct that could lead to a jail sentence; some police departments will arrange for a meeting between the police and the suspected batterer to inform him of the penalties for criminal assault.[106]

In many jurisdictions, the victim can also take advantage of services provided by a domestic abuse shelter or alternative dispute resolution center.

What is a "domestic abuse shelter"?

In many communities there are shelters that provide a variety of services to abuse victims at little or no cost to the victim. Typically these shelters provide victims with

1. food;

2. a place to stay;

3. referral to employment or psychological counseling;

4. medical or legal services;

5. child care;

6. counseling about obtaining public benefits;

7. abuser counseling;

8. outreach and education programs;

9. a 24-hour hotline.

Information about domestic abuse shelters in your area can be obtained from the hotline of a local shelter, the local victim/witness assistance unit in your prosecutor's office, or from local women's groups. If you have difficulty obtaining information in your area, you can contact the National Coalition Against Domestic Violence, 1500 Massachusetts Ave., N.W., Washington, DC (202–347–7017).[107]

What are "alternative dispute resolution centers" and what services can they provide for spouse abuse victims?

Alternative dispute resolution centers provide parties to ongoing conflicts with a forum for mediating their differences and for agreeing to end the dispute without resorting to the courts. Such centers in many communities will mediate spouse abuse cases; in some programs (such as the San Francisco Community Board Program), domestic violence cases constitute the bulk of the disputes resolved by the program. For a further discussion of how such alternative dispute resolution works, see chapter IV. However, a number of domestic violence experts have been critical of the use of such centers to resolve spouse abuse cases. They argue that the premises of mediation—compromise and an admission that both parties are responsible—demeans the victim of spouse abuse who more often that not bears no responsibility for her abuse.

What is a "peace bond"?

In most jurisdictions, judges are permitted to order the abuser to refrain from abuse and to deposit a "peace bond" with the court as a security against any future breach of the peace.[108] Typically, the judge can summarily order the abuser to file a peace bond after determining that there is a serious threat that the abuser will continue to violate the peace by continuing his abuse. In some states, the peace bond is simply a warning to the abuser and posting an actual amount of money is not required. However, in other states, failure to post the required amount of money subjects the defendant to imprisonment.[109]

Once the abuser posts the bond, any subsequent abuse produces forfeiture to the court of the amount of the bond. A number of commentators have questioned the effectiveness of such bonds because the only remedy for further abuse is forfeiture of the bond; violation does not subject the abuser to arrest or imprisonment. Others have criticized the peace bond procedure as an unconstitutional violation of the abuser's rights because it discriminates against indigent abusers who cannot post the bond by imprisoning them in violation of equal protection; and because it subjects all abusers to the summary procedures used to impose peace bonds in violation of the abusers' rights to due process.[110]

If a victim calls the police to report abuse or violation of a protection order, as a practical matter, will the police arrest the abuser?

It depends on the jurisdiction. As a general rule, most police departments still do not make arrests in spouse abuse cases. However, arrests of abusers are becoming more and more likely because of recent changes in the law and in police department policy in many jurisdictions. Until recently, there were a number of serious obstacles to making arrests in a spouse abuse situation. First, many states traditionally allowed warrantless arrests for misdemeanor offenses only if the offense occurred in the presence of the police officer. In most states, the crimes related to spouse abuse were treated as misdemeanors and therefore the officer could not make an arrest without a warrant. Many departments had a policy of discouraging arrests in domestic violence cases because victims were thought to be unwilling to actually prosecute their spouses, or because the police simply did not perceive it as a serious crime.[111]

Is police inability or unwillingness to arrest abusers detrimental to victims?

Yes. A 1983 study conducted by the Police Foundation of police responses to wife abuse in Minneapolis showed that where police separated victims from their abusers for at least 8 hours, there was a 24-percent recurrence of violence; in those cases where the police actually arrested the abuser, there was only a 10-percent recurrence of violence, apparently because these arrests impressed the abusers with the seriousness of their offense and with the likelihood of punishment.[112]

What are these recent changes involving arrests in spouse abuse cases?

There have been several changes. First, 33 states have expanded the police's power to make arrests in domestic abuse cases. In 28 states, the police are now authorized to arrest an abuser without a warrant if the officer has probable cause to believe he has committed a misdemeanor.[113] In almost all of the states, the abuse need not occur in the presence of the police. However, there may be additional requirements before an arrest can be made. Minnesota and New Hampshire, for example, allow warrantless arrest only where the incident took place within a few hours before the police arrived. Minnesota and Nevada only permit warrantless arrests when there is actual physical evidence of abuse.[114]

In addition, in 19 states probable cause that the abuser violated a protection order is also grounds for a warrantless arrest.[115] Such states typically require that the abuser receive a copy of the order and that the police verify that the order is in effect, before an arrest is made. In order to ease verification, such states may also require that the police department maintain a copy of the order in their files along with proof of service on the abuser.[116]

To further encourage the use of warrantless arrest in abuse cases, half of these states have immunized police officers who make such arrests from liability to the abuser in suits for false arrest as long as the officer's actions were taken in a "good faith effort" to enforce the law.[117]

Such special arrest provisions as applied to domestic violence cases have been upheld against a constitutional challenge that they violated equal protection and constitute an irrational classification that singles out married people for special treatment. The Florida Supreme Court, in upholding such a law, held that statutory classifications need not be all inclusive to satisfy equal protection as long as they apply equally to all of the members of a particular class of victims for whom there was a reasonable state interest in providing protection.[118]

Such statutes, and similar statutes allowing for warrantless arrests for out of presence misdemeanors, have been held to satisfy the requirements of the Fourth Amendment as long as the officer had probable cause or "reasonable ground" to believe that the offense had occurred.[119] However, the United States Supreme Court did invalidate a warrantless arrest that took place in a suspect's home on the grounds that the Fourth Amendment's prohibition of unreasonable search or seizure must be broadly interpreted to protect the sanctity of the suspect's activities at home and barred nonconsentual entry into a suspect's home to make a routine felony arrest without first demonstrating probable cause and obtaining a warrant.[120]

In a domestic abuse situation, where police entry into the home may well be at the consent of the victim and where there is an emergency or dangerous situation, there is probably no such Fourth Amendment prohibition.

Has there been any change in police department policy concerning the discretionary use of arrest powers?

Yes. There have long been complaints of police failure to enforce protection orders and criminal laws in domestic abuse cases because of the perception that such offenses are "minor," that they are better served by conciliation or temporary separation of the parties, and that the spouse-victim will not cooperate in the prosecution of spouse abuse.[121] One study of police law enforcement in routine cases (including domestic violence cases) showed that a nonarrest decision was made in 43 percent of all felony situations and 52 percent of all misdemeanor cases in spite of the existence of probable cause; this was found to be the result of departmental policy and inadequate training.[122]

Beginning in the late 1970s, a number of groups concerned about the lack of police response to domestic disputes began negotiations with police departments in different municipalities aimed at changing these practices. Where informal conversations were insufficient to produce a change in department policy, class action suits were begun against police departments alleging that the failure to make arrests violated women's constitutional rights to due process and equal protection under the law.[123] A number of these suits produced consent decrees where police departments agreed to change their training of officers with respect to domestic cases and their patrolman's guides. In New York City, for example, following such a consent decree, police officers were ordered to arrest family members or cohabitants alleged to have been guilty of violent abuse and were specifically prohibited from attempting to informally "adjust" the cases.[124] As a result of such changes, a study indicated that the New York City Police Department significantly improved its handling of domestic violence matters in situations where the victim requested arrest.[125]

After agreeing to a similar consent decree, the Oakland (California) Police Department issued a directive that the police department would no longer employ an arrest avoidance policy in response to incidents of alleged domestic violence and that in cases where the statutory requirements were met, "arrests shall be presumed to be the most appropriate response."[126] In their training program, Oakland policemen are now trained to assume that domestic violence victims will cooperate in subsequent criminal proceedings in making their decision whether to make an arrest.[127]

Legislatures in some states (including Nevada, Virginia, and Texas) have passed resolutions encouraging police departments to institute training programs on intervention in family violence cases.

In addition, both domestic abuse victims' organizations and law enforcement organizations have now prepared extensive training materials and practice guides that are increasingly being adopted (without the need for litigation) by police departments in jurisdictions across the United States.[128]

Despite all of these changes in the law and in official departmental policies, experts on domestic violence report that most police officers still do not perceive spouse abuse as a serious crime and that the arrest of an abuser is the exception, not the rule.

Is arrest for spouse abuse mandatory in any jurisdictions?

Yes. In a number of states—including Delaware, Maine, Massachusetts, Minnesota, North Carolina, Oregon, and Utah—a finding of probable cause that spouse abuse occurred or that an order of protection has been violated leaves a police officer with no discretion about whether to make the arrest.[129] Such arrests are mandatory in these states, although the specific requirements for a mandatory arrest situation vary.

Does the victim have any recourse if the police officer responding to a report of domestic violence fails or refuses to make an arrest?

It depends on the circumstances and the jurisdiction. Where an arrest is discretionary, there probably is no cause of action against the police if the officer appearing on the scene had reasonable grounds for failing to make the arrest. However, in those states where an arrest is mandatory, failure to make an arrest under the circumstances indicated in the statute gives rise to a valid claim for damages against the individual officer and the municipality employing him. The Oregon Supreme Court upheld a damage claim against a policeman and his police department when, despite probable cause to believe that a protection order had been violated, the officer refused to make an arrest. The court found that the statutory requirement for warrantless arrest in such circumstances created a private right for the victim to recover damages caused by further abuse after the police failed to make the arrest.[130]

Even in states where warrantless arrests are not mandatory, in particular circumstances, victims can and have argued that the expansion of arrest powers in spouse abuse cases creates a special duty to protect spouse abuse victims (a designated class of persons identified in the law) and the failure to provide protection by making an arrest constitutes negligence. In one such case in Miami, a visibly injured woman whose husband threatened her in the presence of the police was forced to kill her husband after the police refused to make an arrest; arguing that the police's failure to enforce the law caused her husband's death, the woman sued for damages.[131]

Where there is an outstanding order of protection, the victim can argue that the city or state has undertaken a special duty to protect her and failure to arrest violators constitutes negligence. In one New York case, the police were summoned by a victim who had already obtained an order of protection from the court in connection with prior abusive incidents, but they refused to make an arrest. A New York court held that the government had assumed a special duty to the victim and her family by issuing the order of protection and that failure to provide protection under those circumstances gave rise to a cause of action against the police and against the city for damages.[132]

Besides making an arrest, are the police obligated to assist the victim in any other ways?

It depends on the jurisdiction. There are statutes in eleven states that encourage or require the police to assist the victim by providing transportation to a hospital and in eight states that the victim be provided with transportation to a shelter.[133] Eighteen states have some provision requiring the police officer appearing on the scene to advise the victim of her rights, including her right to seek criminal prosecution or a civil protection order and her right to receive assistance from certain social service agencies.[134] In addition, Massachusetts directs policemen to use all reasonable means to prevent further abuse, including remaining on the scene as long as there is a danger to the victim's physical safety,[135] and Maryland requires police (if requested) to accompany an endangered victim to her residence to remove any personal clothing and effects.[136]

In some states where such requirements have not been enacted by statute, police departments in particular jurisdictions may adopt policies that provide for special services to spouse abuse victims; for example, in California, the Oakland Police Department settled a lawsuit brought by abuse victims by agreeing to provide spouse abuse victims with information on social service resources.[137] As a result of a similar lawsuit, the police department in New York City has agreed to direct police officers to assist the victim in obtaining medical assistance if she so requests.[138]

Are prosecutors required to bring criminal actions in spouse abuse cases?

No. Filing charges in spouse abuse cases, as in all other crimes, is primarily a matter of prosecutorial discretion.[139] Traditionally, prosecutors have been reluctant to commence criminal proceedings in spouse abuse cases because many victims (who are financially or otherwise dependent on the abuser) initially express interest in filing charges but subsequently decide against cooperating with the prosecution. A District of Columbia survey, for example, indicated that lack of witness cooperation accounted for dismissal of 43 percent of the cases involving family members as compared to 17 percent of the dismissals of cases involving strangers.[140] Prosecutors in other jurisdictions have reported that approximately 80 percent of criminal charges filed in domestic cases are dismissed because the victim requested dismissal or because the victim failed to appear for a court hearing or meeting with the prosecutor.[141]

However, recently, prosecutors in such jurisdictions as Seattle, Santa Barbara, Los Angeles, Philadelphia, and Westchester County have instituted special programs aimed at reducing attrition in domestic violence cases by providing additional attention and services for victims. In Seattle, for example, cases are handled by a special battered women's project where caseworkers affiliated with the prosecutor's office—

1. explain the criminal process to the victim;

2. arrange for necessary services;

3. aid in the filing of the complaint and corroborative materials;

4. help the victim obtain a protection order (if necessary);

5. assist the victim in providing input into any sentencing of the abuser.[142]

As a result of these innovations, the Seattle program reports that eighty-three percent of the domestic violence cases for which it files charges result in convictions. In addition, in many jurisdictions, prosecutors are increasingly using complaints signed by prosecutors rather than the victim herself; this prevents the spouse from exerting pressure on the victim to drop the criminal case and has resulted in substantial conviction levels even where the victim failed to appear at trial.[143]

While some jurisdictions have voluntarily created such programs, in other jurisdictions, class actions by spouse abuse victims have produced consent decrees resulting in new prosecutorial policies and increased prosecution. In Cleveland, for example, prosecutors agreed to consider each domestic abuse case on its own merits, investigate cases where police officers fail to arrest alleged abusers and allow victims to request review of a decision not to prosecute.[144]

In other states, state statutes impose special restrictions on prosecutors in spouse abuse cases. In Washington, for example, a prosecutor is required to inform victims within five days whether prosecution will be initiated and to provide victims with information about how the victim can initiate criminal proceedings if the state chooses not to do so.[145]

Where a prosecutor adopts a general policy of not prosecuting spouse abuse cases, are the constitutional rights of victims violated?

Yes. At least one court has held that failure to prosecute where there is a practice or policy of not bringing domestic abuse complaints unreasonably discriminates against spouse abuse victims and violates the victims' rights to due process and equal protection under the laws.[146]

Can a husband be prosecuted for raping his wife?

It depends on the jurisdiction. Although largely unreported, marital rape is a significant problem; one 1980 study in San Francisco revealed that twelve percent of the married women surveyed had been raped at least once by their husbands, a rape rate twice that among strangers.[147] Increasingly (in part because of the widely publicized 1978 Oregon trial of a man accused of raping his wife) attention is being paid to marital rape and the antiquated laws in many jurisdictions that prohibit prosecution for marital rape.

The rule that husbands cannot be guilty of raping their wives is 300 years old and began with a publication written by the British jurist, Sir Matthew Hale, in 1736.[148] Various justifications are proposed for this rule, including that by marriage the wife has irrevocably consented to sex with her husband, that wives are their husbands' "property," and/or that for legal purpose a husband and wife are one "person," while rape requires the rapist to have sex with another.[149] A number of states have adopted this common-law rule in their court decisions in rape cases or have included marital exceptions in their rape laws.[150]

In at least 36 states men who rape their wives cannot be prosecuted if the parties are living together and 13 states have extended this traditional marital rape exemption to prevent prosecution of unmarried cohabitants.[151] Delaware, Hawaii, Maine, North Dakota, and West Virginia have gone so far as to prohibit prosecution for first-degree rape where the victim is a "voluntary social companion" of the rapist; these statutes apply only if the victim previously had sex with the rapist, except in West Virginia where prosecution of `a victim's voluntary social companion is prohibited even if the parties never previously had sex.[152]

However, 11 states—California, Connecticut, Florida, Iowa, Massachusetts, Minnesota, Nebraska, New Jersey, Oregon, and Wisconsin—have abolished or restricted the marital rape exemption; in those states, husbands who rape their wives can be prosecuted under most circumstances.[153]

Despite many recent changes in the law in this area, there is no clear trend. While a number of states have enacted legislation abolishing the exemption, others have extended it for the first time to include unmarried couples living together or even dates. Significantly, courts in three states—New Jersey, Massachusetts, and Florida—have invalidated common-law marital rape exemptions. The New Jersey Supreme Court in February 1981 upheld a rape charge against a husband. The court rejected the traditional rationales for the common-law rape exemption that (1) a woman is the "sexual property of her husband"; (2) by marrying she consents to sexual intercourse; and (3) "after marriage a man and woman no longer retain separate legal existence" and thus "a husband could not be convicted of, in effect, raping himself." The court found these notions clearly outdated in light of a woman's recognized right to make her "own choices regarding reproduction and sexual conduct."[154]

Do services provided to spouse abuse victims receive state funding?

Yes, in most states. However, the character of the funding varies from state to state. In a number of states, services (such as domestic abuse shelters) are funded by surcharges (usually less than ten dollars) on marriage licenses or filing fees for divorce or dissolution of marriage.[155] Such surcharges have been challenged as unconstitutional violations of equal protection on the ground that it is irrational and discriminatory to impose a surcharge on all people who apply for marriage licenses when domestic violence services are utilized by only a small proportion of married people and by unmarried people who pay no surcharge. While courts in Alabama and Nevada have upheld statutes and rejected such constitutional challenges, a trial court in Illinois declared that state's divorce surcharge unconstitutional as a violation of equal protection guarantees.[156]

Can an abuse victim sue her spouse for damages?

Yes. The deliberate abuse of another person (particularly where it involves physical violence) makes the abuser liable for damages. Depending on the circumstances, the victim can allege in a civil complaint that the abuser committed any of a number of intentional torts, including false imprisonment, assault, trespass, and intentional infliction of emotional distress. In one Maryland case, for example, the court ruled that a spouse had a valid claim for damages for intentional outrageous conduct where her husband and his friends allegedly forced the victim's car off the road at gunpoint and then beat and raped her.[157] For a fuller discussion of a victim's right to bring a civil action for damages against a person who commits a crime, see chapter V.

Are such damage suits common?

No. But with the publicity surrounding the problem of spouse abuse and the increasing recognition of the seriousness of spouse abuse, victims are bringing such damage actions more and more frequently. Unlike many victims, the spouse abuse victim is in a position to know the identity and whereabouts of the abuser. Equally important, in many cases, the abuser has sufficient financial resources to satisfy any judgment that the victim may obtain. In one recent case in Roanoke, Virginia, a wife received a judgment of $65,000 for damages resulting from abuse and in another case in Washington, the wife received a judgment of over $18,000 for lost wages, medical bills, and pain and suffering.[158]

Does the abuse victim face any special problems in bringing a civil suit against her spouse?

Yes. At common law there was a marital privilege that could be invoked by either spouse to disqualify the other from providing adverse testimony at trial. The justification for this marital privilege was the preservation of family peace and harmony.

However, most states have modified or abolished this

privilege; even in the remaining states, courts faced with attempts by abusers to invoke the marital testimonial privilege have made an exception and permitted the victim to testify.[159]

The second potential obstacle was the doctrine of interspousal immunity, which traditionally barred tort actions based on personal interest between spouses. The justification for this rule was the preservation of domestic tranquillity, the elimination of fraudulent or frivolous suits, and the availability of other remedies, such as divorce. Once the prevalent rule, most states have now abolished interspousal tort immunity.[160] However, even in those states that have retained interspousal tort immunity for some purposes, exceptions have been made for spouse abuse. The Supreme Court of Virginia, for example (which had generally recognized interspousal immunity), rejected the traditional justification of preserving family harmony in a spouse abuse case and held that the defendant had no immunity from a suit for wrongful death where he was alleged to have intentionally and fatally shot his wife.[161]

Is child abuse a serious problem?

Yes. It is estimated that over a million cases of child abuse (involving physical mistreatment, sexual abuse, and neglect) occur in this country each year.[162] According to the American Humane Association, the number of cases of child abuse reported to state and local authorities doubled from 413,000 in 1976, to 851,000 by 1981. In Florida alone, the number of child abuse reports increased from 35,000 in 1981, to over 45,000 in 1982.[163]

There are between 100,000 and 200,000 reported cases of child sexual abuse alone each year. Although such abuse often takes place in the home, increasingly there are reports of sexual abuse by others—teachers, camp counselors, ministers, and bus drivers—who have close contact with children. In one widely publicized case, staff members of a nursery school in Manhattan Beach, California, were charged with 115 counts of molestation, including rape, sodomy, and child pornography; some of the victims were as young as two years old. Reacting to such abuse, in 1984 Congress authorized drafting of a Model Child Care Standards Act containing minimum licensing requirements (including background checks of employees) for day care centers and group homes. Although such sexual abuse has long been a problem, changes in the law and a growing perception that this is a "serious" crime have led to an increase in prosecutions. Nevertheless, only a small fraction of all such cases are actually reported, and child victims often run the risk of disbelief or outright harassment if they attempt to report instances of sexual abuse.[164]

Recognizing that child abuse is a serious problem, Congress in 1984 enacted legislation which made federal funding for victim assistance dependent on a state's demonstrated record in fighting child abuse and made challenge grants available to states (of up to 25% of expenditures or 50¢ a child) specifically to fund state programs to prevent child abuse and neglect.

Is child abuse a crime?

Yes. Depending on the jurisdiction and the nature of the abuse, child abuse can be prosecuted under a variety of different criminal statutes. Virtually every state has made it a crime (usually a misdemeanor) for a person with custody of a child to knowingly, intentionally, or willfully abuse or neglect the child.[165] Where the abuse takes the form of physical or sexual attacks on the child, it can be prosecuted as assault, battery, sodomy, molestation, or rape (although the definitions of these crimes vary greatly from jurisdiction to jurisdiction).[166] Where there is sexual abuse of the child and the abuser is the child's parent it can be prosecuted as incest in virtually every jurisdiction.[167] Most of the ten states that have made "domestic violence" a separate criminal offense, restrict the definition of the offense to the assault on a "wife," "spouse," or "opposite sex cohabitant." However, some, such as Ohio, have made their domestic violence criminal statutes applicable to family or household members physically harmed by the abuser, including children.[168]

Are civil orders of protection available to prevent child abuse?

Yes. Twenty-seven states have enacted legislation providing for protection orders prohibiting the abuse of minor children of the abuser or his spouse; in these states, evidence of physical abuse of a child is also specified as sufficient basis for issuing a protection order. In virtually all of these states, the parent of the minor victim (or an adult member of the minor's household) can petition the court for the order on the minor's behalf.[169]

Is a parent who allows a child to be abused by the other parent liable to criminal prosecution?

Yes. In at least one such case a mother has been prosecuted for allegedly allowing her child to be physically abused by a third party in the mother's presence. Rejecting the argument that the mother could not be guilty of criminal liability unless she had affirmatively participated in the assault of her child, the North Carolina Supreme Court held that although there is usually no criminal liability for simply being present at the scene of a crime, the mother had an affirmative legal duty to protect her child. Her failure to act could make her criminally liable as an aider and abettor to the assault of her child.[170] A special American Bar Association Committee on intrafamily child sexual abuse, has specifically recommended that a parent be held criminally responsible for the sexual abuse of the child if the parent had actual knowledge of the abuse or intentionally failed to take reasonable steps to prevent its occurrence.[171]

Have any special statutes or procedures been adopted to encourage the reporting and prosecution of child abuse cases?

Yes, although the statutes and procedures vary from jurisdiction to jurisdiction.

Reporting Laws. Beginning in the late '50s and early '60s (particularly after the publication of the book *The Battered Child Syndrome*), a number of states enacted child abuse-reporting statutes, many patterned after the model child abuse reporting law drafted by the Children's Bureau of the United States Department of Health, Education, and Welfare in 1963.[172] Typically, such statutes

1. urge or, in most states, require physicians and others who treat child abuse cases to report cases of suspected child abuse to child protection agencies or to the police;

2. give the reporters immunity from civil liability for making good faith reports;

3. make it a crime punishable by fine or imprisonment (usually a misdemeanor) to fail to report child abuse;

4. require the agency receiving the report to investigate the case and to develop a plan of action to remedy the problem (often through the use of trained interdisciplinary teams);

5. provide confidentiality for case records; and

6. provide a guardian *ad litem* (for the suit) for children in all cases in which a judicial proceeding is pending.

By 1972, all fifty states had enacted such statutes and forty-seven of them had made reporting mandatory.[173]

To assist in the implementation of these reporting laws, Congress passed the Child Abuse Prevention and Treatment Act in 1974, to provide funds to the states to assist them in delivering services to abused and neglected children. One of the requirements for these funds was enactment of an effective statutory scheme for making reporting of child abuse mandatory.[174]

Despite these statutes, one commentator has estimated that at best only 1 out of every 3 abused children is identified and reported, and at worst, only 1 out of 6 cases is reported.[175]

Outreach. Private and publicly funded organizations in many jurisdictions have begun outreach programs designed to publicize the need for identifying, reporting, and treating cases of child abuse; such organizations provide counseling services to parents and children, have begun workshops in school systems (such as the Columbus, Ohio, schools) designed to educate children to recognize and report cases of abuse (particularly sexual abuse), and operate hotlines that allow parents and/or children to report instances of abuse and/or request help.[176]

Special Child Abuse Units. Hospitals and child protective services agencies have created special units to coordinate the handling and treatment of child abuse (such as the one at San Francisco's General Hospital for reviewing sexual abuse cases) and have prepared written protocols that contain specific guidelines for examining, treating, and reporting cases of child abuse.[177] To ease the child victim's role in the prosecution of child abuse, a number of jurisdictions (for example, New York City, through the Victims Services Agency) have established special units in the prosecutor's office trained to deal with child victims. Typically these units provide simplified explanations of the criminal process to the victim, escorts to accompany the victim to all meetings with prosecutors and proceedings and coordinate (with the help of guardians *ad litem* where they are appointed) any simultaneous proceedings in civil and criminal court.[178] In order to ease the strain on the victim, many prosecutors have adopted procedures for reducing the number of pretrial interviews required of the victim and/or utilize special interviewing rooms (such as the one used in Seattle, Washington) which allow for the victim to be interviewed by one person while others observe through a one-way mirror.[179]

Testimony at Trial. To ease the trauma of the victim's trial testimony, a number of states (either by statute or court decision) allow for the exclusion of the public during the child's testimony (particularly in sex crime cases).[180] Several states also specifically provide for videotaped depositions of a child victim's testimony in criminal sex offense cases.[181]

While such procedures may protect the victim, they may also violate the constitutionally protected rights of others. The Supreme Court, for example, has invalidated a Massachusetts statute that required closure of sex offense trials involving children on the grounds that such a blanket prohibition of press coverage violated the public's right to know and the press's right to publish under the First Amendment.[182] Since this decision related solely to the *mandatory* exclusion of the press and public, and the court confirmed the judge's *discretionary* ability to exclude the press and public from certain testimony, such exclusion may well be constitutional in particular cases where the judge makes a finding that public testimony would prevent the child from freely testifying or that it would traumatize the victim.[183]

A more difficult problem is raised by the defendant's Sixth Amendment right to confront opposing witnesses. One court in California has specifically held that seating the defendant in a child abuse case so that he could hear but not see the child witness violated his right to confrontation.[184] However, at least in juvenile court proceedings, an Illinois appellete court upheld the introduction of a child's testimony in a neglect proceeding where that testimony was taken outside the parent's presence in the judge's chambers, on the grounds that the prosecutor and defense counsel were both present and the child could be subjected to effective cross-examination.[185]

Allowing Hearsay in Sex Abuse Cases. A number of jurisdictions have adopted evidentiary rules that allow the admission of out-of-court statements by the child in sex abuse cases that would normally be excluded as hearsay. Some states have permitted statements about the sexual abuse to be introduced as "excited utterances," even though the children made the statements as much as three months after the assault.[186] In Kansas, legislation has been enacted to make a special exception to the hearsay rule, where the child is otherwise unavailable, for statements made by children concerning deprivation or crimes committed against them; in Washington, the statement of a child under the age of ten that describes sexual contact initiated by another may be used as evidence.[187] A third avenue for admitting children's out-of-court statements is the so-called residual hearsay exception that has been adopted in the federal courts and in almost a third of the states that allows any statement to be introduced as evidence that has trustworthiness equivalent to the existing exceptions to the hearsay rule.[188] Under analogous reasoning, the Minnesota Supreme Court admitted a statement about sexual abuse that the child-victim made concerning the defendant during a dream; concluding that the child could not have concocted such a statement, and that there was other evidence of sexual abuse, the court found the statement trustworthy and admitted it despite it being hearsay.[189] The American Bar Association has recommended that states adopt a specific exception to the hearsay rule allowing the admission into evidence of such out-of-court statements by child sexual abuse victims where (1) the witness is reliable; (2) the statement is generally trustworthy; (3) the interests of justice would be served by admitting the statement; (4) the child testifies or there is other corroborative evidence of the abuse.[190]

Are there special problems in admitting testimony by children as evidence in child abuse cases?

Yes. The majority of states by statute or common law require a child to be a certain age before he is presumed to be competent to testify; below that age, the judge has the sole discretion (after observing the child and asking him questions) to admit the child's testimony after the judge satisfies himself that the child (1) has a present understanding of the difference between truth and falsity and realizes he has the obligation to speak the truth; (2) had the mental capacity at the time of the abuse to make accurate observations; (3) has memory sufficient to retain an independent recollection of that observation; and (4) is able to understand simple questions about the abuse and communicate his memory into words.[191] The judge's assessment of the child's competence is subject to review on appeal but will not be set aside except in cases of clear abuse of the judge's discretion.[192]

Some commentators have argued for a more liberal approach to child testimony that would allow all children to testify and allow the judge or jury to consider it (after observing the child) for what it is worth.[193] This approach has been adopted in the federal courts and those state jurisdictions that have rules based on the Federal Rules of Evidence; in such jurisdictions, every person is competent to be a witness and the factors just listed (which previously could render a child incompetent as a witness) can be used by the defendant only to attack the weight and credibility of the child's testimony.[194] In some states, there is, in addition, a special cautionary instruction that must be given to the jury regarding the care with which it should assess a child's testimony for credibility.

In some jurisdictions, there are additional difficulties in admitting a child's testimony in sex abuse cases. A few jurisdictions—including Nebraska and the District of Columbia—require corroboration (other evidence that strengthens, supports, or confirms the testimony about the sexual abuse) in all sex offense cases involving children; in other states, such corroboration is required in certain special instances of sexual abuse.[195] The most frequent reasons given for this requirement of corroboration are the alleged frequency of false reports of sexual offenses, potential bias in favor of the abused child, the difficulty that a falsely accused defendant may have in defending himself, and the idea that children may be susceptible to overt or covert influences by others. Most commentators have dismissed these objections (which were once used to justify corroboration requirements in adult sexual abuse cases and have now been abandoned) and emphasize the great care that goes into qualifying a child's testimony as competent, the use of cautionary instructions for the jury, and the requirement that the state convince the jury beyond a reasonable doubt that the child is telling the truth.[196]

Are there alternatives to imprisonment for persons convicted of child abuse?

Yes. Where the defendant is a nonviolent first offender, he may qualify for the kind of pretrial diversion program discussed in connection with spouse abuse. In addition, in a number of jurisdictions (including Olathe, Kansas; Sacramento,

California; and Everett, Washington) special pretrial diversion programs have been established for offenders in intrafamily child sex abuse cases. A number of states have also enacted sexual psychopath statutes that provide for the commitment to a mental institution (instead of prison) of persons (not otherwise considered insane) who, by a course of repeated misconduct in sexual matters, have evidenced such a lack of power to control their sexual impulses as to be dangerous to other persons.[197] Because of the summary nature of some sexual psychopath proceedings, such statutes have been challenged on a number of constitutional grounds. The Supreme Court has specifically held that such proceedings require the notice and opportunity to be heard guaranteed by the due process clause, and other cases have considered challenges to these statutes on equal protection grounds for failure to provide protections available in civil mental health commitment proceedings.[198] These infirmities as well as the difficulty of determining which defendants may be sexual psychopaths (particularly since this is a legal and not a psychiatric concept) have led a number of commentators to call for the repeal of these statutes; as of late 1981, eight states had repealed such laws.[199]

Can the victim of child abuse sue his or her parents for damages?

Yes. Sexual or physical abuse or neglect can constitute any of a number of intentional torts that would entitle the victim to sue for damages. The nature and requirements for such suits are discussed for victims in general in chapter V.

Child abuse cases raise a number of special problems. If the child is a minor, the nonabusing parent or another adult (usually a guardian *ad litem* appointed by the court) must sue on the child's behalf. In addition, most of the problems with admitting the testimony of children previously discussed in connection with criminal trials also exist in a civil trial for damages.

Despite these problems, increasingly child abuse victims are suing their parents, often only after they reach majority and years after the abuse. The Utah Supreme Court, for example, upheld the right of a victim to sue her stepfather for allegedly subjecting her to eight years of sexual abuse when she was a minor; it rejected the stepfather's arguments that the victim consented to the sexual abuse (as a minor, she was held to be unable to consent to such acts) and that he was immune to suit under a "parental immunity" theory.[200] Although the statute of limitations for such intentional torts is typically short (often only one or two years), courts have held that victims of child abuse can bring such actions years after the abuse, and that the statute of limitations is tolled as long as the victim was a minor.[201]

Is domestic violence against the elderly a problem?

Yes. Like spouses and children, in recent years it has become increasingly apparent that elderly Americans living with their families or others upon whom they are dependent are being physically assaulted, neglected, harrassed, or otherwise abused. One sociologist estimated that 5 percent of dependent elderly Americans are abused.[202]

Do elderly victims of domestic abuse have special rights?

Yes. Where the elderly victim is the parent or relative of the abuser and lives in the same household, 32 states allow the victim to obtain an order of protection under the same statutes that permit spouse abuse victims to obtain such orders. In 20 states, such protection is available to elderly abuse victims who are unrelated members of the abuser's household.[203]

In addition, over 35 states have enacted elderly abuse-reporting laws (similar to the reporting laws applicable to child abuse), and a number of states have enacted or proposed legislation enhancing the punishment of persons convicted of certain crimes against the elderly; such statutes and other rights generally applicable to elderly victims are discussed in chapter IX.

Are domestic violence victims eligible for awards from state victims' compensation boards?

It depends on the jurisdiction. Two thirds of the compensation programs bar or restrict compensation to relatives of the offender, persons living in the same household as the offender, and/or persons engaged in a continuing (sexual) relationship with the offender. Although most of these programs exclude all domestic violence victims, some of them do allow compensation to the victim where it is "in the interests of justice" or where the victim is separated from the offender and cooperates in the prosecution of the crime. In approximately a third of the programs, where they satisfy the other criteria for eligibility and benefits, any domestic violence victim can claim victim compensation. For a fuller discussion of this restriction on eligibility for crime victims' compensation, see chapter III.

Notes

1. "Wife Beating: The Silent Crime," *Time Magazine*, Sept. 5, 1983, at 23.
2. *Id.*; L. Lerman, *Prosecution of Spouse Abuse: Innovations in Criminal Justice Response*, vol. 1, no. 28 (Washington, D.C.: Center for Women Policy Studies, 1981) [hereafter *Prosecution of Spouse Abuse*].
3. *Id.*
4. L. Lerman and F. Livingston, "State Legislation on Domestic Violence," *Response*, vol. 6, no. 5, 2, 5n.7 (Sept./Oct. 1983) [hereafter *State Legislation*], citing E. Stark et al., "Wife Abuse in the Medical Setting" (available on a loan basis from the Center for Women Policy Studies, Washington, D.C.).
5. A. Boylan and N. Taub, *Adult Domestic Violence: Constitutional, Legislative and Equitable Issues* (Legal Services Corp. Research Institute, 1981), pp. 372–75 [hereafter *Adult Domestic Violence*].
6. For detailed discussions of the rights and remedies of spouse abuse victims, *see State Legislation, supra* note 4; *Adult Domestic Violence, supra* note 5; *Prosecution of Spouse Abuse, supra* note 2.
7. Where the number of states that have adopted a particular type of domestic violence statute appear in this chapter, the figure is taken from *State Legislation, supra* note 4.
8. *Id.* at 2.
9. *Id.* at 6. *See, e. g.*, CONN. GEN. STAT. ANN. §46b–38(b)(2) (West Supp. 1983–84).
10. *Adult Domestic Violence, supra* note 5, at 71–2. *See, e.g.*, TEX. FAM. CODE ANN. tit. 4 §71.11(a)(7) (Vernon Supp. 1982–83); CAL. CIV. CODE §4359(a)(6) (West 1983); W VA. CODE §48–2A–6(1) (1980).
11. *Adult Domestic Violence, supra* note 5, at 38–9. *See, e.g.*, TEX. FAM. CODE ANN. tit. 4 §71.11(a)(1)(c) (Vernon Supp. 1982–83); OHIO REV. CODE ANN. §3113.31(E)(1)(g) (Page Supp. 1982) (school); N.D. CENT. CODE §14–07.1–02(4)(b), –03(2)(b) (1981) (shelter).
12. *State Legislation, supra* note 4, at 2, 12n.7A. *See, e.g.*, TEX. FAM. CODE ANN. tit. 4 §71.11(a)(2)(A) (Vernon Supp. 1982–83).
13. *State Legislation, supra* note 4, at 6. *See, e.g.*, IOWA CODE §236.5(2)(b) (West Supp. 1983–84); N.C. GEN. STAT. §50B–3(a)(3) (Supp. 1981).
14. *Adult Domestic Violence, supra* note 5, at 68. *See* KAN. STAT. ANN. §60–3107(e) (Supp. 1982); OHIO REV. CODE ANN. §3113.31(E)(4) (Page Supp. 1982); 35 PA. CONS. STAT. ANN. §10186(c)(Purdon Supp. 1983–84).

15. *Adult Domestic Violence, supra* note 5, at 45; N.H. Rev. Stat. Ann. §173–B:6(II)(Supp. 1981).

16. *Boyle v. Boyle*, 5 Fam. L. Rep. 2916, 2917 (Pa. Ct. C.P., Alleghany Co. Sept. 10, 1979).

17. *State Legislation, supra* note 4, at 6, 13; *compare* Tex. Am. Code Ann. tit. 4 §71.11(a)(5)(Vernon Supp. 1982–83) (mandatory) *to* Ill. Ann. Stat. ch. 40 ¶ 2302–8 §208(5)(Smith-Hurd Supp. 1983–84) (requiring or recommending).

18. *State Legislation, supra* note 4, at 6, 13. *But see* N.H. Rev. Stat. Ann. §173–B:4(I)(b)(counseling for the abuser only).

19. *State Legislation, supra* note 4, at 6, 13. *See, e.g.,* N.D. Cent. Code 14–07.1–02(4)(d)(1981).

20. *State Legislation, supra* note 4, at 6. *See, e.g.,* 35 Pa. Cons. Stat. Ann. §10186(a)(4)(Purdon Supp. 1983–84); Mass. Ann. Laws ch. 209A §3(c); Ill. Ann. Stat. ch. 40 ¶ 2302–8 §208(3)(Smith-Hurd Supp. 1983–84) (Michie/Law. Coop. 1981)(custody); W. Va. Code §48–2A–6(d)(1980) (custody with visitation rights); R.I. Gen. Laws §15–5–19 (Supp. 1982).

21. Ill. Ann. Stat. ch. 40 §602 (Smith-Hurd 1980).

22. *State Legislation, supra* note 4, at 13 n.23. *See, e.g.,* Ill. Ann. Stat. ch. 40 §607 (Smith-Hurd 1980).

23. *State Legislation, supra* note 4, at 6. *See, e.g.,* 35 Pa. Cons. Stat. Ann. §10186(a)(5)(Purdon Supp. 1983–84); Ohio Rev. Code Ann. §3113.31(E)(1)(e)(Page Supp. 1982); N.C. Gen. Stat. §50B–3(a)(6), (7)(Supp. 1981).

24. *State Legislation, supra* note 4, at 6, 13 ns. 24,25. *See, e.g.,* Cal. Civ. Proc. Code §547(c)(West Supp. 1983).

25. *State Legislation, supra* note 4, at 6, 13. *See, e.g.,* Cal. Civ. Code §4359(a)(1)(West 1983); N.H. Rev. Stat. Ann. §173–b:4(I)(b)(1)(Supp. 1981)(awards plaintiff exclusive use of commonly owned property); Tex. Fam. Code Ann. tit. 4 §71.11(a)(1)(E)(Vernon Supp. 1982–83) (prohibiting transfer or encumbrance).

26. *State Legislation, supra* note 4, at 6, 13; Tex. Code Ann. §36–1205 (Supp. 1982).

27. *State Legislation, supra* note 4, at 13. *See, e.g.,* Kan. Stat. Ann. §107(a)(7)(Supp. 1982); N.C. Gen. Stat. §50B–3(a)(10)(Supp. 1981).

28. *State Legislation, supra* note 4, at 6, 14–15; Lerman, *Legal Help for Battered Women* 6 (Washington, D.C.: Center for Women Policy Studies 1981) [hereafter *Legal Help*].

29. *State Legislation, supra* note 4, at 2.

30. *State Legislation, supra* note 4, at 2, 6. *See, e.g.,* 35 Pa. Cons. Stat. Ann. §10182(iii)(Purdon Supp. 1983–84); Kan. Stat. Ann. §60–3102(a)(3) (A)(Supp. 1982); W. Va. Code §48–2A–5 (1980)(requires "clear and convincing evidence"); Tenn. Code Ann. §36–1205 (Supp. 1982); N.H. Rev. Stat. Ann. §173–B: 4 (Supp. 1981).

31. *State Legislation, supra* note 4, at 2, 6. *See, e.g.,* Cal. Civ. Proc. Code §527.6 (West Supp. 1983).

32. *State Legislation, supra* at 2, 6; D.C. CODE ANN. §16–1001(5)(Supp. 1983).

33. *Lucke v. Lucke*, 300 N.W.2d 231 (N.D. 1980).

34. *State Legislation, supra* note 4, at 14 n. 62. *See, e.g.*, N.C. GEN. STAT. 50B–49(c)(1)(Supp. 1981).

35. *State Legislation, supra* note 4, at 8, 15 ns.86–94. *See, e.g.*, OHIO REV. CODE ANN. §3113.31(D)(Page Supp. 1982)(same day).

36. *See, e.g.*, MASS. ANN. LAWS ch. 209(A) §4 (Michie/Law. Coop. 1981).

37. *See, e.g.*, OREG. REV. STAT. §107.705–720 (1981).

38. *State Legislation, supra* note 4, at 8; OHIO REV. CODE ANN. §3113.31(D) (Page Supp. 1982) (hearing within 10 court days); MASS. ANN. ANN. LAWS ch. 209A §4 (Michie/Law. Coop. 1981) (hearing within 5 days of entry of *ex parte* order); CONN. GEN. STAT. ANN. §46b–38(b) (West Supp. 1983–84) (14 days); CAL. CIV. PROC. CODE §§546, 527(a)(20–25 days).

39. *State Legislation, supra* note 4, at 15 n.98.

40. *Id.* at 2–3. *See, e.g.*, N.D. CENT. CODE §14–07.1–08 (1981); KAN. STAT. ANN. §60–3105(a)(Supp. 1982).

41. *Sniadach v. Family Finance Corp.*, 395 U.S. 337 (1969).

42. *Williams v. Marsh*, 626 S.W.2d 223 (Mo. 1982). *See* discussion, *State Legislation, supra* note 4, at 5 n.9, 15 n.87.

43. *State Legislation, supra* note 4, at 5 n.9; *Boyle, supra* note 16; *Ohio v. Heyl*, No. C79BR120 (Mun. Ct., Hamilton Co. 1979).

44. *State Legislation, supra* note 4, at 8. *See, e.g.*, KAN. STAT. ANN. §60–3107(c)(Supp. 1982)(subject to further provisions); OREG. REV. STAT. §107.716(3)(1981).

45. *State Legislation, supra* note 4, at 8. *See, e.g.*, W. VA. CODE §48–2A–6 (1), (2)(30 days).

46. *See, e.g.*, OHIO REV. CODE ANN. §3113.31(E)(3) (Page Supp. 1982) (affects only provisions regarding custody and child support within 60 days of filing); MO. ANN. STAT. §455.060(4)(Vernon Supp. 1983) (entry of decree).

47. *State Legislation, supra* note 4, at 8.

48. *Id.* at 6. *See* FLA. STAT. ANN. §741.30 and §409.602(4)(West Supp. 1983); ARIZ. REV. STAT ANN. §13–3601 (Supp. 1982–83).

49. *State Legislation, supra* note 4, at 6. *See, e.g.*, ILL. ANN. STAT. ch. 40 ¶ 2302–8 §208(1)(Smith-Hurd Supp. 1983–84).

50. *State Legislation, supra* note 4, at 6. *See, e.g.*, N.Y. JUD. LAW §812 (McKinney Supp. 1982–83).

51. *State Legislation, supra* note 4, at 6. *See, e.g.*, W. VA. CODE §48–2A–2(b)(1980).

52. *State Legislation, supra* note 4, at 6.

53. *Id. See, e.g.*, OREG. REV. STAT. §107.705(2)(1981); WASH. REV. CODE ANN. §10.99.020(1)(1980).

54. *Id.* W. VA. CODE §48–2A–2(b)(1980); 35 PA. CONS. STAT. ANN. §10182 (Purdon Supp. 1983–84).

55. *Adult Domestic Violence, supra* note 5, at 84–86. *See also* OHIO REV. CODE ANN. §3113.31(A)(3)(Page Supp. 1982).

56. *See, e.g.*, D. Flynn, "Protection from Abuse Act," 51 *Temple L. Q.* 116, 120 (1978); B. H. Schickling, "Relief for Victims of Intra-Family Assaults," 81 *Dick. L. Rev.* 815, 818–819 (1979).

57. *Cipolla v. Cipolla*, 264 Pa. Super. 53, 398 A.2d 1053, 1054 n.1 (1979).

58. *State Legislation, supra* note 4, at 14 n.51; WISC. STAT. ANN. §46.95(1)(c)(West Supp. 1983–84).

59. *State Legislation, supra* note 4, at 6. *See, e.g.*, N.C. GEN. STAT. §50B–(1)(Supp. 1981).

60. *Id. See, e.g.*, W. VA. CODE §48–2A–2(a)(1980).

61. *State Legislation, supra* note 4, at 14 n.55; KAN. STAT. ANN. §60–3102(a)(Supp. 1982).

62. *State Legislation, supra* note 4, at 6; *Adult Domestic Violence, supra* note 5, at 136–40. *See, e.g.*, 35 PA. CONS. STAT. ANN. §10183 (Purdon 1977); KAN. STAT. ANN. §60–3103 (Supp. 1982) (legal access to residents required).

63. *Adult Domestic Violence, supra* note 5, at 136–40. *See* KY. REV. STAT. ANN. §403.270(2)(Supp. 1982).

64. *State Legislation, supra* note 4, at 6. *See, e.g.*, UTAH CODE ANN. §30–6–7 (Supp. 1981); MINN. STAT. ANN. §518B.01 subd.4(c)(West Supp. 1983).

65. *State Legislation, supra* note 4, at 6; *Lucke, supra* note 33; "In re Gloria C. v. William C." *N.Y.L.J.*, May 16, 1984, at 12, cl.5 (Fam. Ct., Richmond Co.).

66. *State Legislation, supra* note 4, at 6. *See, e.g.*, N.Y. REV. STAT. ANN. §§173–B:3(III), 10 (Supp. 1981).

67. *State Legislation, supra* note 4, at 6. *See, e.g.*, TENN. CODE ANN. §36–1204 (Supp. 1982); UTAH CODE ANN. §30–6–4 (Supp. 1983).

68. *State Legislation, supra* note 4, at 6. *See, e.g.*, MASS. ANN. LAWS ch. 209A §3 (Michie/Law. Coop. 1891); N.H. REV. STAT. ANN. §173–B:3(II)(Supp. 1981).

69. *State Legislation, supra* note 4, at 6. *See, e.g.*, NEB. REV. STAT. §42–926 (1978).

70. *See, e.g.*, UTAH CODE ANN. §30–6–5(2), (4) (Supp. 1981); OREG. REV. STAT. 107.716(5)(1981).

71. *See, e.g.*, COLO. REV. STAT. 14–4–102(4)(Supp. 1982)($10 charge for service).

72. *Minnesota v. Errington*, No. 81–289, Slip Op. (Minn. Oct. 6, 1891) [reported in *Response* (Nov./Dec. 1981)] and cited in Lerman, "Court Decisions on Wife Abuse Laws: Recent Developments," *Response* 4 (May/June 1982) [hereafter "Court Decisions"].

73. *State Legislation, supra* note 4, at 8. *See, e.g.*, CONN. GEN. STAT. ANN. §46b–38(b)(West Supp. 1983–84)(court); MINN. STAT. ANN. §418B.01 subd. 8 (West Supp. 1983)(personal service required).

74. *State Legislation, supra* note 4, at 8. *See, e.g.*, COLO. REV. STAT. §14–4–102(3)(Supp. 1982).

75. *State Legislation, supra* note 4, at 8. *See, e.g.*, TEX. FAM. CODE ANN. tit. 4 §71.17(b)(Vernon Supp. 1982–83); MICH. COMP. LAWS ANN.

§552.14(3)(Supp. 1983–84); Minn. Stat. Ann. §518B.01 subd. 13 (West Supp. 1982) (only at victim's request).

76. *State Legislation, supra* note 4, at 8. *See, e.g.,* W. Va. Code §48–2A–7(2)(1980); Iowa Code Ann. §236.8 (West Supp. 1984–84); Kan. Stat. Ann. §60–3110 (Supp. 1982).

77. *State Legislation, supra* note 4, at 3, 8. *See, e.g.,* Tenn. Code Ann. §36–1212 (Supp. 1982); N.C. Gen. Stat. §50B–4 (Supp. 1981).

78. *State Legislation, supra* note 4, at 3, 8. *See, e.g.,* Mich. Comp. Laws Ann. §552.14(4)(Supp. 1983–84) (indicating that the abuser can be "found guilty" of "contempt" and imprisoned); 35 Pa. Cons. Stat. Ann. §10190(a), (b) (Purdon Supp. 1983–84) (indirect criminal contempt for violation).

79. *State Legislation, supra* note 4, at 3, 8. *See, e.g.,* W. Va. Code §48–2A–7(2)(1980)(30 days imprisonment and $1,000 fine); Tex. Fam. Code Ann. tit. 4 §71.16(a)(Vernon Supp. 1982–83) (6 months imprisonment/$500 fine; up to a year and $2,000 fine if the violation involved violence).

80. *See* Cal. Civ. Proc. Code §1209 (West 1982) (and annotations).

81. *Cippola v. Cippola, supra* note 57, 398 A.2d at 1055–57.

82. 35 Pa. Const. Stat. Ann. §10189(a)(b)(Purdon Supp. 1983–84).

83. *State Legislation, supra* note 4, at 8. *See, e.g.,* Wash. Rev. Code Ann. §10.99.040(2)(Supp. 1983–84); Mass. Ann. Laws ch. 208 §34c (Michie/Law. Coop. 1981).

84. *State Legislation, supra* note 4, at 3, 8. *See, e.g.,* N.D. Cent. Code §14–07.1–06 (1981); Cal. Civ. Code §4458 (West 1983).

85. *State Legislation, supra* note 4, at 3, 8. *See, e.g.,* N.D. Cent. Code §1407.1–06 (1981); Minn. Stat. §518B.01 subd.14(a)(b)(West Supp. 1983).

86. *State Legislation, supra* note 4, at 3, 8. For penalties for contempt *see supra* notes 75 through 80; for misdemeanor penalties, *see, e.g.,* Mass. Ann. Laws ch. 208 §34C (Michie/Law. Coop. 1891); Cal. Penal Code §273.6 (West Supp. 1983).

87. *State v. Allen* (Lebanon Co., Pa.)(Ct. C.P., Oct. 8, 1980), discussed in *Adult Domestic Violence, supra* note 5, at 160.

88. *Trammel v. U.S.,* 445 U.S. 40 (1980); 2 Wigmore, *Evidence* §488 (1979).

89. *State Legislation, supra* note 4, at 3; *Adult Domestic Violence, supra* note 5, at Part II. *See, e.g., Keller v. Keller,* 158 N.W.2d 694 (N.D. 1968); *Carlson v. Carlson,* 234 Minn. 258, 48 N.W.2d 58, 61 (1951); *Scampoli v. Scampoli,* 323 N.Y.S.2d 627, 37 A.D.2d 614 (1971); *Daniel v. Daniel,* 236 So.2d 197 (Fla. App. 1970).

90. *See, e.g., S. v. A.,* 118 N.J. Super. 69, 285 A.2d 588 (Ch. Div. 1972); *Roberts v. Roberts,* 24 Conn. Supp. 146, 187 A.2d 257 (Super. Ct. 1962).

91. *Adult Domestic Violence, supra* note 5, at Part II. *See, e.g., Dickson v. Dickson,* 12 Wash. App. 183, 529 P.2d 476 (1974); *cert. denied,* 423 U.S. 832 (1975); *reh. denied,* 423 U.S. 991 (1975); *Hawks v. Yancey,* 264 S.W. 233 (Tex. Ct. App. 1924); *Webber v.*

Gray, 228 Ark. 289, 307 S.W.2d 80 (1957); *Galella v. Onassis,* 487 F.2d 986 (2d Cir. 1973).

92. *State Legislation, supra* note 4, at 3, 8–9. *See, e.g.,* CAL. PENAL CODE §273.5 (West Supp. 1983); *People v. Cameron,* 53 Cal. App.3d 786, 126 Cal. Rptr. 44 (1975).

93. CAL. PENAL CODE §273.5 (West Supp. 1983).

94. ARK. STAT. ANN. 41–1653–59 (Supp. 1983). *See also State Legislation, supra* note 4, at 17 n.128.

95. R.I. GEN. LAWS §11–5–9 (1981); TENN. CODE ANN. §39–2–105 (1982); OHIO REV. CODE ANN. §2919.25,

96. *State Legislation, supra* note 4, at 10; MINN. STAT. ANN. §629.72 subd. 2 (West 1983).

97. *State Legislation, supra* note 4, at 10; OHIO REV. CODE ANN. §2919.26(E)(Page 1982); N.C. GEN. STAT. §15A–534.1 (Supp. 1981); MASS. ANN. LAWS ch. 276 §42A (Michie/Law. Coop. 1980); N.Y. CRIM. PROC. LAW §530.12.

98. MASS. ANN. LAWS ch. 276 §42A (Michie/Law. Coop. 1980); N .H. REV. STAT. ANN. §651:2(VI)(Supp. 1981).

99. For a general discussion of the availability of restitution in criminal actions, *see* chap. IV.

100. *State Legislation, supra* note 4, at 10, 17 n.141. *See, e.g.,* CAL. PENAL CODE §1000.6 *et. seq.* (West Supp. 1983); WIS. ANN. STAT. §971.38 (West Supp. 1983–84).

101. *State Legislation, supra* note 4, at 10, 17; ARIZ. REV. STAT. ANN. §13–3601(G); cf. N.J. STAT. ANN. §2C:43–12a, b, e (1982). *See also Adult Domestic Violence, supra* note 5, at 304 (discussing Ohio's probation practice concerning diversion).

102. *State Legislation, supra* note 4, at 10. *See* OHIO REV. CODE ANN. §2933.16 (Page 1982); MASS. ANN. LAWS ch. 276 §42A (Michie/Law. Coop. 1980).

103. *State Legislation, supra* note 4, at 10. *See, e.g.,* MINN. STAT. ANN. §5188.01 §16 (West 1983); CONN. GEN. STAT. §46b–38(e)(West Supp. 1983–84).

104. *State Legislation, supra* note 4; at 6.

105. *People v. Revell,* 402 N.Y.S.2d 522 (Dist. Ct., Nassau Co. 1978); N.Y. JUD. LAW §812(2)(e)(McKinney Supp. 1982–83); N.Y. CRIM. PROC. LAW §100.07(2)(McKinney 1981).

106. *Prosecution of Spouse Abuse, supra* note 2, at 64–65.

107. *See Legal Help, supra* note 28, at 13.

108. *See, e.g.,* MICH. COMP. LAWS §§ 772.8, .13(2) (1982); *Adult Domestic Violence, supra* note 5, at 83–85.

109. *Legal Help, supra* note 28, at 7. *See, e.g.,* MICH. COMP. LAWS §772.14a (1982).

110. *See* Note, "Peace and Behavior Bonds—Summary Punishment for Uncommitted Offenses," 52 *Bay. L. Rev.* 914, 926–32 (1966); Note, "Peace Bond—A Questionable Procedure for a Legitimate State Interest," 74 *W. Va. L. Rev.* 326 (1971); *Adult Domestic Violence, supra* note 5, at 84–85 (Pt. 2).

111. *State Legislation, supra* note 4, at 4.
112. L. W. Sherman and R. A. Berk, "Police Responses to Domestic Assault: Preliminary Findings" (1983) (available from the Police Foundation, 1909 K. Street, N.W., Washington, DC 20006).
113. *See, e.g.,* FLA. STAT. ANN. §901.15(6)(West Supp. 1983)(battery); MINN. STAT. ANN. §629.341 (West 1983); UTAH CODE ANN. §§30–6–8(2)(Supp. 1981), 77–36–2(3) (Supp. 1983).
114. MINN. STAT. ANN. §629.341 (West 1983) (within 4 hours); N .H. REV. STAT. ANN. §594:10(I)(Supp. 1981)(within 6 hours); NEV. REV. STAT. §171–124(1)(f)(1979).
115. *State Legislation, supra* note 4, at 4, 10. *See, e.g.,* OREG. REV. STAT. §133.310(3)(1981).
116. *Id.; Adult Domestic Violence, supra* note 5, at 144–46.
117. *State Legislation, supra* note 4, at 4, 10. *See, e.g.,* N.C. GEN. STAT. §14–134.3 (1981); OREG. REV. STAT. §133.315 (1981).
118. *LeBlanc v. State,* 382 So.2d 299 (Fla. 1980). *See also Prosecution of Spouse Abuse, supra* note 2, at 123.
119. *Prosecution of Spouse Abuse, supra* note 2, at 122–23. *See, e.g., City of Columbus v. Herrell,* 18 Ohio App.2d 149, 47 Ohio Ops.2d 254, 247 N.E.2d 770 (1969). *Compare Wong Sun v. U.S.,* 371 U.S. 471, 479–80 (1963).
120. *Payton v. New York,* 455 U.S. 573 (1980); *Welsh v. Wisconsin,* U.S.———(1984). *See also Prosecution of Spouse Abuse, supra* note 2, at 122.
121. *See, e.g., Adult Domestic Violence, supra* note 5, at 207–23; Woods, "Litigation on Behalf of Battered Women," 5 *Women's Rights L. Rptr.* 7 (1978).
122. President's Commission on Law Enforcement and Administration of Justice. *Task Force Report: The Police* 21 (1971).
123. *See, e.g., Bruno v. Codd,* 47 N.Y.2d 582, 419 N.Y.S.2d 901, 393 N.E.2d 976 (1979)(New York City); *Scott v. Hart,* Civ. No. 76–2395 (N.D. Cal.)(consent decree filed on Nov. 9, 1979) (Oakland, Calif.).
124. *See* Procedure No. 110–16, "Desk Appearance Ticket (General Procedure)," and Procedure No. 110–38, "Arrests—Family Offenses," New York City Police Department Patrol Guide (Sept. 1982).
125. E. Connick, J. Chytilo, and A. Person, *Battered Women in the New York City Criminal Justice System* 8 (1980).
126. Lerman, "Elements and Standards for Criminal Justice Programs on Domestic Violence," *Response* 11 (Nov./Dec. 1982) [hereafter "Elements"], quoting Office of the Chief of Police, Oakland Police Department, Special Order No. 3853 (Nov. 1, 1979).
127. *Id.,* quoting "Domestic Violence and Domestic Disputes," Oakland Police Training Bulletin No. III–J (Nov. 1, 1979).
128. *Id.,* quoting Training Key No. 245, International Association of Chiefs of Police (1976). *See, e.g.,* N. Loving, *Spouse Abuse, A Curriculum Guide for Police Trainers* (Washington, D.C.: Police Executive Research Forum, 1981); *State Legislation, supra* note 4, at 18 n.167.

129. *State Legislation, supra* note 4, at 10. *See, e.g.,* OREG. REV. STAT. §133.310(3); MASS. ANN. LAWS ch. 209A §6(4) (Michie/Law. Coop. 1981); UTAH CODE ANN. 30–6–8 (Supp. 1981); ME. REV. STAT. ANN. tit. 19 §770(6)(D)(1981).

130. *Nearing v. Weaver,* 295 Or. 702, 670 P.2d 137 (1983). *Compare Kubitscheck v. Winnett,* No. 8587 (filed Feb. 20, 1980) (settled for an undisclosed but substantial sum of money), discussed in *Court Decisions, supra* note 72, at 3, 21.

131. *Buckhannan v. City of Miami,* No. 80–14830 (Fla. Cir. Ct., filed Mar. 30, 1981), discussed in *Court Decisions, supra* note 72, at 3, 21.

132. *Sorichetti v. City of New York,* 408 N.Y.S.2d 219, 95 Misc.2d 451 (Sup.Ct. 1978). Other cases involving suits against the police for failure to provide protection in domestic violence cases include *Baker v. New York,* 25 App.Div.2d 770, 269 N.Y.S.2d 515 (1966) (protection order); *Benway v. Watertown,* 1 App.Div.2d 465, 151 N.Y.S.2d 485 (1956) (the plaintiff has cause of action against the city for the return of a gun to the plaintiff's husband); *Jones v. County of Herkimer,* 51 Misc.2d 130, 272 N.Y.S.2d 925 (1966) (police and other city officials knew that the husband had threatened and previously assaulted the victim); *Todesco v. Alaska,* No 4FA–81–593 Civ. (Alaska Superior Court, Fourth Dist. filed May 19, 1981).

133. *State Legislation, supra* note 4, at 10. *See, e.g.,* N.C. GEN. STAT. §50B–5(a), (b)(Supp. 1981); WASH. REV. CODE ANN. §10.99.03(4)(Supp. 1983–84); MASS. ANN. LAW ch. 209A §6 (Michie/Law. Coop. 1981).

134. *State Legislation, supra* note 4, at 10. *See, e.g.,* MASS. ANN. LAWS ch. 209A §6 (Michie/Law. Coop. 1981); WASH. REV. CODE ANN. §10.99.033)(a)(Supp. 1983–84); OHIO REV. CODE ANN. §3113.31(J)(Page Supp. 1982).

135. MASS. ANN. LAWS ch. 209A §6(1) (Michie/Law. Coop. 1981).

136. MD. ANN. CODE. art. 27 §11F(a)(1982). At least one critic has complained that officers may accompany victims to their home but often fail to wait for them to emerge safely. J. E. Hamos, *State Domestic Violence Laws and How to Pass Them,* p. 46 (1980).

137. *Scott, supra* note 123, at 8.

138. *Bruno v. Codd,* 90 Misc.2d 1047, 396 N.Y.S.2d 974 (Sup. Ct. 1977), *reversed in part, appeal dismissed in part,* 407 N.Y.S.2d (App. Div. 1978), *aff'd.,* 47 N.Y.2d 582, 419 N.Y.S.2d 901, 393 N.E.2d 976 (1979).

139. *See* the discussion of prosecutorial discretion to file criminal actions in chap. II.

140. *See Prosecution of Spouse Abuse, supra* note 2, at 18, citing B. Forst et al., *What Happens After Arrest?* 28 (1977) (available from Institute for Law and Social Research).

141. *Prosecution of Spouse Abuse, supra* note 2, at 30, n.16.

142. *Elements, supra* note 126, at 9, 12–14.

143. *Prosecution of Spouse Abuse, supra* note 2, at 44–47. For a detailed description of these programs, *see id.* at 33–51.

144. *Raguz v. Chandler*, C. 74–1064 (N.D. Ohio).

145. Wash. Rev. Code Ann. §10.99.060 (1980).

146. *Doe v. City of Belleville*, No. 81–5256 (S.D. Ill. Mar. 22, 1982) (Order denying motion to dismiss; Magistrate's report).

147. Z. Mettger, "A Case of Rape: Forced Sex in Marriage," *Response*, vol. 5, no. 2, Mar./Apr. 1982, at 1 [hereafter "A Case of Rape"].

148. Hale, *History of the Pleas of the Common Crown*, 629 (1736 ed.).

149. *A Case of Rape*, supra note 147, at 2.

150. A complete survey of the laws applicable to marital rape, as of July 1982, is available from the National Center on Women and Family Law, 799 Broadway, New York, NY 10003.

151. States that have expanded the exemption to unmarried cohabitants include Alabama, Connecticut, Delaware, Hawaii, Iowa, Kentucky, Maine, Minnesota, Montana, North Dakota, Pennsylvania, Texas, and West Virginia. *See* "A Case of Rape," supra note 147, at 16 n.11; *State Legislation*, supra note 4, at 5 n.5.

152. "A Case of Rape," supra note 147, at 2; Del. Code Ann. tit. 11 §764 (1979); Hawaii Rev. Stat. §707–730(a)(i) (Supp. 1982); W. Va. Code §61–813–3(a)(iii)(1977)(statutes pertain to first-degree rape only).

153. *State Legislation*, supra note 4, at 5 n.5.

154. *State v. Smith*, 85 N.J. 1983, 426 A.2d 38, 43, 44, 46 (1981). *See* Drucker, Comment: "The Common Law Does Not Support a Marital Exception for Forcible Rape," 5 *Women's Rights L. Rep.* 181 (1979); "A Case of Rape," supra note 147, at 13.

155. *See, e.g.,* W. Va. Code §48–1–24 (Supp. 1983); Nev. Rev. Stat. §122.060 (1981). For descriptions of services provided by various spouse abuse projects across the United States, *see Adult Domestic Violence*, supra note 5, at 313–317. *See, e.g.,* Kan. Stat. Ann. §23–108–110 (Vernon 1982); Me. Rev. Stat. Ann. tit. 22 §8501 (1980); Mo. Ann. Stat. §§455.200–230 (Vernon Supp. 1983); Nev. Rev. Stat. §§217.400–407 (1981).

156. *State Legislation*, supra note 4, at 19 n.183. *See Roberts et al. v. Young*, No. 81–110 (Cir. Ct., Macon Co. Ala. Sept. 29, 1982); *F.T.H. Corp. v. County of Washoe*, No. 81–518765 (County of Wahoe, Nev. Nov. 1981); *Crocker V. Finley and Roswell*, No. 82–Chi (Cir. Ct., Cooke Co., Ill., Co. Dept. Chancery Div. Feb. 1983), *appeal docketed*, Nos. 58056, 58062, 58058 (Ill. Mar. 1983).

157. *Lusby v. Lusby*, 283 Md. 334, 390 A.2d 77 (1978).

158. *See Goldstein v. Goldstein*, Roanoke, Virginia, Clearing House No. 29, 490), (available from Clearing House, 407 S. Dearborn, Suite 400, Chicago, IL. 60605; *Betts v. Betts*, No. 52337/1982 (Wash. Sup. Ct., Cowlitz Co.).

159. *See* 8 Wigmore, *Evidence* §2239 (1961); McCormick, *Evidence*, § § 66, 84 (1972). *See* Prosser, *Torts* §122 (4th Ed. 1971).

160. As of 1978, 18 states retained this rule for at least some suits between spouses: Arizona, Delaware, Florida, Georgia, Hawaii, Illinois, Iowa, Kansas, Louisiana, Maine, Massachusetts, Mississippi, Ohio, Pennsylvania, Rhode Island, Tennessee, Virginia, and

Wyoming. *See Adult Domestic Violence, supra* note 5, at 10 n.32, Pt. II.

161. *Korman v. Carpenter,* 216 Va. 86, 216 S.E.2d 195 (1975). *Compare Lusby, supra* note 157 (holding that the traditional justification for immunities did not apply in this case of wife assault and rape).

162. D. J. Besharov, "The Legal Aspects of Reporting Known and Suspected Abuse and Neglect," 23 *Vill. L. Rev.* 458 (1977–78).

163. "Wife Beating, " *supra* note 1, at 18, 20. 164. N. Brozan, "Light on Child Sex Abuse," *N.Y. Times,* 1984, at 1.

164. N. Brozan, "Light on Child Sex Abuse," *N.Y. Times,* 1984, at 1.

165. *See, e.g.,* ARIZ. REV. STAT. §13–3620 (A) (Supp. 1982–83); CAL. PENAL CODE §273A (West Supp. 1983); DEL. CODE tit. 11, §1102 (1979). A state-by-state summary of such provisions is available from Herner and Company, 1700 N. Moore St., Arlington, VA 22209.

166. For a discussion of rape statutes and their application to sex with children, *see* chap. XI. Some statutes, such as the Tennessee assault statute, explicitly make aggravated assault a crime "regardless of whether the victim is . . . a child." TENN. CODE ANN. §39–2–106 (1982).

167. *See, e.g.,* N.Y. PENAL LAW §255.25 (McKinney 1980).

168. CAL. PENAL CODE 273.5 (West Supp. 1983) (sex cohabitant); ARK. STAT. ANN. 41:1653 (Supp. 1983) (wife).

169. *State Legislation, supra* note 4, at 6. *See, e.g.,* OHIO REV. CODE ANN. §2919.25 (Page 1982).

170. *State v. Walden,* 306 N.C. 466, 293 S.E.2d 780 (1982).

171. *Recommendations for Improving Legal Intervention in Intra-Family Child Sexual Abuse Cases* (ABA, National Legal Resource Center for Child Advocacy and Protection, 1982), pp. 28–30 [hereafter *Intra-Family Child Abuse*].

172. Children's Bureau, U.S. Department of Health, Education and Welfare. *The Abused Child—Principles and Suggested Language for Legislation and Reporting of the Physically Abused Child* (1963). For a discussion of the history of the enactment of the child abuse reporting statutes in the United States, *see* J. Bergman, "Elder Abuse Reporting Laws: Protection or Paternalism" (1982), pp. 4–23.

173. M. Thomas, Jr., "Child Abuse and Neglect, Part I: Historical Overview, Legal Matrix and Social Perspectives," 50 *N.C.L. Rev.* 293, 332 (1972).

174. 42 U.S.C. §§5101–5106.

175. K. Katz, "Elder Abuse," 18 *J. Fam. L.* 695, 707 (1979–80).

176. "Wife Beating," *supra* note 1, at 22.

177. *Intra-Family Child Abuse, supra* note 171, at 13.

178. *Id.* at 6–16.

179. *Id.* at 11.

180. *See* 6 Wigmore, *Evidence* §1835 (1976).

181. *See, e.g.,* FLA. STAT. ANN. §918,17 (West Supp. 1983). For a list of such statutes, *see* ABA, *Child Sexual Abuse and the Law* (ABA,

National Legal Resource Center for Child Advocacy and Protection, 1982) (3d ed.), ch. 10 [hereafter *Child Sexual Abuse*].

182. *Globe Newspaper Co. v. Superior Court*, 457 U.S. 596 (1982).

183. *Intra-Family Child Abuse*, *supra* note 171, at 12.

184. *Herbert v. Superior Court of Sacramento County*, 117 Cal.App.3d 66, 172 Cal.Rptr. 850 (1981).

185. *In the Interest of Brooks*, 63 Ill.App.3d 328, 379 N.E.2d 872 (1978). *But see In re S. Children*, 102 Misc. 1015, 424 N.Y.S.2d 1004 (Fam.Ct. 1980) (holding that the right to confront witnesses may only be abridged in juvenile court where emotional trauma to the child can be clearly established).

186. *See, e.g., People v. Gage*, 62 Mich. 271, 28 N.W. 835 (1886) (superceded by statute as stated in *People v. Kreiner*, 415 Mich. 372, 329 N.W.2d 716 (1982). *See also* 83 A.L.R.2d 1368 (1962).

187. KAN. STAT. ANN. §60–460(dd)(Supp. 1982) (provided the child is disqualified or unavailable as a witness); WASH. REV. CODE ANN. §9A.44.120 (Supp. 1983–84) (provided the child testifies at the proceedings or is unavailable as a witness, in which case the statement serves only as corroborative evidence).

188. *See, e.g.*, Rule 803. *See* Anderson, "Evidence—New Confusion Under the Hearsay Rule: State v. Harris," 59 *Oreg. L. Rev.* (1981) for a complete listing of state statutes and court decisions adopting the residual exception.

189. *State v. Posten*, 302 N.W.2d 638 (Minn. 1981).

190. *Intra-Family Child Abuse*, *supra* note 171, at 34–35.

191. *Id*. For a list of competency statutes, *see* 8 Wigmore, *Evidence* §488 (1979). For a discussion of the factors judges use to determine whether a child witness is competent, *see* 81 Am. Jur.2d "Witnesses" §88 (1962); 2 Wigmore, *Evidence* §506; Stafford, "The Child as Witness," 37 *Wash. L. Rev.* 303, 304–5 (1962).

192. *State v. Manlove*, 441 F.2d 229, 231 (8th Cir. 1968).

193. 2 Wigmore *Evidence* §509.

194. F.R.E., Rule 601.

195. *See generally Intra-Family Child Abuse*, *supra* note 171, at ch. 5.

196. *Id*. at 32–33.

197. As of late 1981, 17 states had sexual psychopath statutes. *See id*. at ch. 4.

198. *See Specht v. Patterson*, 386 S.E. 605, 608 (1976); *People v. Feagley*, 14 Cal.3d 338, 535 P.2d 373, 121 Cal.Rptr. 509 (1975); *State ex rel Farrell v. Stovall*, 59 Wis.2d 148, 207 N.W.2d 809 (1973).

199. These states are California, Indiana, Iowa, Missouri, Ohio, South Dakota, Vermont, and Wisconsin. *See* discussion in *Intra-Family Child Sexual Abuse*, *supra* note 171, at 26–27.

200. *C. v. Foust*, 6 Fam. L. Rep. 2916 (Utah Sup. Ct. 1980). *See also Taylor v. Taylor*, Superior Court, State of Washington, Kings County (available as Clearing House No. 32,982) (settlement); *Walker v. Cohea*, no. 73390 (Sup.Ct., Butte Co.) (Cal. 1980) (Clearing House No. 33002) ($50,000 settlement).

201. *See, e.g.*, N.Y.C.P.L.R. §208.

202. "Private Violence," *Time*, Sept. 5, 1983, p. 19.

203. *State Legislation, supra* note 4, at 6. *See, e.g.*, N.Y. FAM. CT. ACT §812(1)(a); COLO. REV. STAT. §14–4–101(2)(Supp. 1982); NEV. REV. STAT. §217.400(3)(1981). In Vermont, such orders are explicitly available to persons living in the same household as the abuser who were related by blood or marriage if such persons are 60 years of age or older. VT. STAT. ANN. tit. 15 §1101(2)(Supp. 1983).

XI

The Rights of Rape Victims

What is "rape"?

The definition of *rape* varies from jurisdiction to jurisdiction. Since the mid 1970s, attempts to make the offense gender neutral, so that a person of either sex can be convicted of rape or be a victim of a rape,[1] as well as attempts to define the crime as one of violence rather than as a sexual offense, have affected the definition of the offense.[2] Generally, however, a person is guilty of rape if that person engages in sexual intercourse with another person when that other person has not consented, is incapable of consent, or is below a statutorily mandated age, thereby making consent irrelevant.[3] The definition of *sexual intercourse* varies from jurisdiction to jurisdiction, with some jurisdictions including homosexual intercourse and sexual assault with an object,[4] and with other jurisdictions limiting the definition to heterosexual vaginal intercourse.[5]

Have rape victims traditionally faced any special legal problems?

Yes. Rape is an act of brutal violence perpetrated by means of an intimate sexual act. This unusual combination of intimacy and brutality has historically made the law on rape unique. Historically, the law seemed more concerned with the victim's actions than the defendant's, and trials of rape cases were nothing short of ordeals for the victim.[6] Reflecting a skepticism and undue fear of "frame-ups" found in no similar degree with respect to any other crime, numerous procedural hurdles were imposed on the prosecution. States, for example, required corroboration of the victim's testimony before a jury could convict the defendant.[7] Failure of the victim to file a "prompt report" with the police would make conviction impossible.[8] The victim's consent could be implied from her sexual history and reputation for chastity, proof of which was admissible as a matter of course.[9] Only females could be raped, and every state had a spousal exception making it legal for a husband to rape his wife.[10]

Has this situation changed?

Yes. Since the mid 1970s, these traditional approaches toward rape have undergone significant changes.[11] A grass roots, nationwide reform movement has resulted in rape reform legislation in a majority of the states[12] and a voluminous amount of literature on the subject.[13] The general trend is away from a focus on the victim's conduct and toward a focus on the objective circumstances surrounding the offense.[14] In California, for example, state and local governmental agencies are expressly prohibited from requiring a rape victim to submit to a polygraph examination as a prerequisite to filing a complaint.[15] In addition, many states have enacted legislation providing for the judge's screening of evidence of the victim's sexual history before it can be presented to the jury.[16]

Indeed, the movement urging reform of rape laws is so active that information published on the status of the legal rights of rape victims is in danger of being outdated by the time the publication is in print. For this reason, it is particularly important that the victim of a sexual assault consult the specific statutes in her jurisdiction rather than rely for a definitive answer on the information reported in this chapter. This chapter is designed solely to provide an overview of the subject; it is not a comprehensive study of the offense in each jurisdiction.

Can a woman be guilty of raping a man?

In most states, yes. Most states have enacted gender neutral rape statutes that illegalize forcible sexual intercourse regardless of the sex of the victim or the assailant.[17] Some states use neutral terms to describe the actors, but limit rape to heterosexual intercourse by narrowly defining *sexual intercourse*.[18] In such jurisdictions, a male or female could not be convicted of raping someone of his or her own sex. Other jurisdictions limit the offense even further by defining *sexual intercourse* as penetration of the female by the male.[19] Such a definition restricts rape to forcible sexual intercourse by the male with the female.

Can a person be convicted of raping his spouse?

Usually, no. Although a growing number of states have expressly rejected a spousal exception to their rape laws,[20] most states have retained such exceptions, thereby making it legal to rape one's spouse.[21] Indeed, many of these statutory exceptions include those who are living together as husband and wife, even if they are not married.[22] It should be noted, however, that these exceptions are so technical and complicated that formulating accurate generalizations would be impossible. Each jurisdiction's statutes must therefore be consulted to determine the precise scope of the exception within that jurisdiction.

Many states have limited their spousal exceptions in a variety of ways. Some exclude from the exemption those couples who are separated pursuant to an agreement.[23] Some exclude those persons who have filed for divorce or who have reached a certain stage toward obtaining a divorce.[24] A couple of states do not apply the exception to situations in which there was a previous finding of adult abuse or in which a protective order has previously been issued.[25] Several states do not apply the exception where an injury has occurred.[26] Others apply it only in cases of consensual sexual intercourse with a minor.[27] Finally, many states expressly allow for a spouse's conviction if he was an accomplice to a third person's rape of the victim.[28]

What defenses may the defendant assert against a charge of rape?

The traditional defense against a charge of rape is the claim that the victim consented to sexual intercourse with the defendant.[29] Indeed, almost all jurisdictions recognize this defense.[30] In some jurisdictions, however, consent is not a defense if the defendant has inflicted serious injury on the victim.[31] North Carolina does not recognize the consent defense if the victim was in the custody of the defendant or the defendant's employer at the time of the rape.[32]

In addition, consent is not a defense to a charge of sexual intercourse with a minor.[33] However, such a charge, commonly referred to as statutory rape, often permits a defense that the defendant made a reasonable mistake as to the age of the victim.[34] Under this defense, the victim usually must be over a certain statutorily mandated age for the defense to be valid.[35]

Some jurisdictions permit less common defenses for accused rapists. Several states provide a "voluntary social companion" defense to certain types of rape. In some of these jurisdictions, the defendant may maintain that the victim was in his company voluntarily and, therefore, a rape in the first degree did not occur.[36] Hawaii limits this defense by not recognizing it if there was serious injury.[37] Montana recognizes the defense only if the victim's lack of consent resulted from an incapability to consent and if the victim voluntarily took a substance that incapacitated her while she was a voluntary social companion of the defendant.[38]

A couple of states allow the defendant to use as a defense the victim's failure to report the offense "promptly" to the authorities.[39] Other jurisdictions find that the defendant's reasonable belief that the victim was capable of consenting is a defense to a charge of raping someone who was incapable of consenting.[40] Finally, Texas and Mississippi recognize the defense of lack of chastity of the victim to a charge of statutory rape.[41]

Must the victim resist the assault in order for the rapist to be convicted?

It depends. Only a few jurisdictions expressly require that the victim resist her attacker.[42] The resistance requirement for a conviction of raping an adult is qualified. Some jurisdictions do not require resistance when the victim was physically helpless,[43] involuntarily unconscious,[44] or under a serious threat of great harm.[45] In those jurisdictions where resistance is required before one can be convicted of raping an adult, a conviction for raping a minor when consent of the minor is no defense does not require resistance of the minor.[46]

On the other hand, few jurisdictions totally dismiss any resistance requirement.[47] Most jurisdictions rest any determination of whether the victim should have resisted on the circumstances surrounding the case.[48] Factors such as the age of the victim,[49] the fear evoked by the incident,[50] and the force used by the assailant[51] have been found to be determinative.

Must the victim's testimony be corroborated before the defendant can be convicted?

Usually, no. Most jurisdictions have expressly rejected, either by common law or statute, any requirement that evidence be introduced to corroborate the victim's testimony.[52] Some courts, however, espousing a widely held belief of questionable validity that minors tend to fantasize about sexual assaults, require corroboration for a conviction of sexual assault of a minor.[53] In addition, some jurisdictions require corroboration for a conviction of forcible rape if the defendant and the victim had a previous "friendly or loving or intimate" relationship.[54] Texas common law suggests that corroboration is necessary if the victim did not file a prompt report of the incident with the police.[55] In addition, some cases have held that corroboration is necessary if the victim's testimony is "contradictory or incredible, or inherently improbable."[56]

Is evidence of the victim's prior sexual conduct admissible at trial?

It depends. Almost all states expressly provide for hearings outside the presence of the jury to determine whether to admit evidence of the victim's prior sexual acts.[57] At such hearings, the judge balances the materiality and relevance of the evidence against the prejudicial effect it will have on the jury and the invasion of the victim's privacy caused by publicizing the information.[58]

The type of evidence that the judge may consider admitting varies widely from jurisdiction to jurisdiction. Some jurisdictions allow the judge to consider any evidence.[59] Other jurisdictions limit potentially admissible evidence to facts concerning the victim's prior sexual contact with the defendant or the source of semen or pregnancy.[60] Other jurisdictions allow the judge to consider evidence of previous false claims by the victim,[61] a distinct pattern of the victim's sexual conduct,[62] prior convictions for prostitution,[63] or information that may impeach the prosecutor's witnesses.[64] In North Carolina, the judge may consider evidence of the victim's psychological fantasies.[65] In addition, some states admit impeachment evidence even without a prior determination at a hearing.[66]

What are some of the sentencing alternatives for a convicted rapist?

The standard sentence for a convicted rapist in all jurisdictions is a term of imprisonment. Not all such sentences are, however, identical. Some jurisdictions impose a mandatory minimum term that must be served in prison before the offender becomes eligible for release.[67] Others impose a mandatory minimum term for a defendant previously convicted of a felony.[68] Still others impose mandatory minimum sentences on those previously convicted of rape.[69] Finally, if the defendant used a firearm during the rape, a mandatory minimum sentence may be imposed[70] or the sentence may be increased.[71]

In addition to prison sentences, many jurisdictions also impose fines or require the defendant to pay restitution to his victim.[72] Some jurisdictions also have available less traditional sentencing alternatives. Such jurisdictions sometimes require a convicted rapist to submit to a psychiatric examination as part of his sentence.[73] California does not allow plea-bargaining agreements to govern the sentencing of rapists.[74] Tennessee increases the offender's prison sentence by five years if the victim contracted venereal disease, became pregnant or developed a serious mental disease as a result of the rape.[75]

Rape has traditionally been a narrowly defined offense[75a] carrying serious penalties.[76] The reform movement's attempt to expand the definition of *sexual assault* has, however, resulted in the enactment of sexual assault statutes providing a series of graded offenses and sentences.[77] This legislation enables particularization of the offense charged and the sentence it carries, as well as providing lesser offenses to which the defendant can plead guilty without being able to escape conviction for sexual assault.[78]

Do victims generally report rapes?

No. It is estimated that only 3.5 to 10 percent of the rapes committed each year are reported to law enforcement agencies.[79] Reasons for not reporting a rape vary, ranging from a feeling of guilt or embarrassment, to a feeling that nothing will be done about it, to a fear of retaliation.[80] Another contributing factor to this low reporting rate is the high number of "acquaintance" rapes: roughly half of the rape victims are raped by people they know,[81] often making them more reticent to report the incident. "Acquaintance" rapes are particularly common among child victims, constituting as many as two thirds of all rapes of minors.[81a] There is, however, an indication that this reluctance to report a rape is decreasing.

The Justice Department reports a steady rise in reported rapes, with a 35-percent increase in 1981.[82] Most of this increase has been attributed to the victim's increasing willingness to report the offense.[83]

Should the victim report the rape to the police?

It depends. There are two conflicting interests involved in the decision whether to report a rape. On the one hand, from society's perspective rape is a serious offense and the goals of law enforcement to prevent the assailant from raping others and to convict the assailant for the rape already committed are best met if the victim reports the offense.[84] On the other hand, from the victim's perspective rape is a traumatic experience, and reliving that trauma in grueling pretrial interrogation and cross-examination at trial is very painful. There is therefore no simple answer to the question as to whether the victim should report the rape. Many Rape Crisis centers answer this question by leaving it up to the victim to decide, and consciously avoid influencing that decision.[85]

What services are available to the rape victim?

A growing number of jurisdictions provide training for medical personnel, law enforcement officers, and district attorneys on how to minimize the victim's trauma.[86] Services include a meeting between the prosecutor and the victim before the preliminary hearing, and the availability of female police officers to interview female victims.[87] Indeed, some jurisdictions, for example, Los Angeles and Manhattan, have organized specially trained rape prosecution units within the district attorney's office and within the police department.[88]

In addition, there are more than 700 Rape Crisis centers nationwide, usually providing 24-hour on call counseling for the victim.[89] Specially trained volunteer counselors are available through these centers to provide support for the victim over the telephone, during medical examinations, during the filing of the police report, and at subsequent criminal proceedings.[90]

Recent litigation in Pennsylvania and Rhode Island highlighted the seriousness with which Rape Crisis counselors view their role. In Rhode Island, the director of the Rape Crisis Center was imprisoned for refusing to turn over counseling records after receiving a subpoena from the public defender's office.[91] In Pittsburgh, the director of the Rape

Crisis Center was held in contempt for refusing to hand over files containing statements of the victim.[92] The court recognized the importance of the confidentiality between counselor and victim, but ordered victim statements relevant to the offense to be turned over upon the defendant's request.[93] The Pennsylvania legislature, in response to this ruling, enacted a statute protecting a Rape Crisis Center counselor from being examined as a witness without prior written consent of the victim.[94]

What happens to the victim after the incident is reported to the police or the hospital?

If the victim reports the offense to the police, the police will question the victim about the incident much as they do when any crime is reported. Some jurisdictions provide specially trained personnel to conduct this questioning.[95] In addition, the police will usually transport the victim to a hospital for a medical examination.[96] This medical examination is the same whether the victim has reported the rape to the police or goes to the hospital without reporting the crime. The purpose of the examination is twofold: first, it treats any injuries that would be sustained during an assault; second, it allows doctors to gather evidence, such as semen and pubic hairs, to aid in any future prosecution.[97]

Must the rape victim pay for her medical examination after the rape?

Often, no. Over one-fourth of the states provide that a state organization will pay at least part of the medical costs of rape victims.[98] The organization designated to pay these costs differs from jurisdiction to jurisdiction. Depending on the jurisdiction, payment may be made by, for example, the local government,[99] the state board of health,[100] the state,[101] the district attorney's office,[102] or the commission of corrections.[103]

Nevada has enacted comprehensive legislation providing for reimbursement of up to $1,000 for medical and emotional treatment of the victim, as well as emotional treatment of the victim's spouse.[103a]

Most states that pay a victim's costs for the examination reimburse medical examiners only for treatment performed to gather evidence; the victim, it would seem, must pay for treatment for any injuries.[104] Some states further limit reimbursement by paying medical costs only if the victim has reported the crime to the local law enforcement agency.[105]

Minnesota pays only when the victim is not otherwise reimbursed by, for example, an insurance company.[106]

Victims in jurisdictions not providing reimbursement for medical expenses must rely on restitution[107] or compensation[108] programs.

Is the victim's identity withheld from the general public?

Generally, no. The majority of states have enacted some legislation aimed at protecting the victim's privacy,[109] but most of this legislation does not keep the victim's identity from being disclosed.

The Supreme Court has recently ruled that it is unconstitutional to require a judge to close a rape trial to the general public.[110] Over one-fourth of the states, however, provide the judge with the discretionary power to clear the court of bystanders.[111] Such provisions are often limited to trials in which a minor was the victim.[112] In Florida, all those not witnesses or otherwise necessary to the proceeding, except for the media, are excluded from trials in which the alleged victim is under sixteen years of age.[113]

Several jurisdictions attempt to protect a victim who is a minor by allowing the victim's testimony to be videotaped and played for the jury so that the victim can avoid testifying in open court.[114] Several other jurisdictions make it unlawful for the media to publish the names of rape victims,[115] although the Supreme Court has held such statutes unconstitutional to the extent that they prohibit disclosure of information contained in public court documents.[115a] Still others require that the district attorney's office and law enforcement agencies refrain from unnecessary pretrial disclosures of either the victim's or the defendant's identity.[116] Finally, some states allow the prosecutor to move to exclude the victim's address and telephone number if the information would threaten the victim's safety.[117]

Can a victim sue her assailant in a civil action?

Classic tort law permits the victim of an assault or battery to sue his or her assailant.[118] On occasion, rape victims have employed this principle in suits against their assailants. In one such instance, a 15-year-old victim sued her assailant after he was sentenced to 5 months in prison; the victim subsequently received a judgment for $22,500 in damages.[119] Such an action may be particularly beneficial if the assailant has some financial resources.[120] Even if the defendant has no such resources, the victim can collect on the judgment by attaching the defendant's assets.[121]

A prior conviction for the same incident addressed in the victim's civil suit is particularly beneficial to the victim.[122] However, since the applicable burden of proof in criminal proceedings is more stringent than the applicable burden of proof in civil proceedings, the defendant may be acquitted in a criminal proceeding but found liable in a civil proceeding.[123]

Can a victim sue a third party for rape?

There have been numerous civil suits, most of them unsuccessful, against a third party who the victim claims may be indirectly responsible for a criminal assault.[124] Some of these suits have been brought by rape victims.[125] Indeed, one court in New York cited the state law limiting admissibility in a criminal proceeding[126] of evidence concerning the victim's sexual history as support for its decision to limit investigation into the plaintiff's sexual history in a civil suit brought by a rape victim against her landlord.[127]

Numerous persons and organizations, including landlords, transportation authorities, employers, universities, and hotels, have been named as defendants in such actions.[128] In one case, a landlord agreed to settle a claim against him for $150,000 for refusing to fix a lock on a window that a rapist used to enter the victim-plaintiff's apartment.[129] Rape victims have successfully sued Conrail, Howard Johnson's, and Catholic University.[130]

Notes

1. *See infra* pp.——.
2. Bienan, "Rape III—National Developments in Rape Reform Legislation," 6 *Women's Rights L. Rep.* 170, 174 (Spring 1980) [hereafter "Rape III"].

    These definitional changes potentially have far-reaching consequences. A woman recently obtained a $9,000 libel judgment against a newspaper that reported that she had been raped. Under Iowa's revised sex offense laws, enacted in 1977, the woman's assailant had been charged with the crime of "sexual abuse," which does not require penetration. *The National L.J.*, Feb. 13, 1984, p. 8.
3. *See* Rape III at 172–76 (discussing the changing definition).
4. *See, e.g.*, MICH. COMP. LAWS ANN. §750.520a; WASH. REV. CODE §9A.44.010.
5. *See, e.g.*, TEX. PENAL CODE ANN. §21.02; ME. REV. STAT. ANN. tit. 17–A §251.B.

6. Rape III, *supra* note 2, at 172. *See also* Berger, "Man's Trial, Woman's Tribulation: Rape Cases in the Courtroom," 77 *Colum. L. Rev.* 1, 7 (1977) [hereafter "Man's Trial"].

7. Rape III *supra* note 2, at 175. *See also infra* p. 149.

8. *Id*. Rape III at 175.

9. *Id*. at 180; Bocchino, Tanford, "Rape Victim Shield Laws and the Sixth Amendment," 128 *U. Penn. L. Rev.* 544 (1980) [hereafter "Rape Victim Shield Laws"].

10. Man's Trial *supra* note 6, at 9. *See also infra* p. 146–47.

11. Rape III *supra* note 2, at 171.

12. *Id*.

13. *Id*. [citing Field and Barnett, "Forcible Rape: An Updated Bibliography," 68 *J. Crim. L. and Criminology* 146 (1977) which reported 371 pieces on the subject as of 1977].

14. *Id*. at 172.

15. Cal. Penal Code §637.4. *See also* Women Organized Against Rape, *Legal Information*, 14 (1983) (reporting that the decision to take the polygraph examination is voluntary in Pennsylvania) [hereafter "*Legal Information*"].

16. Rape Victim Shield Laws. *See infra* p. 66.

17. *See, e.g.*, WASH. REV. CODE §9A.44.010 (defining *rape* as an act by a "person" against another "person"); WYO. STAT. §6–2–302 (defining *rape* as an act by an "actor" against a "victim"). *But see* GA. CODE §16–6–1 (requiring the rapist to be male and the victim to be female); IDAHO CODE §18–6101 (same).

18. *See, e.g.*, MONT. CODE ANN. §45–5–501; Ind. Code §35–42–4–1.

19. *See, e.g.*, MO. REV. STAT. §566.010; Ind. Code §35–42–4–1.

20. *See, e.g.*, N.J. REV. STAT. §2C: 14–5; WIS. STAT. §940.255(6).

21. *See, e.g.*, Mich. Comp. Laws §750.5201; LA. REV. STAT. §14:41; N.Y. Penal Law §130.00(4).

22. *See, e.g.* ARIZ. REV. STAT. ANN. §13–1401, COLO. REV. STAT. §18–3–409.

23. *See, e.g.* IND. CODE §35–42–4.1; OHIO REV. CODE ANN. §2907.01(L).

24. *See, e.g.*, OHIO REV. CODE ANN. §2907.01; TENN. CODE ANN. §39–2–610.

25. *See*, N.D. Cent. Code §12.1–20–01; Ind. Code §35–42–4.1.

26. *See, e.g.* CONN GEN. STAT. §53a–70b; Cal. Penal Code §262.

27. *See, e.g.*, N.H. REV. STAT. ANN. §632–A:5.

28. *See, e.g.*, OKLA. STAT. tit. 21, §1111; 18 PA. CONS. STAT. §3103.

29. Rape III, *supra* note 2, at 180–82.

30. *See, e.g.*, Cal. Penal Code §261.6; Del. Code Ann. tit. 11, §767. *See also* Weiner, "Shifting the Communication Burden: A Meaningful Consent Standard in Rape," 6 *Harv. Women's L. J.* 143 (1983); Rape III, *supra* note 2, at 180–84 (discussing changing definitions of consent).

31. *See, e.g.*, MO. REV. STAT. §565.080; N.J. REV. STAT. §2C:2–10.

32. N.C. GEN. STAT. §14–27.7 (the defendant is, in such an instance, charged with a class G felony).

33. *See, e.g.*, UTAH CODE ANN. §76–5–407; MASS. GEN. LAWS ANN. ch. 265, §23.

34. *See, e.g.*, MO. REV. STAT. §565.080; MONT. CODE ANN. §45–5–511.

35. *See, e.g.*, Mont. Rev. Code Ann. §45–5–511 (the defense is valid only if the minor was at least 14 years old). Colo. Rev. Stat. §18–3–406 (the minor must have been at least 15 years old).

36. *See, e.g.*, Del. Code Ann. tit 11, §764 (defense to rape in the first degree); W. Va. Code §61–8B–3 (defense to first-degree sexual assault).

37. Haw. Rev. Stat. §707.730.

38. Mont. Code Ann. §45–5–511.

39. N.H. Rev. Stat. §632–A:7 (must be reported within 6 months of the incident); Utah Code Ann. §76–5–407 (must be reported within 3 months of the incident).

40. *See, e.g.*, Conn. Gen. Stat. Ann. §53a–67; Wash. Rev. Code §9A.44.030.

41. Tex. Penal Code Ann. §21.09; Miss. Code Ann. §97–3–67.

42. *See, e.g.*, Ala. Code §13A–6–60; Kan. Stat. Ann. §21–3502.

43. *See, e.g.*, *Rusk v. State*, 43 Md. App. 476, 406 A.2d 624 (Ct. Spec. App. 1979), *rev'd on other grounds*, 289 Md. 230, 424 A.2d 720 (1981); Ky. Rev. Stat. Ann. §510.040.

44. *See, e.g.*, Miss. Code Ann. §97–3–65; Kan. Stat. Ann. §21–3502.

45. *See, e.g.*, Idaho Code §18–6101.

46. *See, e.g.*, P.R. Laws Ann. tit. 33, §4061; La. Rev. Stat. Ann. §14:42.

47. *But see* Minn. Stat. §609.347 (expressly rejecting any resistance requirement); 18 Pa. Cons. Stat. §3107 (same).

48. *See, e.g.*, *Cortez v. People*, 155 Colo. 317, 394 P.2d 346 (1964) (the degree of resistance required depends on the circumstances surrounding the case); *State v. Dighera*, 617 S.W.2d 524 (Mo. Ct. App. 1981) (resistance is not required if circumstances show that the victim was put in a state of fear).

49. Cal. Penal Code §261.

50. *Arnold v. U.S.*, 358 A.2d 335 (D.C. 1976).

51. S.C. Code Ann. §16–3–651; *State v. Havens*, 264 N.W.2d 918 (S.D. 1978).

52. *See, e.g.*, *Perry v. State*, 154 Ga. App. 385, 268 S.E.2d 747 (1980); Mich. Comp. Laws §750.520h.

53. Bienen, "A Question of Credibility: John Henry Wigmore's Use of Scientific Authority in Section 924a of the Treatise on Evidence," 19 *Cal. W. L. Rev.* 235, 244 (1983) [hereafter "Credibility"] (providing a study of this common reaction to child complainants).

   With amendments to New York's penal law (§§130.16 and 260.11) eliminating the corroboration requirement, effective November 1, 1984, only Nebraska and Washington, D.C. maintain the corroboration requirement in sexual assault cases involving minors. *N.Y. L.J.*, Apr. 19, 1984, p. 3.

54. P.R. Crim. P.R. 154.

55. *Villareal v. State*, 511 S.W.2d 500 (Tex. Crim. App. 1974).

56. *Robinson v. Commonwealth*, 459 S.W.2d 147, 150 (Ky. 1970). *See also State v. True*, 438 A.2d 460, 471 (Me. 1981) (uncorroborated testimony is sufficient unless it "does not meet the test of common sense").

57. *See, e.g.*, Cal. Evid. Code §782; Ala. Code §12–21–203; N.Y. Crim. Proc. Law §60.42.

58. *See, e.g.*, Alaska Stat. §12.45.045; Ky. Rev. Stat. §510.145. *See also* Rape Victim Shield Laws (providing an exhaustive study of the history of admissibility of such evidence, a survey of state law as of 1980, and an argument that the same test employed in deciding the admissibility of other evidence should be employed in determining the admissibility of evidence of the rape victim's prior sexual conduct); Man's Trial, *supra* note 6, at 52–84 (supporting the liberal granting of motions for hearings on the admissibility of such evidence).

59. *See, e.g.*, Wyo. Stat. §6–2–312; Alaska Stat. §12.45.045.

60. *See, e.g.*, Ind. Code §35–1–32.5–1; *et seq.*; Mich. Comp. Laws Ann. §750.520.j.

61. Wis. Stat. 972.11; Vt. Stat. Ann. tit. 13, §3255; *People v. Mandel*, 48 N.Y.2d 952, 425 N.Y.S.2d 63,401 N.E.2d 185 (1979) (suggesting that such evidence may be admissible if prior claims were proven false, and a pattern casting substantial doubt on the validity of present charges was proven).

62. Minn. Stat. Ann. §609.347; N.C. Gen. Stat. §8–58.6.

63. N.Y. Crim. Proc. Law §60.42 (if there was a conviction within the past 3 years).

64. *See, e.g.*, Minn. Stat. Ann. §609.347; Md. Ann. Code art. 27, 461A.

65. N.C. Gen. Stat. §8–58.6.

66. *See, e.g.*, W. Va. Code §61–8B–12; *In re JWY*, 363 A.2d 674 (App. D.C. 1976).

67. *See, e.g.*, Conn. Gen. Stat. §53a–70 (1-year minimum sentence imposed for first-degree rape); La. Rev. Stat. Ann. §42.1 (2-year minimum sentence imposed for rape).

68. *See, e.g.*, Md. Ann. Code art. 27, §643B (mandatory life sentence upon fourth conviction of a violent felony); Del. Code Ann. tit. 11, §4214 (same).

69. *See, e.g.*, Neb. Rev. Stat. §28–319(3); R.I. Gen. Laws §11–37–10.

70. *See, e.g.*, Iowa Code Ann. §902.7; Hawaii Rev. Stat. §706–660.1(a).

71. *See, e.g.*, Me. Rev. Stat. Ann. tit. 17–A, §1252.4 (increase of sentence by 1 level); N.M. Stat. Ann. §31–18–16 (increase of sentence by 1 year).

72. *See, e.g.*, Mont. Code Ann. §45–5–503; N.J. Rev. Stat. §§2C:43–3; 2C:43–3.

73. *See, e.g.*, Nev. Rev. Stat. §200.375 (parole was conditioned on board certification that the offender was under psychiatric supervision and is not dangerous); Ohio Rev. Code Ann. §2907.27 (submitting to treatment must be a condition of parole).

74. Cal. Penal Code §1192.5.

75. Tenn. Code Ann. §39–2–609.

76. Rape III, *supra* note 6, at 173.

77. *Id.* at 172.

78. *Id.* at 172–73.

79. "Rape: The Sexual Weapon," *Time*, 27 (Sept. 5, 1983).

80. *See id.* at 28.

81. *Id.*

81a. Credibility, *supra* note 53, at 239, n.11.

82. *Id*. at 27 (reporting the Justice Department figures).

83. *Id*.

84. *See supra*, at p. 604–05.

85. *See, e.g.*, R.I. Rape Crisis Center, *Rape: It Can Happen to Anyone* (stressing the fact that whether to report the offense is the victim's decision).

86. Rape III, *supra* note 6, at 179, 212.

87. *Legal Information*, at 12 (outlining legal statistics in Philadelphia).

88. *Time*, *supra* note 79, at 29.

89. *Id*. at 27.

90. *Id*. at 28.

91. United Press International, Jan. 13, 1983 (AM cycle).

92. *In re Pittsburgh Action Against Rape*, 494 Pa. 15, 428 A 2d 126 (1981).

93. *Id*.

94. 42 Pa. Cons. Stat. §5945.1.

95. *Time*, *supra* note 79, at 29.

96. *See* WOAR, *Legal Steps in the Criminal Justice System* (1978).

97. *Id*.

98. *See, e.g.*, Ark. State. Ann. §41–1821; Iowa Code Ann. §709.10; Vt. Stat. Ann. tit. 32, §1407.

99. *See, e.g.*, Cal. Govt. Code §13961.5.

100. *See, e.g.*, Ind. Code §16–10–1.5–7.

101. *See, e.g*, Iowa Code Ann. §709.10.

102. *See, e.g.*, Me. Rev. Stat. Ann. tit. 30, §507.

103. Minn. Stat. §241.57.

103a. Nev. Rev. Stat. §17.280. *et seq*.

104. *See, e.g.*, Ark. Stat. Ann. §41–1822; Ohio Rev. Code Ann. §2907.28; Kan. Stat. Ann. §65–448. *But see* Vt. Stat. Ann. tit. 32, §1407 (providing for state payment of medical and psychological examinations).

105. *See, e.g.*, Ark. Stat. Ann. §41–1821; Me. Rev. Stat. Ann. tit. 30, §507.

106. Minn. Stat. §241.57.

107. *See, e.g.*, Fla. Stat. §775.087; N.D. Cent. Code §12.1–32–02. *See also supra* pp. 605.

108. *See, e.g.*, Alaska Stat. §18.67.010 *et seq*.; Mich. Comp. Laws §18.354. *See also* 8 WOARpath No. 11, p. 3 (Fall 1982).

109. *See supra*, at 603–04.

110. *Globe Newspaper Co. v. Supreme Court for the County of Norfolk*, 457 U.S. 596 (1982). *See also supra*, at 107–09. Man's Trial, *supra*, note 6, at 88–96 (the author argues that absent substantial reason for closing the trial, a rape trial should be open to the public).

111. *See, e.g.*, Ala. Code §12–21–202; Minn. Stat. §631.045. *See also* 39 A.L.R.3d 852.

112. *See, e.g.*, Mass. Gen. Laws Ann. 278 §16A; N.H. Rev. Stat. Ann. §632–A:8.

113. Fla. Stat. Ann. §918.16.

114. *See, e.g.*, Alaska Stat. §12.45.047; N.M. Stat. Ann. §30–9–17.

115. *See, e.g.*, Ga. Code §16–6–23. S.C. CODE ANN. §16–3–730. *See also* 36 A.L.R.3d 80; 56 A.L.R.3d 386. *Compare Doe v. Sarasota— Bradenton Television*, 436 So. 2d 328 (Fla. Dist. Ct. App. 1983) (a television station that broadcasted videotapes of a victim's testimony was found not liable for invasion of privacy or violation of a statute making it unlawful to publish information identifying a rape victim, despite the victim's agreement to testify only if there was no such publicity).

115a. *Cox Broadcasting Corp. v. Cohn*, 420 U.S. 469 (1975).

116. *See, e.g.*, ME. REV. STAT. ANN. tit. 30, §508 (as to minor victims); S.D. CODIFIED LAWS ANN. §23A–6–22.

117. *See, e.g.*, NEV. REV. STAT. §48.071; OHIO REV. CODE ANN. §2907.11.

118. Prosser, Law of Torts §§ 9, 10 (4th ed. 1971).

119. "Rape Redress," *Time*, p. 59 (Aug. 25, 1980). *See also Cianci v. New Times Publishing Co.*, 639 F.2d 54 (2d Cir. 1980) (a defamation suit brought by the ex-mayor of Providence, Rhode Island, after the defendant published an article concerning the plaintiff's settlement of a civil suit concerning an alleged rape that supposedly occurred 12 years previously).

120. 8 WOARpath No. 11, p. 3 (Fall 1982).

121. *Id.*

122. *Id.*

123. *Id.*

124. *See*, 43 A.L.R.3d 331 (citing suits concerning the duty of landlord). 10 A.L.R.3d 619 (citing suits concerning the duty of private person). 70 A.L.R.2d 628 (citing suits concerning the duty of an innkeeper or restaurateur). *See also Virginia D. v. Madesco Invest. Corp.*, 648 S.W.2d 881, 886 (Mo. 1983) (citing these annotations).

125. *See, e.g., Virginia D., supra. See also* 8 WOARpath No. 11 p. 3 (citing several such cases).

126. *See supra*, at 603–4.

127. *Mason v. Cohn*, 108 Misc. 2d 674, 438 N.Y.S.2d 462 (Sup. Ct. 1981).

128. 8 WOARpath No. 11, p. 3; *Virginia D., supra. See also* The Associated Press, Jan. 5, 1980 (PM Cycle); *N.Y. Times*, Mar. 24, 1980 (reporting a suit by a female truck driver against her employer for firing her "for her own good" after she was raped while awaiting assistance after her truck broke down. One contention of the plaintiff was that the defendant's mechanics had refused to help her when her truck broke down.) (Research uncovered no publication on resolution of the suit.)

129. *N.Y. Times*, Nov. 5, 1980.

130. 8 WOARpath No. 11, p. 3.

Appendix A

State-by-State Analysis of Victim Compensation Laws

This state-by-state analysis of victim compensation programs was prepared for the National Institute of Justice, U.S. Department of Justice by ABT Associates, Inc. under contract No. J-LEAA-013-78 entitled *Compensating Victims of Crime: An Analysis of American Programs* by Daniel McGillis and Patricia Smith (May 1983). The abbreviated version of this chart first appeared in National Organization for Victim Assistance, *The Victim Service System: A Guide to Action* 70–71 (1983), and was updated by NOVA in 1984.

All programs cover the injured victim(s) of crimes causing physical injury and compensate for medical losses. Two types of physical injury crimes may be excluded: those that involve a perpetrator who lives in the same household, is a relative of, or has had a continuing relationship with, the victim; and those that have been the result of a motor vehicle crime. The following chart indicates the variation on those issues and others affecting eligibility and benefits.

Program Elements	AL	AK	CA	CO	CT	DE	FL	HI	IL	IN	IA	KS	KY	LA	MA	MD	MI	MN	MO	MT
Eligibility:																				
Interveners		X	X		X		X	X	X	X	X	X	X	X	X	X	X	X	X	X
Dependents	X	X	X	X	X	X	X	X	X	X	X	X	X	X	X	X	X	X	X	X
Third Parties[1]	X	X	X	X	X	X		X	X			X		X			X	X		
Family Exclusion[2] ?				X[6]	X		X			X[3]		X	X	X[6]	X		X[4]	X[5]	X	X[6]
Residents Only[11]			X	X	X[7]	X[7]	X						X[7]	X	X				X	
Motor Vehicles Excluded							X	X		X								X		X
Reckless MV Included[8]	X		X						X					X						
Means Test					X		X					X	X		X					
Recovery:																				
Counseling[11]	X	X	X	X	X	X	X	X	X	X	?	X	X	X	X	X	X	X	X	X
Disability	X	X	X	X	X	X	X		X	X	?	X	X	X	X	X	X	X	X	
Rehabilitation	X	X	X	X	X	X	X		X	X	?	X	X	X	X	X	X	X	X	X
Loss/Earnings	X	X	X	X	X	X	X	X	X	X	X	X	X	X	X	X	X	X	X	X
Loss/Support	X	X	X	X	X	X	X	X	X	X	X	X	X	X	X	X	X	X	X	X
Funeral	X	X	X	X	X	X	X	X	X	X	X	X	X	X	X	X	X	X	X	X

Replacement Services	X	X	X	X¹⁰	X	X	X	X	X	X	X	X	X	X	X	X	X	X
Pain/Suffering					X	X												
Other Expenses	X	X	X	X	X	X	X	X	X	X	X¹⁰	X		X		X		X
Benefits:																		
Maximum (in thousands)	10	40	23	10	10	20	10	10	15	18	10	15	10	45	15	25	10	25
Minimum Loss	0	0	25	100	0	25	0	0	200	0	100	100	100	100	100	100	200	0
Deductible	0	0	0	100	0	0	0	0	200	0	100	100	100	0	0	0	200	0
Attorney Fees	?	X	X	X	X	X	X	X	X	X	X	X	X	X	X	X	X	X
Emerg. Award	?	1500	1000	500	500	X	500	0	0	0	0	500	500	1000	500	500	100	0
Reduced by Contribution	X	X	X	X	X	X	X	X	X		X		X	X	X	X	X	X
Denied by Contribution	X	X	X	X	X	X	X	X	X	X	X	X	X	X	X	X	X	X
Source of Funds:																		
General Rev.		X					X								X	X		
Penalty Assess.	X	X	X	X	X	X	X	X	X	X		X	X			X	X	
Fines	X	X	X	X	X	X	X	X	X	X	X	X	X	X	X	X	X	X

Program Elements	States NC[12]	NB	NV	NJ	NM	NY	ND	OH	OK	OR	PA	RI	SC	TN	TX	VA	WA	WV	WI	DC
Eligibility:																				
Intervenors	X	X	X	X	X	X	X	X	X	X	X	X	X	X	X	X	X	X	X	X
Dependents	X	X	X	X	X	X	X	X	X	X	X	X	X	X	X	X	X	X	X	X
Third Parties[1]	X	X	X	X	X		X	X	X	X	X	X	X	X	X	X	X	X	X	X
Family Exclusion[2]	X[6]	X	X	X	X	X	X[6]	X[6]	X	X	X	X	X[6]	X	X	X	X	X[6]	X[6]	X[6]
Residents Only[11]			X		X								X[7]	X	X	X[7]				
Motor Vehicles Excluded[8]	X	X	X	X	X	X	X	X	X	X	X	X				X				X
Reckless MV Included													X					X	X	
Means Test			X			X									X					X
Recovery:																				
Counseling[11]	X	X	X	X	X	X		X	X	X	X	X	X	X	X	X	X	X	X	X
Disability	X					X	X		X											X
Rehabilitation	X	X	X	X	X	X	X	X	X	X	X	X	X	X	X	X	X	X	X	X
Loss/Earnings	X	X	X	X	X	X	X	X	X	X	X	X	X	X	X	X	X	X	X	X

402

Category																				
Loss/Support	X		X	X	X	X	X	X	X	X	X	X	X	X	X	X	X	X	X	X
Funeral	X	X	X	X	X	X	X	X	X	X	X	X	X	X	X	X	X	X	X	X
Replacement Services	X			X			X			X				X		X			X	
Pain/Suffering									X				X							
Other Expenses		X	X	X	X	X		X		X				X	X	X		X	X	
Benefits: Maximum (in thousands)	20	10	15	25	12	20	25	25	10	23	25	25	10	5	25	12.5	15	20	10	25
Minimum Loss	100	0	100	100	0	0	100	0	0	250	100	0	300	100	0	100	0	0	0	100
Deductible	0	0	0	0	0	0	0	0	0	250	0	0	0	0	0	100	200	0	0	0
Attorney Fees	X	X	X	X	X	X	X		X	X	X	X	X	X	X		X	X	X	X
Emerg. Award	0	500	1500	1500	1500	0	500	1000	500	1000	1000	0	1500	500	0	1000	0	500	0	1000
Reduced by Contribution	X		X	X	X		X		X	X		X		X		X		X		X
Denied by Contribution	X	X	X	X	X	X	X	X	X	X	X	X	X	X	X	X	X	X	X	X

Program Elements	NC[12]	NB	NV	NJ	NM	NY	ND	OK	OH	OR	PA	RI	SC	TN	TX	VA	WA	WV	WI	DC
Source of Funds:																				
General Rev.	X	X	9	X	X	X	X	X		X									X	
Penalty Assess.			X						X	X	X	X	X	X	X	X	X	X		X
Fines									X	X	X	X	X	X	X	X				

[1] Third Parties refer to programs that will reimburse persons other than the victim who paid bills or who provided services for the victim.

[2] Family exclusion includes those programs that exclude relatives, cohabitants of a household, or persons who have maintained a continuous relationship with the accused.

[3] In Indiana the spouse of the offender is ineligible for compensation. There is a separate fund for spouse abuse victims in the state.

[4] A victim residing with the accused is ineligible to receive an award in Michigan; however, the victim's out-of-pocket expenses may be paid directly to a medical care provider.

[5] The ineligibility-of-a-relative provision can be waived if there is formal or permanent separation in cases involving a spouse and the spouse prosecutes the offender; if it is an incest case; and in cases involving mental derangement.

[6] These programs may waive the family exclusion "in the interests of justice."

[7] These programs restrict recovery to residents but allow nonresidents to recover if the state in which they reside has reciprocity with the state in which the crime took place.

[8] Injuries caused by motor vehicles are excluded in these states unless there was intent on the part of the accused to use the vehicle to commit the crime.

[9] Nevada's compensation fund is generated by bond forfeitures and Son of Sam moneys.

[10] Louisiana compensates for catastrophic property loss. Colorado compensates elderly and handicapped victims for loss of security-related property and the deductible from insurance coverage. New York compensates elderly and handicapped victims for loss of essential property.

[11] Since federal funding is available only to programs which compensate non-residents and for counseling, after 1984 more states can be expected to provide such compensation.

[12] As of 1984, North Carolina's program was not operating due to lack of appropriations and the legislature was considering substantial amendments to scale down the program's benefits.

Appendix B

This list of addresses and telephone numbers of administrators of state compensation programs was prepared as Appendix C to D. McGillis and P. Smith, *Compensating Victims of Crime: An Analysis of American Programs* (Washington, D.C.: Department of Justice, May 1983), with the assistance of Robert W. Armstrong, Director, Virginia Division of Crime Victims' Compensation.

Crime Victims' Compensation Programs
(Effective 1983)

Ms. Anita Armstrong
  Morgan
Exec. Dir.
Crime Victims' Compensation
  Commission
P.O. Box 1283
Montgomery, AL 36104
205–261–4007

Ms. Nola K. Capp
Admin.
Violent Crime Compensation
  Bd.
Pouch N
Juneau, AK 99811
907–465–3040

Mr. Fred Buenrostro
Asst. Exec. Secy.
Victim Indemnification
  Program

State Board of Control
926 J St., Suite 300
Sacramento, CA 95814
916–422–4426

Barbara Kendall
V/W Assist. Unit
20th Jud. Dist.
D.A.'s Office
Boulder Co. Justice Center
P.O. Box 471
Boulder, CO 80306
303–441–3700

Mr. James D. O'Connor
Chairman
Criminal Injuries Compensation Bd.
101 Lafayette St.
Hartford, CT 06115
203–566–4156

Robert Bailey
Office of Crim. Justice Plans
  & Analysis
Old Lansbury Bldg.
421–8th St., N.W.
Washington, DC 20004
202–727–6537

Mr. Oakley Banning, Jr.
Violent Crime Compensa-
  tion Bd.
800 Delaware Ave., Suite 601
Wilmington, DE 19801
302–571–3030

Mr. Herbert G. Parker
Bureau of Crime
  Compensation
Div. of Workers'
  Compensation
Dept. of Labor and Employ-
  ment Security
2562 Exec. Center Circle
Montgomery Bldg., Suite 201
Tallahassee, FL 32301
904–488–0848

Mr. Wilfred S. Pang
Exec. Secy.
Criminal Injuries Compensa-
  tion Commission
P.O. Box 339
Honolulu, HI 96809
808–548–4680

Ms. Sarah Ellsworth
Div. Chief
Crime Victims Div.
Office of the Atty. Gen.
188 W. Randolf, Suite 2200
Chicago, IL 60601
312–793–2585

Mr. John N. Shanks
Dir.

Violent Crimes Compensation
  Div.
601 State Office Bldg.
100 North Senate Ave.
Indianapolis, IN 46204
317–232–7101

Crime Victim Reparation
  Program
Dept. of Human Serv.
Des Moines, IA
515–286–3838 or 3832

Mr. Kenneth Bahr
Dir.
Crime Victims' Reparations Bd.
503 Kansas Ave., Suite 212
Topeka, KS 66603
913–296–2359

Ms. Addie Stokley
Exec. Dir.
Crime Victims' Compensation
  Bd.
113 E. Third St.
Frankfort, KY 40601
502–564–2290

Mr. Bob Wirtz
Crime Victims' Reparations Bd.
1885 Wooddale Blvd.,
  Rm. 610
Baton Rouge, LA 70806
504–925–4437

Mr. Martin I. Moylan
Exec. Dir.
Criminal Injuries Compensation Bd.
1123 North Eutaw St.
601 Jackson Towers
Baltimore, MD 21201
301–523–5000

Ms. Roberta Brown
Asst. Atty. Gen.

Commonwealth of
  Massachusetts
Torts Div.
One Ashburton Place
Boston, MA 02108
617–727–5025

Ms. Jessie Slayton
Chairman and Exec. Dir.
Crime Victims' Compensation
  Bd.
P.O. Box 30036
Lansing, MI 48909
517–373–7373

Mr. Duane E. Woodworth
Exec. Dir.
Crime Victims' Reparations Bd.
702 American Center Bldg.
160 E. Kellogg Blvd.
St. Paul, MN 55101
612–296–7080

Richard R. Rousselot
Div. of Workers'
  Compensation
Dept. of Public Safety
P.O. Box 58
Jefferson City, MO 65102
314–751–4231

Mr. William R. Palmer
Asst. Admin.
Workers' Compensation Div.
815 Front St.
Helena, MT 59604
406–449–2047

Crime Victims' Reparation
  Bd.
P.O. Box 94946
State Office Bldg., 3rd Fl.
301 Centennial Mall S.
Lincoln, NB 68509
402–471–2828

Mr. Howard E. Barrett
The Board of Examiners
Blasdel Bldg.
209 E. Musser St., Room 205
Carson City, NV 89710
702–885–4065

Mr. Kenneth Welch
Chairman
Violent Crimes Compensation
  Bd.
60 Park Place
Newark, NJ 07102
201–648–2107

Mr. Daniel Martinez
Dir.
Crime Victims' Reparations
  Commission
P.O. Box 871
Albuquerque, NM 87103
505–841–4694

Mr. Ronald A. Zweibel
Chairman
Crime Victims Bd.
270 Broadway
New York, NY 10007
212–587–5160

Mr. James R. Scarcella
Dir.
Victim & Justice Services
P.O. Box 27687
Raleigh, NC 27611
919–733–7974

Mr. Joseph Larson
Exec. Admin.
Crime Victims' Reparations
Workmens' Compensation
  Bureau
Russel Bldg.
Highway 83 North
Bismarck, ND 58505
701–224–2700

Mr. Charles W. Wood
Admin.
Crime Victims' Compensation
 Bd.
3033 North Walnut St., Suite
 100 W.
Oklahoma City, OK 73105
405–521–2330

Mr. Jerry L. Flakus
Dir.
Crime Victims' Compensation
 Program
Dept. of Justice
100 State Office Bldg.
Salem, OR 97310
503–378–5348

Mr. Marvin E. Miller
Crime Victims' Compensation
 Bd.
Justice Dept.
Strawberry Sq., Room 1432
Harrisburg, PA 17120
717–783–5153

Mr. Robert Harrell
Deputy Admin.
Administrative Office of
 State Courts
Providence County
 Courthouse
250 Benefit St.
Providence, RI 02903
401–227–3266

Mr. J. Robert Turnbull
Workers' Compensation Fund
1026 Sunter St.
Columbia, SC 29201
803–758–6500

Ms. Karen Kendrick
Asst. Atty. Gen.
Criminal Injuries
 Compensation Bd.
State Board of Claims

450 James Robertson
 Parkway
Nashville, TN 37219
615–741–2734

Mr. Jerry Belcher
Texas Industrial Accident Bd.
Crime Victim Div.
P.O. Box 12757
Capitol Station
Austin, TX 78701
512–475–8362

Mr. Robert B. Belz
Dir.
Victims of Crime Div.
Court of Claims
255 E. Main St., 2nd Fl.
Columbus, OH 43215
614–466–7190

Ms. Gwendolyn C. Blake
Exec. Secy. of Social Welfare
Crime Victims'
 Compensation Commission
P.O. Box 550
St. Thomas, VI 00801
809–774–1166

Mr. Robert W. Armstrong
Dir.
Div. of Crime Victims'
 Compensation
P.O. Box 1784
Richmond, VA 23214
704–786–5170

Mr. G. David Hutchins
Asst. Dir.
Crime Victim Compensa-
 tion Section
Dept. of Labor and
 Industries
Gen. Admin. Bldg.
Olympia, WA 98504
206–753–6318

Ms. Cheryle M. Hall
Clerk
West Virginia Court of
  Claims
Crime Victims' Reparation
  Div.
State Capitol
Charleston, WV 25305
304–348–3470

Mr. Richard H. Anderson
Exec. Dir.
Crime Victims'
  Compensation Program
P.O. Box 7951
Madison, WI 53707
304–348–3470
608–266–6470

Appendix C

Suggestions for Retaining an Attorney

Crime victims' rights and representation of crime victims is a new and rapidly expanding field. While increasing numbers of attorneys are gaining experience in representing crime victims in civil and criminal proceedings, the number of attorneys with actual experience or special knowledge of crime victims' problems and rights is still relatively small.

Whether a knowledge of recent developments in this area is necessary will depend on the victim's needs. If, for example, the victim is interested in commencing a civil action for damages against a known criminal for intentional injury or destruction of property or against a third party for negligence, the victim may have ready access to local attorneys skilled in tort actions, personal injury cases, or "white-collar crime" who could provide excellent representation. If the victim wishes to retain a lawyer to assist in preparation of a claim for compensation, personal injury attorneys familiar with similar kinds of claims (including specialists in workmen's compensation) may well satisfy the need.

However, if the victim is faced with the need for representation in an ongoing criminal proceeding, is faced with a complex restitution question or wishes to compel a prosecutor to bring charges in a particular case, he may have need of an attorney with special knowledge of the developing law discussed in this book and, in particular, how it affects the victim's rights in the victim's particular jurisdiction. In such a case, victims should carefully question potential attorneys about their knowledge and experience in this area.

If the victim has difficulty finding an experienced attorney, the victim might consider contacting any of the following for names of attorneys experienced and knowledgeable about the particular problem the victim faces:

1. the local victims' assistance agency or victim/witness unit of a local prosecutor's office;

2. the local bar association (the victim should specify in connection with any inquiry that he is interested only in attorneys knowledgable and experienced in the crime victims' area);

3. the National Organization for Victim Assistance, 1757 Park Road, N.W., Washington, DC 20010 (a nationwide clearinghouse for information on victims' assistance, including legal representation);

4. the Victims' Assistance Legal Organization (VALOR) F & M Bldg., 210 Laskin Rd., Suite 9, Virginia Beach, VA 23451 (to be relocating in 1984–85 to McGeorge School of Law, Sacramento, Calif. (an organization of lawyers and other professionals interested in victims' legislation and litigation);

5. the American Civil Liberties Union, 132 W. 43 St. New York, NY.

Appendix D

This list of names and addresses of dispute resolution programs is taken from the *1983 Dispute Resolution Program Directory* compiled by the Special Committee on Alternative Dispute Resolution of the Public Services Activities Division of the American Bar Association, Washington, D.C. It is reproduced with the permission of the Special Committee on Alternative Dispute Resolution.

Dispute Resolution Programs

Conflict Resolution Center
P.O. Box 210
Anchorage, AK 99510

Family Mediation Center
6900 E. Camelback Rd.,
  Suite 700
Scottsdale, AZ 85251

The Problem Solvers
6560 North Scottsdale Rd.,
  Suite GO23
Scottsdale, AZ 85253

Community Mediation
Program
% Family Crisis Serv.
2555 E. First St., #102
Tucson, AZ 85716

Humanists as Mediators
College of Liberal Arts
University of Arkansas
33rd & University
Little Rock, AR 72204

Small Claims Program
Little Rock Municipal Ct.
102 Palaski Co.
  Courthouse
Little Rock, AR 72201

Family Law
  Counseling Serv.
1600 Shattuck Ave.,
  Suite 200
Berkeley, CA 94709

Housing Alliance of Contra
  Costa County
2480 Pacheco St.
Concord, CA 94520

American Assoc. for
  Mediated Divorce
5435 Balboa Blvd., Suite 208
Encino, CA 91318

Christian Conciliation
  Serv.; San Joaquin Valley
P.O. Box 1348
Fresno, CA 93715

Dist. Atty.'s Hearing
  Officer Program
1800 Crim. Courts Bldg.
210 W. Temple St.
Los Angeles, CA 90012

Endispute of Southern
  California, Inc.
3345 Wilshire Blvd., #407
Los Angeles, CA 90010

L.A. City Atty. Program
1700 City Hall E.
200 North Main St.
Los Angeles, CA 90012

Family Ct. Serv. of the
  Supreme Ct.
928 Main St.
Martinez, CA 94553

Mountain View Rental
  Housing Mediation Group
650 Castro
Mountain View, CA 94040

Pastoral Mediation Serv.
Holy Names College
3500 Mountain Blvd.
Oakland, CA 94619

Family Mediation Serv.
285 Hamilton Ave.
Palo Alto, CA 94301

Rental Housing Mediation
  Task Force (RHMTA)
City Hall
250 Hamilton Ave.
Palo Alto, CA 94303

The New Family Center
210 California Ave., Suite G
Palo Alto, CA 94306

Center for Collaborative
  Problem Solving
2822 Van Ness Ave.
San Francisco, CA 94109

Community Bd. Program
149 Ninth St.
San Francisco, CA 94103

Community Dispute
  Services
American Arbitration Assoc.
445 Bush St., 5th Fl.
San Francisco, CA 94108

Neighborhood Mediation
  & Conciliation Serv.
70 W. Hedding St.
San Jose, CA 95110

Neighborhood Small Claim
  Night Ct.
200 W. Hedding St.
San Jose, CA 95110

San Jose Housing Serv.
425 Stockton Ave.
San Jose, CA 95126

Family Mediation Center
  of Marin County
610 D St.
San Rafael, CA 94901

Mediation Serv.
Admin. Bldg.
Civic Center, Rm. 243
San Rafael, CA 94903

Program for Consumer
   Affairs
701 Ocean St., Rm. 240
Santa Cruz, CA 95060

Rental Info. and
   Mediation Serv.
Nelson Community
   Center
301 Center St., Rm. 7
Santa Cruz, CA 95060

Divorcing Family Clinic
Center for Legal Psychiatry
2424 Wilshire Blvd.
Santa Monica, CA 90403

Neighborhood Justice
   Center
1320 Santa Monica Mall
Santa Monica, CA 90401

Family Ct. Serv.
Courthouse
222 E. Weber Ave.,
   Rm. 501
Stockton, CA 95202

Boulder Mediation Center
Ketchum 223
Campus Box 331
Boulder, CO 80309

Family Mediation Center, Inc.
P.O. Box 1978
Boulder, CO 80306

Neighborhood Justice
   Center
11 E. Vermijo Ave.
Colorado Springs, CO
   80903

Center for Dispute
   Resolution
430 W. Ninth Ave.
Denver, CO 80302

Divorce and Custody
   Mediators
1720 Emerson
Denver, CO 80218

Fair Haven Community
   Mediation Program, Inc.
162 Fillmore St.
New Haven, CT 06513

Waterbury Superior Ct.
Mediation Program
Superior Ct. Bldg.
Family Serv. Div.
Waterbury, CT 06722

Family Div. of
   Connecticut Superior Ct.
80 S. Main St.
West Hartford, CT 06107

Family Ct. of Delaware
Delaware Diversion
900 King St.
P.O. Box 2359
Wilmington, DE 19899

Fee Dispute Conciliation
   and Mediation Committee
Delaware State Bar Assoc.
820 North French St.
Wilmington, DE 19801

Wilmington Citizen's
   Dispute Settlement
   Center
800 North French St.
Wilmington, DE 19801

Civil Arbitration Program
Civil Div.
DC Superior Ct.

500 Indiana Ave.
Washington, DC 20001

DC Mediation Serv.
  (DCMS)
& DC Citizen's Complaint
  Center (CCC)
Superior Ct., Bldg. A
Washington, DC 20001

14th Street Inter-Agency
  Community Serv. Center
3031–14 St., N.W.
Washington, DC 20010

Citizen Dispute
  Settlement Program
Hall of Justice, State Atty.
Bartow, FL 33830

Community Arbitration
  Program
State Atty.'s Office
125 E. Orange Ave.
Daytona Beach, FL 32014

Citizen Dispute
  Settlement Program
305 S. Andrews Ave.
Fort Lauderdale, FL 33301

Family Conciliation Unit
One River Plaza, Suite 210
305 S. Andrews Ave.
Fort Lauderdale, FL 33301

Citizen Dispute
  Settlement
2115 Second St.
P.O. Box 398
Fort Meyers, FL 33902

Citizens Dispute
Settlement Program
P.O. Box 1437
Gainesville, FL 32602

Citizen's Dispute
Settlement Program
330 E. Bay St.
Jacksonville, FL 32202

Citizen's Settlement
  Program
1351 N.W. 12th St.,
  Rm. 214
Miami, FL 33125

Citizen Dispute Program
Bldg. A, Rm. 81
Collier County
  Courthouse
Naples, FL 33942

Citizen Dispute Settlement
  Program
880 North Orange Ave.
Orlando, FL 32801

Community Juvenile
  Arbitration
1800 St. Mary's Ave.,
  Box 5
Pensacola, FL 32501

Citizen Dispute
Settlement Program
150 Fifth St., N., Rm. 166
St. Petersburg, FL 33701

Seminole County Juvenile
  Office of the State Atty.
Seminole County
  Courthouse
Sanford, FL 32771

Citizen's Dispute
  Settlement Program
Hillsborough County
  Courthouse
Tampa, FL 33602

Citizen's Dispute Settlement
  Program

County Courthouse
Titusville, FL 32780

Citizen Dispute
Settlement Program
Courthouse, Rm. 430
West Palm Beach, FL
33401

Divorce Mediation Assoc.
2959 Piedmont Rd.
Atlanta, GA 30305

Fee Arbitration Program
State Bar of Georgia
84 Peachtree St., 11th Fl.
Atlanta, GA 30303

Neighborhood Justice
Center of Atlanta
1118 Euclid Ave., N.E.
Atlanta, GA 30307

Neighborhood Justice
Center of Honolulu
1538 Makiki St.
Honolulu, HI 96822

Maui Neighborhood
Justice Center, Inc.
P.O. Box 326
Makawao, HI 96768

Endispute of Chicago, Inc.
116 South Michigan Ave.,
Suite 300
Chicago, IL 60603

Neighborhood Justice of
Chicago, Inc.
4753 N. Broadway,
Suite 1122
Chicago, IL 60640

Divorce Mediation Serv.
1580 N. Northwest Highway
Park Ridge, IL 60068

Victim Offender
Reconciliation Program of
Elkhart County Pact
220 W. High St.
Elkhart, IN 46516

Night Prosecutor's Program
Prosecutor's Office Bldg.
County-City Bldg., 6th Fl.
South Bend, IN 46601

Polk County Atty.'s
Neighborhood Mediation
Center
112–11th St.
Des Moines, IA 50309

Midwest Mediation Serv.
Route 1, P.O. Box 235
Lawrence, KS 66044

Kenton-Campbell Pretrial
Kenton Municipal Bldg.
3rd and Court Sts.,
Rm. 308A
Covington, KY 41011

Fayette Mediation
Program
170 North Walnut St.
Lexington, KY 40507

Pretrial Serv.
430 W. Muhammad Ali
Blvd., Rm. 206
Louisville, KY 40202

Ct. Mediation Serv.
% Ninth District Ct.
142 Fed. St.
Portland, ME 04101

Community Arbitration
Juvenile Serv. Admin.
102 Cathedral St.
Annapolis, MD 20401

Divorce Mediation Serv. of
   Greater Baltimore
411 E. Lake Ave.
Baltimore, MD 21212

Community Relations Serv.
Dept. of Justice
5550 Friendship Blvd.
Chevy Chase, MD 20815

Family & Child Associates
414 Hungerford Dr.,
   Suite 240
Rockville, MD 20850

Montgomery County Office
   of Consumer Affairs
611 Rockville Pike,
   Rm. 201
Rockville, MD 20852

Mediation Project
University of Massachusetts
Rm. 125, Hasbrouck
Amherst, MA 01002

Mediation Program
Boston Municipal Court
Crime and Justice
   Foundation
19 Temple Place
Boston, MA 02111

Cambridge Dispute
   Settlement Center
One West St.
Cambridge, MA 02139

Children's Hearings Project
797 Cambridge St.
Cambridge, MA 02141

Harvard Small Claims and
   Mediation Project
Harvard Law School
Cambridge, MA 02138

Massachusetts Institute of
   Technology
Grievance Procedure
Room 10–213
Cambridge, MA 02139

Urban Court Mediation
   Component
560-A Washington St.
Dorchester, MA 02124

Framingham Ct.
Mediation, Inc.
600 Concord St.
Framingham, MA 01701

Community Mediation
   Serv.
Lynn Youth Resource
   Bureau
19 Sutton St.
Lynn, MA 01901

Bristol County Probate
   and Family Ct.
Mediation Serv.
441 County St.
New Bedford, MA 02740

Salem Mediation Program
Salem Dist. Ct.
65 Washington St.
Salem, MA 01970

Ann Arbor Mediation
   Center
338 S. State St.
Ann Arbor, MI 48104

Family Counseling and
   Mediation Div. of
   Friend of the Ct.
1045 First National Bldg.
Detroit, MI 48226

Volunteer Mediation
   Program

Detroit Human Rights Dept.
150 Michigan Ave., 4th Fl.
Detroit, MI 48226

Lansing Neighborhood Justice Center
City Hall, 6th Fl.
Lansing, MI 48933

Citizen's Dispute Settlement Program
40700 Romeo Plank Rd.
Mt. Clemens, MI 48044

Minnesota Mediation and Counseling Center
7260 University Ave., Suite 105
Fridley, MN 55432

Citizen's Dispute Settlement Program
A-1700 Hennepin County Government Center
Minneapolis, MN 55487

Mediation Center, Juvenile Offender Mediation Program
402 Powers Bldg.
430 Marquette Ave.
Minneapolis, MN 55401

Mediation Center, Legal Assistance Program
402 Powers Bldg.
430 Marquette Ave.
Minneapolis, MN 55401

Conciliation Ct.
County-City Bldg.
Lincoln, NB 68508

Willard Crime Prevention-Justice Center

1245 S. Folsom St.
Lincoln, NM 68522

Douglas County Conciliation Ct.
Hall of Justice, First Floor
Omaha, NB 68183

New Hampshire Mediation Program
8 Loudon Rd.
Concord, NH 03301

Family Counseling Unit
East Orange Municipal Ct.
221 Freeway Drive, E.
East Orange, NJ 07018

Neighborhood Dispute Center
355 Main St.
Hackensack, NJ 07601

Small Claims Settlement Program, Bergen County District Court
Courthouse
Hackensack, NJ 07601

Neighborhood and Family Dispute Settlement Project
595 Newark Ave., Rm. 404
Jersey City, NJ 07306

Millville Neighborhood Dispute Panel
18 S. High St.
Millville, NJ 08332

Citizen's Dispute Settlement Program
129 Church St.
New Brunswick, NJ 08901

Family and Neighborhood
Serv. Div.
Municipal Ct.
31 Green St.
Newark, NJ 07102

The Community Justice
Institute of Atlantic County
Stockton State College
Pomona, NJ 08240

Informal Hearing Program
Mercer County Courthouse
Broad and Market Sts.
Trenton, NJ 08650

Office of Dispute
Settlement
Dept. of the Public
Advocate, CN 850
Trenton, NJ 08625

Christian Conciliation
Serv. of New Mexico, Inc.
315 Arno N.E.
Albuquerque, NM 87102

Albany Dispute
Mediation Program
727 Madison Ave.
Albany, NY 12208

Family Mediation
Component
Neighborhood Youth
Diversion Program
1910 Arthur Ave.
Bronx, NY 10457

Brooklyn Mediation
Center
210 Joralemon St.,
Rm. 618
Brooklyn, NY 11201

Dispute Resolution Center
1106 James Hall

Brooklyn College
Brooklyn, NY 11210

Community Dispute
Resolution Project
Dispute Settlement Center
775 Main St.
Buffalo, NY 14203

Community Mediation
Program
356 Middle County Rd.
Coram, NY 11727

Neighborhood Justice
Project
300 Lake St.
Elmira, NY

Nassau County
Community
Dispute Center
585 Stewart Ave., Suite 302
Garden City, NY 11530

Volunteer Mediation Center
Div. of Volunteer
Counseling Serv.
151 S. Main St.
New City, NY 10956

Family Mediation Serv.
of New York
111 Fourth Ave., Suite IN
New York, NY 10003

IMCR Dispute Resolution
Center
425 W. 144 St.
New York, NY 10031

PINS Mediation Project
105 E. 22 St., Rm. 514
New York, NY 10010

Washington Heights-Inwood
Coalition Community
Mediation Project

31 Bennett Ave., Apt. 42
New York, NY 10033

Community Mediation
  Center
Village (Belle Terre)
  Burgemot
P.O. Box 112
Port Jefferson, NY 11777

Mediation Alternative
  Project
382 Main St.
Port Washington, NY
  11050

Queens Mediation Center
119–45 Union Turnpike
Kew Gardens
Queens, NY 11415

Center for Dispute
  Settlement
36 W. Main St.
Rochester, NY 14614

Dispute Resolution
  Program of the Volunteer
  Center, Inc.
103 E. Water St.
Syracuse, NY 13202

Resolve—A Center for
  Dispute Settlement, Inc.
812 Loew Bldg.
Syracuse, NY 13202

Community Dispute
  Settlement
35 State St.
Troy, NY 12180

Family Mediation
  Associates
62 Waller Ave.
White Plains, NY 10606

Dispute Settlement
  Center
205 Columbia St.
P.O. Box 464
Chapel Hill, NC 27514

Guilford County Dispute
  Settlement Center
1105 E. Wendover Ave.
Greensboro, NC 27405

Neighborhood Justice
  Program
New Hanover Courthouse
316 Princess St.
Wilmington, NC 28401

Family Service Mediation
First Union Bldg., Suite 735
310 W. Fourth St.
Winston-Salem, NC 27101

Fee Arbitration Panel
P.O. Box 2136
Bismarck, ND 58502

Private Complaint Program
City Prosecutor's Office
222 E. Central Parkway,
  Rm. 201B
Cincinnati, Ohio 45202

Cleveland Prosecutor
  Mediation Program
1200 Ontario Ave., 8th Fl.
Cleveland, OH 44113

Community Dispute
  Settlement Program
215 Euclid Ave., Rm. 930
Cleveland, OH 44114

Little Italy Dispute
  Settlement Program
12510 Mayfield Rd.
Cleveland, OH 44106

Family Mediation Center
Severence Medical Bldg.
5 Severence Circle
Cleveland Heights, OH
   44118

Night Prosecutor's Program
Municipal Ct. Bldg.
375 S. High St.
Columbus, OH 43215

Small Claims Div.
Franklin County
   Municipal Ct.
375 South High Street
Columbus, OH 43215

Night Prosecutor's
   Program
Safety Bldg., Rm. 338
335 W. Third St.
Dayton, OH 45402

Citizen Dispute
   Settlement Program
555 North Erie St.
Toledo, OH 43624

Dispute Mediation Program
Dist. Atty.'s Office
Cleveland County Office
   Bldg.
201 S. Jones
Norman, OK 73069

Citizen's Dispute
   Settlement Program
700 Couch Dr.
Oklahoma City, OK 73102

Dispute Serv.
Oklahoma State University
Stillwater, OK 74078

Project Early Settlement
600 Civic Center
Tulsa, OK 74103

Family Mediation Serv.
711 Country Club Rd.
Eugene, OR 97401

Family Mediation Center
3434 S.W. Kelly St.
Portland, OR 97201

Neighborhood Mediation
   Center
4815 N.E. Seventh, Rm. 20
Portland, OR 97211

Community Dispute
   Settlement Program of
   Delaware County
884-B Main St.
Darby, PA 19023

Lancaster Mediation Center
900 E. King St.
P.O. Box 1078
Lancaster, PA 17603

Arbitration Div.
Philadelphia Municipal Ct.
City Hall Annex,
   Rm. 1224
Philadelphia, PA 19107

Dispute Resolution Program
Commission on Human
   Relations
601 City Hall Annex
Philadelphia, PA 19107

Pittsburgh Mediation
   Center, Inc.
Highland Bldg., Suite 421
121 S. Highland Ave.
Pittsburgh, PA 15206

Baptist Center
   Dispute Program
1230 W. Scott St.
Knoxville, TN 37921

Memphis Citizen Dispute
128 Adams St., Rm. 120
Memphis, TN 38103

Dispute Mediation Service
of Dallas
1310 Annex at Live Oak,
#203
Dallas, TX 75204

Dispute Resolution Serv. of
Tarrant County
600 Texas St.
Fort Worth, TX 76102

Neighborhood Justice, Inc.
403 Caroline, 2nd Fl.
Houston, TX 77002

Arlington Juvenile and
Domestic Relations Ct.
Mediation Serv.
1400 North Courthouse Rd.
Arlington, VA 22201

Family Mediation of Greater
Washington
1515 North Courthouse Rd.,
Suite 605
Arlington, VA 22201

Neighborhood Justice
Project
OAR/USA
409 E. High St.
Charlottesville, VA 22901

Center for Separation and
Divorce Mediation
3705 S. George Mason Dr.
Falls Church, VA 22041

Community Mediation
Center
298 Green St.
Harrisonburg, VA 22801

Washington Mediation
Center
6827 Curran St.
McLean, VA 22101

Northwest Mediation
Serv., Inc.
27–100 N.E.
Bellevue, WA 98005

King County Office of
Citizen Complaints—
Ombudsman
213 King County
Courthouse
Seattle, WA 98104

Washington Justice Center
for Dispute Resolution
5009–37 Ave. S.
Seattle, WA 98118

Milwaukee Mediation Center
University of Wisconsin
929 North Sixth St.
Milwaukee, WI 53203

Appendix E

State Domestic Violence Laws

This list of domestic violence statutes was prepared by Lisa Lerman and Franci Livingston (with the assistance of Vicky Jackson) and is reprinted from 6 *Response* 1, 6–13 (Sept./Oct. 1983). It contains a state-by-state citation of domestic violence legislation enacted as of July 1983. It is reproduced with the permission of the authors and the Center for Women Policy Studies, publisher of *Response*.

Following is a list of citations of state statutes pertaining to domestic violence. Statutes that cannot be found in a law library may be obtained from the legislative counsel's office at the state capitol.

Citations for the statutes are listed alphabetically by state in the left-hand column. In the right-hand column entitled "Type of Provision," the statutes are categorized as follows:

• **Protection order** is listed beside a statute that provides for civil injunctive relief for victims of abuse. Only statutes that make protection orders available independent of any other proceeding are listed.

• **Order pending divorce** is listed beside a statute that provides for temporary injunctive relief during a divorce, separation, or custody proceeding.

• **Criminal law** is listed beside a statute that creates a new substantive criminal offense for physical abuse of a family or household member or that provides new procedures for disposition of criminal charges in domestic violence cases, such as conditions on pretrial release, deferred prosecution, or conditions on probation. General criminal statutes that may be the basis of charges against abusive mates are not listed.

• **Police intervention** is listed beside a statute that provides for warrantless arrest based on probable cause in domestic violence cases or that imposes duties on law enforcement officials handling disturbance calls.

• **Data collection and reporting** is listed beside a statute that requires agencies that offer services to violent families to keep records on cases handled or to write statistical or other reports on family violence.

• **Funding and shelter services** is listed beside a statute that appropriates funds for services to violent families or that establishes standards for operation of shelter for battered women.

In addition, citations are listed for some unusual statutes that are not included on the chart. The subject areas of these laws are listed in parentheses. The above categories also refer to sections of the Chart of State Legislation on Domestic Violence. More detailed information about each statute may be obtained by referring to the chart.

Citation	Type of Provision
ALABAMA	
ALA. CODE §§30–5–1 to 35–5–11 (Supp. 1982)	protection order
ALA. CODE §§30–6–1 to 30–6–13 (Supp. 1982)	data collection and reporting, funding and shelter services
ALASKA	
ALASKA STAT. §§09.55.600 to 09.55.640 (Supp. 1982)	protection order, police intervention
ALASKA STAT. §§18.65.5 10, 18.65.520 (1981 & Supp. 1982)	police intervention
ALASKA STAT. §§9.55.200, 9.55.205 (1973 & Supp. 1982)	order pending divorce
ALASKA STAT. §§11.46.350, 11.61.120, 12.25.030, 12.30.025, 12.55.135 (Supp. 1982)	criminal law
ALASKA STAT. §§18.66.010 to 18.66.900(1981)	funding and shelter services
ARIZONA	
ARIZ. REV. STAT. ANN. §§13–3601, 13–3602 (Supp. 1982–1983)	protection order, police intervention, criminal law
ARIZ. REV. STAT. ANN. §25–315 (1956 & Supp. 1982)	order pending divorce
ARIZ. REV. STAT. ANN. §25–324(1956)	order pending divorce
ARIZ. REV. STAT. ANN. §§25–311.01, 11–554 (Supp. 1982)	funding and shelter services
ARIZ. REV. STAT. ANN. §§36–3001 to 36–3007 (Supp. 1982)	funding and shelter services
ARKANSAS	
ARK. STAT. ANN. §§41–1653 to 41–1659 (Supp. 1981)	criminal law

Citation	Type of Provision
CALIFORNIA	
CAL. CIV. CODE §§4359, 5102 (West Supp. 1983)	protection order
CAL. CIV. PROC. CODE §§540–543, 545–553 (West Supp. 1983)	protection order
CAL. CIV. CODE §§4357, 4359, 4370, 4458, 4516, 4601.5, 7020, 7021 (West 1970 & Supp. 1983)	order pending divorce
CAL. PENAL CODE §§273.5, 273.6, 836, 1000.6 to 1000.11 (West Supp. 1983)	criminal law
CAL. GOVT. CODE §§26840.7, 26840.8, 26841 (West Supp. 1983)	funding and shelter services
CAL. WELF. & INST. CODE §§18291 to 18307 (West Supp. 1983)	funding and shelter services
CAL. CIV. PROC. CODE §527.6 (West Supp. 1983)	other injunctive relief (order restraining harassment)
COLORADO	
COLO. REV. STAT. §§14-4-101 to 14-4-105, 13-6-104, 13-6-105 (1973 & Supp. 1982)	protection order, police intervention
COLO. REV. STAT. §§14-10-108, 14-10-109 (1973 & Supp. 1982)	order pending divorce
Colo. H.B. 1479, _____ Leg., _____ Sess., 1983 Colo. Sess. Laws.	order pending divorce
Colo. H.B. 1050, _____ Leg., _____ Sess., 1983 Colo. Sess. Laws.	funding and shelter services
CONNECTICUT	
CONN. GEN. STAT. ANN. §46b-38 (West Supp. 1982)	protection order
Conn. H.B. 7364, _____ Leg., _____ Sess. 1983 Conn. Acts	protection order
CONN. GEN. STAT. ANN. §§46b-56, 46b-83 (West Supp. 1982)	order pending divorce
CONN. GEN. STAT. ANN. §54-1F (West Supp. 1982)	criminal law
CONN. GEN. STAT. ANN. §17-31L (West Supp. 1982)	data collection and reporting
CONN. GEN. STAT. ANN. §17-31K (West Supp. 1982)	funding and shelter services
Conn. S.B. 206, _____ Leg., _____ Sess., 1983 Conn. Acts	funding and shelter services

DELAWARE

DEL. CODE ANN. tit. 10, §§901(9), 902, 921(6), 925(15), 950(5) (1974 & Supp. 1982);   protection order
Family Court Rules 140

DEL. CODE ANN. tit. 13, §§1509, 1510 (1981 Repl. Vol.)   order pending divorce, police intervention

DEL. CODE ANN. tit. 10, §§341, 342 (1974 & Supp. 1982)   order pending divorce
DEL. CODE ANN. tit. 11, §1904 (1979 Repl. Vol.)   police intervention

DISTRICT OF COLUMBIA

D.C. CODE ANN. §§16–1001 to 16–1006(1981) *as amended by* 29 D.C. Reg. 3131 (1982)   protection order, criminal law

D.C. CODE ANN. §16–911 (1981)   order pending divorce
29 D.C. Reg. 3131 (1982)   police intervention

FLORIDA

FLA. STAT. ANN. §741.30 (West Supp. 1983)   protection order
FLA. STAT. ANN. §§409.607, 901.15(6) (West Supp. 1983)   police intervention
FLA. STAT. ANN. §§61.071, 61.08, 61.09, 61.13 (West 1969 & Supp. 1983)   order pending divorce
FLA. STAT. ANN. §409.606 (West Supp. 1983)   data collection and reporting
FLA. STAT. ANN. §§409.602, 409.603, 409.605, 741.01 (West Supp. 1983)   funding and shelter services

GEORGIA

GA. CODE ANN. §§19–13–1 to 19–13–5 (1982 & Supp. 1982)   protection order
GA. CODE ANN. §§19–6–3, 19–6–10, 19–6–14 (1982)   order pending divorce
GA. CODE ANN. §17–4–20 (1982)   police intervention
GA. CODE ANN. §19–13–20 to 19–13–22 (1982) *as amended by* H.B. 142,_____ Leg.,_____   funding and shelter services
Sess., 1983 Ga. Laws._____

Citation	Type of Provision
HAWAII	
HAWAII REV. STAT. §586 (Supp. 1982) *as amended by* H.B. 1102, 12th Leg., 1983 Hawaii Sess. Laws.	protection order
Hawaii S.B. 1186, 12th Leg., 1983 Hawaii Sess. Laws.	protection order
HAWAII REV. STAT. §§580–9 to 580–12 (1976 Repl. Vol.) *as amended by* H.B. 1037, 12th Leg., 1983 Hawaii Sess. Laws	order pending divorce
HAWAII REV. STAT §709–906 (1976 & Supp. 1982) *as amended by* H.B. 1294, 12th Leg., 1983 Hawaii Sess. Laws.	criminal law, police intervention
Hawaii H.B. 34, 12th Leg., 1983 Hawaii Sess. Laws.	data collection and reporting
IDAHO	
IDAHO CODE §32–704 (1946 & Supp. 1982)	order pending divorce
IDAHO CODE §19–603 (1947 & Supp. 1982)	police intervention
IDAHO CODE §§39–5201 to 39–5213 (Supp. 1982)	funding and shelter services
ILLINOIS	
ILL. ANN. STAT. ch. 40, §§2301–1 to 2301–3, 2302–1 to 2302–13 (Smith-Hurd Supp. 1982) *as amended by* 1982 Ill. Laws 2021 and H.B. 1963, 83rd Gen. Assembly, Sess., 1983 Ill. Laws.	protection order
ILL. ANN. STAT. ch. 40, §§501, 602, 607, 608 (Smith-Hurd 1980 & Supp. 1982)	order pending divorce
ILL. ANN. STAT. ch. 38, §§109–1, 111–8 (Smith-Hurd 1980 & Supp. 1982)	criminal law
ILL. ANN. STAT. ch. 38, §§1005–6–3, 1005–6–3.1 (Smith-Hurd 1973 & Supp. 1982)	criminal law
ILL. ANN. STAT. ch. 40, §§2303–1, 2303–4, 2303–5. (Smith-Hurd Supp. 1982)	police intervention
ILL. ANN. STAT. ch. 85, §507–a (Smith-Hurd 1979)	police intervention
ILL. ANN. STAT. ch. 40, §§2303–2, 2303 3 (Smith-Hurd Supp. 1982)	data collection and reporting

ILL. ANN. STAT. ch. 38, §206–5.1 (Smith-Hurd Supp. 1982)   data collection and reporting
ILL. ANN. STAT. ch. 40, §§2401 to 2403 (Smith-Hurd Supp. 1982) *as amended by*
1982 Ill. Laws 2021
ILL. ANN. STAT. ch. 25, §§27.1(a)(3), 27.2(1)(c), (d)(Smith-Hurd Supp. 1982)   funding and shelter services
ILL. ANN. STAT. ch. 53, §§35–18, 73–3 (Smith-Hurd Supp. 1982)   funding and shelter services
    funding and shelter services

INDIANA
Ind. S.B. 295, _____ Leg.,_____ Sess., 1983 Ind. Acts_____   protection order
IND. CODE ANN. §31–1–11.5–7 (Burns Supp. 1982)   order pending divorce
IND. CODE ANN. §35–42–2–1 (2)(D)(Burns Supp. 1982)   criminal law
IND. CODE ANN. §§4–23–17.5 to 4–23–17.5–9 (Burns 1982 Repl. Vol.)   funding and shelter services

IOWA
IOWA CODE ANN. §§236–1 to 236–8 (West Supp. 1982–1983)   protection order
IOWA CODE ANN. §598.11 (West 1981)   order pending divorce
IOWA CODE ANN. §236–11 (West Supp. 1982–1983)   police intervention
IOWA CODE ANN. §§236–9, 236–10 (West Supp. 1982–1983)   data collection and reporting

KANSAS
KAN. CIV. PROC. CODE ANN. §§60–3101 to 60–3111 (Vernon Supp. 1982) *as amended*   protection order
by H.B. 2206, _____ Leg.,_____ Sess., 1983 Kan. Sess. Laws _____
KAN. CIV. PROC. CODE ANN. §60–1607 (Vernon 1967 & Supp. 1979)   order pending divorce
KAN. CRIM. CODE ANN. §21–3721 (Vernon Supp. 1983)   criminal law
KAN. STAT. ANN. §§23–108 to 23–110 (Vernon 1982)   funding and shelter services

Citation	Type of Provision
KENTUCKY	
KY. REV. STAT. §403.710 (1982 Supp.)	protection order
KY. REV. STAT. §§209.010, 209.020, 209.040, 209.130 (1982 Repl. Vol.)	protection order
KY. REV. STAT. §403.160 (Supp. 1982)	order pending divorce
KY. REV. STAT. §431.005 (Supp. 1982)	police intervention
KY. REV. STAT. §§209.010 to 209.030, 209.050, 209.130, 209.140 (1982 Repl. Vol.)	data collection and reporting
KY. REV. STAT. §64.012 (Supp. 1982)	funding and shelter services
KY. REV.STAT. §209.160 (1982 Repl. Vol.)	funding and shelter services
1982 Ky. Acts 1273	funding and shelter services
LOUISIANA	
LA. REV. STAT. ANN. §46.2131 to 46.2139 (West 1982) *as amended by* H.B. 1288, _____ Leg., Reg. Sess., 1983 La. Acts.	protection order
LA. REV. STAT. ANN. §§9:306 to 9:308 (West Supp. 1982)	order pending divorce
LA. CODE CIV. PROC. ANN. art. 3604 (West Supp. 1983) *as amended by* H.B. 260, _____ Leg., Reg. Sess., 1983 La. Acts.	order pending divorce
LA. CODE CRIM. PROC. ANN. art. 213 (West 1982)	criminal law, police intervention
La. S.B. 490, _____ Leg., Reg. Sess., 1983 La. Acts.	criminal law, police intervention
La. S. RES. 21, _____ Leg., Reg. Sess., 1977 La. Acts.	data collection and reporting
LA. REV. STAT. ANN. §46:2125 (West 1982)	data collection and reporting
LA. REV. STAT. ANN. §§46:2121 to 46:2128 (West 1982) *as amended by* H.B. 24 and H.B. 30, _____ Leg., Extra. Sess., 1981 La. Acts.	funding and shelter services

430

MAINE

ME. REV. STAT. ANN. tit. 19, §§761–770 (1964 and Supp. 1982–1983) — protection order
ME. REV. STAT. ANN. tit. 19, §214 (Supp. 1982–1983) — order pending divorce
ME. REV. STAT. ANN. tit. 19, §§693, 694, 722B (1964 & Supp. 1982–1983) — order pending divorce
ME. REV. STAT. ANN. tit. 15, §301 (Supp. 1982–1983). — criminal law, police intervention
ME. REV. STAT. ANN. tit. 19, §§769, 770 (1964 & Supp. 1982–1983) — police intervention
ME. REV. STAT. ANN. tit. 17-A, §15(1)(A)(5–a)(1983) — police intervention
ME. REV. STAT. ANN. tit. 19, §770 (1964 & Supp. 1982–1983) — data collection and reporting
ME. REV. STAT. ANN. tit. 25, §1544 (1964 & Supp. 1982–1983) — data collection and reporting
ME. REV. STAT. ANN. tit. 22, §8501 (1964) — funding and shelter services

MARYLAND

MD. CTS. & JUD. PROC. CODE ANN. §§4-404, 4-501 to 4-506 (Supp. 1982) — protection order
MD. CTS. & JUD. PROC. CODE ANN. §§3-602, 3-603, 3-6A-06 (1980 Repl. Vol. & Supp. 1982) — order pending divorce

MD. ANN. CODE art. 27, §11F (1982 Repl. Vol.) — criminal law, police intervention
Md. H.J. Res. 32, ___ Leg. ___ Sess., 1977 Md. Laws.___ — data collection and reporting
MD. ANN. CODE art. 88A, §§101 to 105 (1979 Repl. Vol. & Supp. 1982) — funding and shelter services
MD. ANN. CODE art. 62, §14 (Supp. 1982) — funding and shelter services

MASSACHUSETTS

MASS. GEN. LAWS ANN. ch. 209A §§1 to 6, ch. 208 §34C (West Supp. 1982–1983) — protection order
MASS. GEN. LAWS ANN. ch. 208 §§17 to 20, 34B, 34C (West 1958 & Supp. 1982–1983) — order pending divorce

MASS. GEN. LAWS ANN. ch. 276 §§28, 42A (West 1972 & Supp. 1982–1983) — criminal law, police intervention
MASS. GEN. LAWS ANN. ch. 266 §120 (West Supp. 1970–1982) — criminal law

Citation	Type of Provision
MICHIGAN	
MICH. COMP. LAWS ANN. §§552.14, 552.15 (West 1967 and Supp. 1982–1983)	order pending divorce
MICH. COMP. LAWS ANN. §§764.15(a), 764.15(b), 769.4a, 772.13, 772.14a (West 1982)	police intervention, criminal law
MICH. COMP. LAWS ANN. §§28.251 to 28.257 (West Supp. 1980–1981)	data collection and reporting
MICH. COMP. LAWS ANN. §§400.1501 to 400.1510 (West Supp. 1982–83) as amended by H.B. 5992, 81st Leg., Reg. Sess., 1982 Mich. Pub Acts.___	funding and shelter services
MICH. COMP. LAWS ANN. §§551.103, 551.331 to 551.344 (West Supp. 1982–1983)	funding and shelter services
MINNESOTA	
MINN. STAT. ANN. §518B.01 (West Supp. 1983) as amended by S.F. 240, ___ Leg.,___ Sess., 1983 Minn. Laws.___	protection order, police intervention
MINN. STAT. ANN. §629.341 (West Supp. 1983) as amended by S.F. 297, ___ Leg.,___ Sess. 1983 Minn. Laws.___	police intervention
MINN. STAT. ANN. §§609.135(5), 629.72 (West Supp. 1983)	criminal law
MINN. STAT. ANN. §§241.62(5), 241.66 (West Supp. 1982–1983)	data collection and reporting
MINN. STAT. ANN. §§241.61 to 241.65, 256D.05(3) (West Supp. 1982–1983)	funding and shelter services
MINN. STAT. ANN. §§357.021, 571.08 (West Supp. 1983)	funding and shelter services
MISSISSIPPI	
MISS. CODE ANN. §§93–21–1 to 93–21–29 (Supp. 1982)	protection order, data collection and reporting
Miss. H.B. 670,___ Leg.,___ Sess., 1983 Miss. Laws.___	funding and shelter services

432

MISSOURI

MO. REV. STAT. §§455.010 to 455.085 (Supp. 1983) — protection order, police intervention
MO. REV. STAT. §§452.315, 452.380 (1978) — order pending divorce
MO. REV. STAT. §§455.200 to 455.230 (Supp. 1983) — funding and shelter services

MONTANA

MONT. CODE ANN. §40-4-106 (3) (1981) — protection order
MONT. CODE ANN. §40-4-106 (1981) — order pending divorce
MONT. CODE ANN. §40-2-402 (1981) — data collection and reporting
MONT. CODE ANN. §§40-2-401 to 40-2-405, 40-1-202 (1981) *as amended by* H.B. 45, 48th Leg., 2nd. Sess., 1983 Mont. Laws. — funding and shelter services

NEBRASKA

NEB. REV. STAT. §§42-901 to 42-903, 42-924 to 42-926 (Vol. III 1978) — protection order
NEB. REV. STAT. §42-357 (Vol. III 1978) *as amended by* L.B. 371, 88th Leg., 1st Sess. 1983 Neb. Laws. — order pending divorce
NEB. REV. STAT. §§29-2219, 29-2262 (Vol. IIA 1979 & Supp. 1982) — criminal law
NEB. REV. STAT. §42-927 (Vol. III 1978) — police intervention
NEB. REV. STAT. §§42-904 to 42-923 (Vol. III 1978 & Supp. 1982) — data collection and reporting, funding and shelter services

NEVADA

NEV. REV. STAT. §33.020 (1979) — protection order
NEV. REV. STAT. §§125-040 to 125-060, 125-200, 125-220 (1981) — order pending divorce
NEV. REV. STAT. §171.124 (1981) — police intervention
NEV. REV. STAT. §§217.400 to 217.470, 122.060 (1981) — funding and shelter services

Citation	Type of Provision

NEW HAMPSHIRE

Citation	Type of Provision
N.H. REV. STAT. ANN. §§173–B:1 to 173–B:11 (Supp. 1979) *as amended by 1981* N.H. Laws 777	protection order
N.H. REV. STAT. ANN. §458.16 (Supp. 1979)	order pending divorce
N.H. REV. STAT. ANN. §§597:7–a; 651:2VI, 651:41 (Supp. 1979)	criminal law
N.H. REV. STAT. ANN. §635.2 (Supp. 1979)	criminal law
N.H. REV. STAT. ANN. §594:10–1 (Supp. 1979)	police intervention
N.H. REV. STAT. ANN. §106–B:14 (Supp. 1979) as amended by 1981 N.H. Laws 226	data collection and reporting
1981 N.H. Laws 226	funding and shelter services

NEW JERSEY

Citation	Type of Provision
N.J. STAT. ANN. §§2C:25–1 to 2C:25–16 (West 1982)	protection order
N.J. STAT. ANN. §2A:34–23 (West 1952 & Supp. 1982–83)	order pending divorce
N.J. STAT. ANN. §§2C:25–3, 2C:25–10, 2C:25–11, 2C:12–1; 2C:33–4 (West 1982)	criminal law
N.J. STAT. ANN. §2C:25–4 to 2C:25–7 (West 1982)	police intervention
N.J. STAT. ANN. §§2C:25–8, 2C:25–16 (West 1982)	data collection and reporting
N.J. STAT. ANN. §§30:14–1 to 30:14–14 (West 1981)	funding and shelter services
N.J. STAT. ANN. §§37:1–12, 37:1–12.1 to 37:1–12.3 (West 1968 & Supp. 1982–1983)	funding and shelter services
14 N.J. Admin. Reg. 197 (1982)	funding and shelter services
N.J. STAT. ANN. §§40:55D–66.1, 40:55D–66.2 (West Supp. 1982–1983)	(shelter zoning law)

NEW MEXICO

Citation	Type of Provision
N.M. STAT. ANN. §40–4–7 (1978)	order pending divorce
N.M. STAT. ANN. §31–1–7 (Supp. 1981)	police intervention

434

NEW YORK

N.Y. FAM. CT. ACT. §§153-C, 155, 168, 216—a, 262(a)(ii), 812, 813, 817, 818, 821 to 828, 832 to 836, 838, 841 to 847 (McKinney 1975 & Supp. 1976–1982) — protection order

N.Y. FAM. CT. ACT. §§430, 446, 550, 551, 655, 656, 1029, 1056, _____ (McKinney 1975 & Supp. 1976–1982) *as amended by* A5264-B, 206th Leg., _____ Sess., 1983 N.Y. Laws. — order pending divorce

N.Y. DOM. REL. LAW §§240(2), 252 (McKinney Supp.1982–1983) *as amended by* A5264-B, 206th Leg., _____ Sess., 1983 N.Y. Laws. — order pending divorce

N.Y. FAM. CT. ACT §§ 155, 168 (McKinney 1975 & Supp. 1976–1982) *as amended by* A6274, 206th Leg., _____ Sess., 1983 N.Y. Laws. — criminal law, police intervention

N.Y. JUD. LAW §§216, 751(1) (McKinney Supp. 1982–1983) — criminal law, police intervention

N.Y. CRIM. PROC. LAW §100.07 (McKinney 1981) — criminal law

N.Y. CRIM. PROC. LAW §170.55 (McKinney 1982) — criminal law

N.Y. CRIM. PROC. LAW §§530.11, 530.12 (McKinney Supp. 1982–1983) — criminal law

N.Y. SOC. SERV. LAW §2-31(a), (b) (McKinney Supp. 1982–1983) — funding and shelter services

9 NYCRR 3.90 (1979) — funding and shelter services

N.Y. Exec. Order No. 19 (Mario M. Cuomo, Gov., June 1, 1983), 9 NYCRR _____ — funding and shelter services

18 NYCRR 492.1 to 492.28 (1982) — funding and shelter services

NORTH CAROLINA

N.C. GEN. STAT. §§50B–1 to 50B–7 (Supp. 1981) — protection order, police intervention

N.C. GEN. STAT. §§50–13.5, 50–16.6 (Repl. Vol. 1976 & Supp. 1981) — order pending divorce

N.C. GEN. STAT. §14.134.3 (Repl. Vol. 1981) — criminal law

N.C. GEN. STAT. §15A–401(b)(3), 15A–534.1 (1978 & Supp. 1981) — criminal law

N.C. H.B. 1148, _____ Leg., _____ Sess., 1982 N.C. Sess. Laws. — funding and shelter services

435

Citation	Type of Provision

NORTH DAKOTA

Citation	Type of Provision
N.D. CENT. CODE §§14–07.1–01 to 14–07.1–08 (1981 Repl. Vol. 3A & Supp. 1981)	protection order, police intervention
N.D. CENT. CODE §29–01–15(4) (1981 Repl. Vol. 5A)	protection order, police intervention
N.D. CENT. CODE §14–05–23 (1981 Repl. Vol. 3A)	order pending divorce
N.D. Rules of Court 8.2 (1981 Repl. Vol. 5B)	order pending divorce
N.D. CENT. CODE §§14–03–21, 14–03–22 (1981 Repl. Vol. 3A)	funding and shelter services
N.D. CENT. CODE §§14–07.2–01 to 14–07.2–05 (1981 Repl. Vol. 3A)	funding and shelter services

OHIO

Citation	Type of Provision
OHIO REV. CODE ANN. §§1901.18, 1901.19, 1909.02 (Page Supp. 1982)	protection order
OHIO REV. CODE ANN. §2919.26 (Page 1982)	protection order
OHIO REV. CODE ANN. §3113.31 (Page 1980 & Supp. 1981)	protection order
OHIO REV. CODE ANN. §§2919.25, 2919.26, 2933.16 (Page 1982)	criminal law
OHIO REV. CODE ANN. §§109.73, 109.77, 737.11 (Page Supp. 1982)	police intervention
OHIO REV. CODE ANN. §2935.03 (Page 1982)	police intervention
OHIO REV. CODE ANN. §3113.29 (Page 1980)	data collection and reporting
OHIO REV. CODE ANN. §§3113.33 to 3113.39 (Page 1980 & Supp. 1981)	funding and shelter services

OKLAHOMA

Citation	Type of Provision
OKLA. STAT. ANN. tit. 22, §§60 to 60.6 (West Supp. 1982–1983) *as amended by* S.B. 103, 39th Leg., 1st Sess., 1983 Okla. Sess. Laws.	protection order
OKLA. STAT. ANN. tit. 12, §1276 (West Supp. 1982–1983)	order pending divorce
OKLA. STAT. ANN. tit. 22, §§40 to 40.3 (West Supp. 1982–1983)	police intervention
Okla. S.B. 47 _____ Leg., _____ Sess., 1983 Okla. Sess. Laws.	funding and shelter services
OKLA. STAT. ANN. tit. 43A, §§613 to 622 (West Supp. 1982–1983)	(mental health facilities to provide services to victims of domestic violence)

OREGON

OR. REV. STAT. §§107.700 to 107.720, 133.055, 133.310, 133.381 (1977 & 1981 Repl. Vol.) *as amended by* S.B. 476., _____ Leg., _____ Sess., 1983 Or. Laws. — protection order, criminal law, police intervention, data collection and reporting

OR. REV. STAT. §33.060 (1981 Repl. Vol.) *as amended by* S.B. 476., _____ Leg., _____ Sess., 1983 Or. Laws _____ — protection order

OR. REV. STAT. §107.095 (1981 Repl. Vol.) — order pending divorce

OR. REV. STAT. §§106.045, 108.610 to 108.660 (Vol. 1, 1981 Repl. Vol.) — funding and shelter services

PENNSYLVANIA

35 PA. CONS. STAT. ANN. §§10182 to 10190 (Purdon 1977 & Supp. 1982–1983) — protection order

42 PA. CONS. STAT. ANN. R.C.P. RULES 1901 to 1905 (1981) — protection order

23 PA. CONS. STAT. ANN. §§403, 502 (Purdon Supp. 1982–1983) — order pending divorce

18 PA. CONS. STAT. ANN. §§4954 to 4956 (Purdon Supp. 1982–1983) — criminal law

1982 Pa. Legis. Serv. 851 (Purdon) — funding and shelter services

RHODE ISLAND

R.I. GEN. LAWS §§15-15-1 to 15-15-6 (Supp. 1982) *as amended by* S. 597, _____ Leg.; _____ Sess., 1983 R.I. Pub. Laws. — protection order

R.I. GEN. LAWS §§15-5-19, 15-5-19.1 (Supp. 1982) — order pending divorce

R.I. GEN. LAWS §§11-5-9, 12-7-3 (1981 Reenact.) — criminal law, police intervention

R.I. GEN. LAWS §15-5-5 (Supp. 1982) — police intervention

SOUTH CAROLINA

S.C. CODE ANN. §20-3-110 (Law. Co-op. 1976) — order pending divorce

S.C. CODE ANN. §20-7-420 (Law. Co-op. Supp. 198___ — order pending divorce

437

Citation	Type of Provision

SOUTH DAKOTA

Citation	Type of Provision
S.D. CODIFIED LAWS ANN. §§25-10-1 to 25-10-14 (Supp. 1982)	protection order, police intervention
S.D. CODIFIED LAWS ANN. §§25-4-34, 25-4-38, 25-4-40, 25-4-45 (1976 & Supp. 1982)	order pending divorce
S.D. CODIFIED LAWS ANN. §§22-18-1, 23A-3-2	criminal law
S.D. H.B. 1086 ____ Leg., ____ Sess., 1983 S.D. Sess. Laws ____	funding and shelter services

TENNESSEE

Citation	Type of Provision
TENN. CODE ANN. §§36-1201 to 36-1215 (Supp. 1982)	protection order, police intervention
TENN. CODE ANN. §§39-2-101, 39-2-105 (1982 Repl. Vol.)	criminal law

TEXAS

Citation	Type of Provision
TEX. FAM. CODE ANN. §§71.01 to 71.19 (Vernon Supp. 1982) *as amended by* S.B. 878 and 997, 68th Leg., ____ Sess., 1983 Tex. Gen. Laws.	protection order, police intervention
TEX. FAM. CODE ANN. §§3.58, 3.59 (Vernon 1975 & Supp. 1982–1983) *as amended by* S.B. 997, 68th Leg. ____ Sess. 1983 Tex. Gen. Laws.	order pending divorce
TEX. CODE CRIM. PROC. ANN. art. 6.01 to 6.07 (Vernon 1977 & Supp. 1982–1983)	criminal law, police intervention
TEX. PENAL CODE ANN. §§22.01(c), 22.02(a) (Vernon Supp. 1982–1983)	criminal law
Tex. S.B. 997, 68th Leg., ____ Sess., 1983 Tex. Gen. Laws.	criminal law
Tex. S. Con. Res. 87, 68th Leg., ____ Sess., 1983 Tex. Gen. Laws.	criminal law
TEX. CODE CRIM. PROC. ANN. art. 14.03 (Vernon Supp. 1982–1983)	police intervention
Tex. S. Con. Res. 88, 68th Leg., ____ Sess., 1983 Tex. Gen. Laws	data collection and reporting
TEX. HUM. RES. CODE ANN. §§51.001 to 51.011 (Vernon Supp. 1982–1983)	funding and shelter services
Tex. S. Con. Res. 82 to 86, 89, 68th Leg., ____ Sess., 1983 Tex. Gen. Laws.	funding and shelter services

UTAH

UTAH CODE ANN. §§30–6–1 to 30–6–8 (Supp. 1981) *as amended by* H.B. 23., 1983 Gen. Sess., 1983 Utah Laws._____ | protection order, police intervention

UTAH CODE ANN. §30–3–3 (Second Repl. Vol. 3, 1953 & Supp. 1981) | order pending divorce
UTAH CODE ANN. §76–5–108 (Supp. 1981) | criminal law
Utah H.B. 24, 1983 Gen. Sess., 1983 Utah Laws._____ | criminal law
UTAH CODE ANN. §30–6–9 (Supp. 1981) | funding and shelter services

VERMONT

VT. STAT. ANN. tit. 15, §§1101 to 1107 (Supp. 1981) *as amended by* 1982 Vt. Acts 362 | protection order
VT. RULES OF CIV. PROC., Rule 80 (1971 & Supp. 1982) | order pending divorce
VT. STAT. ANN. tit. 13, §2451 (Supp. 1981) | order pending divorce
VT. STAT. ANN. tit. 32, §1712(1)(1981) *as amended by* 1982 Vt. Acts 33 | funding and shelter services
VT. STAT. ANN. tit. 3, §18 (1981) *as amended by* 1982 Vt. Acts 33 | funding and shelter services

VIRGINIA

VA. CODE §20–103 (1983 Repl. Vol.) | order pending divorce
VA. CODE §16.1–279(L) (1983 Repl. Vol.) | order pending divorce
VA. CODE §19.2–81 (1983 Repl. Vol.) | criminal law
Va. H.J. Res. 27,_____ Leg.,_____ Sess., 1978 Va. Acts. | police intervention
Va. H.J. Res. 31,_____ Leg.,_____ Sess., 1978 Va. Acts. | funding and shelter services
VA. CODE §§63.1–315 to 63.1–319 (1983 Repl. Vol.) | funding and shelter services
VA. CODE §20–15 (1983 Repl. Vol.) | funding and shelter services

Citation	Type of Provision
WASHINGTON	
WASH. REV. CODE ANN. §26.09.060 (Supp. 1982)	order pending divorce
WASH. REV. CODE ANN. §§10.99.010 to 10.99.070 (1980 & Supp. 1982)	criminal law, police intervention, data collection and reporting
WASH. REV. CODE ANN. §§70.123.010 to 70.123.900 (Supp. 1982)	funding and shelter services
WEST VIRGINIA	
W.VA. CODE §§48-2A-1 to 48-2A-8, 48-2A-10 (1980 Repl. Vol. & Supp. 1982)	protection order
W.VA. CODE §48-2-13 (1980 Repl. Vol.)	order pending divorce
W.VA. CODE §48-2A-9 (Supp. 1982)	data collection and reporting
W.VA. CODE §§48-2C-1 to 48-2C-9, 48-1-24 (Supp. 1982)	data collection and reporting, funding and shelter services
WISCONSIN	
WIS. STAT. ANN. §§767.23, 813.025 (2)(a) (1981 & West. Supp. 1982-1983)	protection order
WIS. STAT. ANN. §940.33 (1982)	protection order
WIS. STAT. ANN. §247.23 (1957 & West Supp. 1982-1983)	order pending divorce
WIS. STAT. ANN. §940.19 (1982)	criminal law
WIS. STAT. ANN. §971.37 (West Supp. 1982-1983)	criminal law
WIS. STAT. ANN. §165.85(4)(b) (West Supp. 1982-1983)	police intervention
WIS. STAT. ANN. §§15.197(16), 20.435(8)(c), 46.95, 50.01(1), 973.05, 973.055 (West Supp. 1982-1983)	funding and shelter services
WYOMING	
WYO. STAT. §§35-21-101 to 35-21-107 (Supp. 1982)	protection order
WYO. STAT. §§20-2-106(c), 20-2-109 to 20-2-112 (Supp. 1982)	order pending divorce
WYO. STAT. §§9-3-104, 9-3-105 (Supp. 1982)	funding and shelter services

440